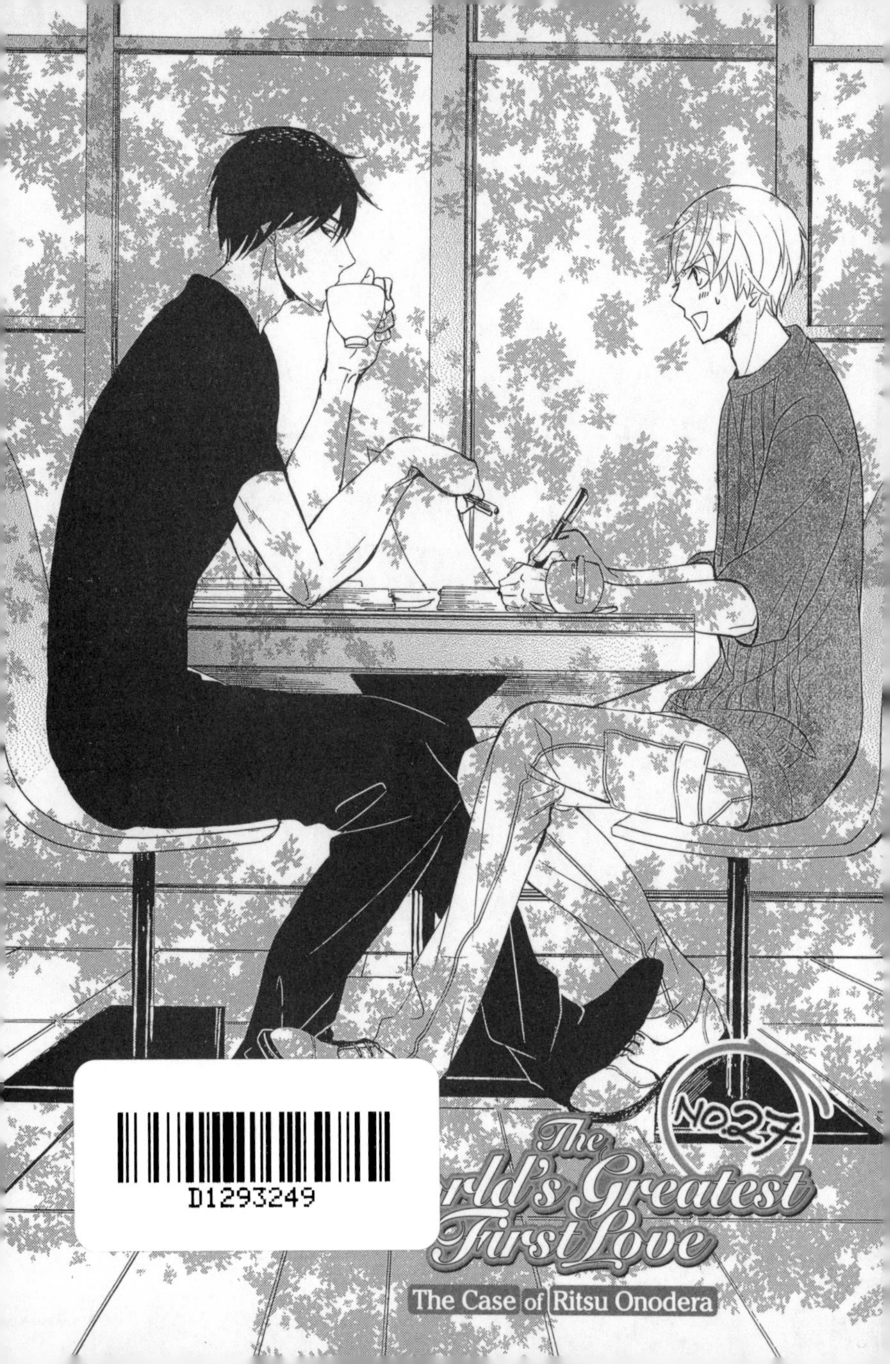

NO.27
The
rld's Greatest
First Love
The Case of Ritsu Onodera

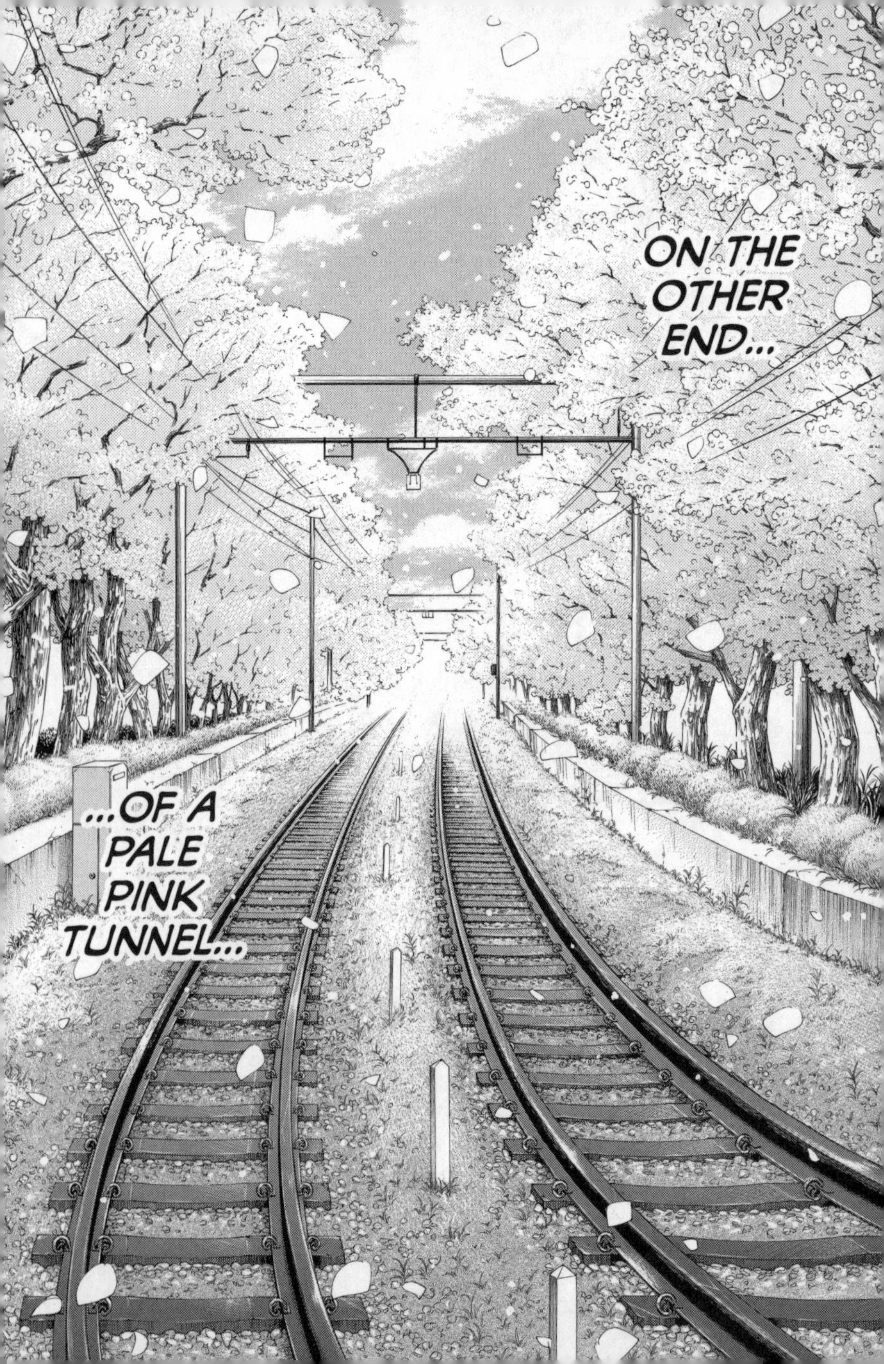
ON THE OTHER END...
...OF A PALE PINK TUNNEL...

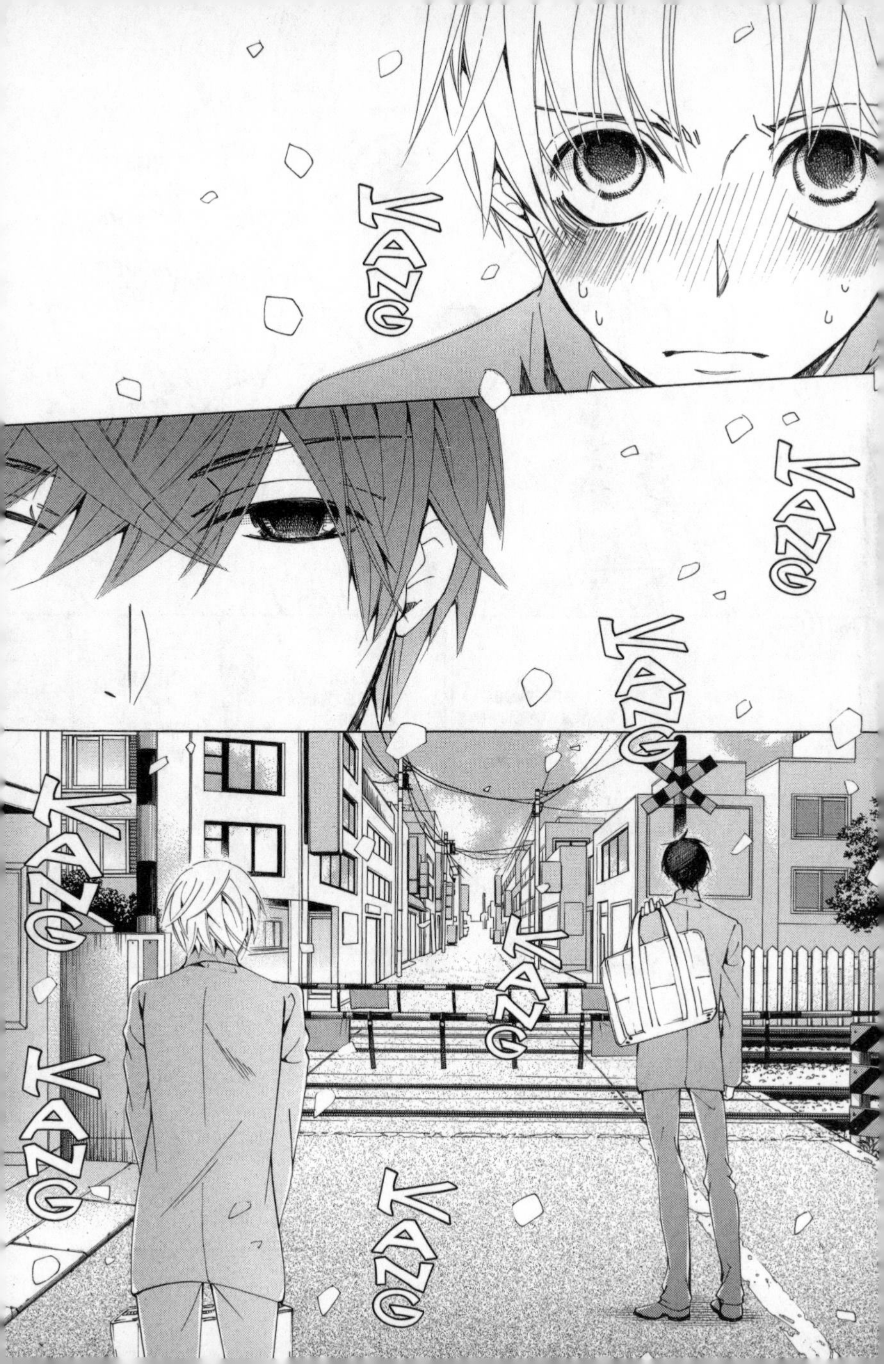
KANG
KANG
KANG
KANG
KANG
KANG
KANG

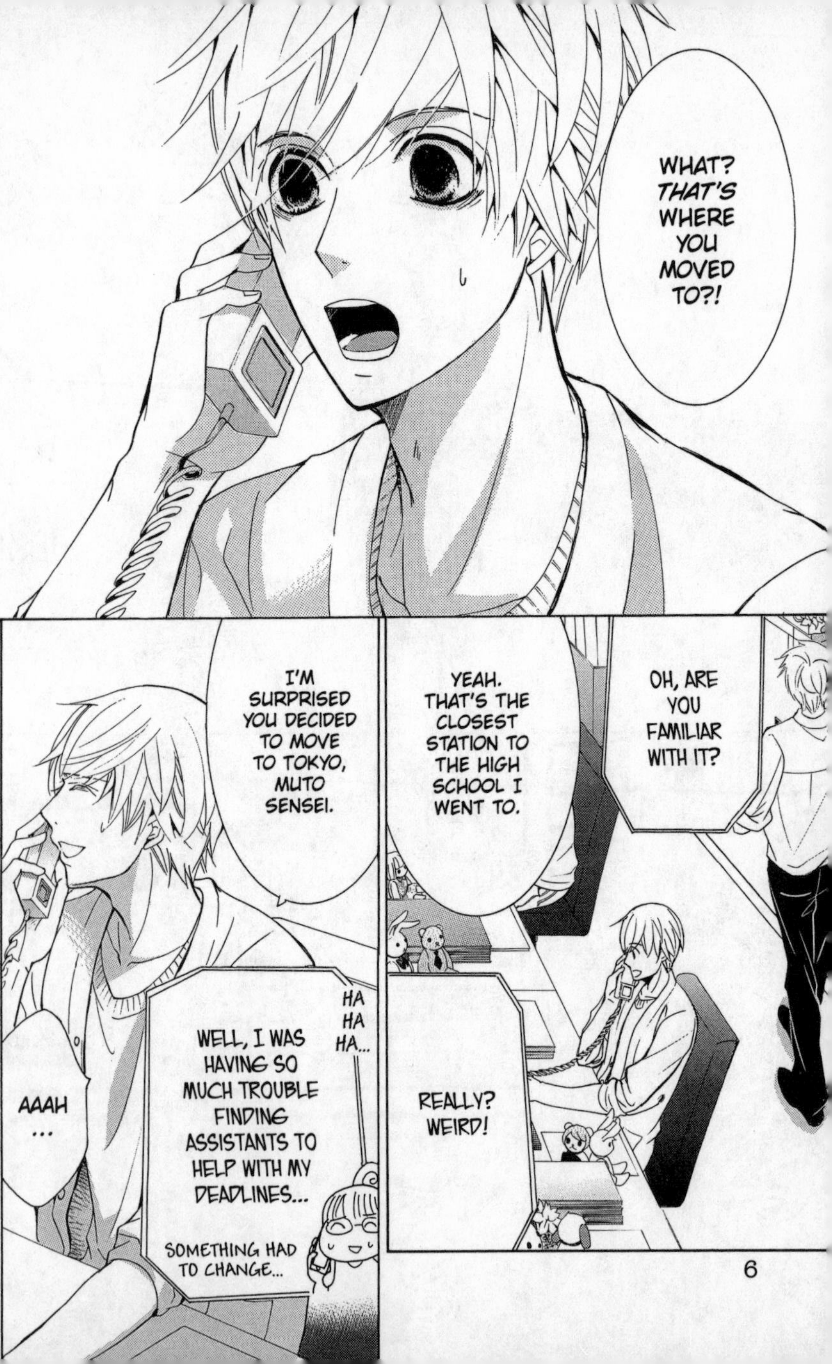
WHAT? THAT'S WHERE YOU MOVED TO?!
OH, ARE YOU FAMILIAR WITH IT?
YEAH. THAT'S THE CLOSEST STATION TO THE HIGH SCHOOL I WENT TO.
REALLY? WEIRD!
I'M SURPRISED YOU DECIDED TO MOVE TO TOKYO, MUTO SENSEI.
HA HA HA...
WELL, I WAS HAVING SO MUCH TROUBLE FINDING ASSISTANTS TO HELP WITH MY DEADLINES...
SOMETHING HAD TO CHANGE...
AAAH ...

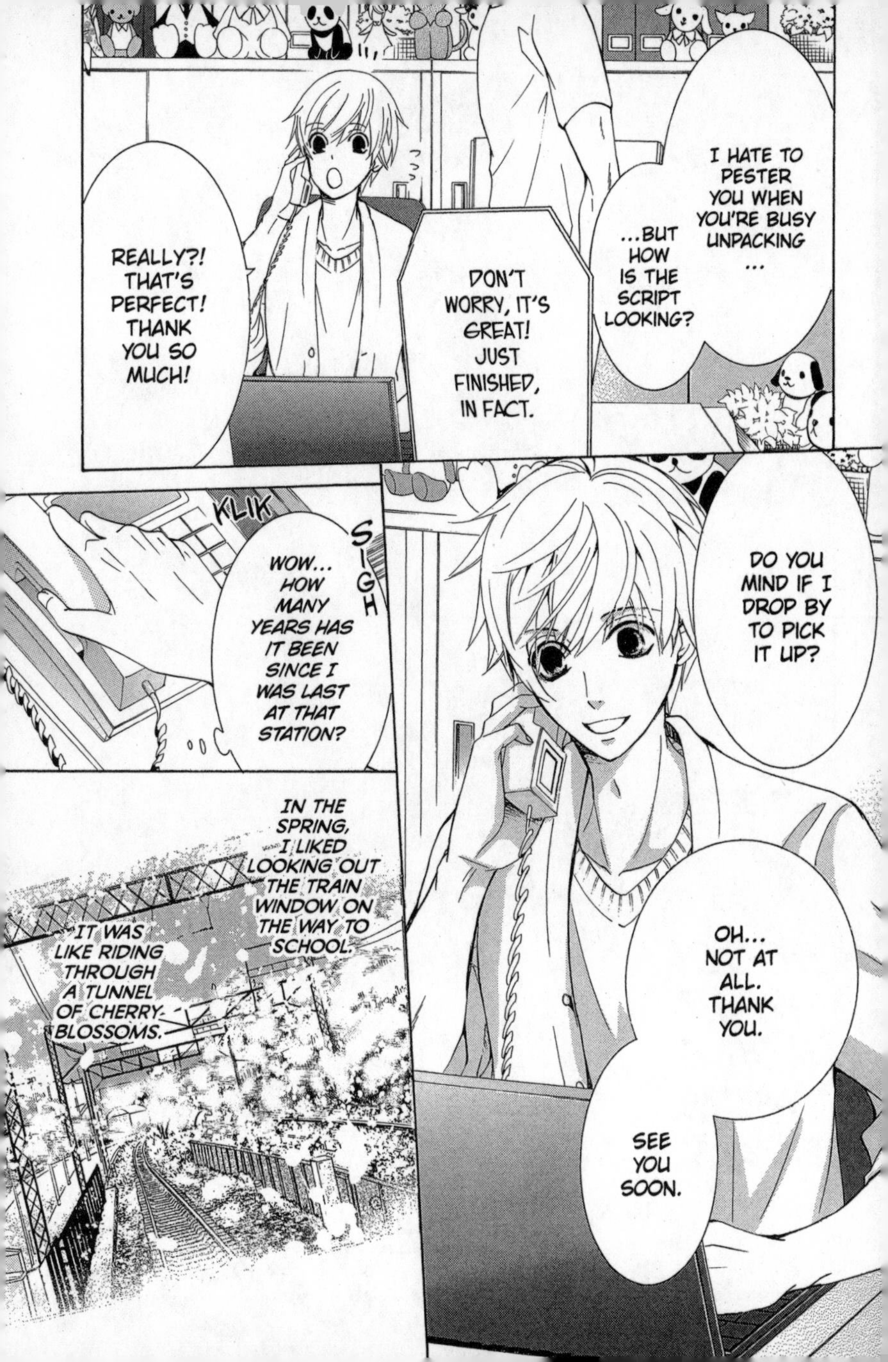
I HATE TO PESTER YOU WHEN YOU'RE BUSY UNPACKING ...
...BUT HOW IS THE SCRIPT LOOKING?
DON'T WORRY, IT'S GREAT! JUST FINISHED, IN FACT.
REALLY?! THAT'S PERFECT! THANK YOU SO MUCH!
DO YOU MIND IF I DROP BY TO PICK IT UP?
OH... NOT AT ALL. THANK YOU.
SEE YOU SOON.
KLIK
SIGH
WOW... HOW MANY YEARS HAS IT BEEN SINCE I WAS LAST AT THAT STATION?
IN THE SPRING, I LIKED LOOKING OUT THE TRAIN WINDOW ON THE WAY TO SCHOOL.
IT WAS LIKE RIDING THROUGH A TUNNEL OF CHERRY BLOSSOMS.

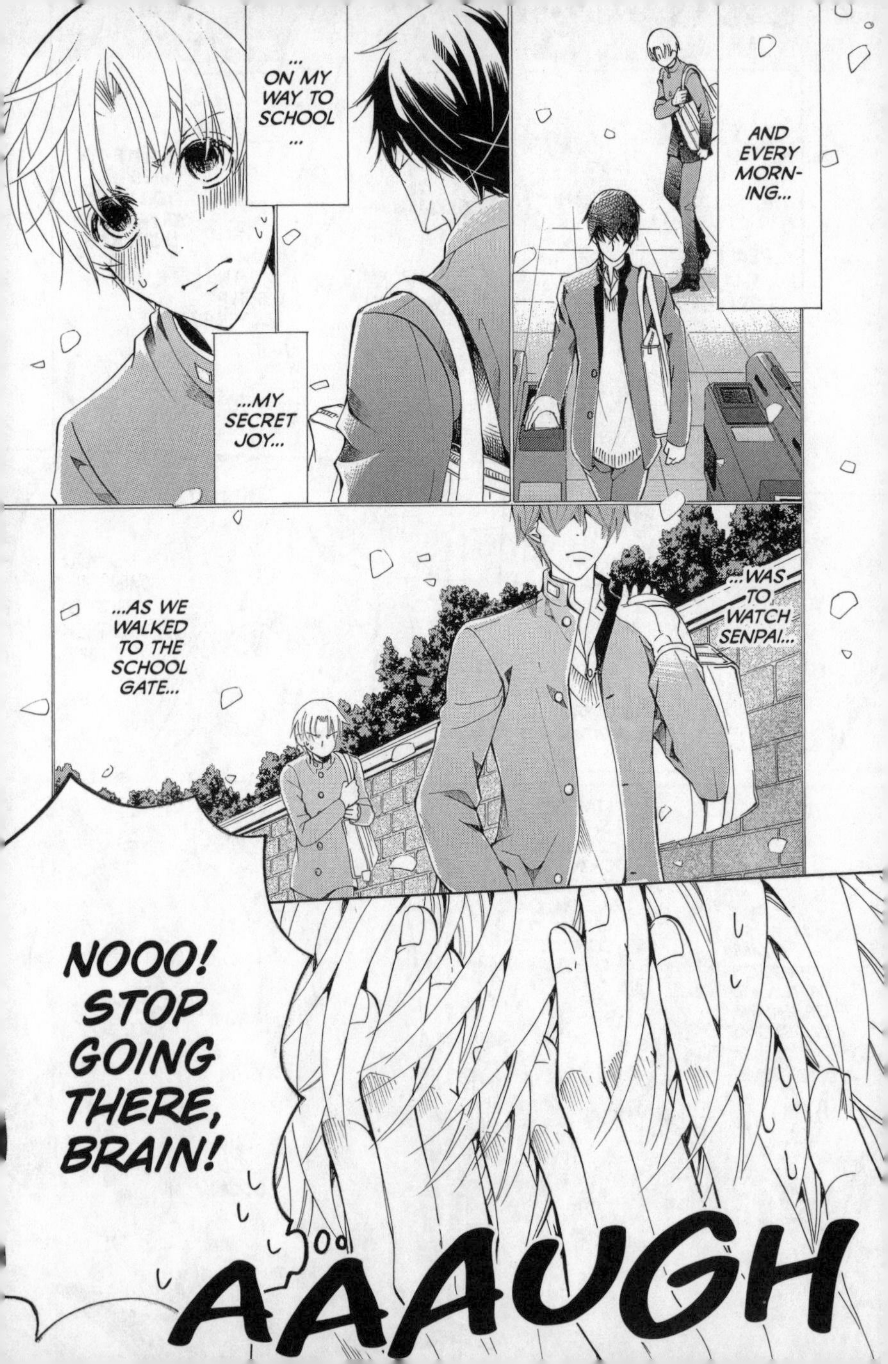
AND EVERY MORNING...
... ON MY WAY TO SCHOOL ...
...MY SECRET JOY...
...WAS TO WATCH SENPAI...
...AS WE WALKED TO THE SCHOOL GATE...
NOOO! STOP GOING THERE, BRAIN!
AAAUGH

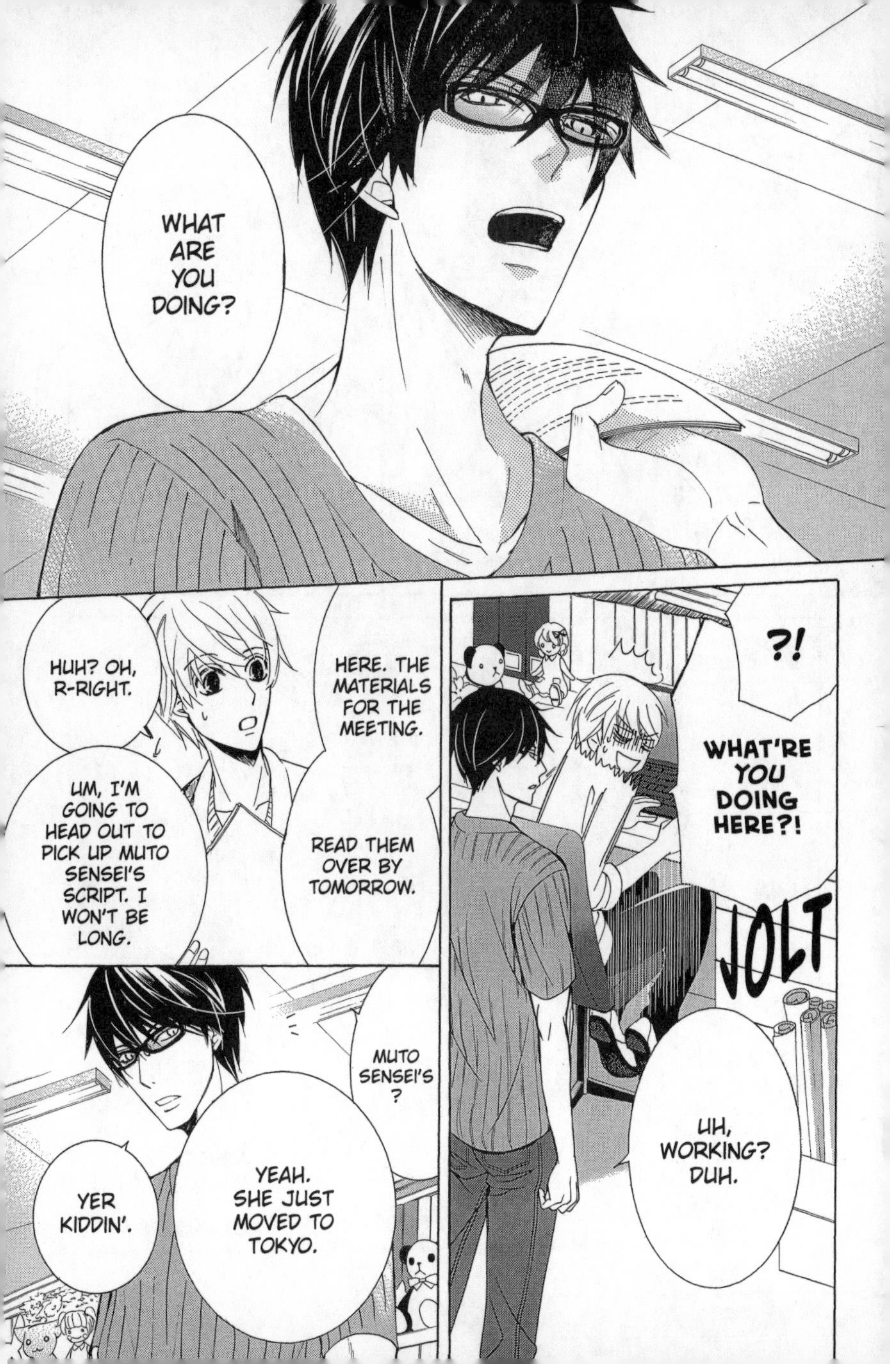
WHAT ARE YOU DOING?
?!
WHAT'RE YOU DOING HERE?!
JOLT
UH, WORKING? DUH.
HERE. THE MATERIALS FOR THE MEETING.
HUH? OH, R-RIGHT.
READ THEM OVER BY TOMORROW.
UM, I'M GOING TO HEAD OUT TO PICK UP MUTO SENSEI'S SCRIPT. I WON'T BE LONG.
MUTO SENSEI'S?
YEAH. SHE JUST MOVED TO TOKYO.
YER KIDDIN'.

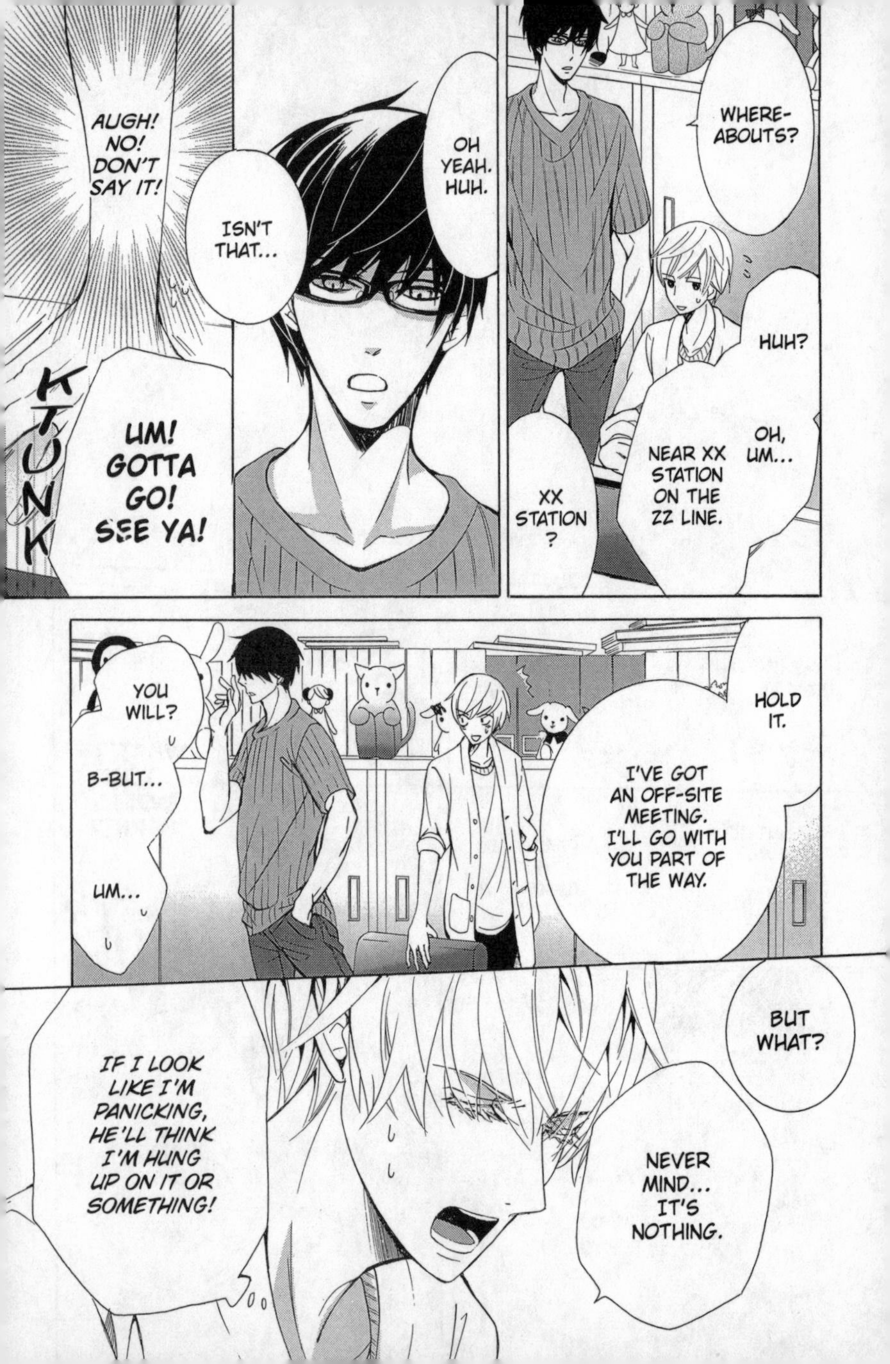
WHERE-ABOUTS?
HUH?
OH, UM...
NEAR XX STATION ON THE ZZ LINE.
XX STATION?
OH YEAH. HUH.
ISN'T THAT...
AUGH! NO! DON'T SAY IT!
UM! GOTTA GO! SEE YA!
KTUNK
HOLD IT.
I'VE GOT AN OFF-SITE MEETING. I'LL GO WITH YOU PART OF THE WAY.
YOU WILL?
B-BUT...
UM...
BUT WHAT?
NEVER MIND... IT'S NOTHING.
IF I LOOK LIKE I'M PANICKING, HE'LL THINK I'M HUNG UP ON IT OR SOMETHING!

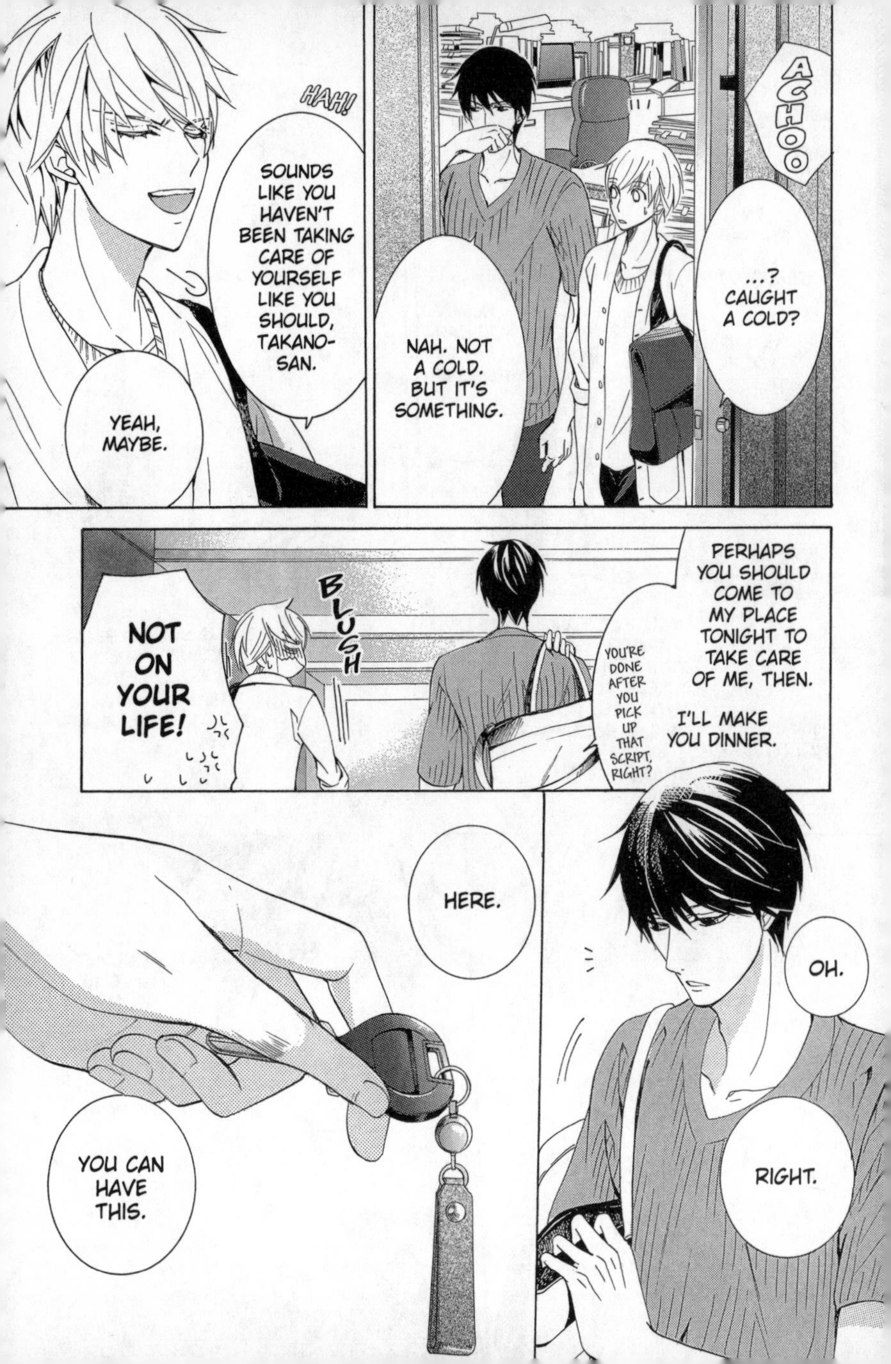
ACHOO
...? CAUGHT A COLD?
NAH. NOT A COLD. BUT IT'S SOMETHING.
HAH!
SOUNDS LIKE YOU HAVEN'T BEEN TAKING CARE OF YOURSELF LIKE YOU SHOULD, TAKANO-SAN.
YEAH, MAYBE.
PERHAPS YOU SHOULD COME TO MY PLACE TONIGHT TO TAKE CARE OF ME, THEN.
I'LL MAKE YOU DINNER.
YOU'RE DONE AFTER YOU PICK UP THAT SCRIPT, RIGHT?
BLUSH
NOT ON YOUR LIFE!
OH.
RIGHT.
HERE.
YOU CAN HAVE THIS.

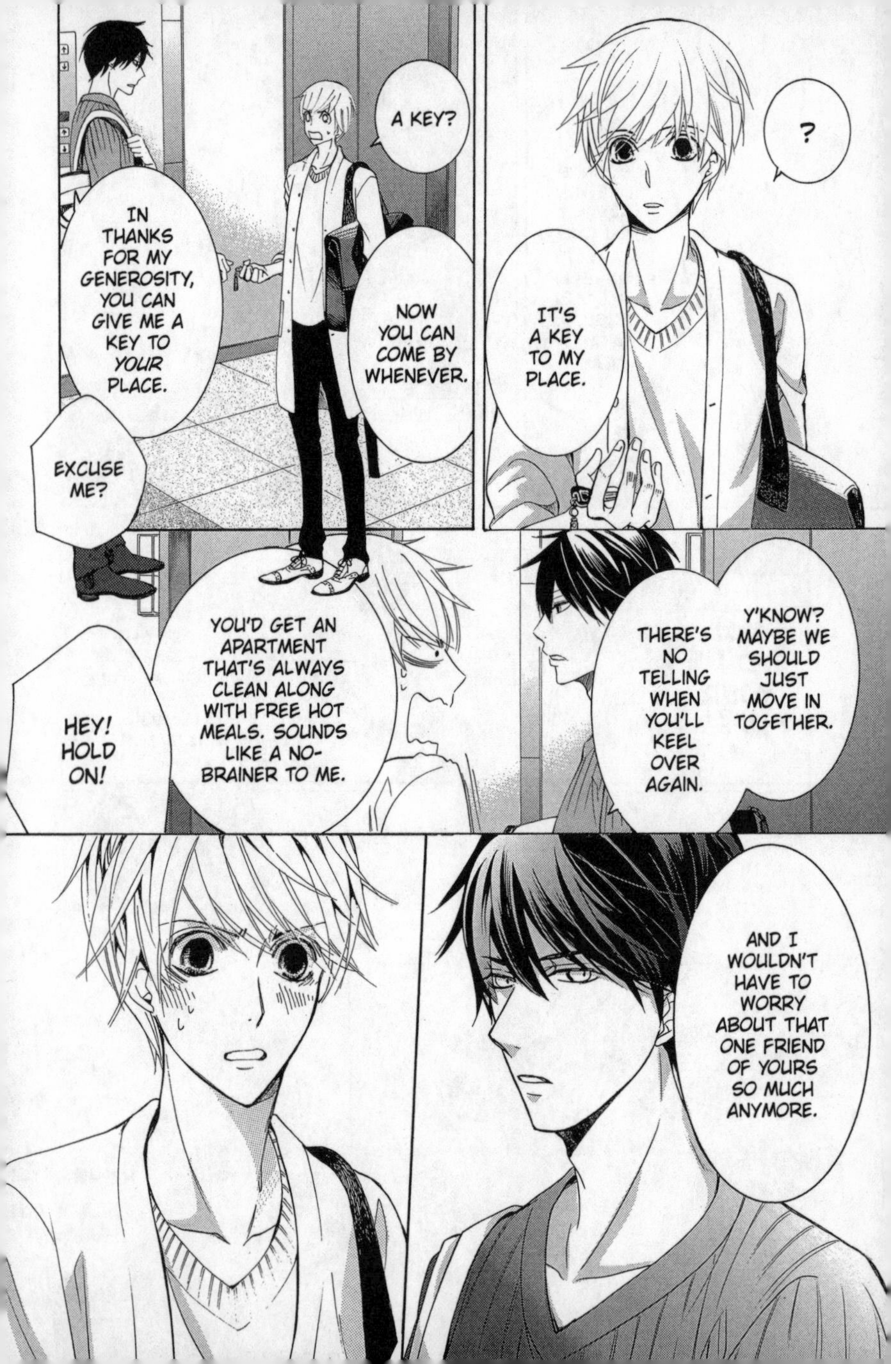
?
IT'S A KEY TO MY PLACE.
A KEY?
NOW YOU CAN COME BY WHENEVER.
IN THANKS FOR MY GENEROSITY, YOU CAN GIVE ME A KEY TO *YOUR* PLACE.
EXCUSE ME?
Y'KNOW? MAYBE WE SHOULD JUST MOVE IN TOGETHER.
THERE'S NO TELLING WHEN YOU'LL KEEL OVER AGAIN.
YOU'D GET AN APARTMENT THAT'S ALWAYS CLEAN ALONG WITH FREE HOT MEALS. SOUNDS LIKE A NO-BRAINER TO ME.
HEY! HOLD ON!
AND I WOULDN'T HAVE TO WORRY ABOUT THAT ONE FRIEND OF YOURS SO MUCH ANYMORE.

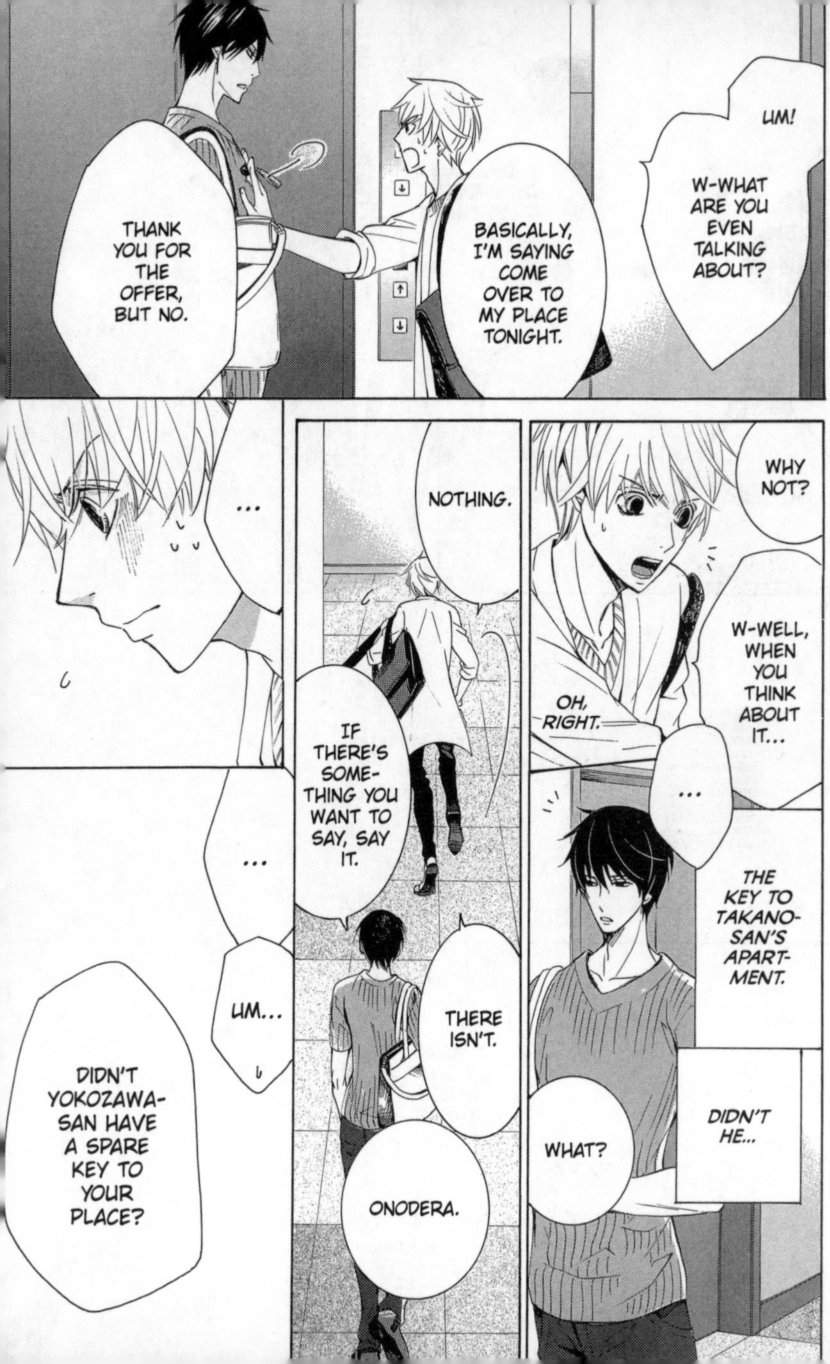
UM!
W-WHAT ARE YOU EVEN TALKING ABOUT?
BASICALLY, I'M SAYING COME OVER TO MY PLACE TONIGHT.
THANK YOU FOR THE OFFER, BUT NO.
WHY NOT?
W-WELL, WHEN YOU THINK ABOUT IT...
OH, RIGHT.
...
THE KEY TO TAKANO-SAN'S APARTMENT.
DIDN'T HE...
WHAT?
NOTHING.
IF THERE'S SOME-THING YOU WANT TO SAY, SAY IT.
THERE ISN'T.
ONODERA.
...
...
UM...
DIDN'T YOKOZAWA-SAN HAVE A SPARE KEY TO YOUR PLACE?

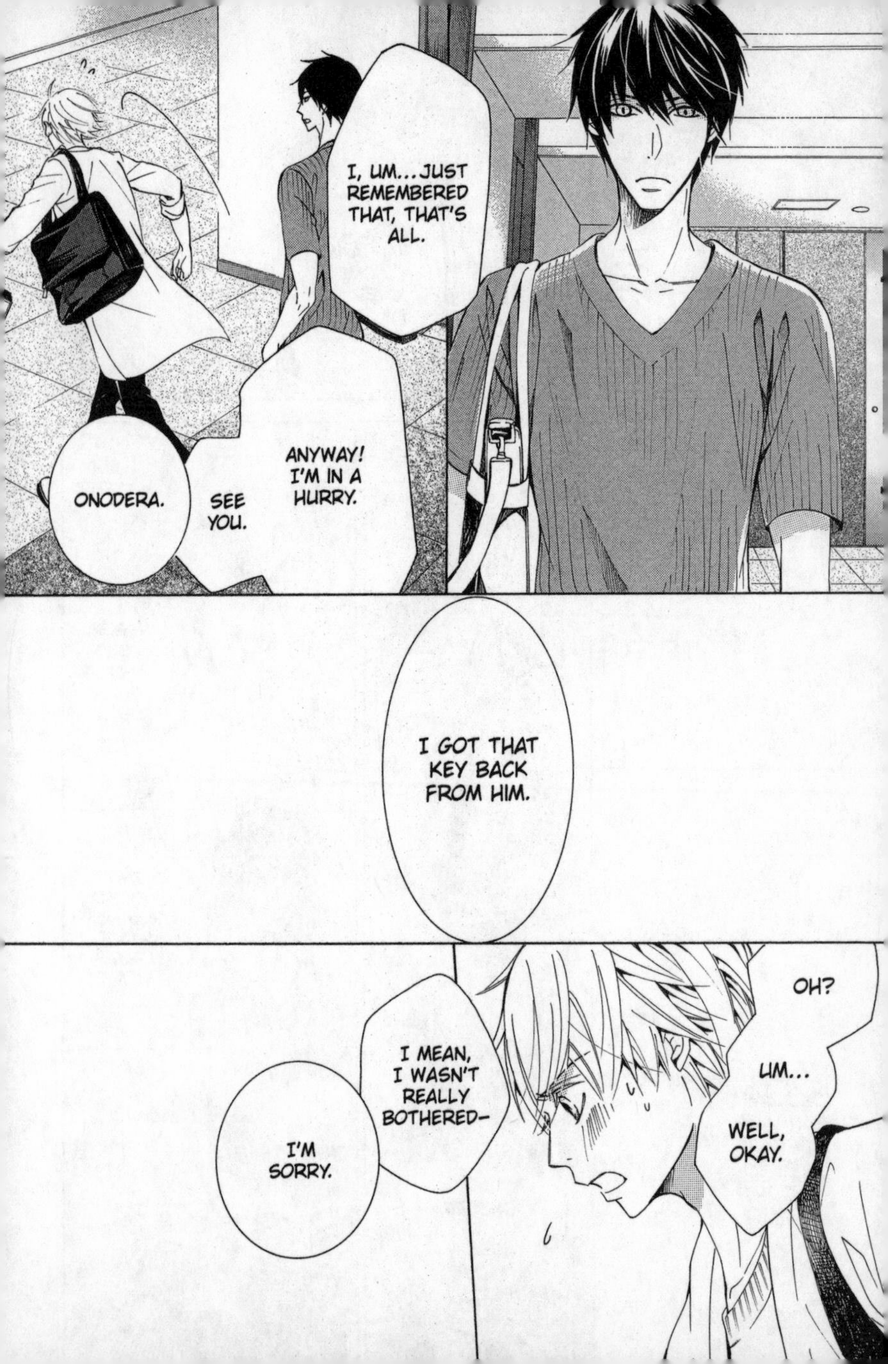
I, UM...JUST REMEMBERED THAT, THAT'S ALL.
ANYWAY! I'M IN A HURRY.
SEE YOU.
ONODERA.
I GOT THAT KEY BACK FROM HIM.
OH?
UM...
WELL, OKAY.
I MEAN, I WASN'T REALLY BOTHERED–
I'M SORRY.

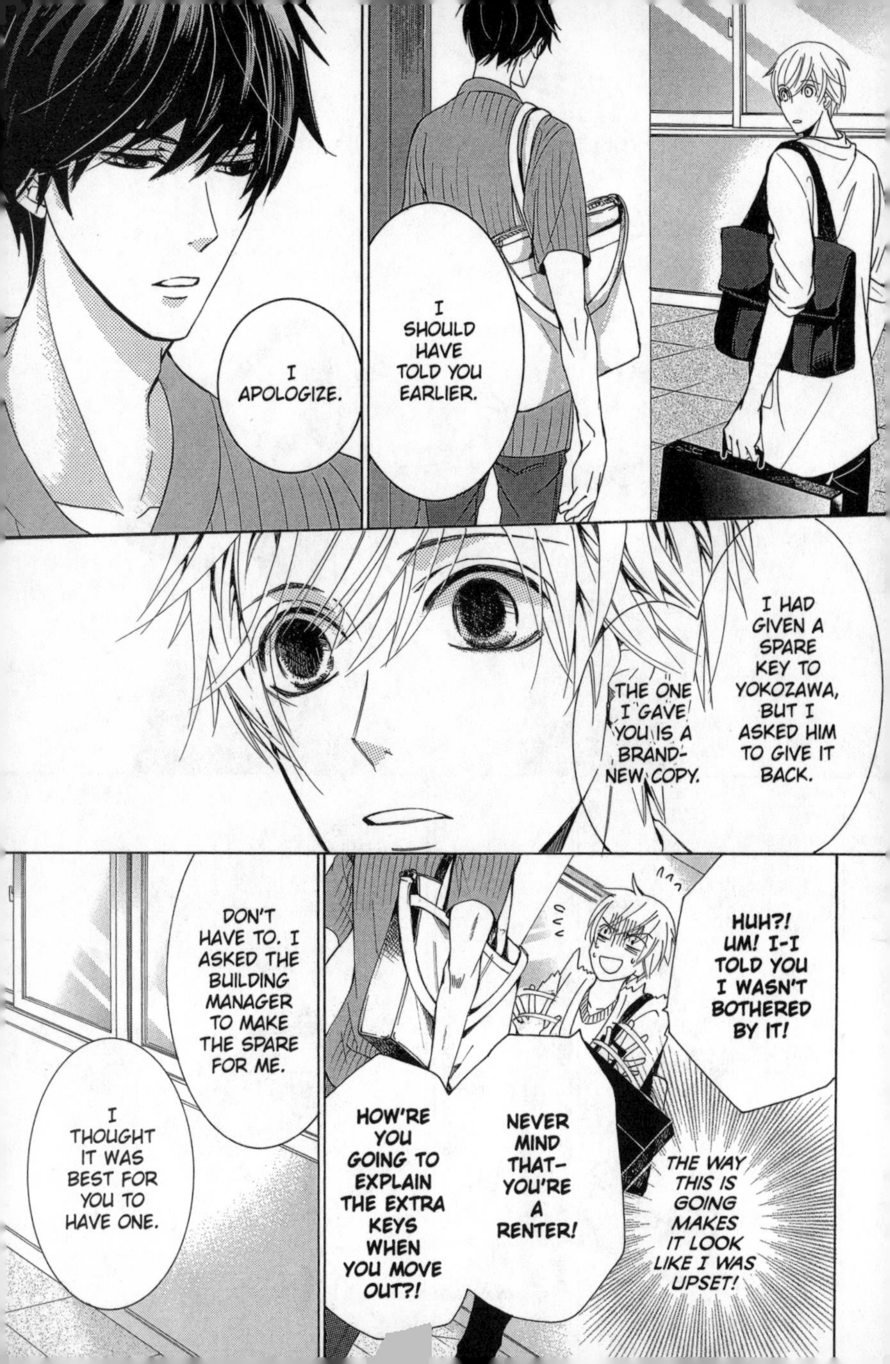
I SHOULD HAVE TOLD YOU EARLIER.
I APOLOGIZE.
I HAD GIVEN A SPARE KEY TO YOKOZAWA, BUT I ASKED HIM TO GIVE IT BACK.
THE ONE I GAVE YOU IS A BRAND-NEW COPY.
HUH?! UM! I-I TOLD YOU I WASN'T BOTHERED BY IT!
THE WAY THIS IS GOING MAKES IT LOOK LIKE I WAS UPSET!
NEVER MIND THAT— YOU'RE A RENTER!
HOW'RE YOU GOING TO EXPLAIN THE EXTRA KEYS WHEN YOU MOVE OUT?!
DON'T HAVE TO. I ASKED THE BUILDING MANAGER TO MAKE THE SPARE FOR ME.
I THOUGHT IT WAS BEST FOR YOU TO HAVE ONE.

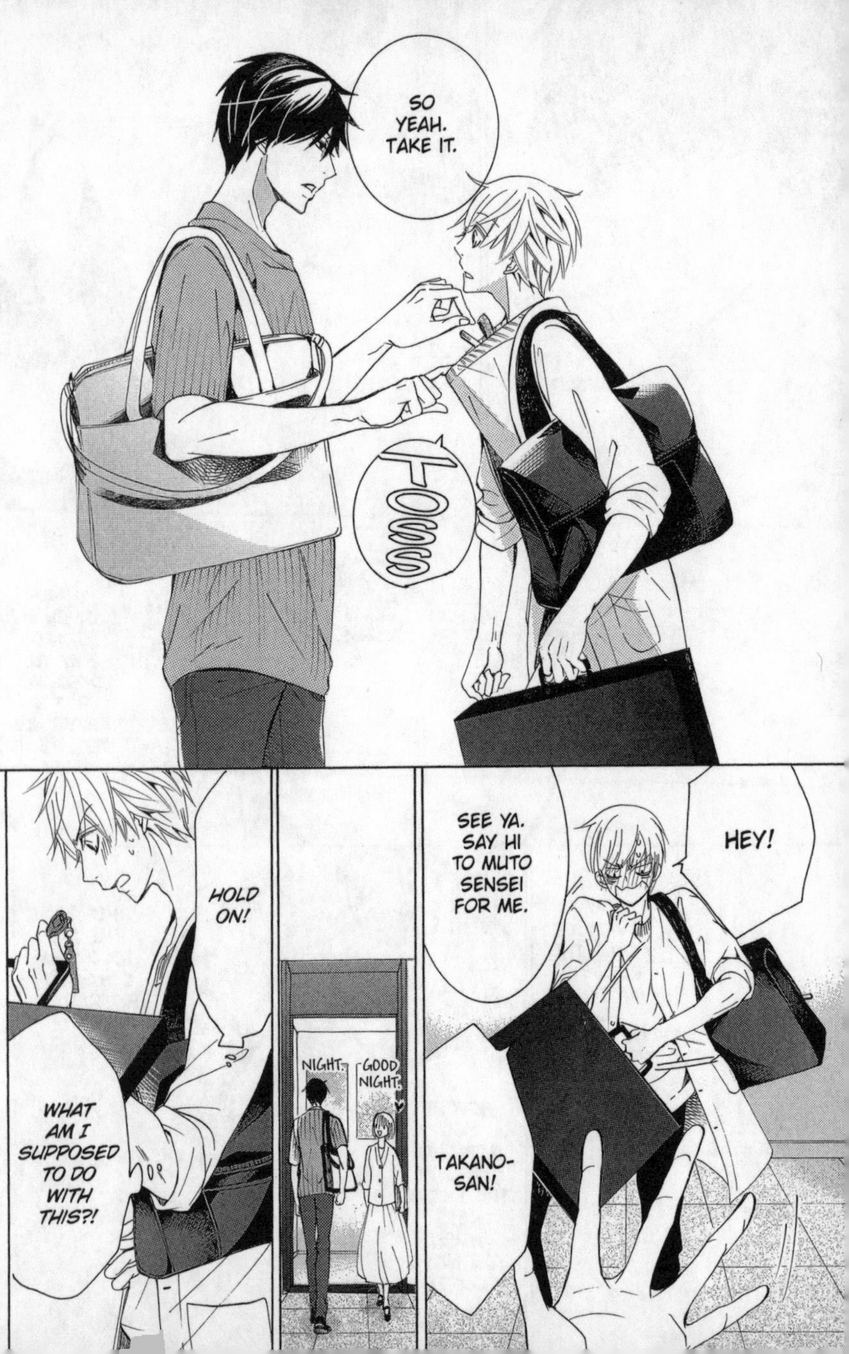
SO YEAH. TAKE IT.
TOSS
HEY!
SEE YA. SAY HI TO MUTO SENSEI FOR ME.
TAKANO-SAN!
GOOD NIGHT.
NIGHT.
HOLD ON!
WHAT AM I SUPPOSED TO DO WITH THIS?!

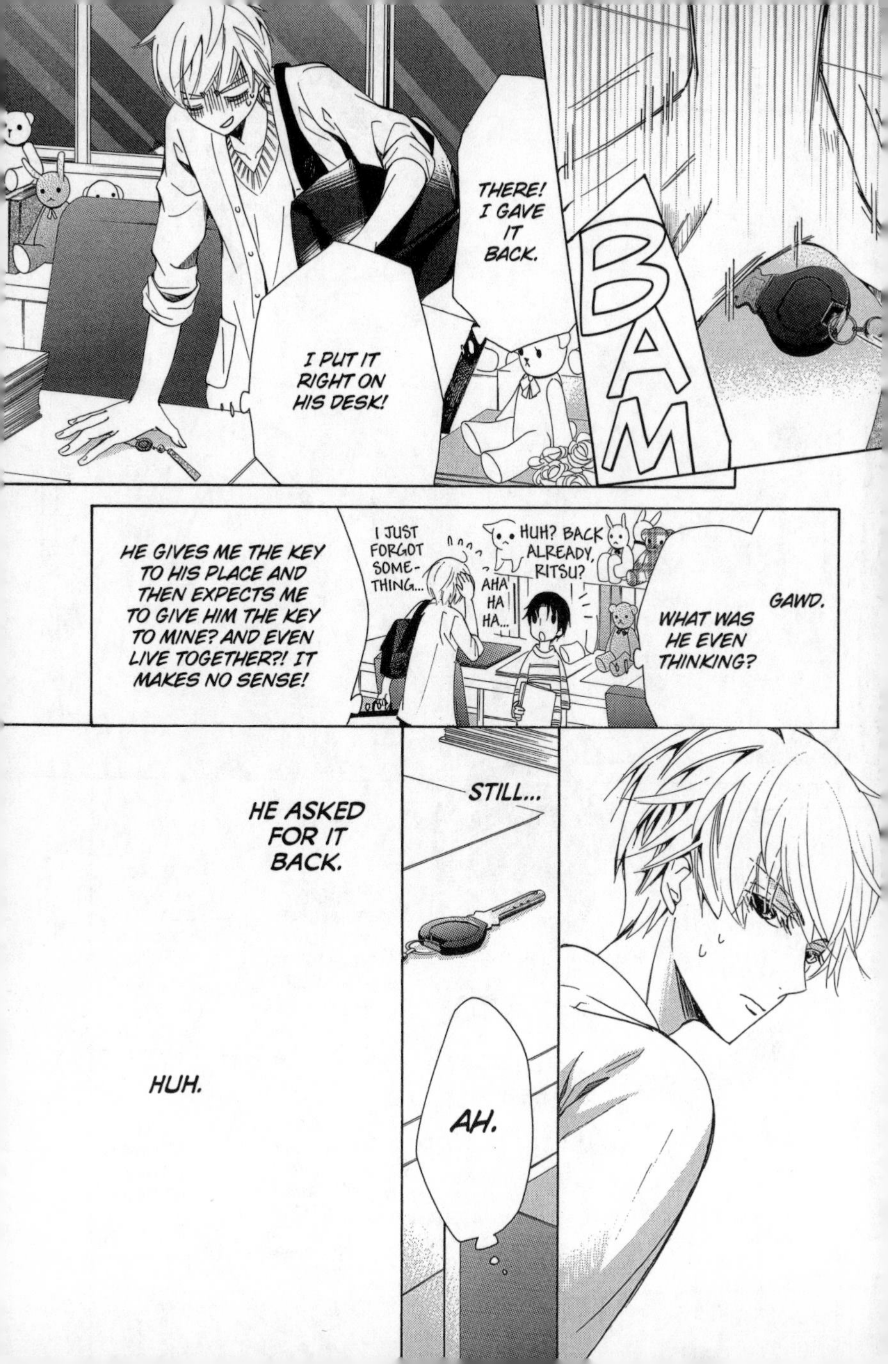
BAM
THERE! I GAVE IT BACK.
I PUT IT RIGHT ON HIS DESK!
GAWD.
WHAT WAS HE EVEN THINKING?
HUH? BACK ALREADY, RITSU?
I JUST FORGOT SOME-THING...
AHA HA HA...
HE GIVES ME THE KEY TO HIS PLACE AND THEN EXPECTS ME TO GIVE HIM THE KEY TO MINE? AND EVEN LIVE TOGETHER?! IT MAKES NO SENSE!
STILL...
AH.
HE ASKED FOR IT BACK.
HUH.

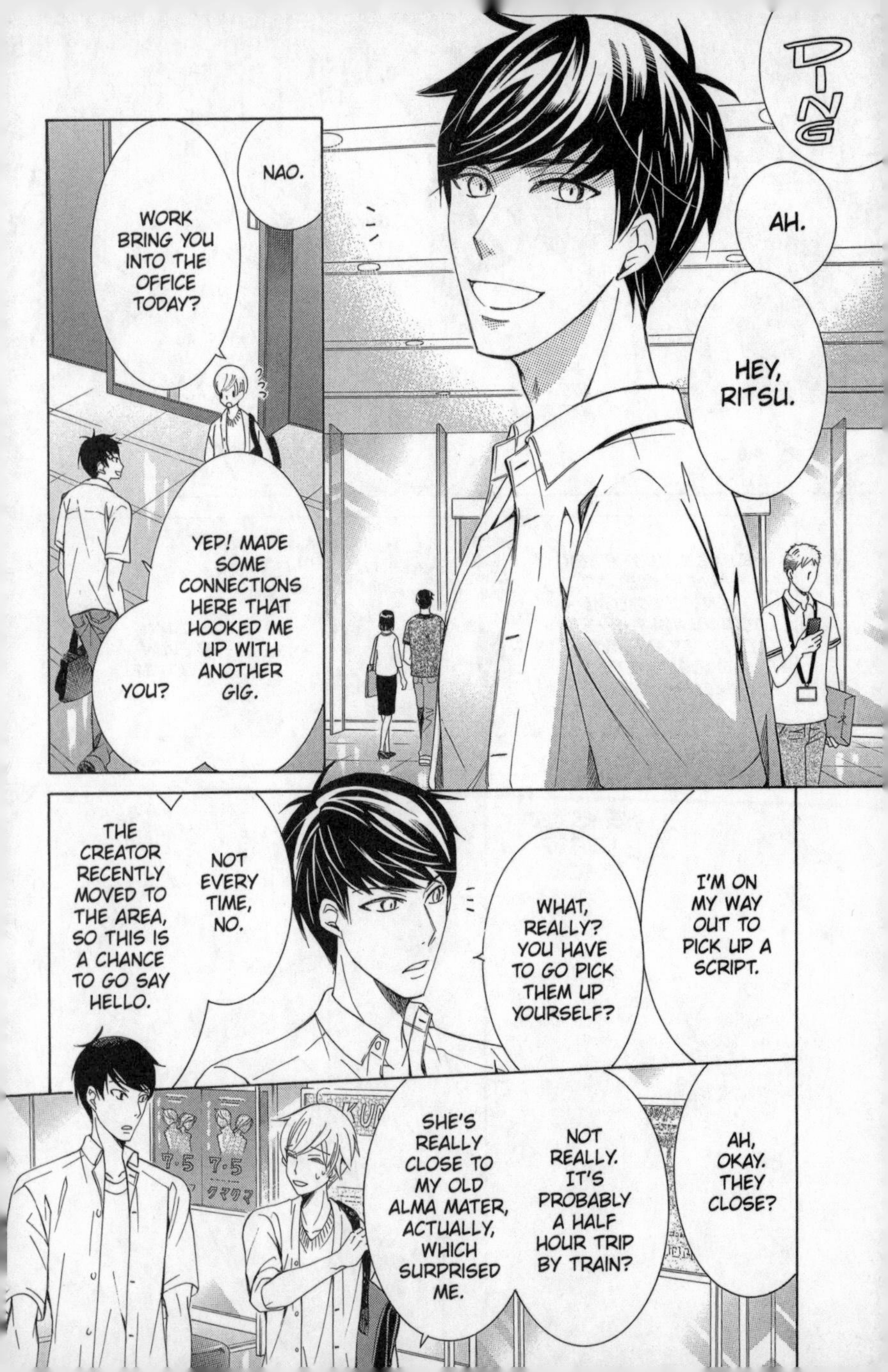
DING
AH.
HEY, RITSU.
NAO.
WORK BRING YOU INTO THE OFFICE TODAY?
YEP! MADE SOME CONNECTIONS HERE THAT HOOKED ME UP WITH ANOTHER GIG.
YOU?
I'M ON MY WAY OUT TO PICK UP A SCRIPT.
WHAT, REALLY? YOU HAVE TO GO PICK THEM UP YOURSELF?
NOT EVERY TIME, NO.
THE CREATOR RECENTLY MOVED TO THE AREA, SO THIS IS A CHANCE TO GO SAY HELLO.
AH, OKAY. THEY CLOSE?
NOT REALLY. IT'S PROBABLY A HALF HOUR TRIP BY TRAIN?
SHE'S REALLY CLOSE TO MY OLD ALMA MATER, ACTUALLY, WHICH SURPRISED ME.

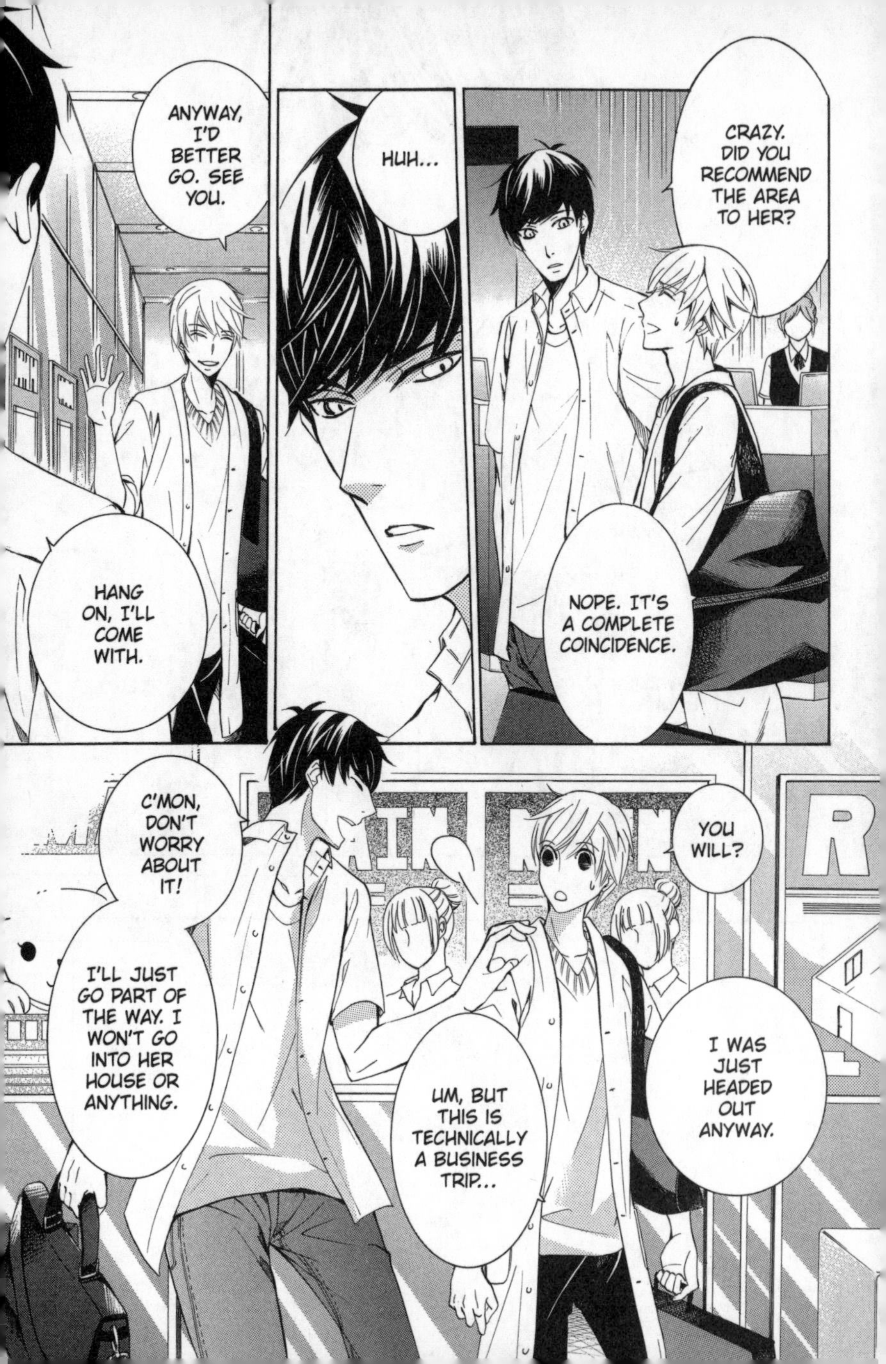
CRAZY. DID YOU RECOMMEND THE AREA TO HER?
NOPE. IT'S A COMPLETE COINCIDENCE.
HUH...
ANYWAY, I'D BETTER GO. SEE YOU.
HANG ON, I'LL COME WITH.
YOU WILL?
I WAS JUST HEADED OUT ANYWAY.
UM, BUT THIS IS TECHNICALLY A BUSINESS TRIP...
C'MON, DON'T WORRY ABOUT IT!
I'LL JUST GO PART OF THE WAY. I WON'T GO INTO HER HOUSE OR ANYTHING.

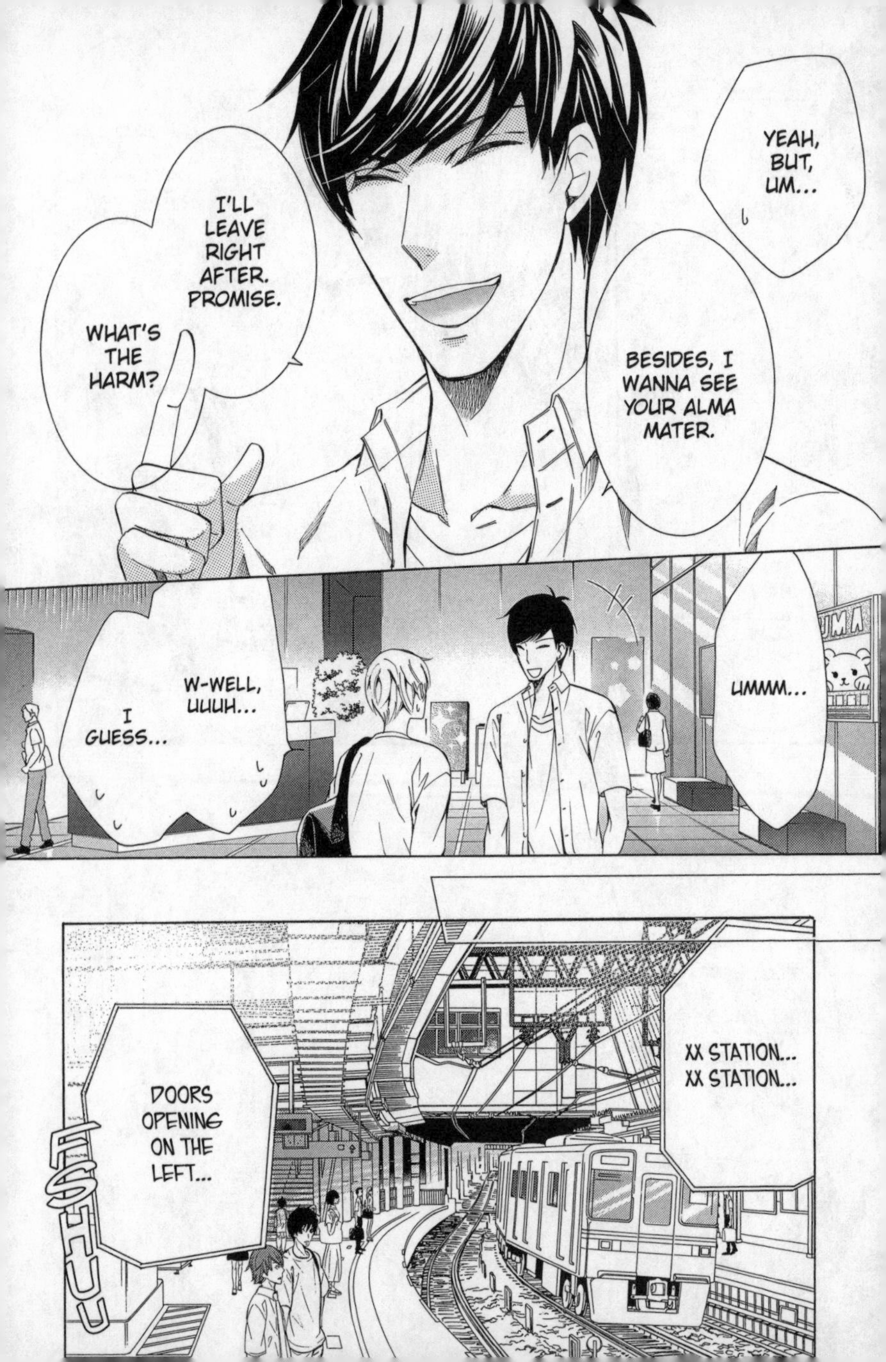
YEAH, BUT, UM...
BESIDES, I WANNA SEE YOUR ALMA MATER.
I'LL LEAVE RIGHT AFTER. PROMISE.
WHAT'S THE HARM?
UMMM...
W-WELL, UUUH...
I GUESS...
XX STATION... XX STATION...
DOORS OPENING ON THE LEFT...
FSHUU

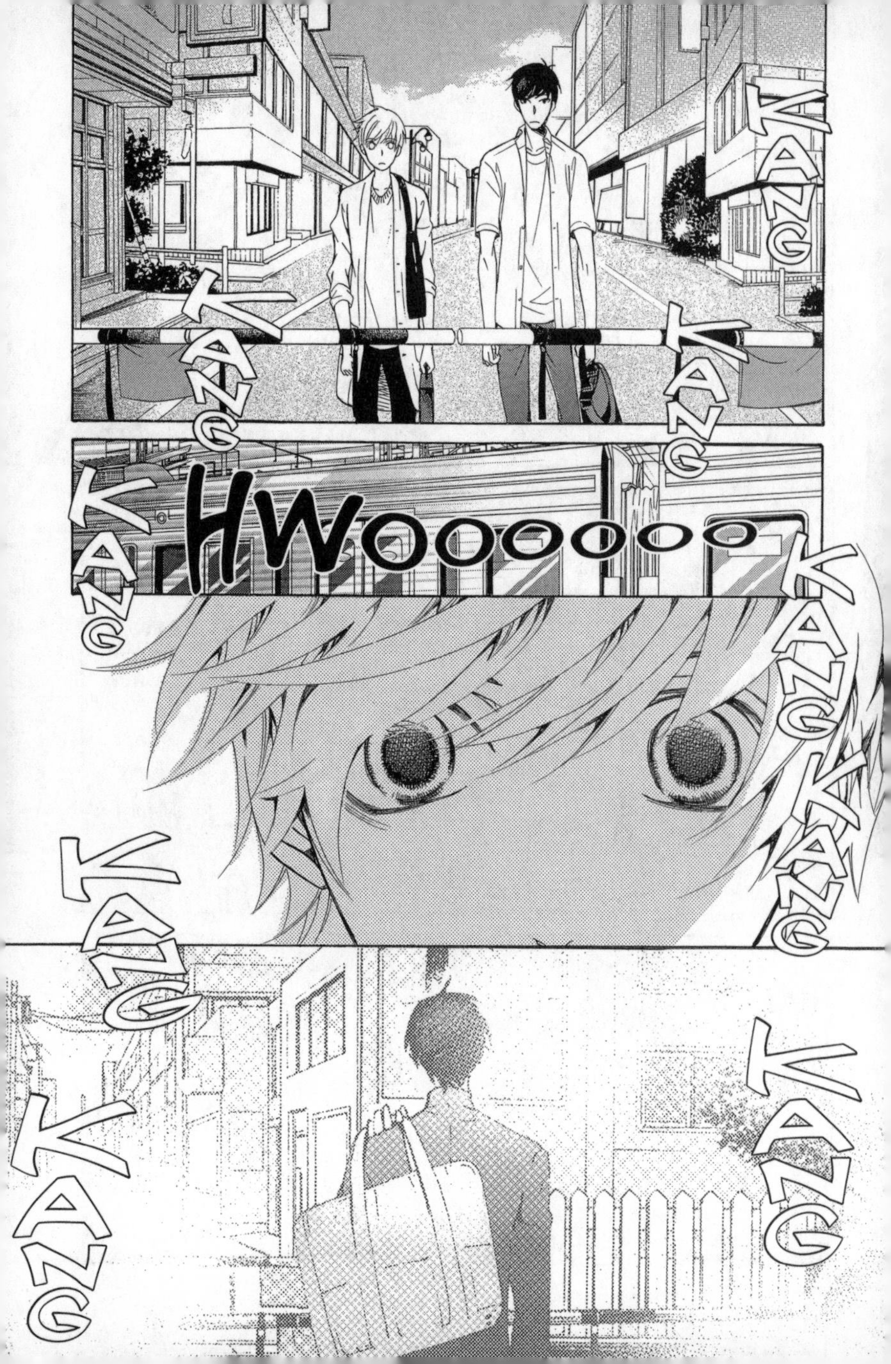
KANG
KANG
KANG
HWOOOOOO
KANG
KANGKANG
KANG
KANG
KANG
KANG

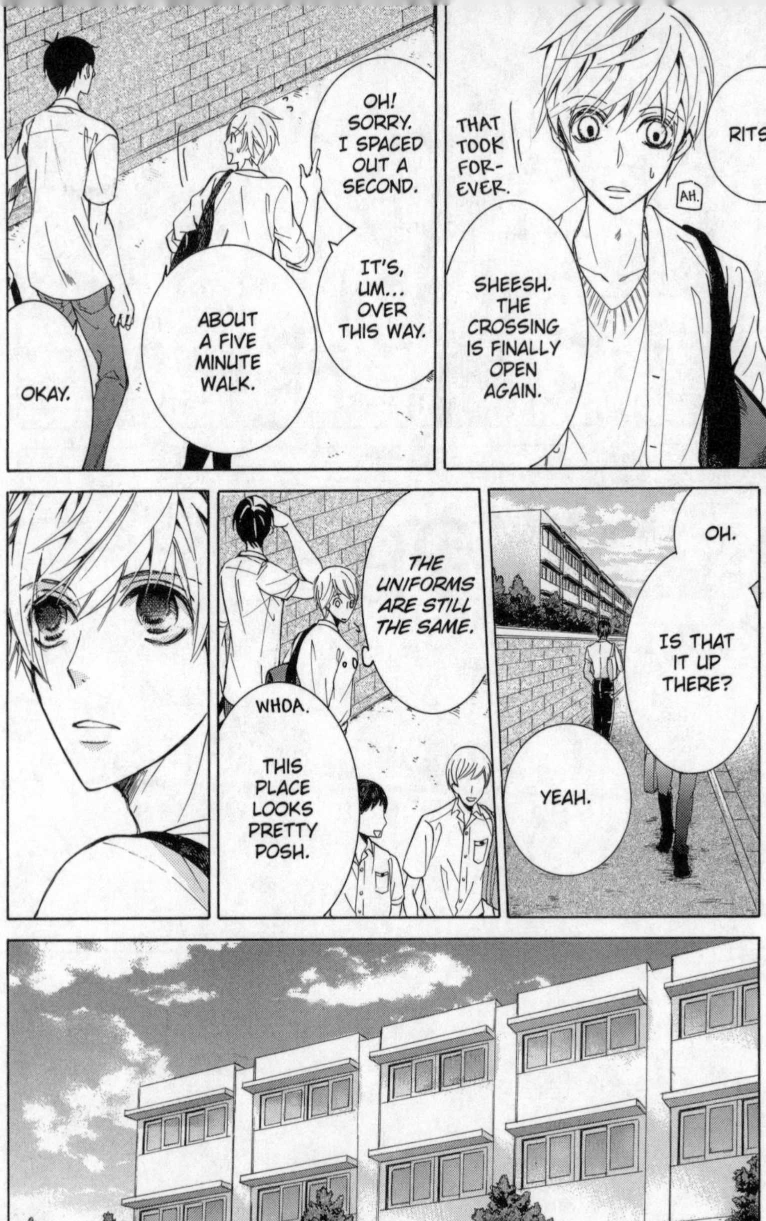
RITSU?
AH.
THAT TOOK FOR-EVER.
SHEESH. THE CROSSING IS FINALLY OPEN AGAIN.
OH! SORRY. I SPACED OUT A SECOND.
IT'S, UM... OVER THIS WAY.
ABOUT A FIVE MINUTE WALK.
OKAY.
OH.
IS THAT IT UP THERE?
YEAH.
THE UNIFORMS ARE STILL THE SAME.
WHOA.
THIS PLACE LOOKS PRETTY POSH.

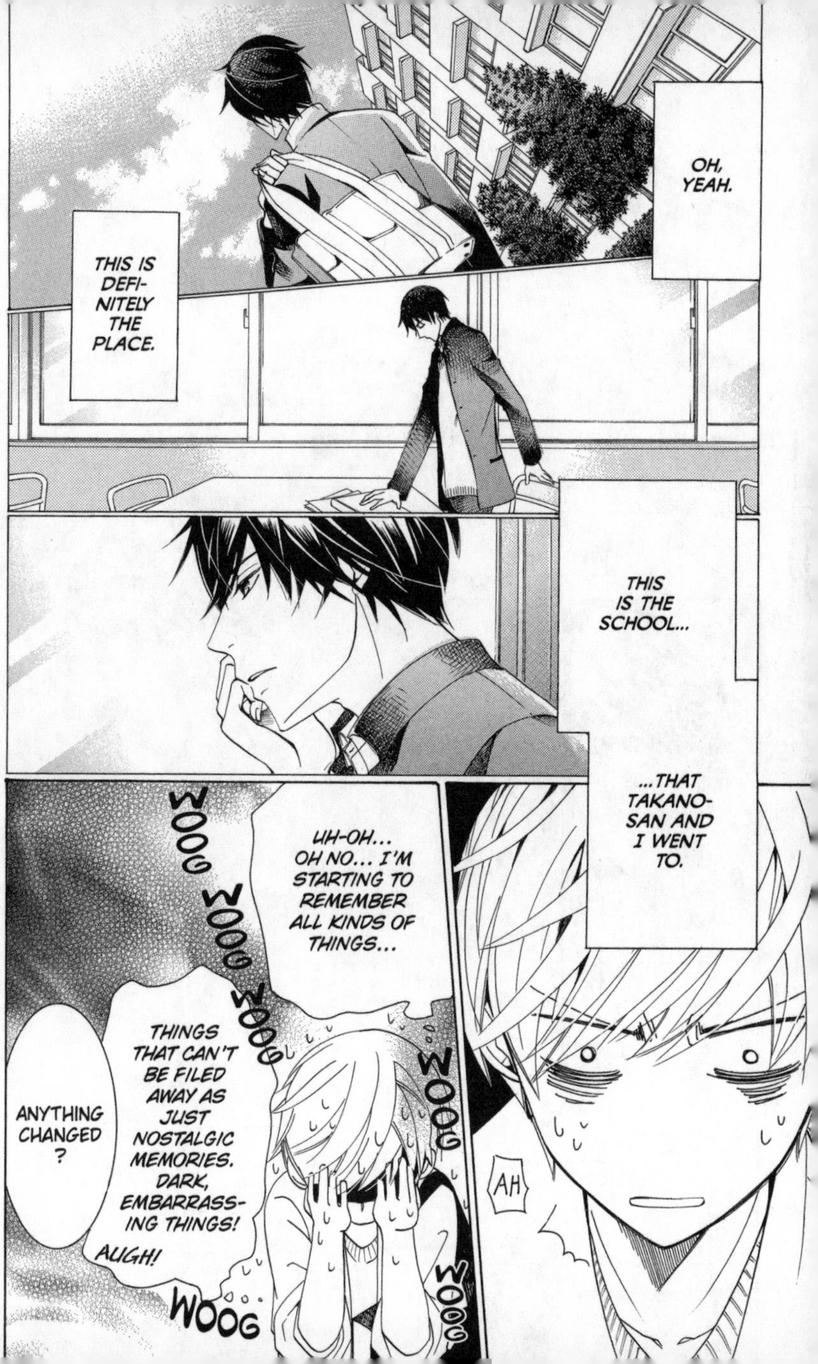
OH, YEAH.
THIS IS DEFI-NITELY THE PLACE.
THIS IS THE SCHOOL...
...THAT TAKANO-SAN AND I WENT TO.
AH
WOOG WOOG WOOG
UH-OH... OH NO... I'M STARTING TO REMEMBER ALL KINDS OF THINGS...
WOOG
THINGS THAT CAN'T BE FILED AWAY AS JUST NOSTALGIC MEMORIES. DARK, EMBARRASS-ING THINGS!
WOOG
ANYTHING CHANGED?
AUGH!
WOOG

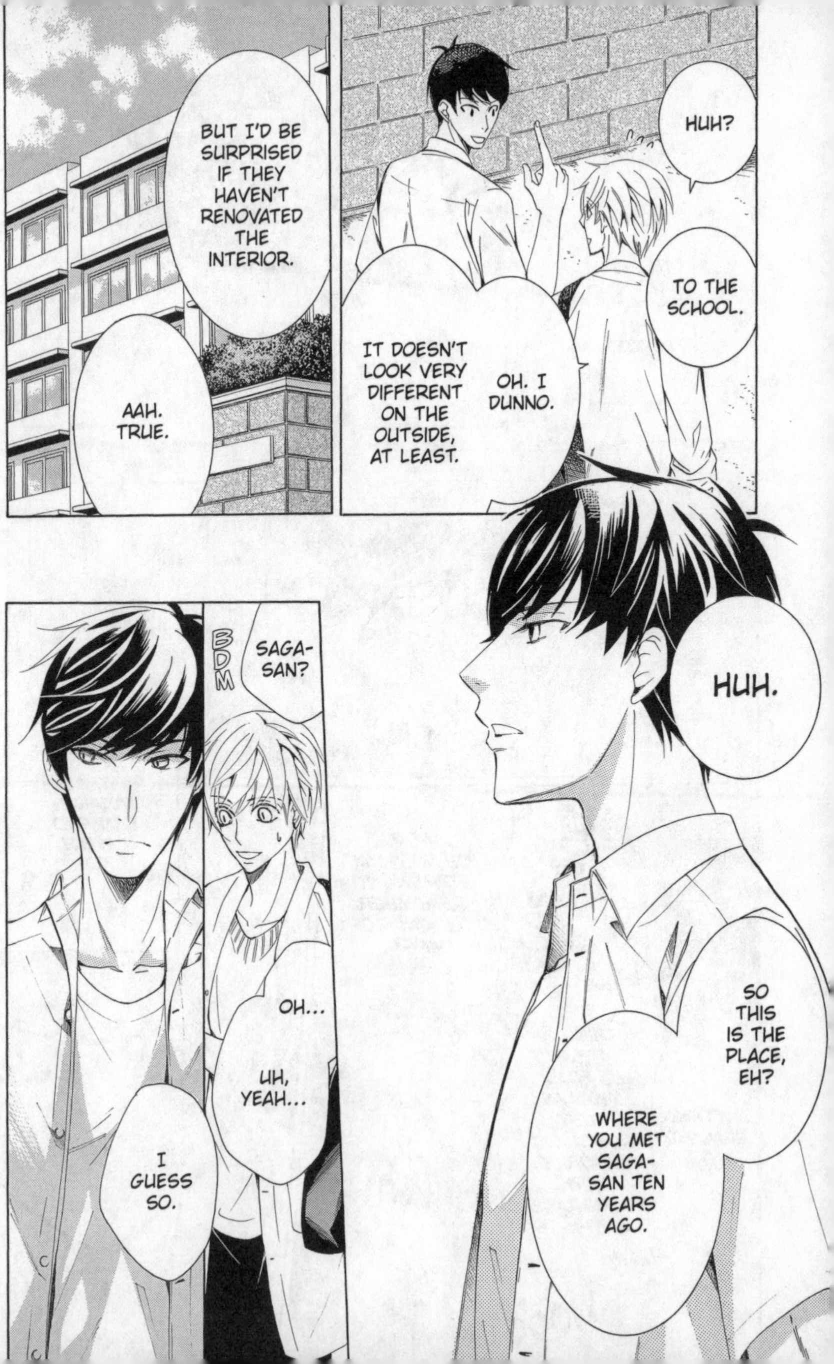
HUH?
TO THE SCHOOL.
OH. I DUNNO.
IT DOESN'T LOOK VERY DIFFERENT ON THE OUTSIDE, AT LEAST.
BUT I'D BE SURPRISED IF THEY HAVEN'T RENOVATED THE INTERIOR.
AAH. TRUE.
HUH.
SO THIS IS THE PLACE, EH?
WHERE YOU MET SAGA-SAN TEN YEARS AGO.
BDM
SAGA-SAN?
OH...
UH, YEAH...
I GUESS SO.

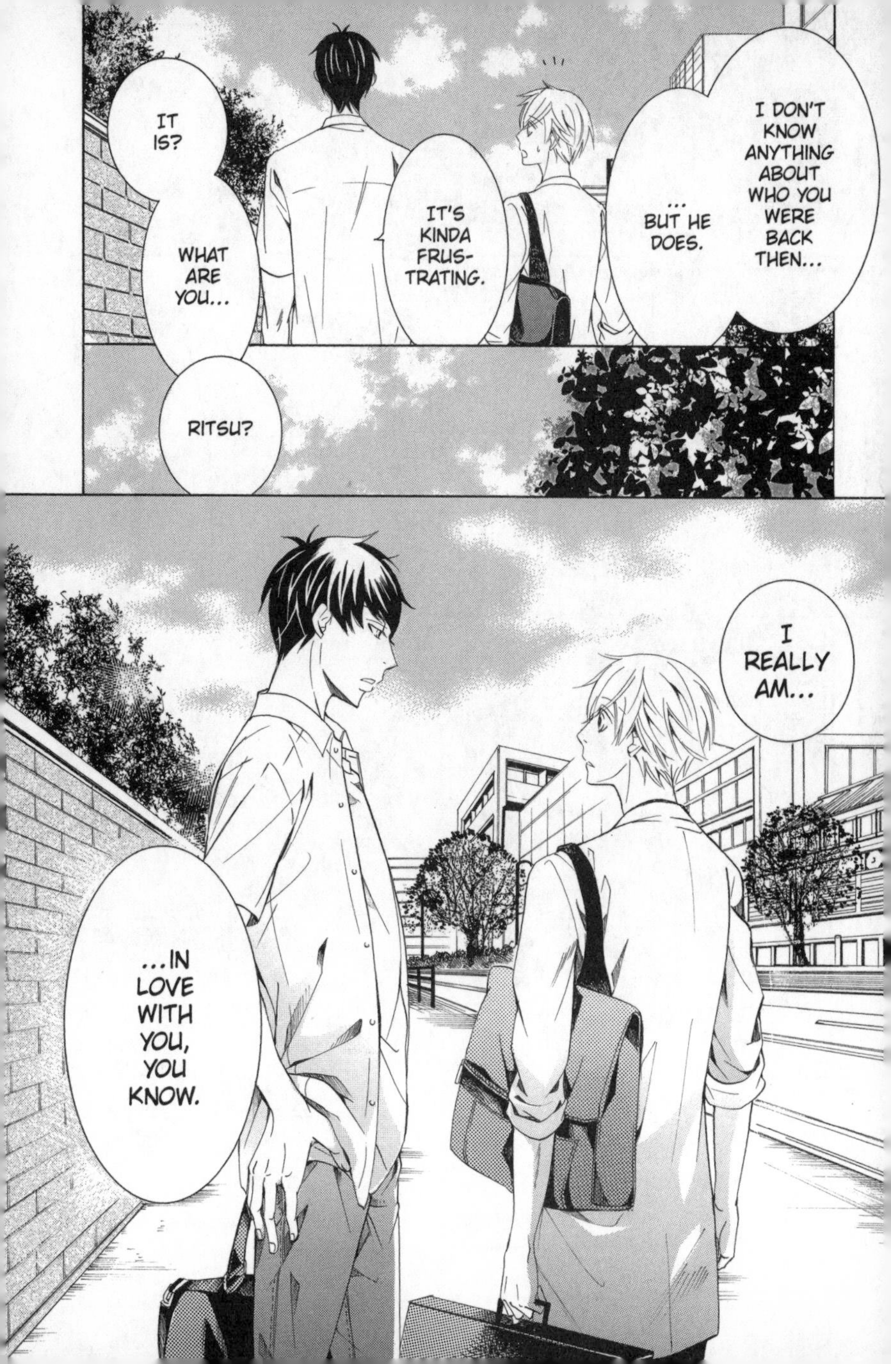
I DON'T KNOW ANYTHING ABOUT WHO YOU WERE BACK THEN...
...BUT HE DOES.
IT'S KINDA FRUS-TRATING.
IT IS?
WHAT ARE YOU...
RITSU?
I REALLY AM...
...IN LOVE WITH YOU, YOU KNOW.

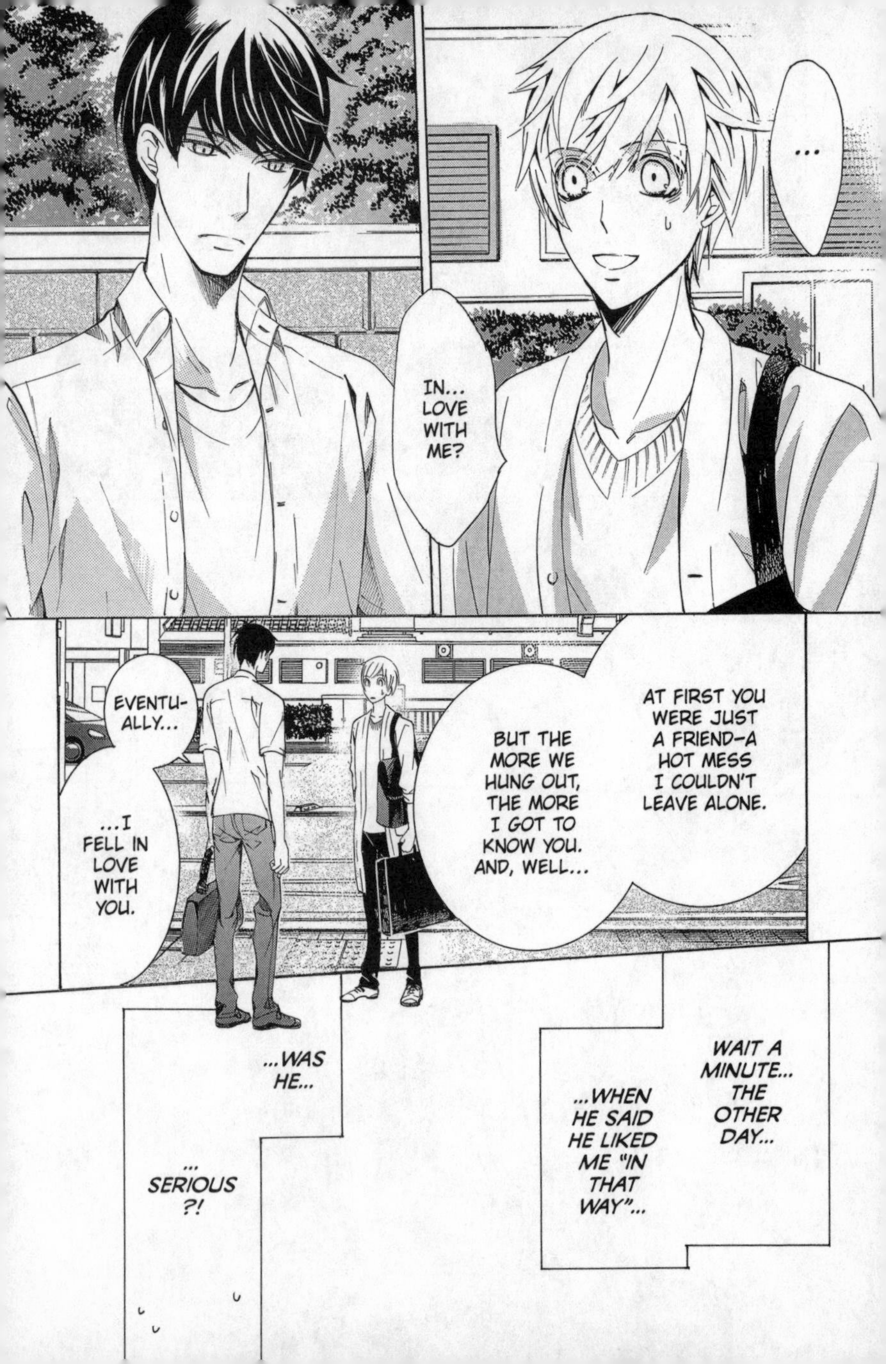
...
IN... LOVE WITH ME?
AT FIRST YOU WERE JUST A FRIEND—A HOT MESS I COULDN'T LEAVE ALONE.
BUT THE MORE WE HUNG OUT, THE MORE I GOT TO KNOW YOU. AND, WELL...
EVENTU-ALLY...
...I FELL IN LOVE WITH YOU.
WAIT A MINUTE... THE OTHER DAY...
...WHEN HE SAID HE LIKED ME "IN THAT WAY"...
...WAS HE...
... SERIOUS ?!

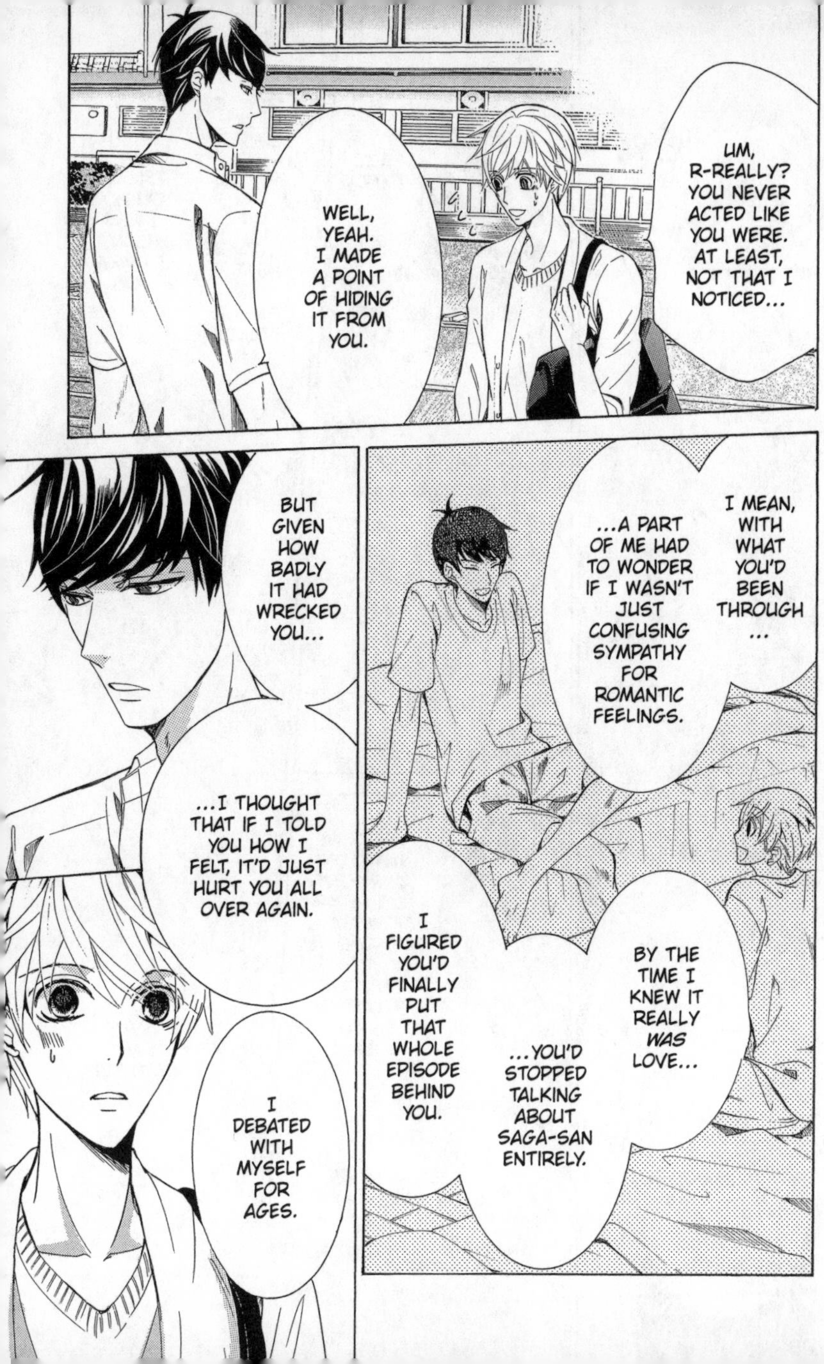
UM, R-REALLY? YOU NEVER ACTED LIKE YOU WERE. AT LEAST, NOT THAT I NOTICED...
WELL, YEAH. I MADE A POINT OF HIDING IT FROM YOU.
I MEAN, WITH WHAT YOU'D BEEN THROUGH...
...A PART OF ME HAD TO WONDER IF I WASN'T JUST CONFUSING SYMPATHY FOR ROMANTIC FEELINGS.
BY THE TIME I KNEW IT REALLY *WAS* LOVE...
...YOU'D STOPPED TALKING ABOUT SAGA-SAN ENTIRELY.
I FIGURED YOU'D FINALLY PUT THAT WHOLE EPISODE BEHIND YOU.
BUT GIVEN HOW BADLY IT HAD WRECKED YOU...
...I THOUGHT THAT IF I TOLD YOU HOW I FELT, IT'D JUST HURT YOU ALL OVER AGAIN.
I DEBATED WITH MYSELF FOR AGES.

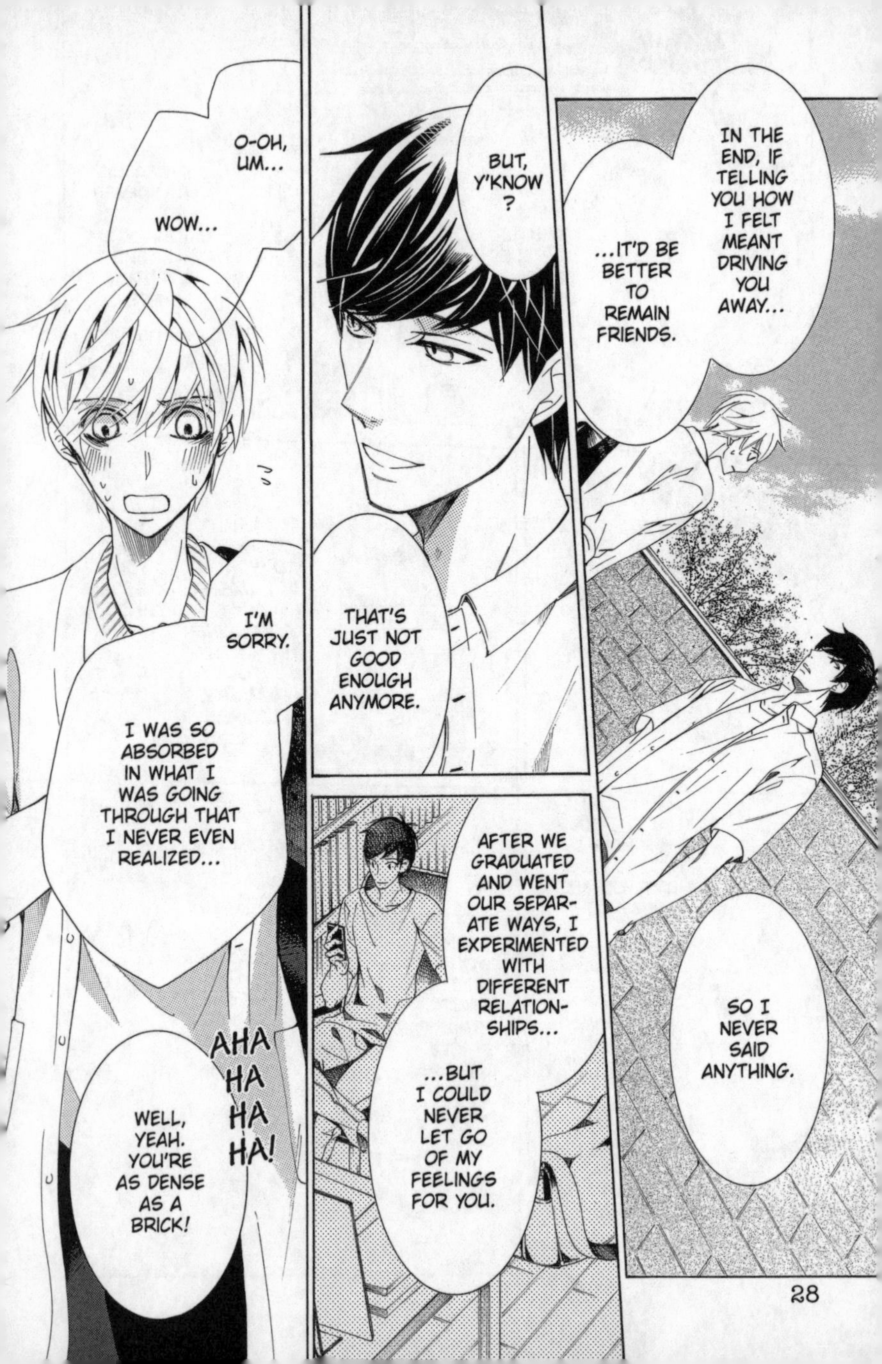
IN THE END, IF TELLING YOU HOW I FELT MEANT DRIVING YOU AWAY...
...IT'D BE BETTER TO REMAIN FRIENDS.
SO I NEVER SAID ANYTHING.
BUT, Y'KNOW?
THAT'S JUST NOT GOOD ENOUGH ANYMORE.
AFTER WE GRADUATED AND WENT OUR SEPAR-ATE WAYS, I EXPERIMENTED WITH DIFFERENT RELATION-SHIPS...
...BUT I COULD NEVER LET GO OF MY FEELINGS FOR YOU.
O-OH, UM...
WOW...
I'M SORRY.
I WAS SO ABSORBED IN WHAT I WAS GOING THROUGH THAT I NEVER EVEN REALIZED...
AHA HA HA HA!
WELL, YEAH. YOU'RE AS DENSE AS A BRICK!

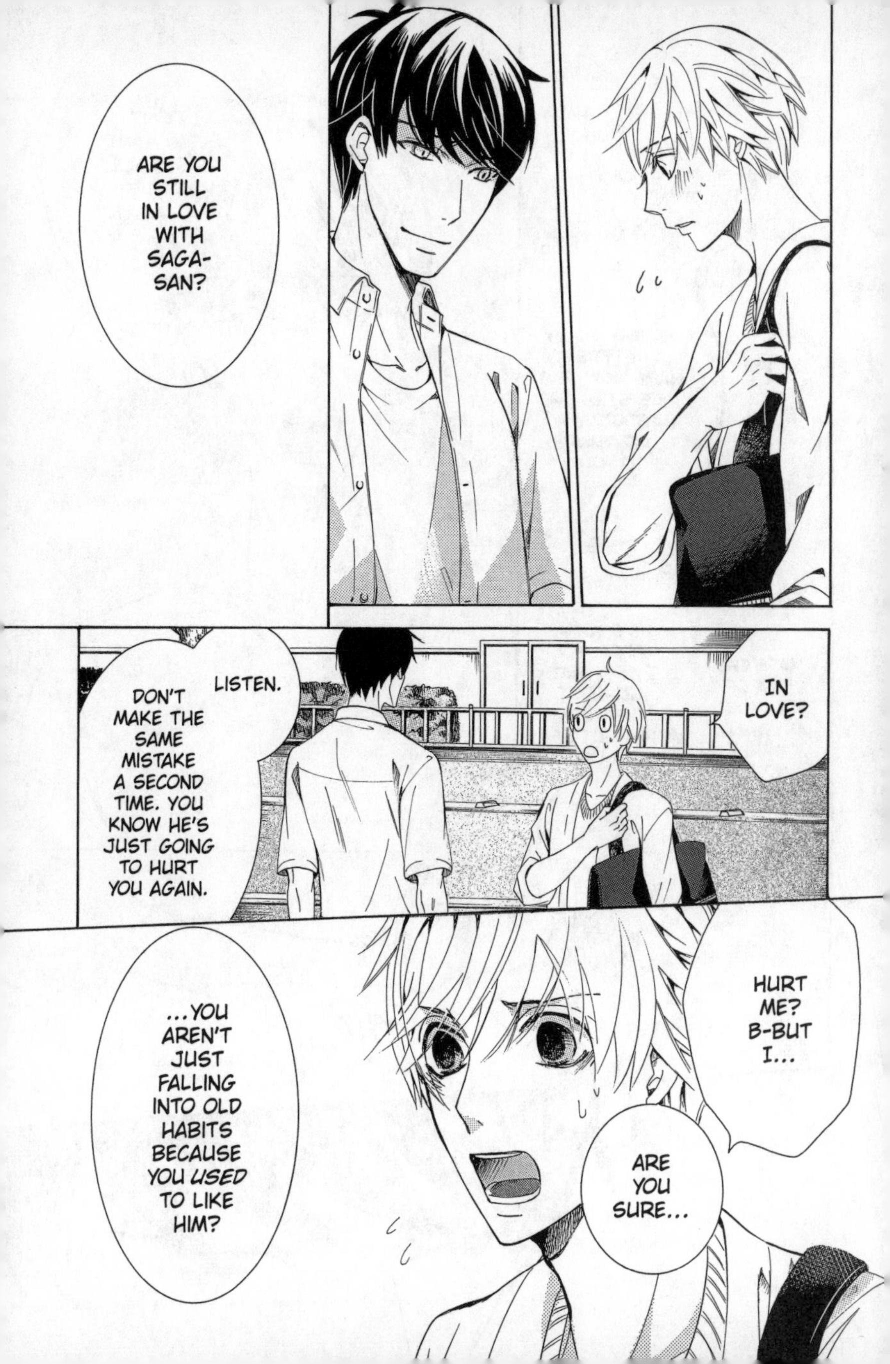
ARE YOU STILL IN LOVE WITH SAGA-SAN?
IN LOVE?
LISTEN.
DON'T MAKE THE SAME MISTAKE A SECOND TIME. YOU KNOW HE'S JUST GOING TO HURT YOU AGAIN.
HURT ME? B-BUT I...
ARE YOU SURE...
...YOU AREN'T JUST FALLING INTO OLD HABITS BECAUSE YOU *USED* TO LIKE HIM?

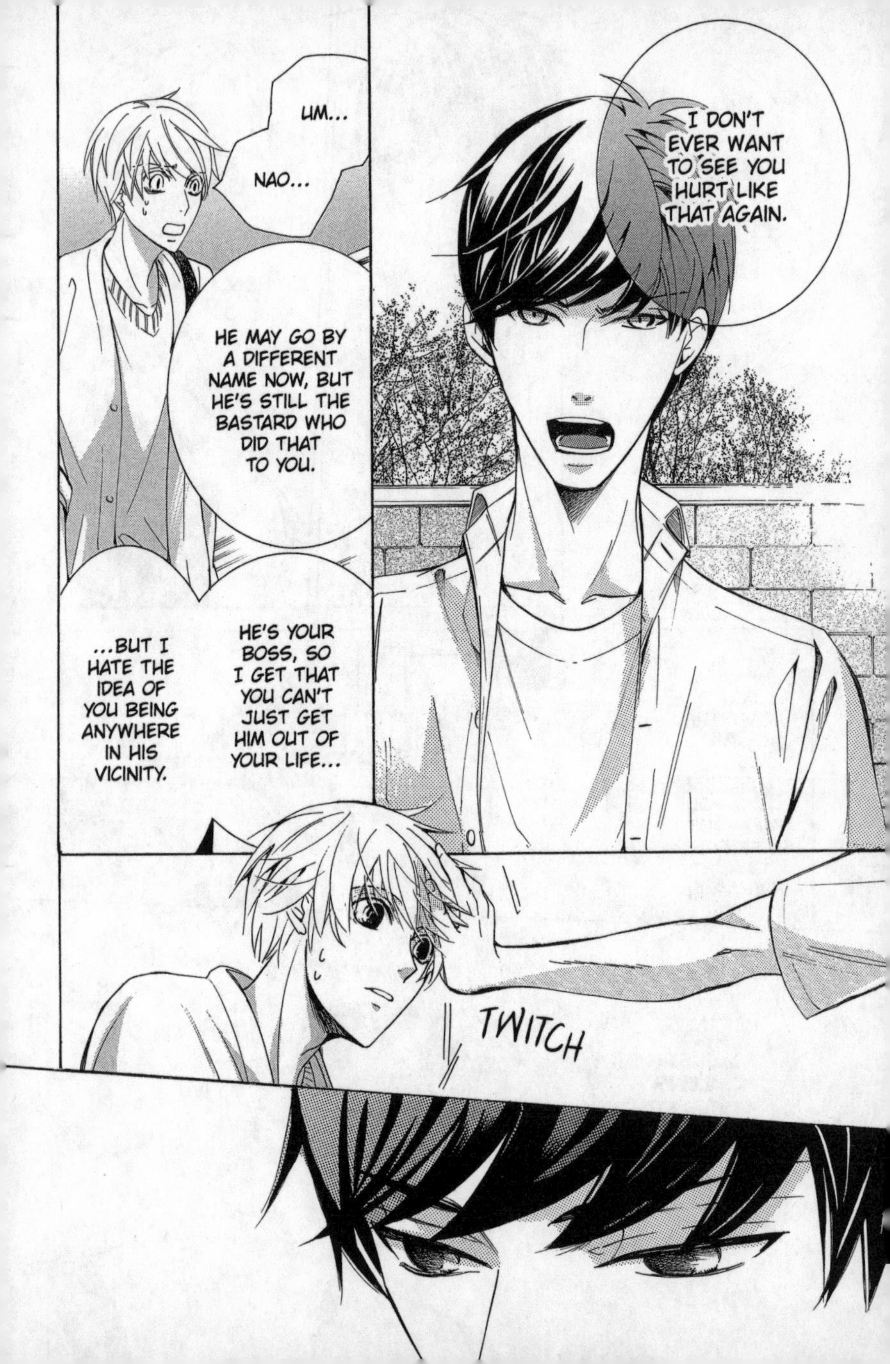
I DON'T EVER WANT TO SEE YOU HURT LIKE THAT AGAIN.
UM...
NAO...
HE MAY GO BY A DIFFERENT NAME NOW, BUT HE'S STILL THE BASTARD WHO DID THAT TO YOU.
HE'S YOUR BOSS, SO I GET THAT YOU CAN'T JUST GET HIM OUT OF YOUR LIFE...
...BUT I HATE THE IDEA OF YOU BEING ANYWHERE IN HIS VICINITY.
TWITCH

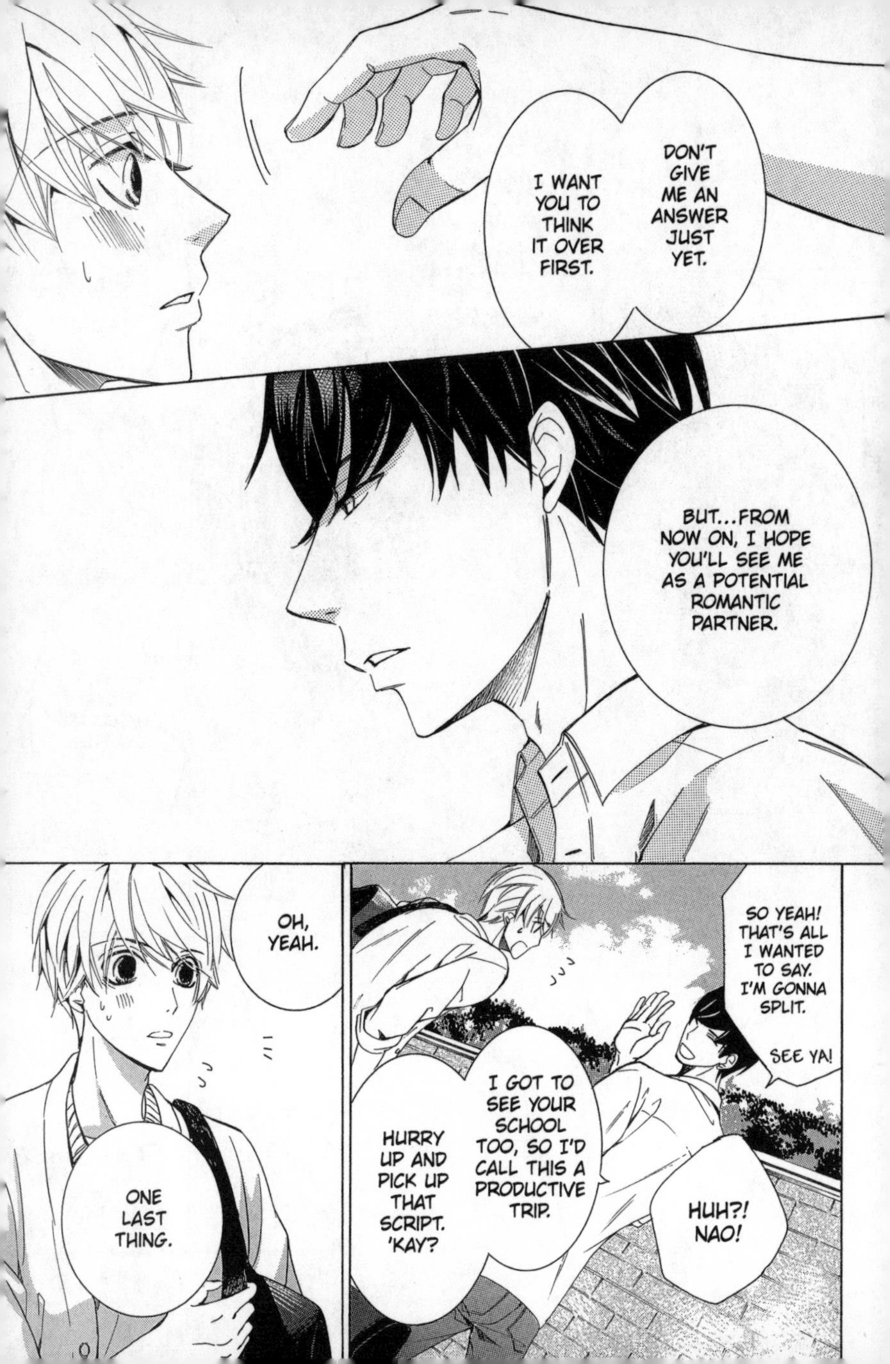
DON'T GIVE ME AN ANSWER JUST YET.
I WANT YOU TO THINK IT OVER FIRST.
BUT...FROM NOW ON, I HOPE YOU'LL SEE ME AS A POTENTIAL ROMANTIC PARTNER.
SO YEAH! THAT'S ALL I WANTED TO SAY. I'M GONNA SPLIT.
SEE YA!
HUH?! NAO!
I GOT TO SEE YOUR SCHOOL TOO, SO I'D CALL THIS A PRODUCTIVE TRIP.
HURRY UP AND PICK UP THAT SCRIPT. 'KAY?
OH, YEAH.
ONE LAST THING.

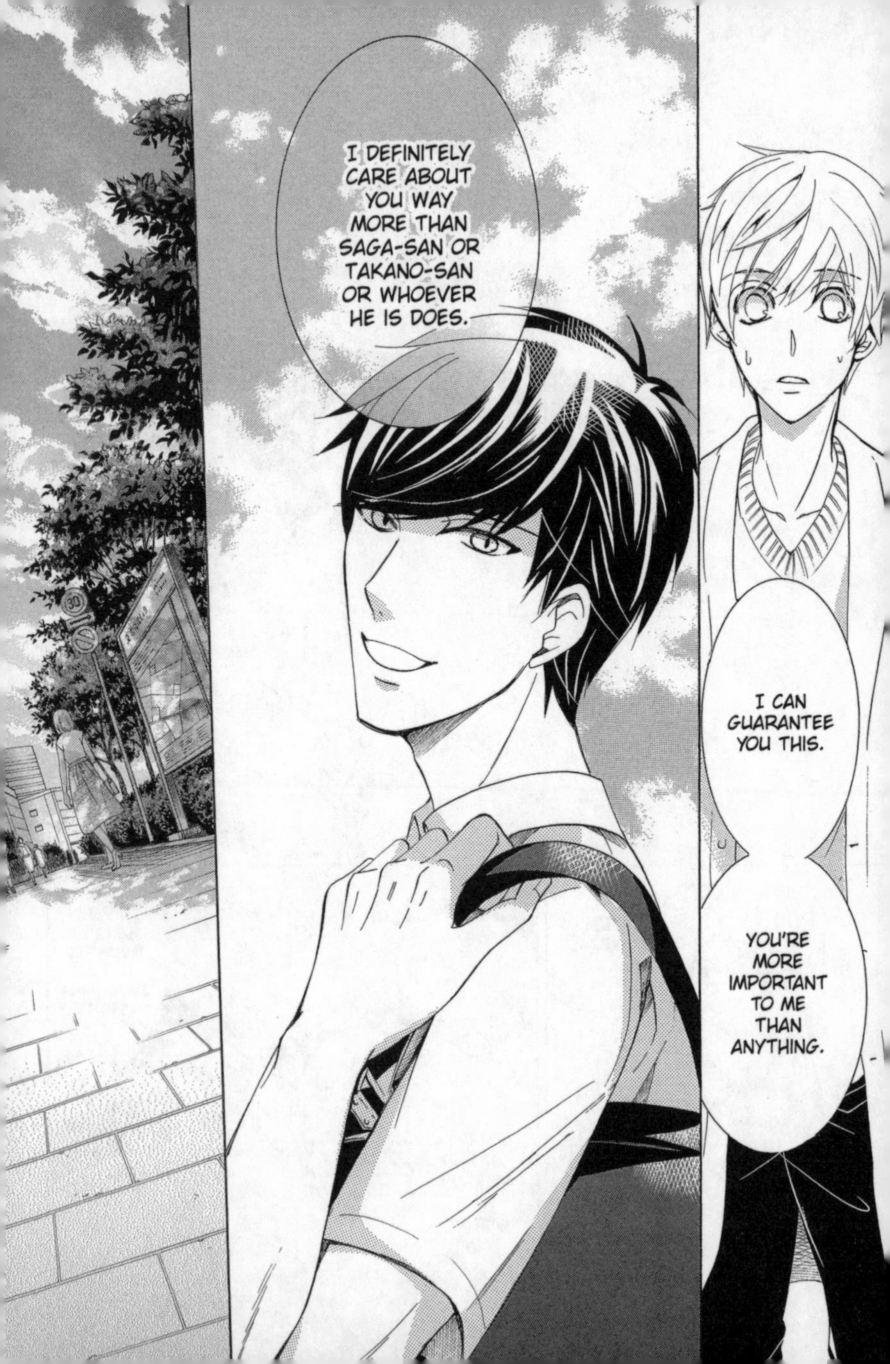
I CAN GUARANTEE YOU THIS.
YOU'RE MORE IMPORTANT TO ME THAN ANYTHING.
I DEFINITELY CARE ABOUT YOU WAY MORE THAN SAGA-SAN OR TAKANO-SAN OR WHOEVER HE IS DOES.

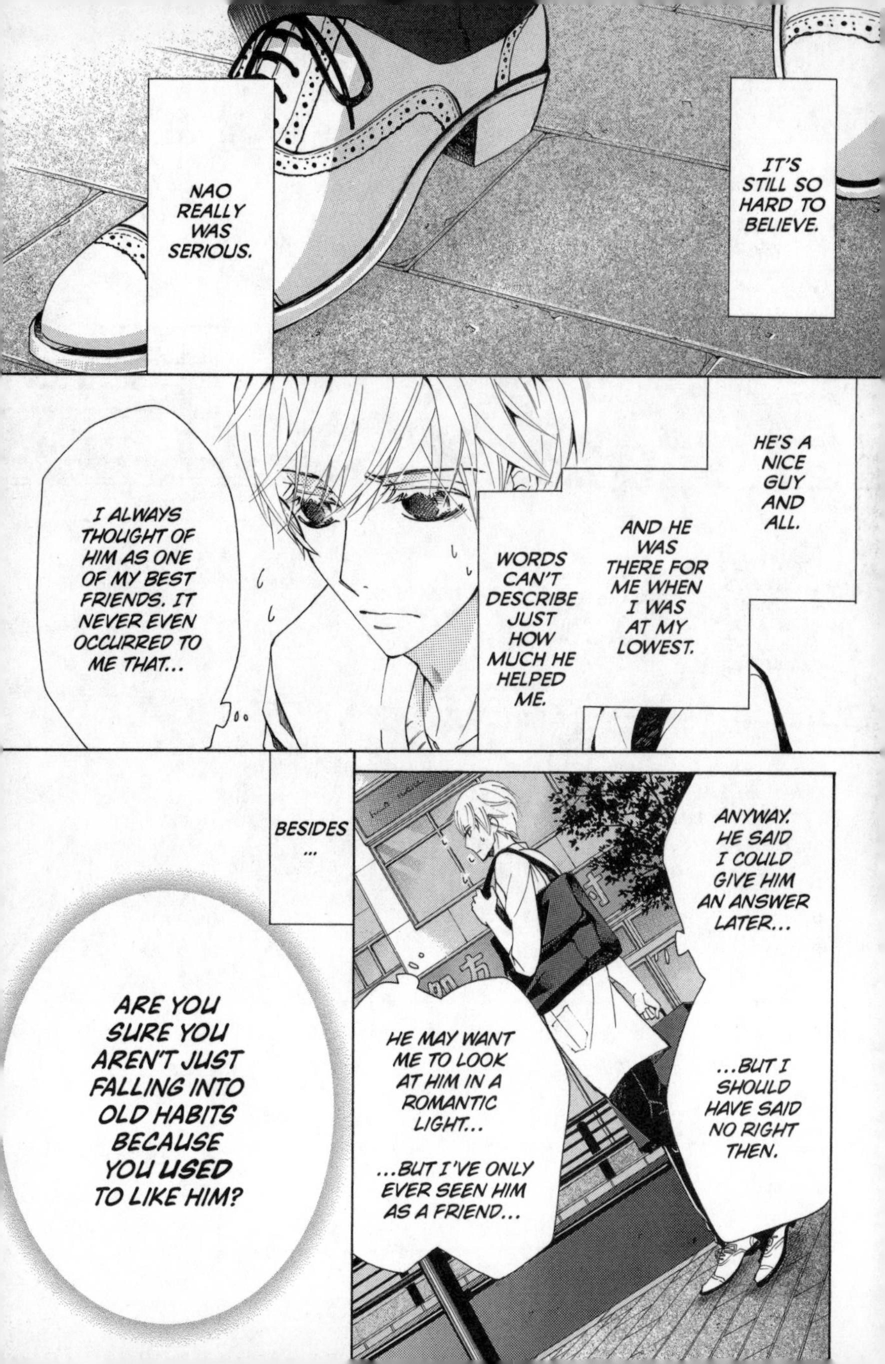
IT'S STILL SO HARD TO BELIEVE.
NAO REALLY WAS SERIOUS.
HE'S A NICE GUY AND ALL.
AND HE WAS THERE FOR ME WHEN I WAS AT MY LOWEST.
WORDS CAN'T DESCRIBE JUST HOW MUCH HE HELPED ME.
I ALWAYS THOUGHT OF HIM AS ONE OF MY BEST FRIENDS. IT NEVER EVEN OCCURRED TO ME THAT...
ANYWAY. HE SAID I COULD GIVE HIM AN ANSWER LATER...
...BUT I SHOULD HAVE SAID NO RIGHT THEN.
HE MAY WANT ME TO LOOK AT HIM IN A ROMANTIC LIGHT...
...BUT I'VE ONLY EVER SEEN HIM AS A FRIEND...
BESIDES...
ARE YOU SURE YOU AREN'T JUST FALLING INTO OLD HABITS BECAUSE YOU USED TO LIKE HIM?

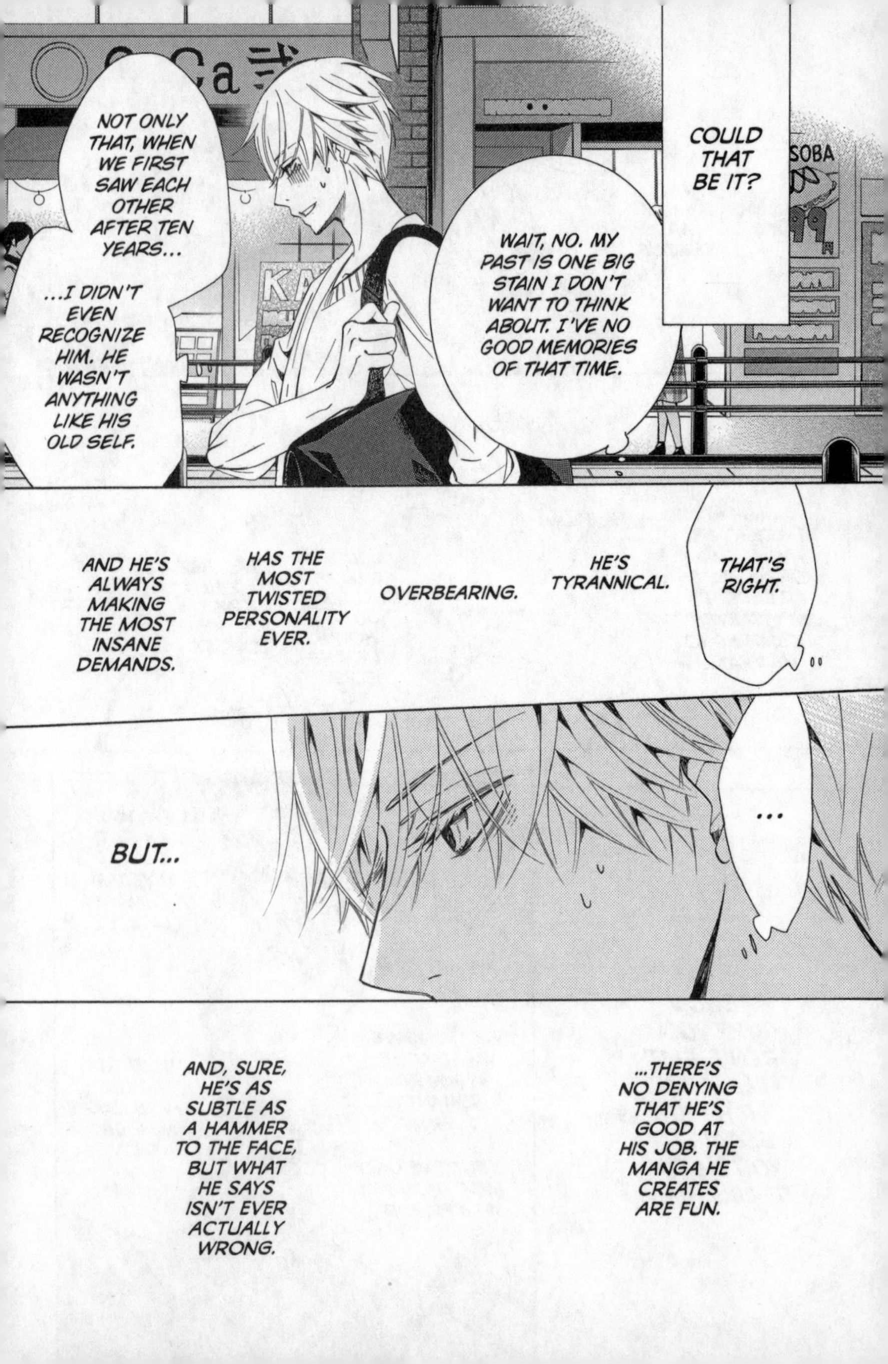
COULD THAT BE IT?
WAIT, NO. MY PAST IS ONE BIG STAIN I DON'T WANT TO THINK ABOUT. I'VE NO GOOD MEMORIES OF THAT TIME.
SOBA
NOT ONLY THAT, WHEN WE FIRST SAW EACH OTHER AFTER TEN YEARS...
...I DIDN'T EVEN RECOGNIZE HIM. HE WASN'T ANYTHING LIKE HIS OLD SELF.
THAT'S RIGHT.
HE'S TYRANNICAL.
OVERBEARING.
HAS THE MOST TWISTED PERSONALITY EVER.
AND HE'S ALWAYS MAKING THE MOST INSANE DEMANDS.
...
BUT...
...THERE'S NO DENYING THAT HE'S GOOD AT HIS JOB. THE MANGA HE CREATES ARE FUN.
AND, SURE, HE'S AS SUBTLE AS A HAMMER TO THE FACE, BUT WHAT HE SAYS ISN'T EVER ACTUALLY WRONG.

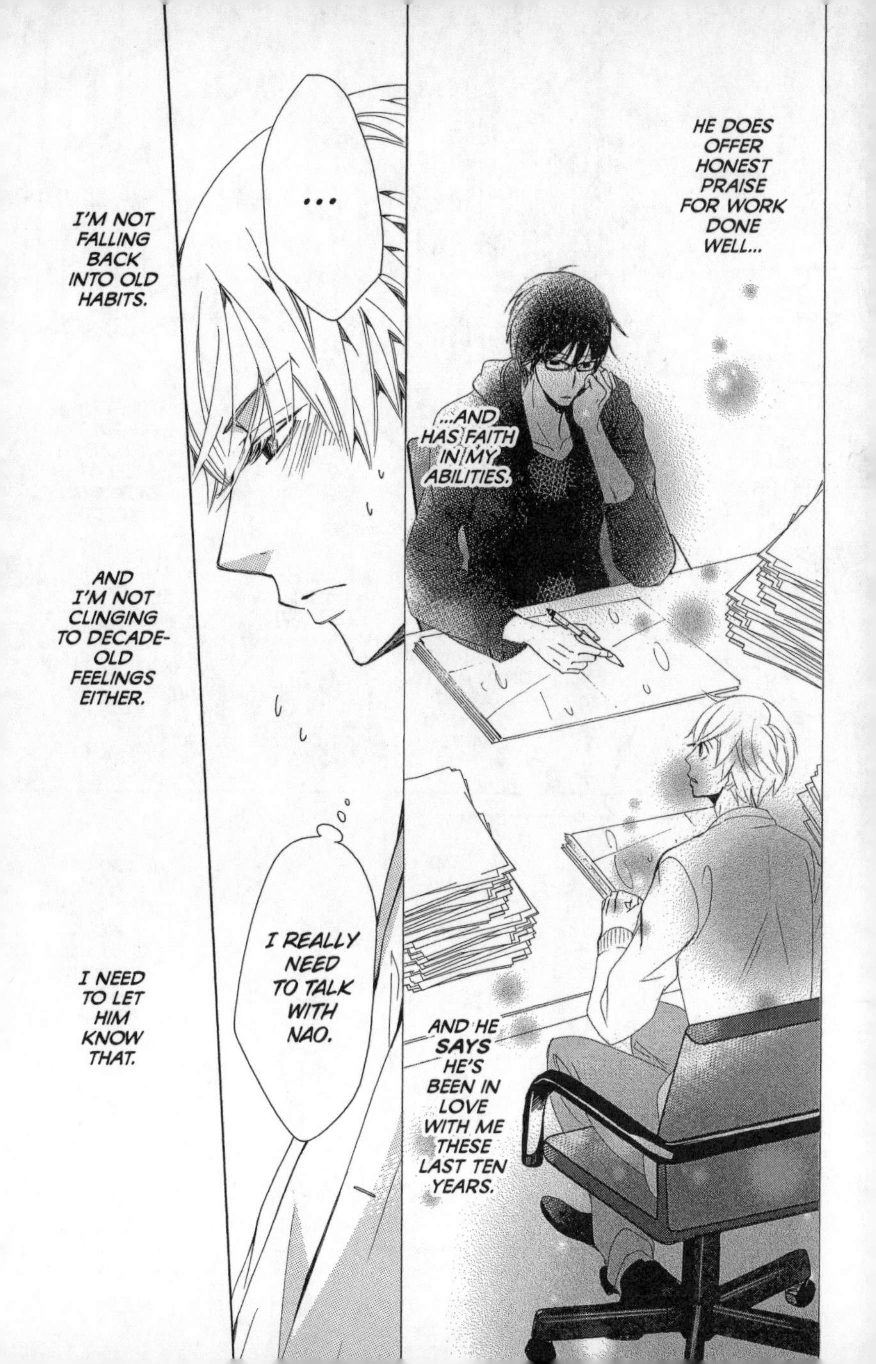
HE DOES OFFER HONEST PRAISE FOR WORK DONE WELL...
...AND HAS FAITH IN MY ABILITIES.
AND HE SAYS HE'S BEEN IN LOVE WITH ME THESE LAST TEN YEARS.
...
I REALLY NEED TO TALK WITH NAO.
I'M NOT FALLING BACK INTO OLD HABITS.
AND I'M NOT CLINGING TO DECADE-OLD FEELINGS EITHER.
I NEED TO LET HIM KNOW THAT.

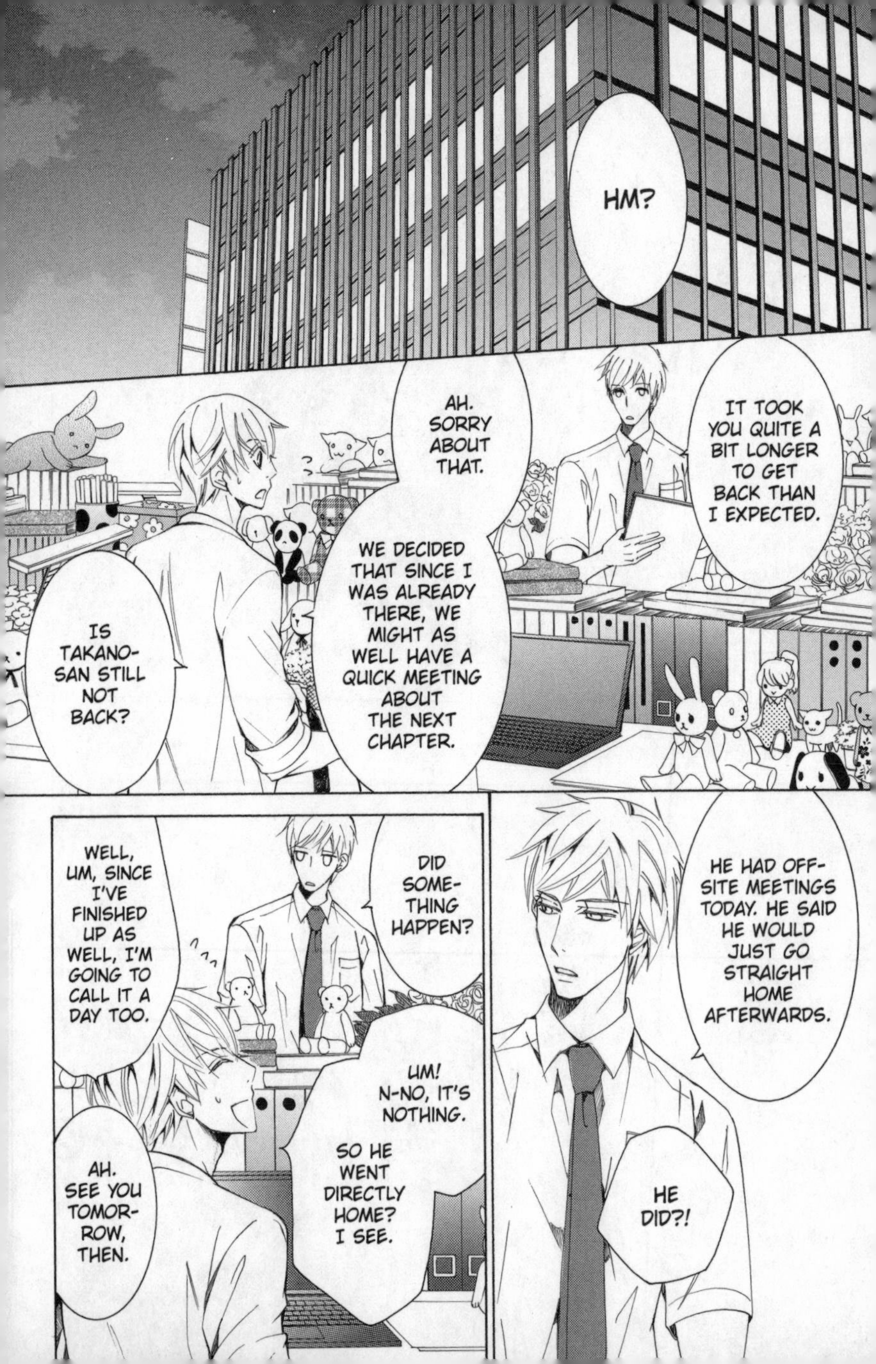
HM?
IT TOOK YOU QUITE A BIT LONGER TO GET BACK THAN I EXPECTED.
AH. SORRY ABOUT THAT.
WE DECIDED THAT SINCE I WAS ALREADY THERE, WE MIGHT AS WELL HAVE A QUICK MEETING ABOUT THE NEXT CHAPTER.
IS TAKANO-SAN STILL NOT BACK?
HE HAD OFF-SITE MEETINGS TODAY. HE SAID HE WOULD JUST GO STRAIGHT HOME AFTERWARDS.
HE DID?!
DID SOMETHING HAPPEN?
UM! N-NO, IT'S NOTHING.
SO HE WENT DIRECTLY HOME? I SEE.
WELL, UM, SINCE I'VE FINISHED UP AS WELL, I'M GOING TO CALL IT A DAY TOO.
AH. SEE YOU TOMORROW, THEN.

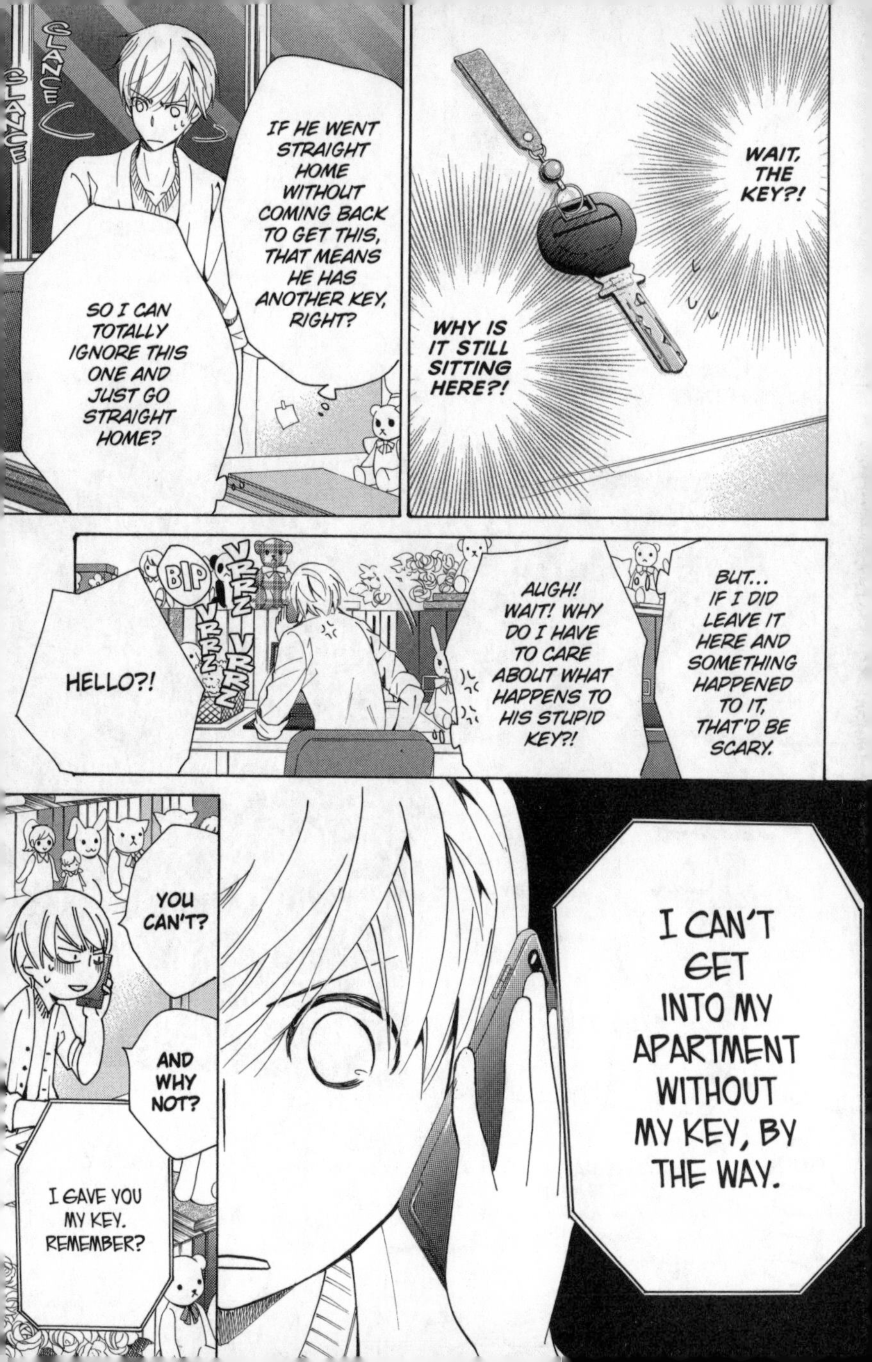
WAIT, THE KEY?!
WHY IS IT STILL SITTING HERE?!
GLANCE
GLANCE
IF HE WENT STRAIGHT HOME WITHOUT COMING BACK TO GET THIS, THAT MEANS HE HAS ANOTHER KEY, RIGHT?
SO I CAN TOTALLY IGNORE THIS ONE AND JUST GO STRAIGHT HOME?
BUT... IF I DID LEAVE IT HERE AND SOMETHING HAPPENED TO IT, THAT'D BE SCARY.
AUGH! WAIT! WHY DO I HAVE TO CARE ABOUT WHAT HAPPENS TO HIS STUPID KEY?!
VRRZ
VRRZ
VRRZ
BIP
HELLO?!
I CAN'T GET INTO MY APARTMENT WITHOUT MY KEY, BY THE WAY.
YOU CAN'T?
AND WHY NOT?
I GAVE YOU MY KEY. REMEMBER?

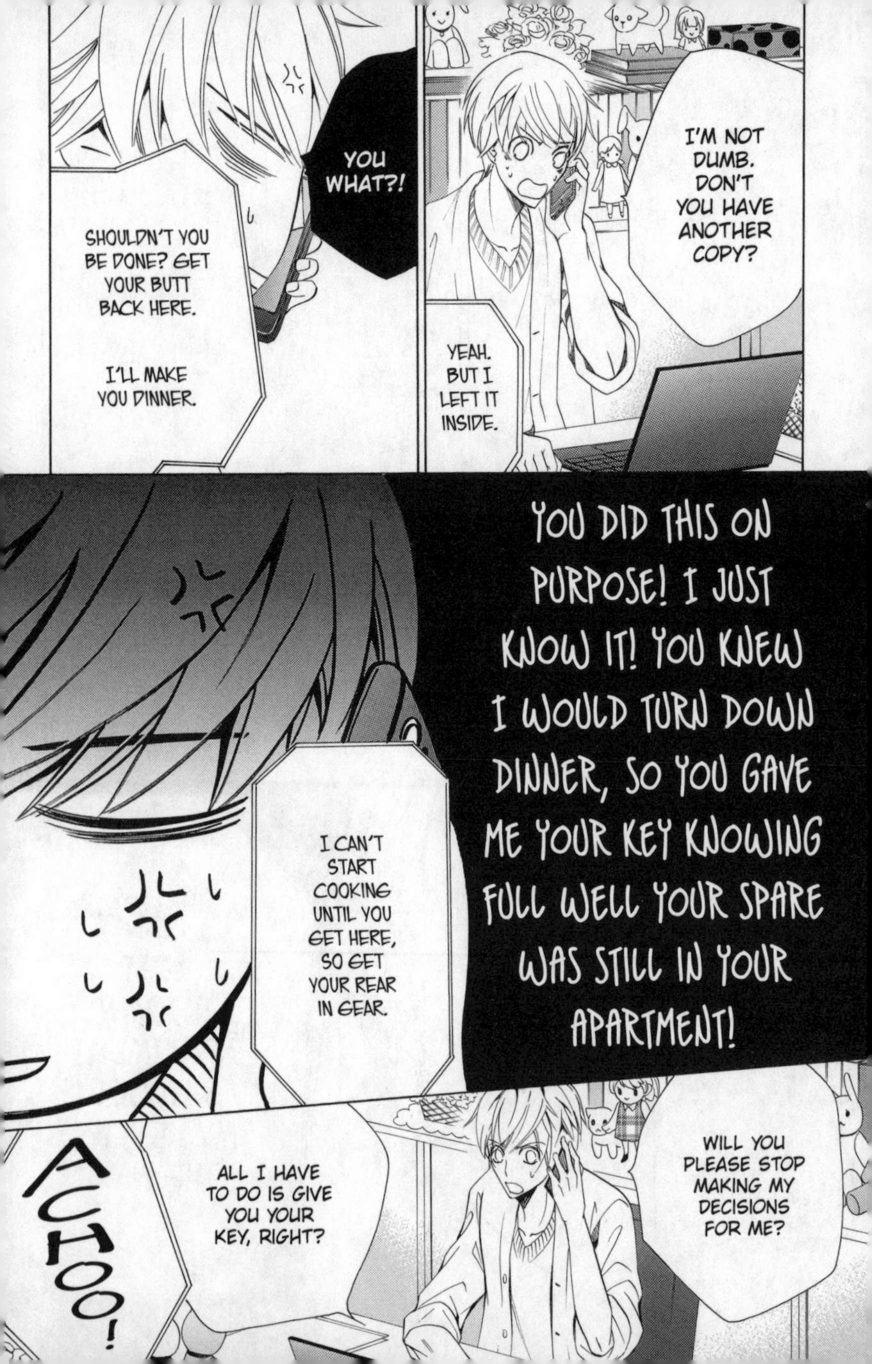
I'M NOT DUMB. DON'T YOU HAVE ANOTHER COPY?
YEAH. BUT I LEFT IT INSIDE.
YOU WHAT?!
SHOULDN'T YOU BE DONE? GET YOUR BUTT BACK HERE.
I'LL MAKE YOU DINNER.
YOU DID THIS ON PURPOSE! I JUST KNOW IT! YOU KNEW I WOULD TURN DOWN DINNER, SO YOU GAVE ME YOUR KEY KNOWING FULL WELL YOUR SPARE WAS STILL IN YOUR APARTMENT!
I CAN'T START COOKING UNTIL YOU GET HERE, SO GET YOUR REAR IN GEAR.
WILL YOU PLEASE STOP MAKING MY DECISIONS FOR ME?
ALL I HAVE TO DO IS GIVE YOU YOUR KEY, RIGHT?
ACHOO!

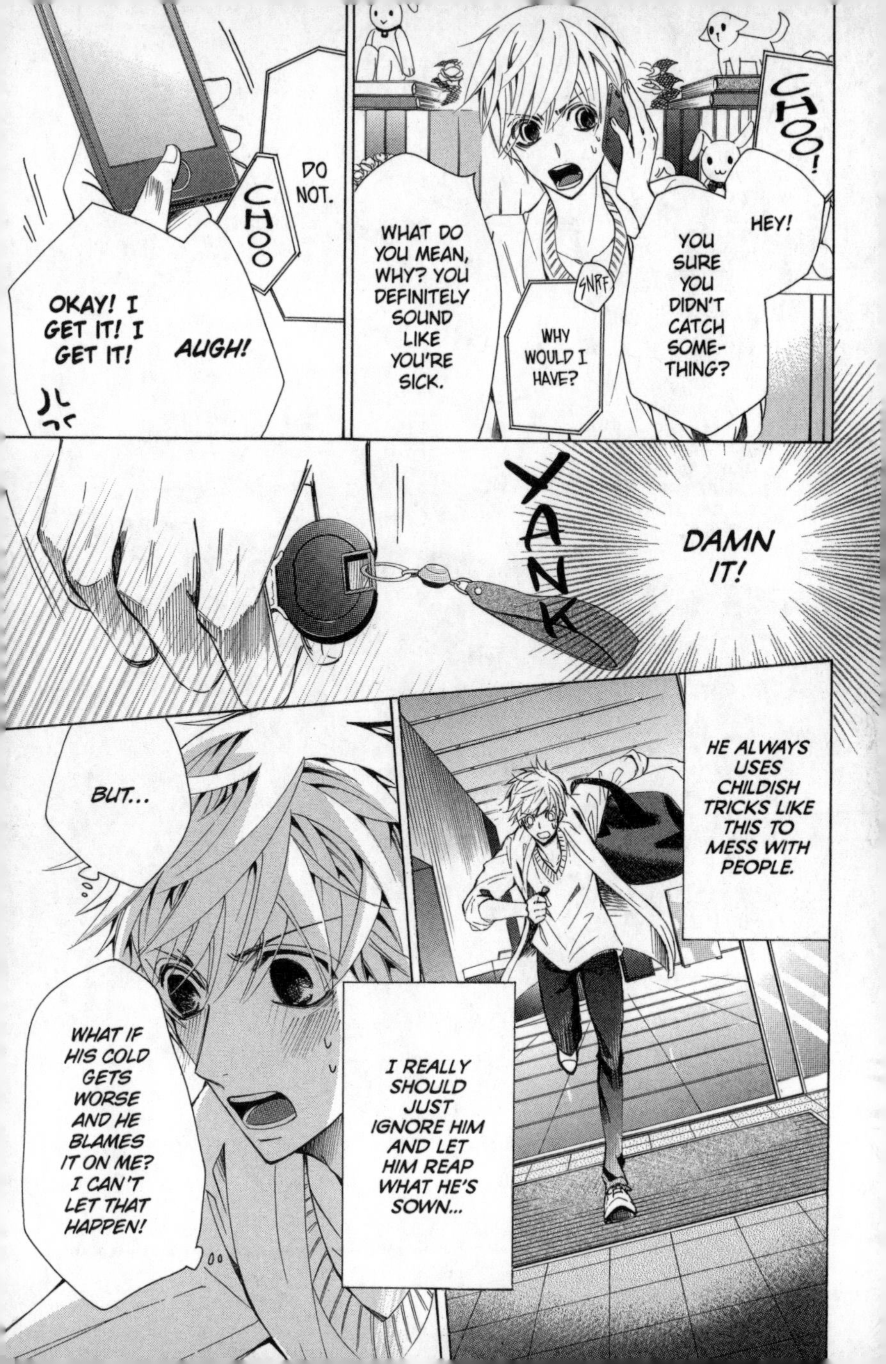
HEY!
YOU SURE YOU DIDN'T CATCH SOME-THING?
CHOO!
SNRF
WHY WOULD I HAVE?
WHAT DO YOU MEAN, WHY? YOU DEFINITELY SOUND LIKE YOU'RE SICK.
DO NOT.
CHOO
AUGH!
OKAY! I GET IT! I GET IT!
DAMN IT!
YANK
HE ALWAYS USES CHILDISH TRICKS LIKE THIS TO MESS WITH PEOPLE.
I REALLY SHOULD JUST IGNORE HIM AND LET HIM REAP WHAT HE'S SOWN...
BUT...
WHAT IF HIS COLD GETS WORSE AND HE BLAMES IT ON ME? I CAN'T LET THAT HAPPEN!

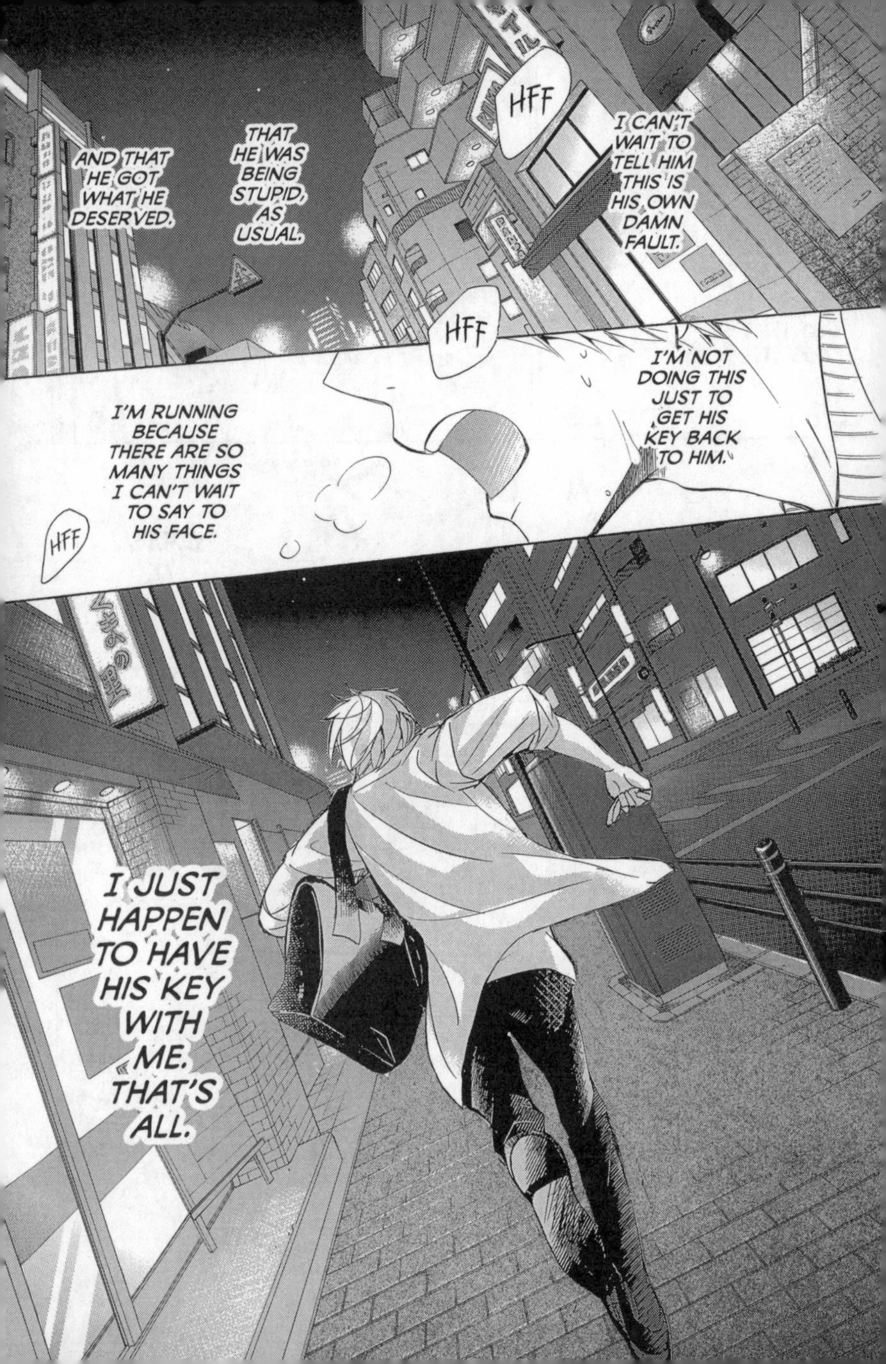
I CAN'T WAIT TO TELL HIM THIS IS HIS OWN DAMN FAULT.
HFF
THAT HE WAS BEING STUPID, AS USUAL.
AND THAT HE GOT WHAT HE DESERVED.
HFF
I'M NOT DOING THIS JUST TO GET HIS KEY BACK TO HIM.
I'M RUNNING BECAUSE THERE ARE SO MANY THINGS I CAN'T WAIT TO SAY TO HIS FACE.
HFF
I JUST HAPPEN TO HAVE HIS KEY WITH ME. THAT'S ALL.

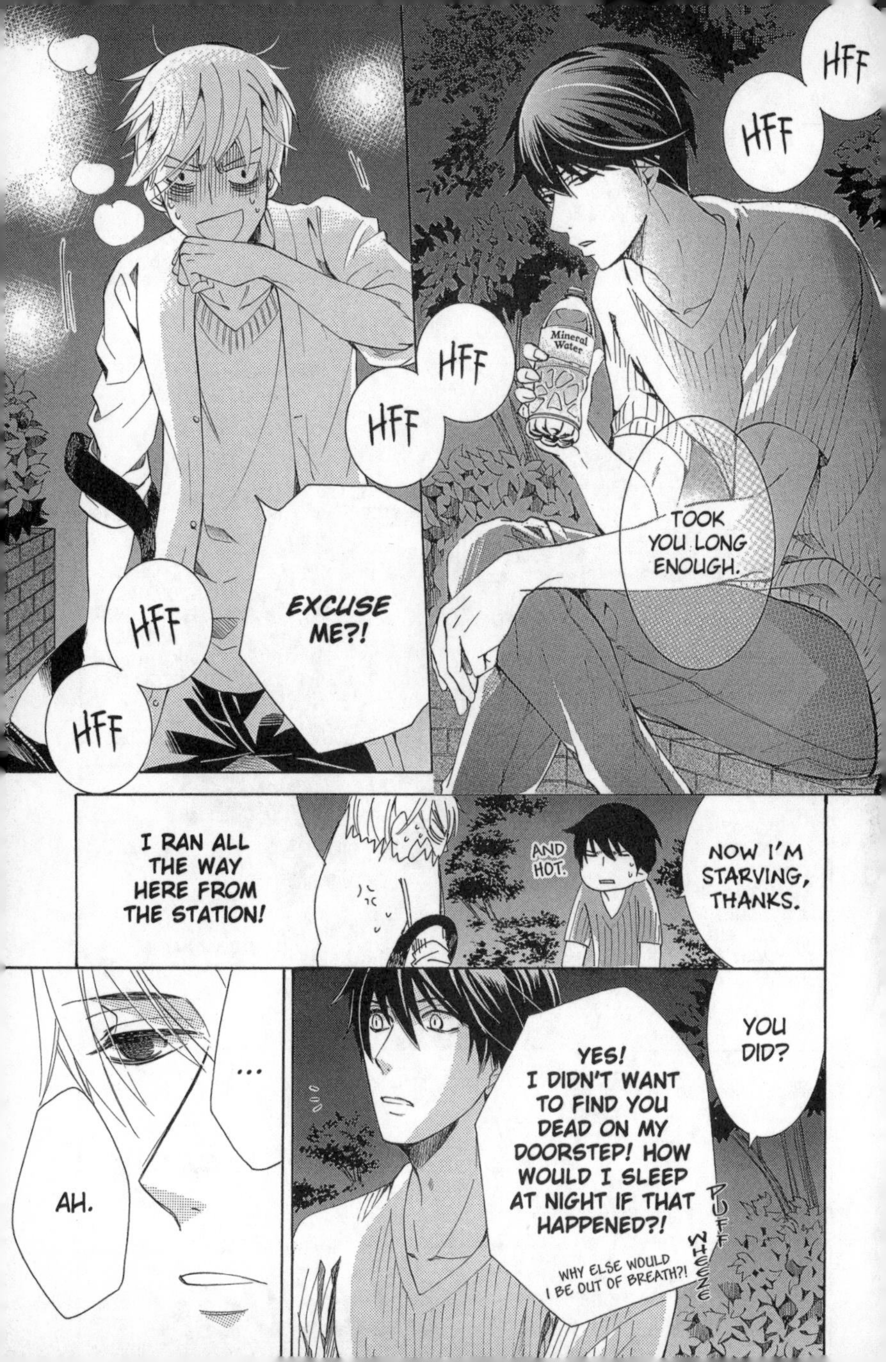
HFF
HFF
Mineral Water
HFF
HFF
TOOK YOU LONG ENOUGH.
EXCUSE ME?!
HFF
HFF
NOW I'M STARVING, THANKS.
AND HOT.
I RAN ALL THE WAY HERE FROM THE STATION!
YOU DID?
YES! I DIDN'T WANT TO FIND YOU DEAD ON MY DOORSTEP! HOW WOULD I SLEEP AT NIGHT IF THAT HAPPENED?!
PUFF
WHEEZE
WHY ELSE WOULD I BE OUT OF BREATH?!
...
AH.

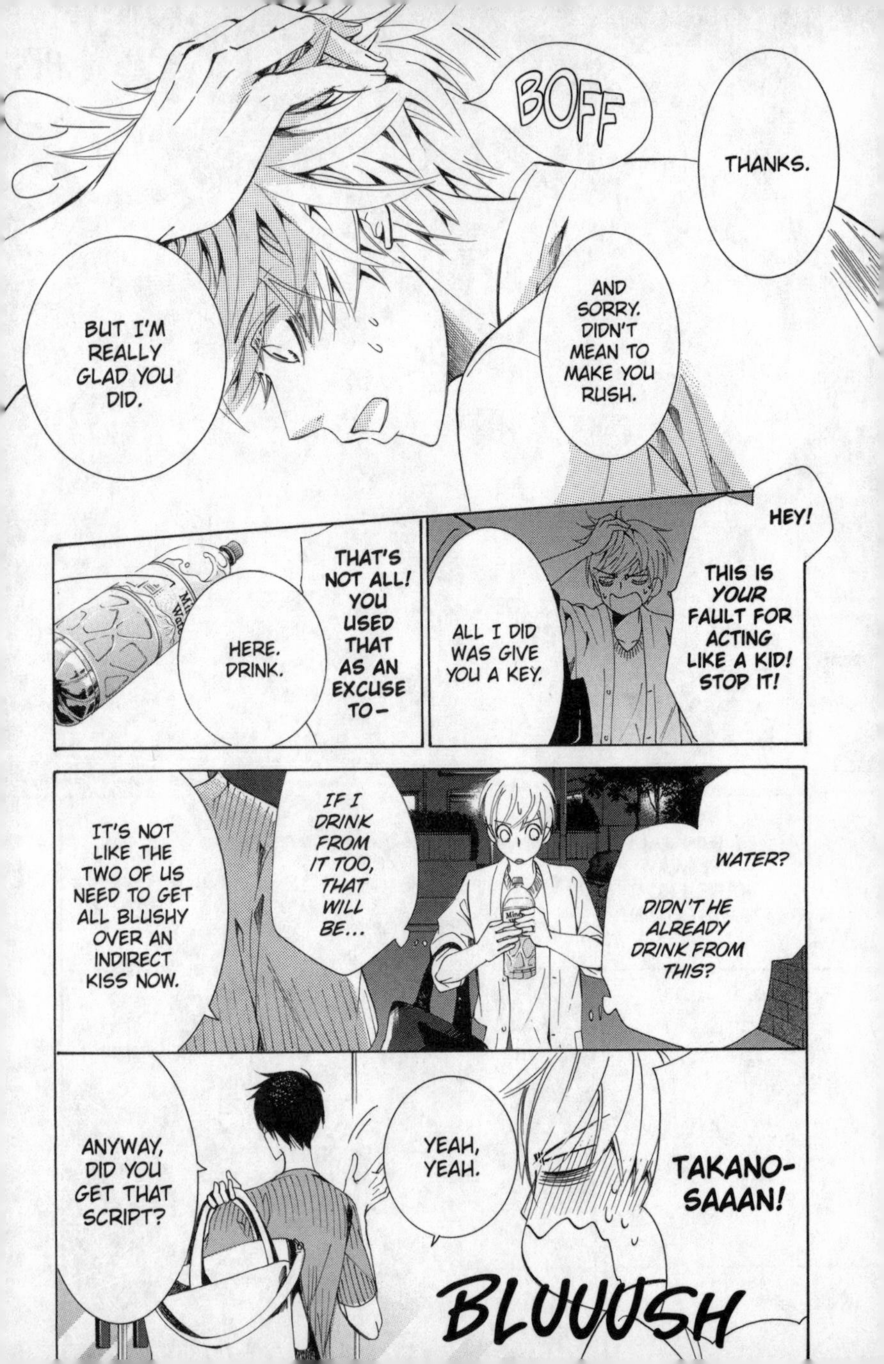
BOFF
THANKS.
AND SORRY. DIDN'T MEAN TO MAKE YOU RUSH.
BUT I'M REALLY GLAD YOU DID.
HEY!
THIS IS YOUR FAULT FOR ACTING LIKE A KID! STOP IT!
ALL I DID WAS GIVE YOU A KEY.
THAT'S NOT ALL! YOU USED THAT AS AN EXCUSE TO—
HERE. DRINK.
WATER?
DIDN'T HE ALREADY DRINK FROM THIS?
IF I DRINK FROM IT TOO, THAT WILL BE...
IT'S NOT LIKE THE TWO OF US NEED TO GET ALL BLUSHY OVER AN INDIRECT KISS NOW.
TAKANO-SAAAN!
BLUUUSH
YEAH, YEAH.
ANYWAY, DID YOU GET THAT SCRIPT?

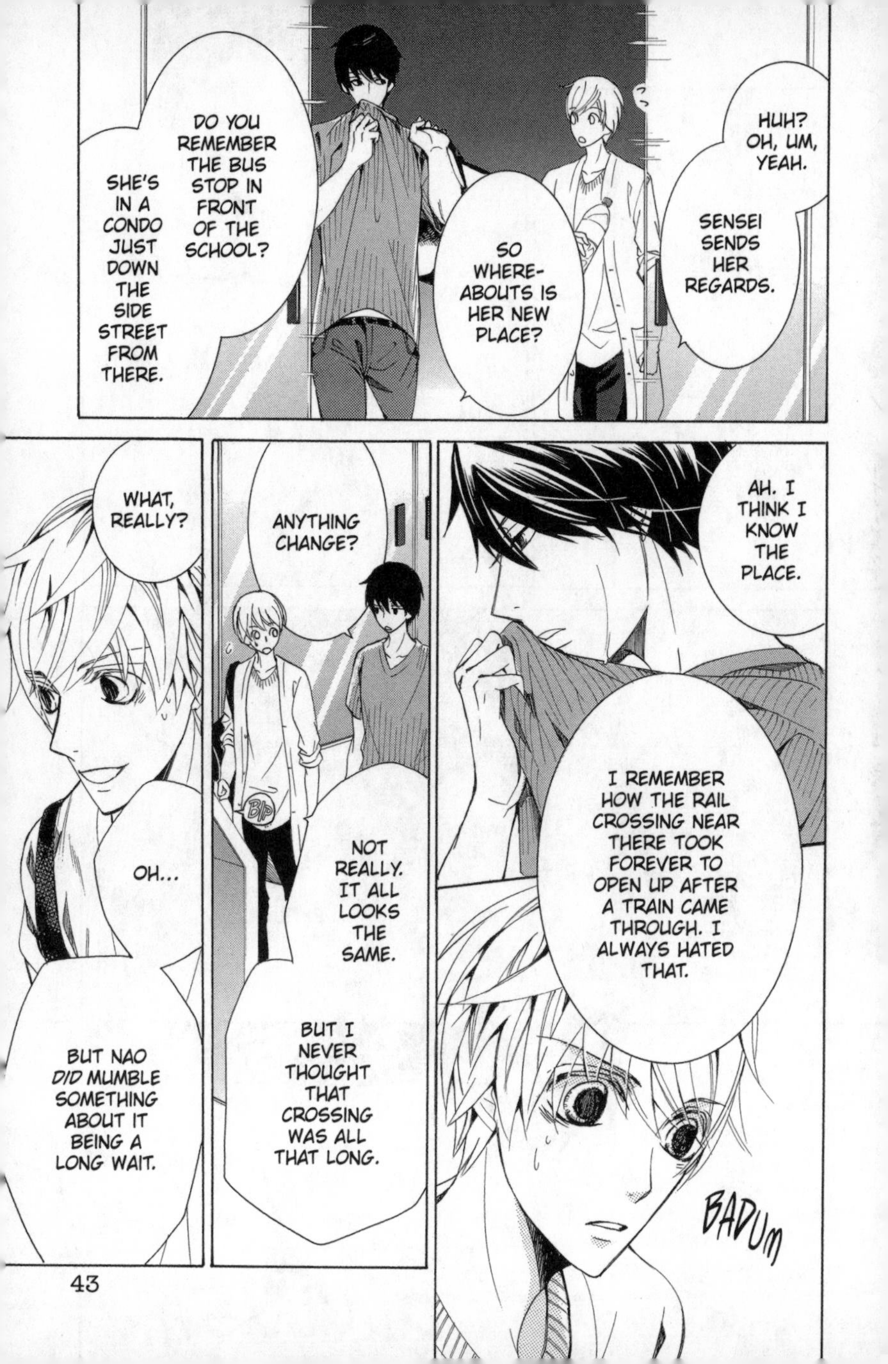
HUH? OH, UM, YEAH.
SENSEI SENDS HER REGARDS.
SO WHERE-ABOUTS IS HER NEW PLACE?
DO YOU REMEMBER THE BUS STOP IN FRONT OF THE SCHOOL?
SHE'S IN A CONDO JUST DOWN THE SIDE STREET FROM THERE.
AH. I THINK I KNOW THE PLACE.
I REMEMBER HOW THE RAIL CROSSING NEAR THERE TOOK FOREVER TO OPEN UP AFTER A TRAIN CAME THROUGH. I ALWAYS HATED THAT.
BADUM
ANYTHING CHANGE?
BIP
NOT REALLY. IT ALL LOOKS THE SAME.
BUT I NEVER THOUGHT THAT CROSSING WAS ALL THAT LONG.
WHAT, REALLY?
OH...
BUT NAO *DID* MUMBLE SOMETHING ABOUT IT BEING A LONG WAIT.

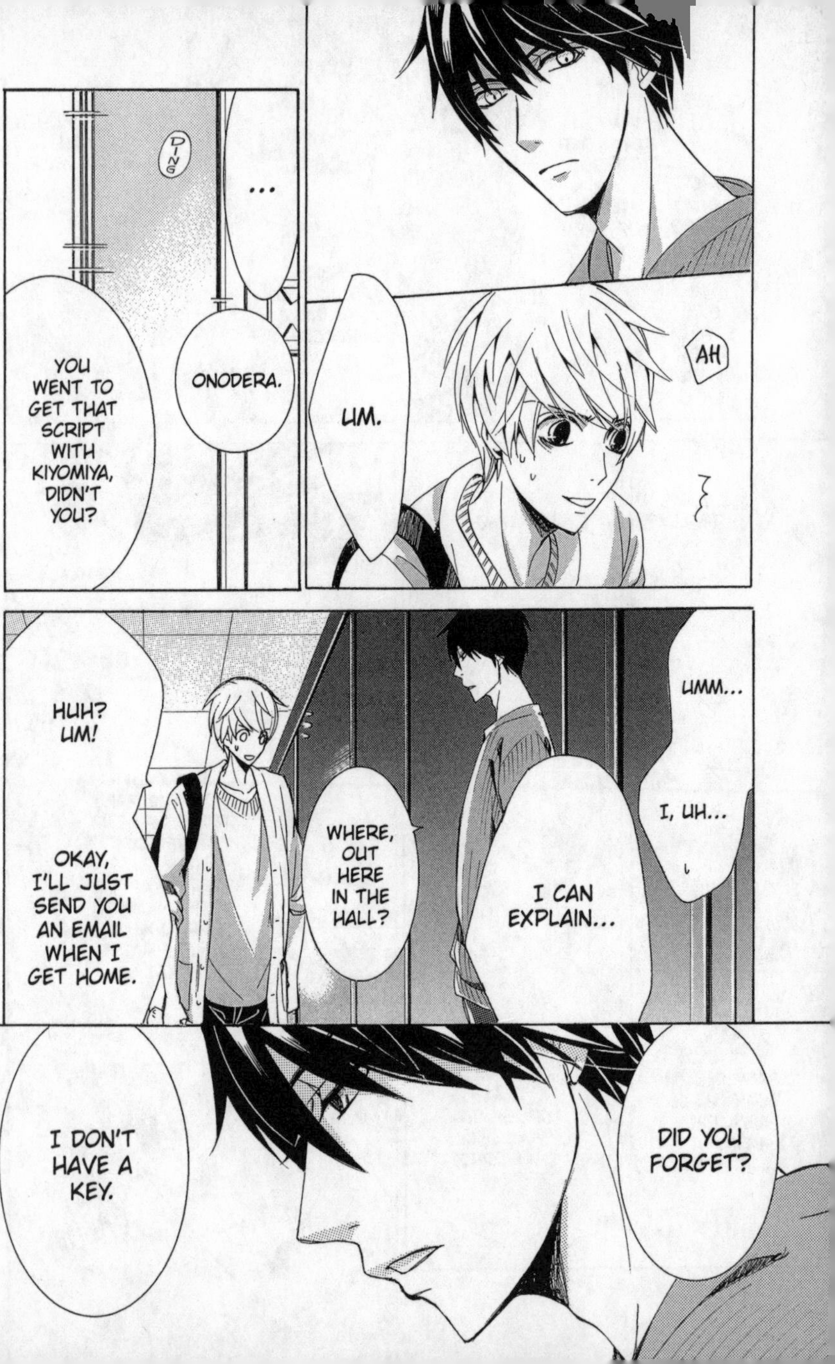
AH
UM.
DING
...
ONODERA.
YOU WENT TO GET THAT SCRIPT WITH KIYOMIYA, DIDN'T YOU?
UMM...
I, UH...
I CAN EXPLAIN...
WHERE, OUT HERE IN THE HALL?
HUH? UM!
OKAY, I'LL JUST SEND YOU AN EMAIL WHEN I GET HOME.
DID YOU FORGET?
I DON'T HAVE A KEY.

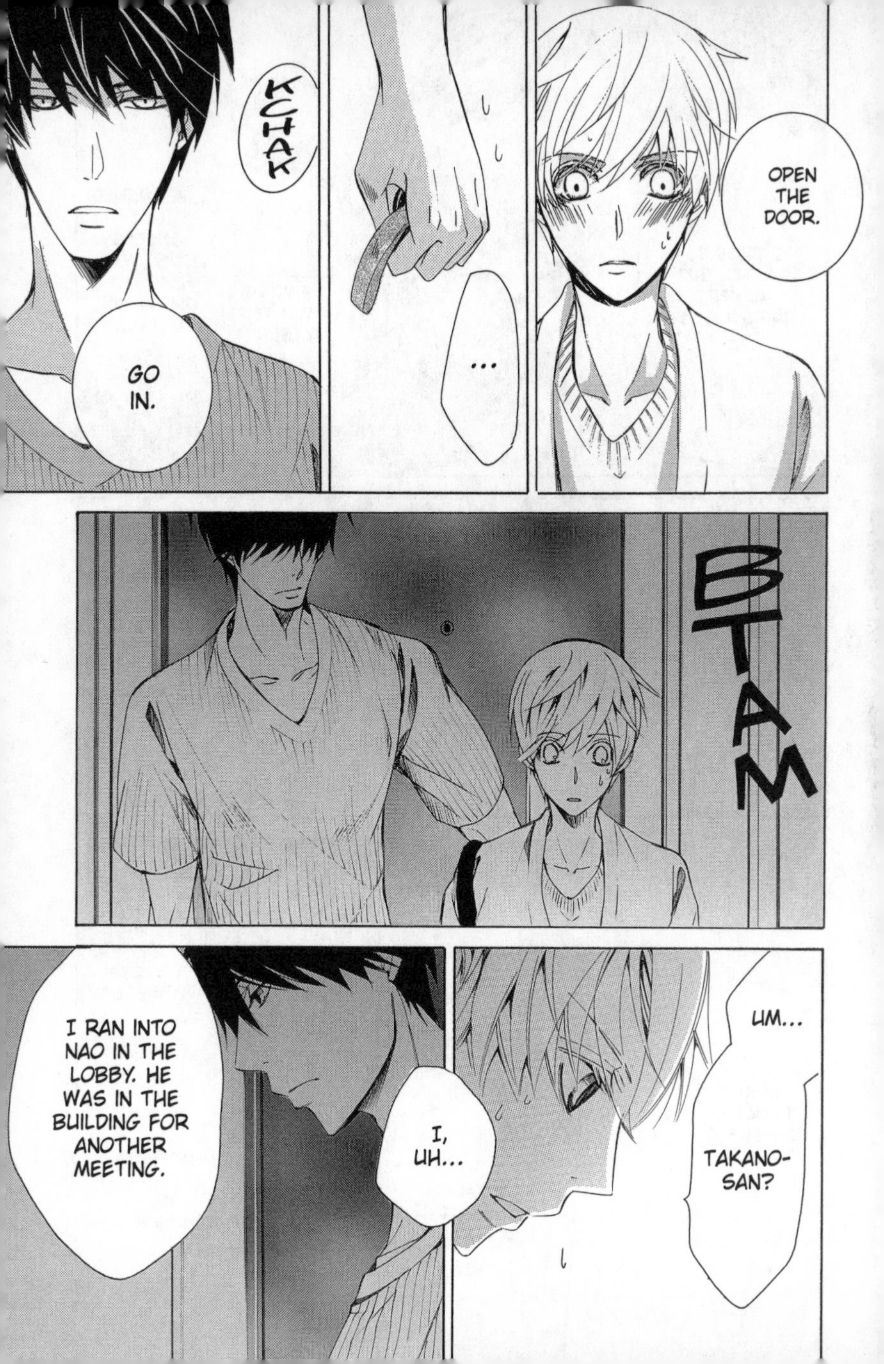
OPEN THE DOOR.
...
KCHAK
GO IN.
BTAM
UM...
TAKANO-SAN?
I, UH...
I RAN INTO NAO IN THE LOBBY. HE WAS IN THE BUILDING FOR ANOTHER MEETING.

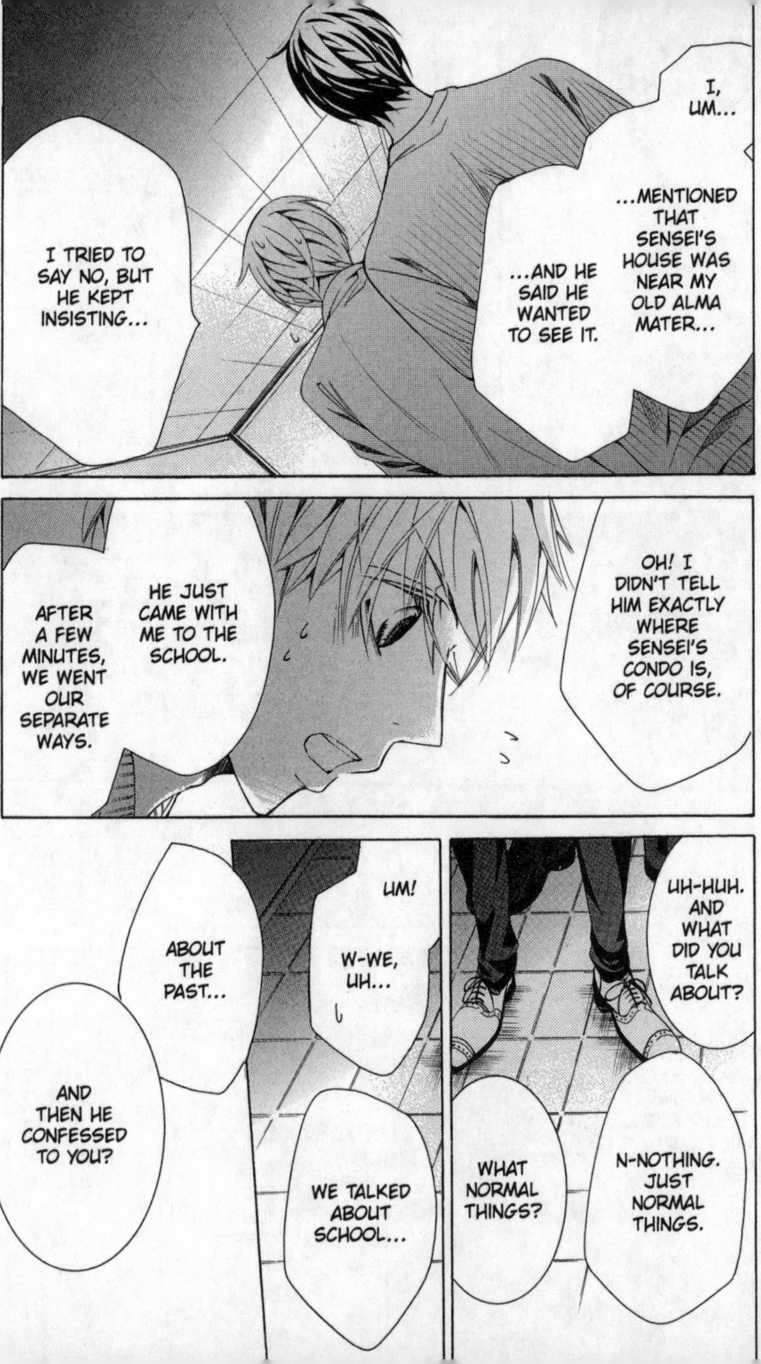
I, UM...
...MENTIONED THAT SENSEI'S HOUSE WAS NEAR MY OLD ALMA MATER...
...AND HE SAID HE WANTED TO SEE IT.
I TRIED TO SAY NO, BUT HE KEPT INSISTING...
OH! I DIDN'T TELL HIM EXACTLY WHERE SENSEI'S CONDO IS, OF COURSE.
HE JUST CAME WITH ME TO THE SCHOOL.
AFTER A FEW MINUTES, WE WENT OUR SEPARATE WAYS.
UH-HUH. AND WHAT DID YOU TALK ABOUT?
N-NOTHING. JUST NORMAL THINGS.
WHAT NORMAL THINGS?
UM!
W-WE, UH...
WE TALKED ABOUT SCHOOL...
ABOUT THE PAST...
AND THEN HE CONFESSED TO YOU?

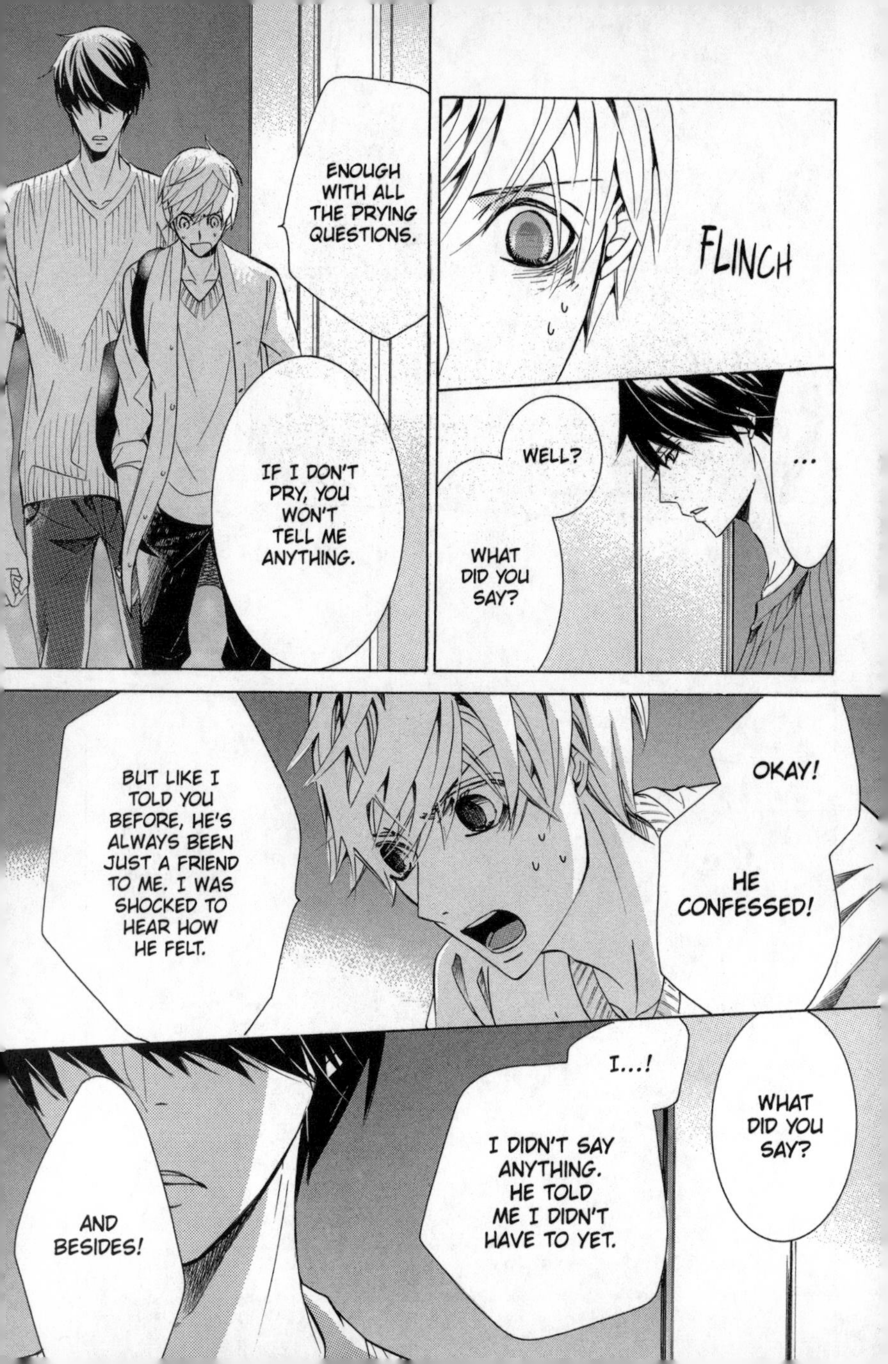
FLINCH
...
WELL?
WHAT DID YOU SAY?
ENOUGH WITH ALL THE PRYING QUESTIONS.
IF I DON'T PRY, YOU WON'T TELL ME ANYTHING.
OKAY!
HE CONFESSED!
BUT LIKE I TOLD YOU BEFORE, HE'S ALWAYS BEEN JUST A FRIEND TO ME. I WAS SHOCKED TO HEAR HOW HE FELT.
WHAT DID YOU SAY?
I...!
I DIDN'T SAY ANYTHING. HE TOLD ME I DIDN'T HAVE TO YET.
AND BESIDES!

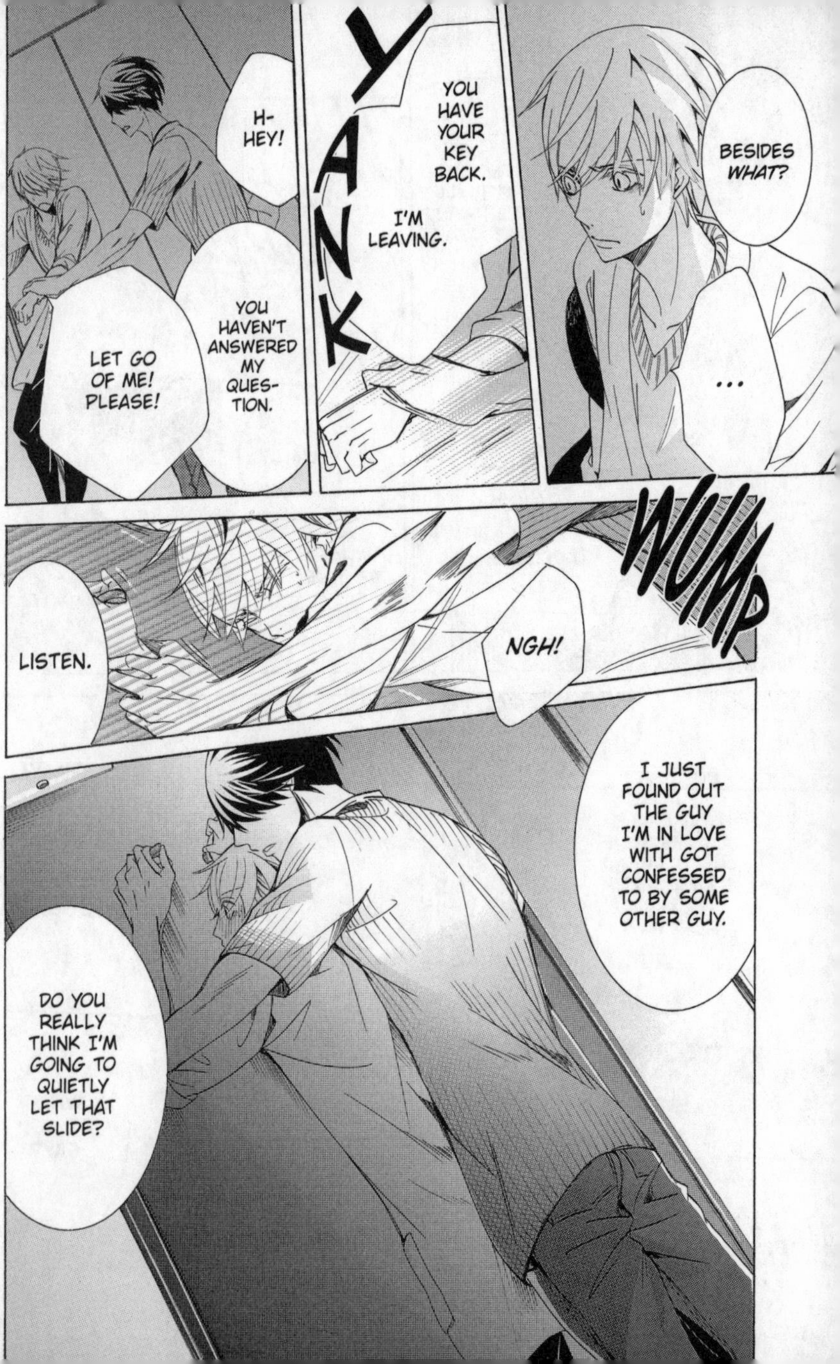
BESIDES WHAT?
...
YANK
YOU HAVE YOUR KEY BACK.
I'M LEAVING.
H-HEY!
YOU HAVEN'T ANSWERED MY QUESTION.
LET GO OF ME! PLEASE!
WUMP
NGH!
LISTEN.
I JUST FOUND OUT THE GUY I'M IN LOVE WITH GOT CONFESSED TO BY SOME OTHER GUY.
DO YOU REALLY THINK I'M GOING TO QUIETLY LET THAT SLIDE?

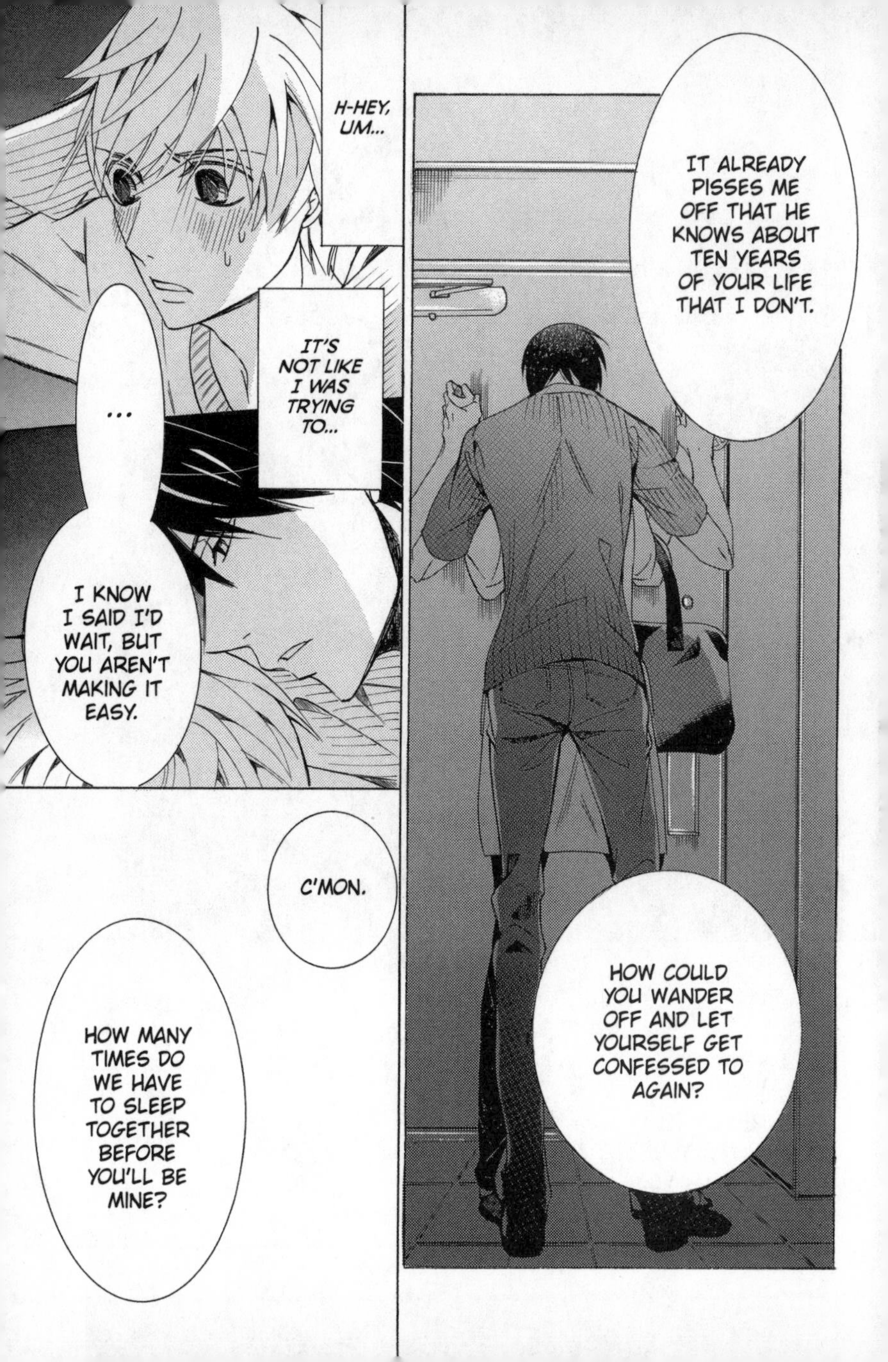
IT ALREADY PISSES ME OFF THAT HE KNOWS ABOUT TEN YEARS OF YOUR LIFE THAT I DON'T.
HOW COULD YOU WANDER OFF AND LET YOURSELF GET CONFESSED TO AGAIN?
H-HEY, UM...
IT'S NOT LIKE I WAS TRYING TO...
...
I KNOW I SAID I'D WAIT, BUT YOU AREN'T MAKING IT EASY.
C'MON.
HOW MANY TIMES DO WE HAVE TO SLEEP TOGETHER BEFORE YOU'LL BE MINE?

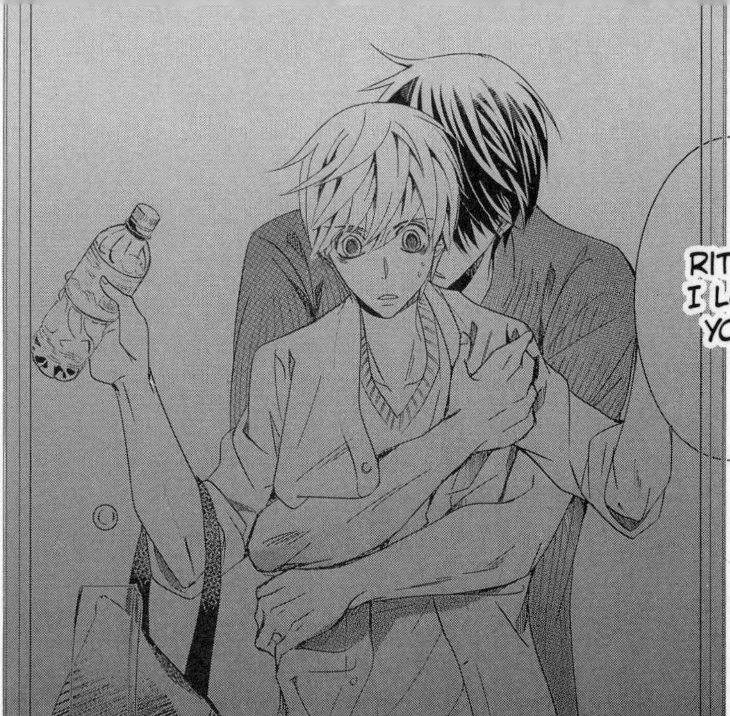
RITSU. I LOVE YOU.
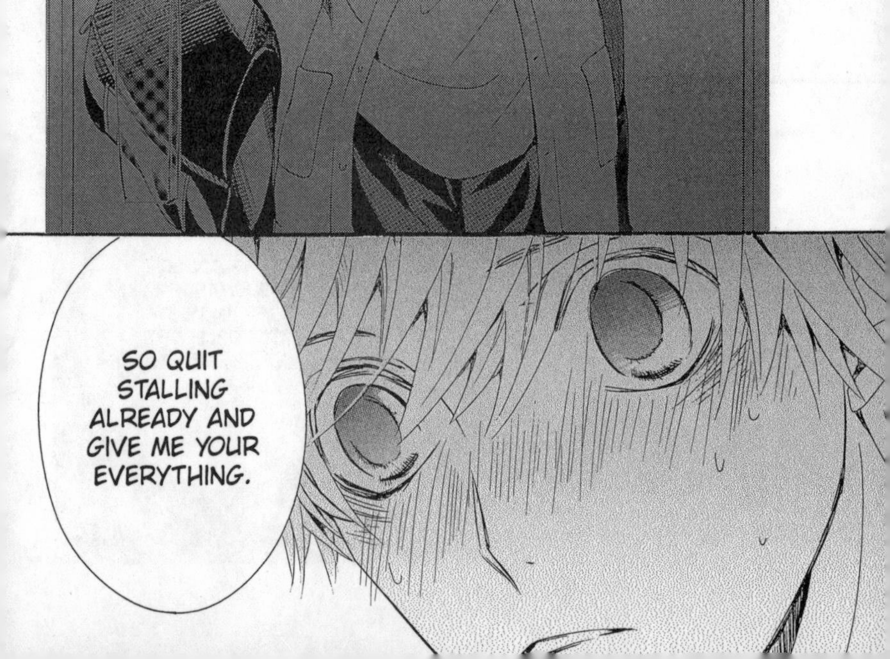
SO QUIT STALLING ALREADY AND GIVE ME YOUR EVERYTHING.

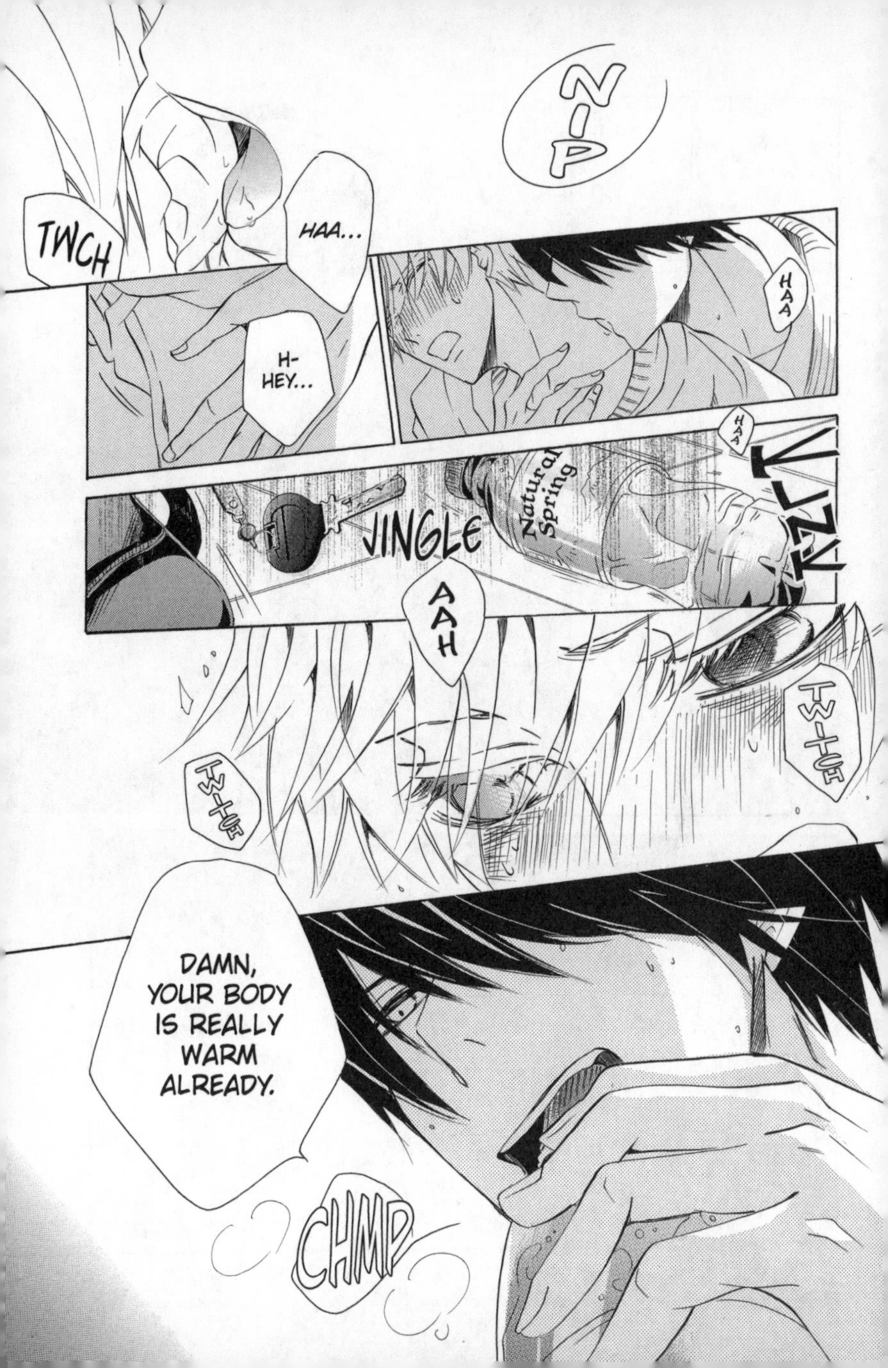
NIP
HAA...
TWCH
HAA
H-HEY...
HAA
Natural Spring
JINGLE
AAH
TWITCH
TWITCH
DAMN, YOUR BODY IS REALLY WARM ALREADY.
CHMP

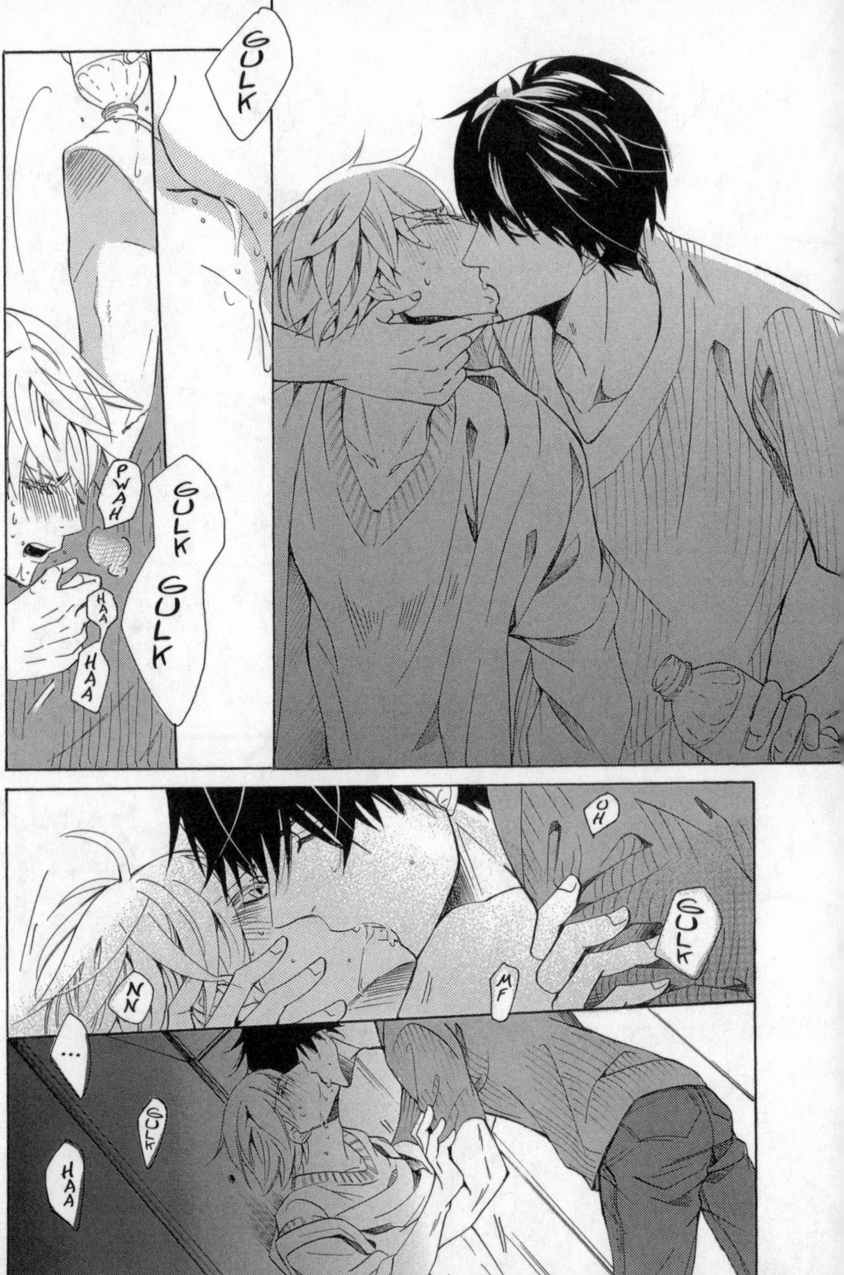
GULK
PWAH
GULK GULK
HAA HAA
UH
GULK
MF
NN
...
GULK
HAA

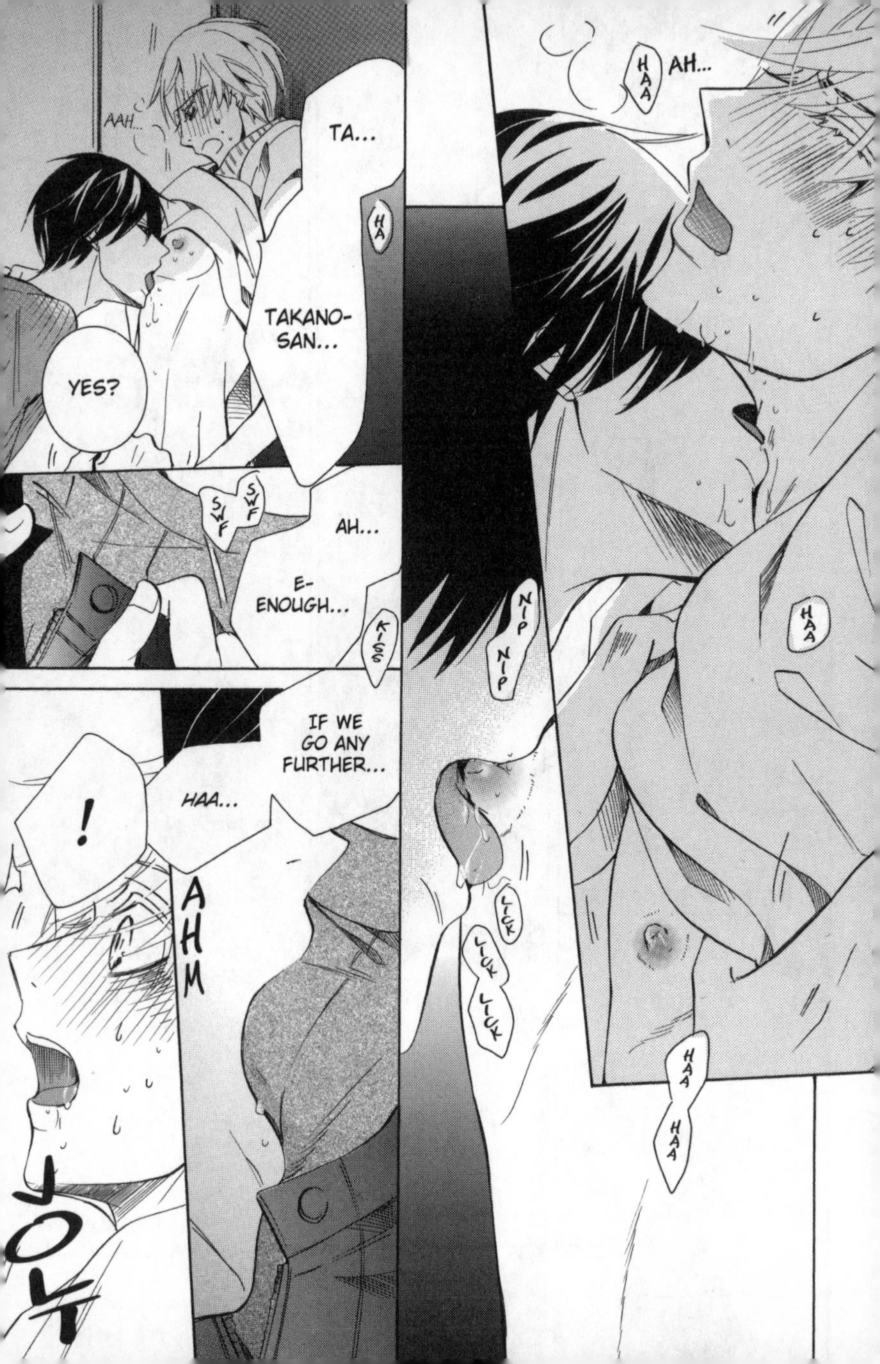
HAAA
AH...
NIP NIP
HAA
LICK
LICK LICK
HAA HAA
TA...
HA
AAH...
TAKANO-SAN...
YES?
SWF SWF
AH...
E-ENOUGH...
KISS
IF WE GO ANY FURTHER...
HAA...
!
AHM
JOLT

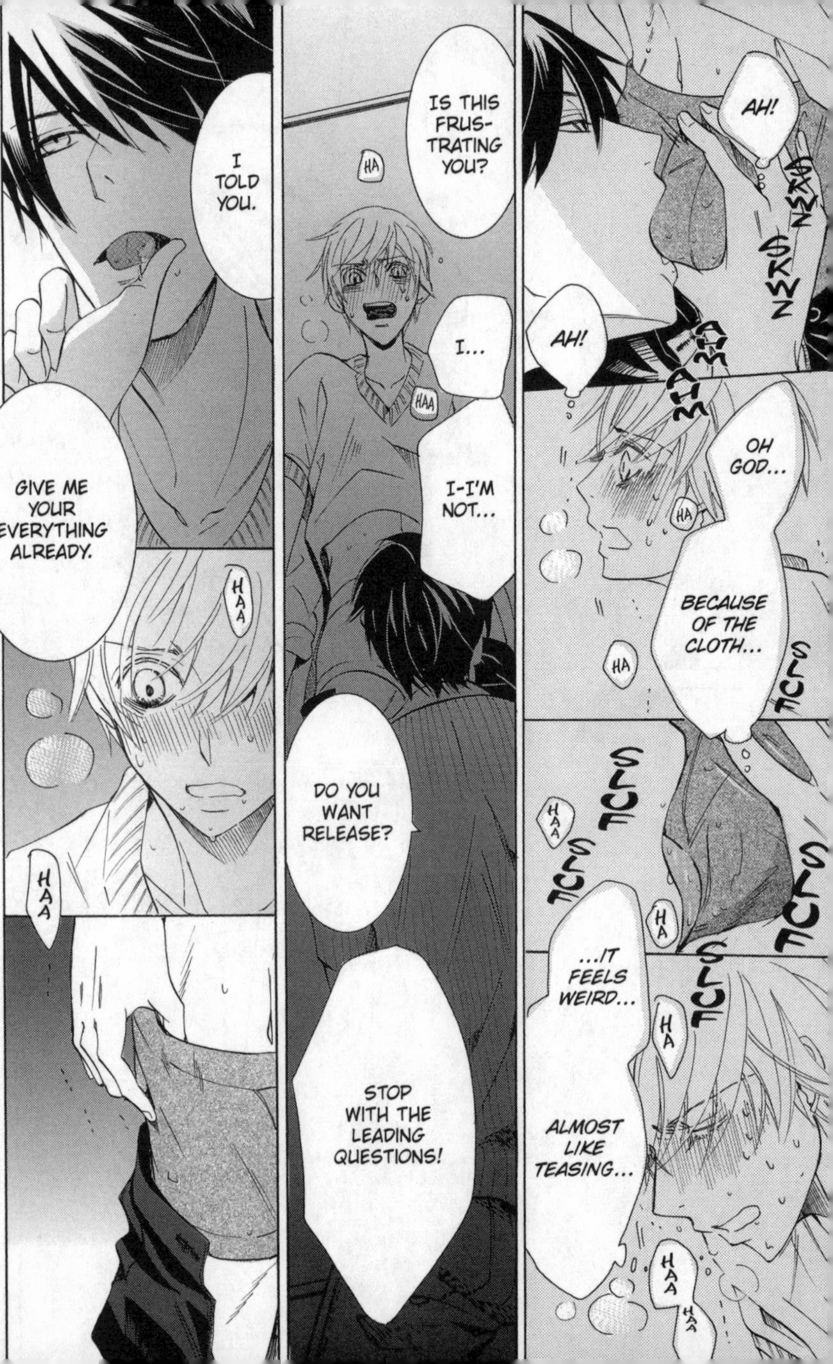
AH!
SKWZ
SKWZ
AH!
AHM
AHM
OH GOD...
HA
BECAUSE OF THE CLOTH...
HA
SLUF
SLUF
HAA
SLUF
HA
SLUF
SLUF
...IT FEELS WEIRD...
HA
ALMOST LIKE TEASING...
HAA
HAA
IS THIS FRUS-TRATING YOU?
HA
I...
HAA
I-I'M NOT...
DO YOU WANT RELEASE?
STOP WITH THE LEADING QUESTIONS!
I TOLD YOU.
GIVE ME YOUR EVERYTHING ALREADY.
HAA
HAA

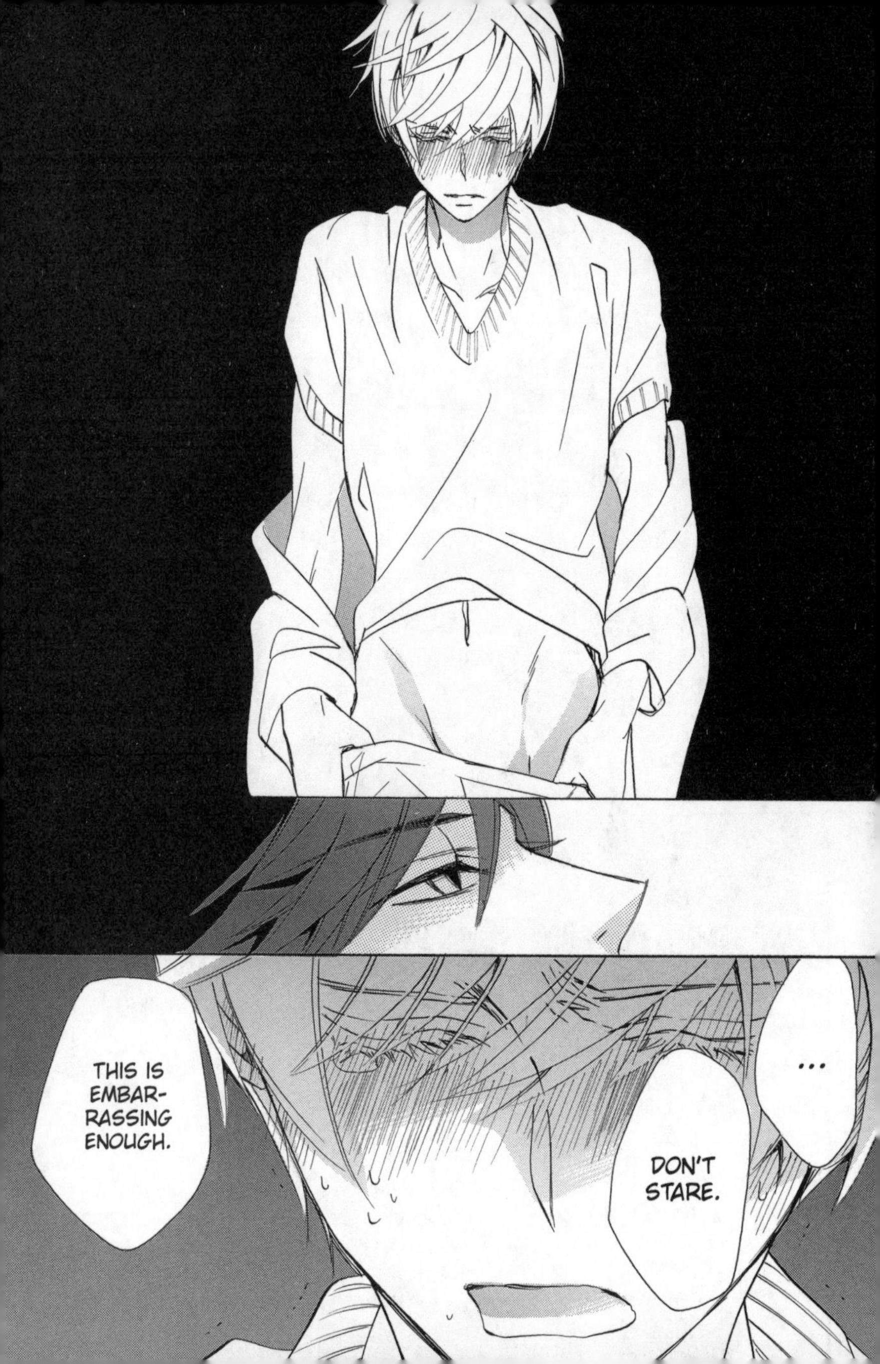
...
DON'T STARE.
THIS IS EMBAR-RASSING ENOUGH.

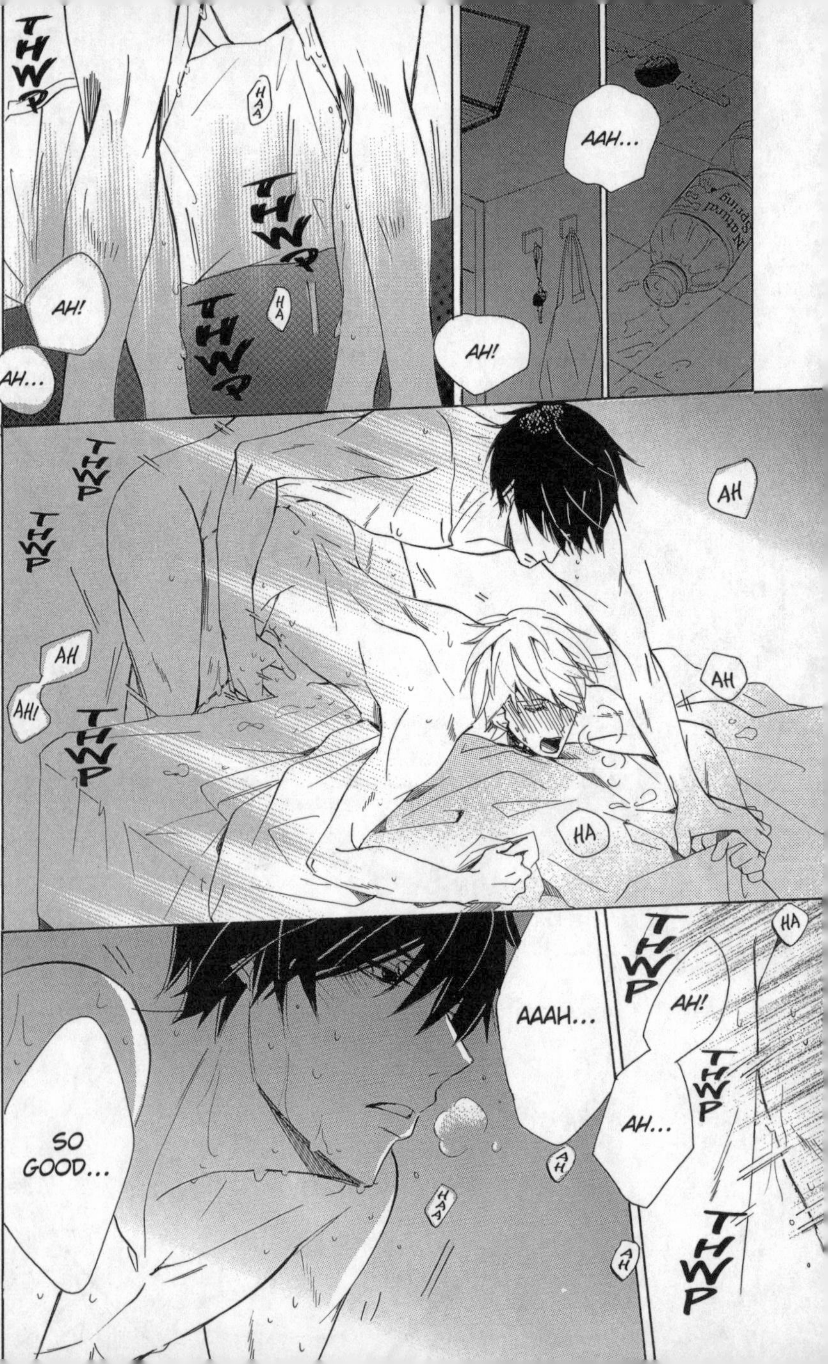
AAH...
Natural
Spring
AH!
HAA
THWP
THWP
THWP
HA
AH!
AH...
AH
THWP
THWP
AH
AH
AH!
THWP
HA
HA
THWP
AH!
THWP
AH...
THWP
AAAH...
SO GOOD...
AH
HAA
AH

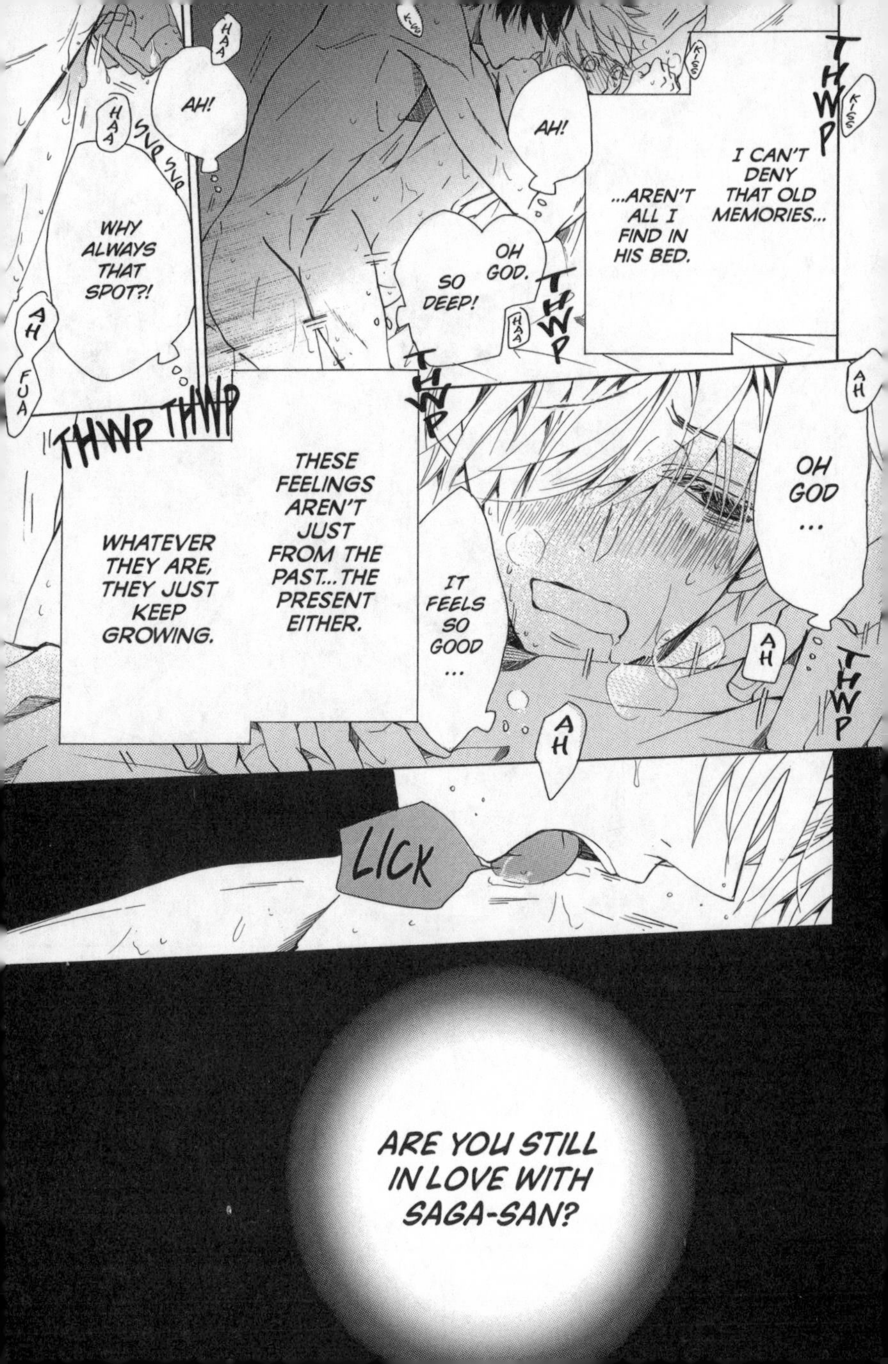
KISS
KISS
KISS
THWP
I CAN'T DENY THAT OLD MEMORIES...
...AREN'T ALL I FIND IN HIS BED.
AH!
OH GOD.
SO DEEP!
HAA
THWP
HAA
AH!
HAA
SVP SVP
WHY ALWAYS THAT SPOT?!
AH
FUA
THWP THWP
AH
OH GOD...
THWP
AH
IT FEELS SO GOOD...
AH
THWP
THESE FEELINGS AREN'T JUST FROM THE PAST...THE PRESENT EITHER.
WHATEVER THEY ARE, THEY JUST KEEP GROWING.
LICK
ARE YOU STILL IN LOVE WITH SAGA-SAN?

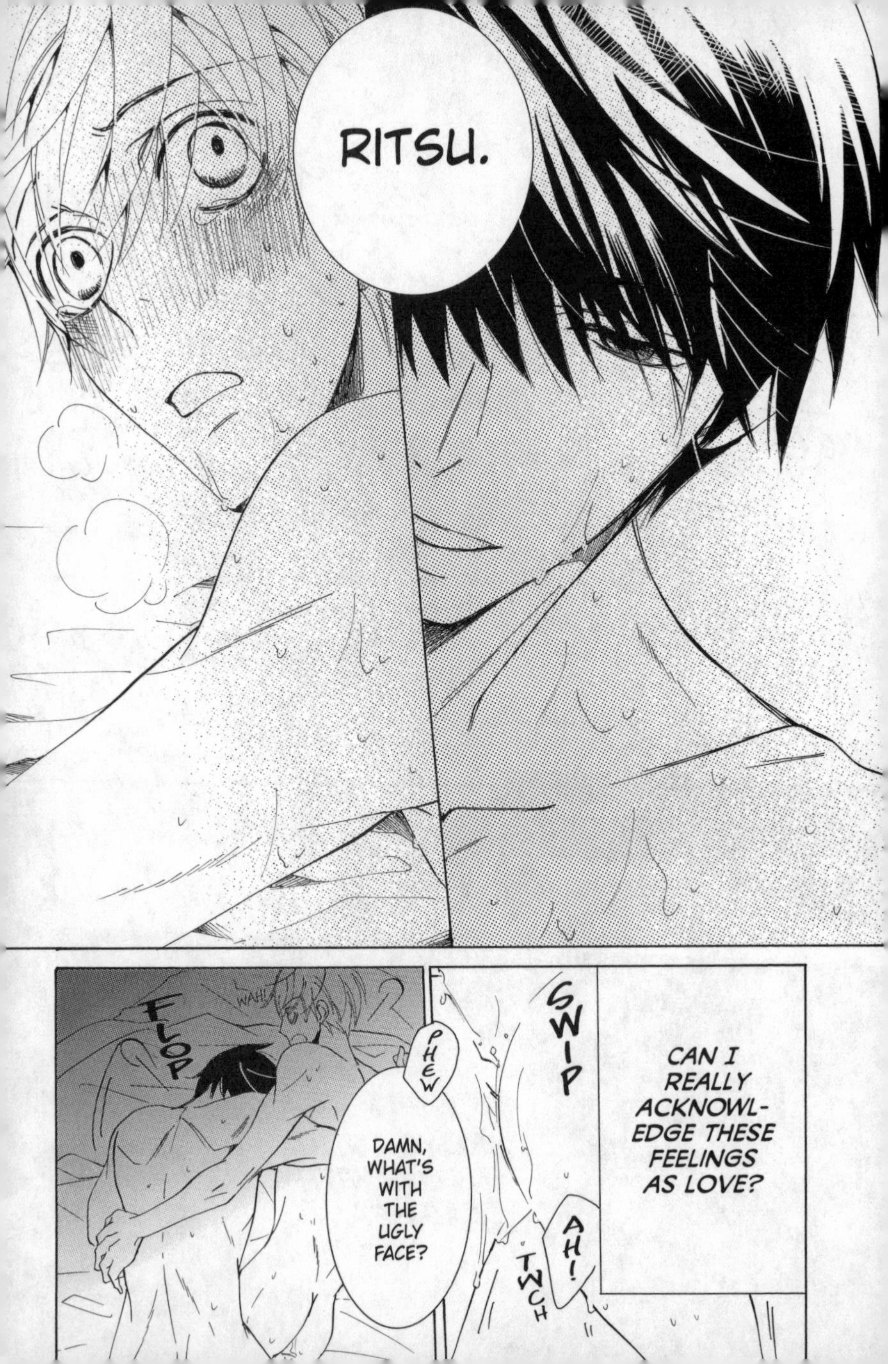
RITSU.
CAN I REALLY ACKNOWL-EDGE THESE FEELINGS AS LOVE?
SWIP
AH!
TWCH
PHEW
DAMN, WHAT'S WITH THE UGLY FACE?
WAH!!
FLOP

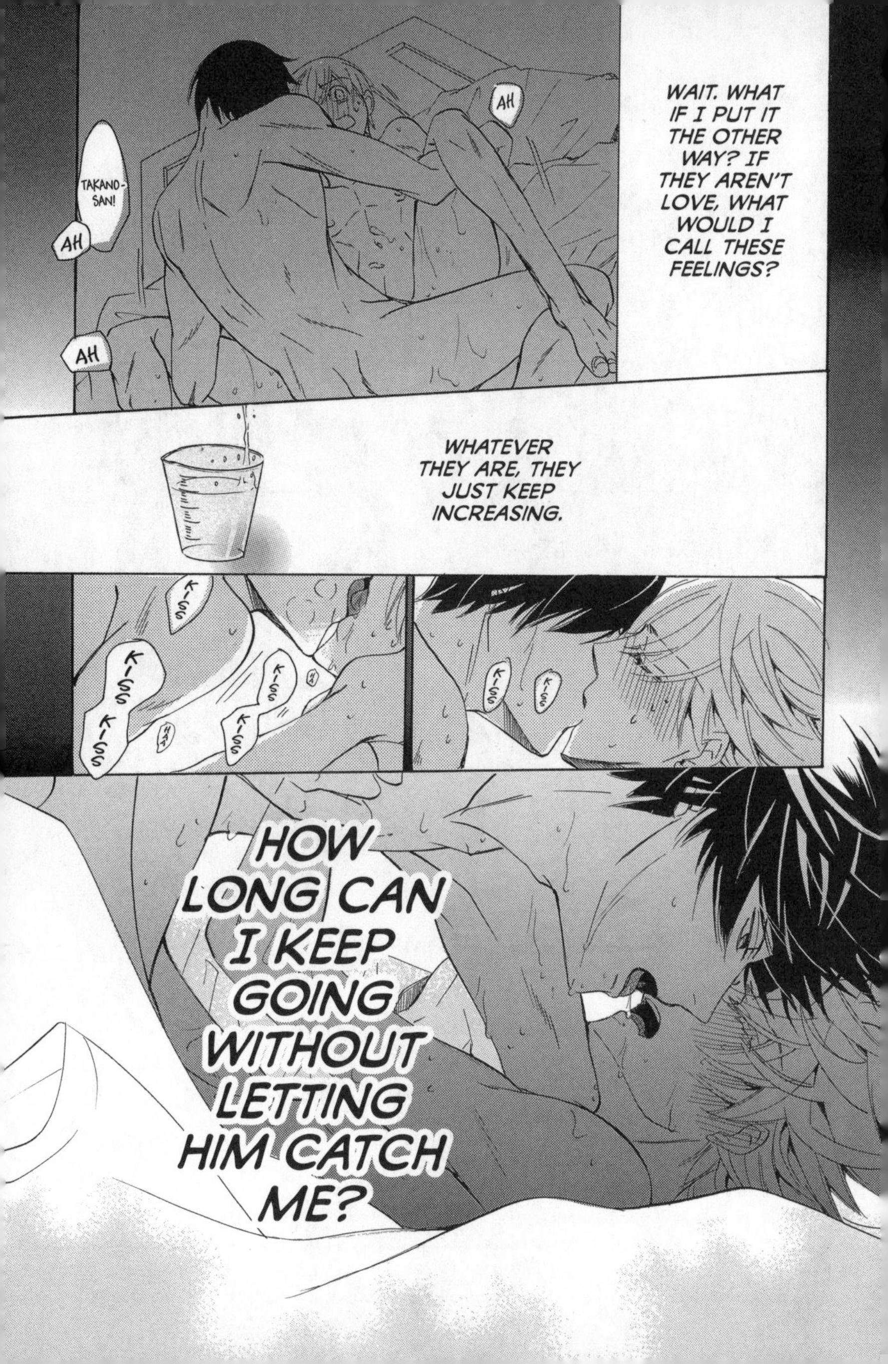

WAIT. WHAT IF I PUT IT THE OTHER WAY? IF THEY AREN'T LOVE, WHAT WOULD I CALL THESE FEELINGS?
AH
TAKANO-SAN!
AH
AH
WHATEVER THEY ARE, THEY JUST KEEP INCREASING.
KISS
KISS
KISS
KISS KISS
KISS
KISS
HOW LONG CAN I KEEP GOING WITHOUT LETTING HIM CATCH ME?

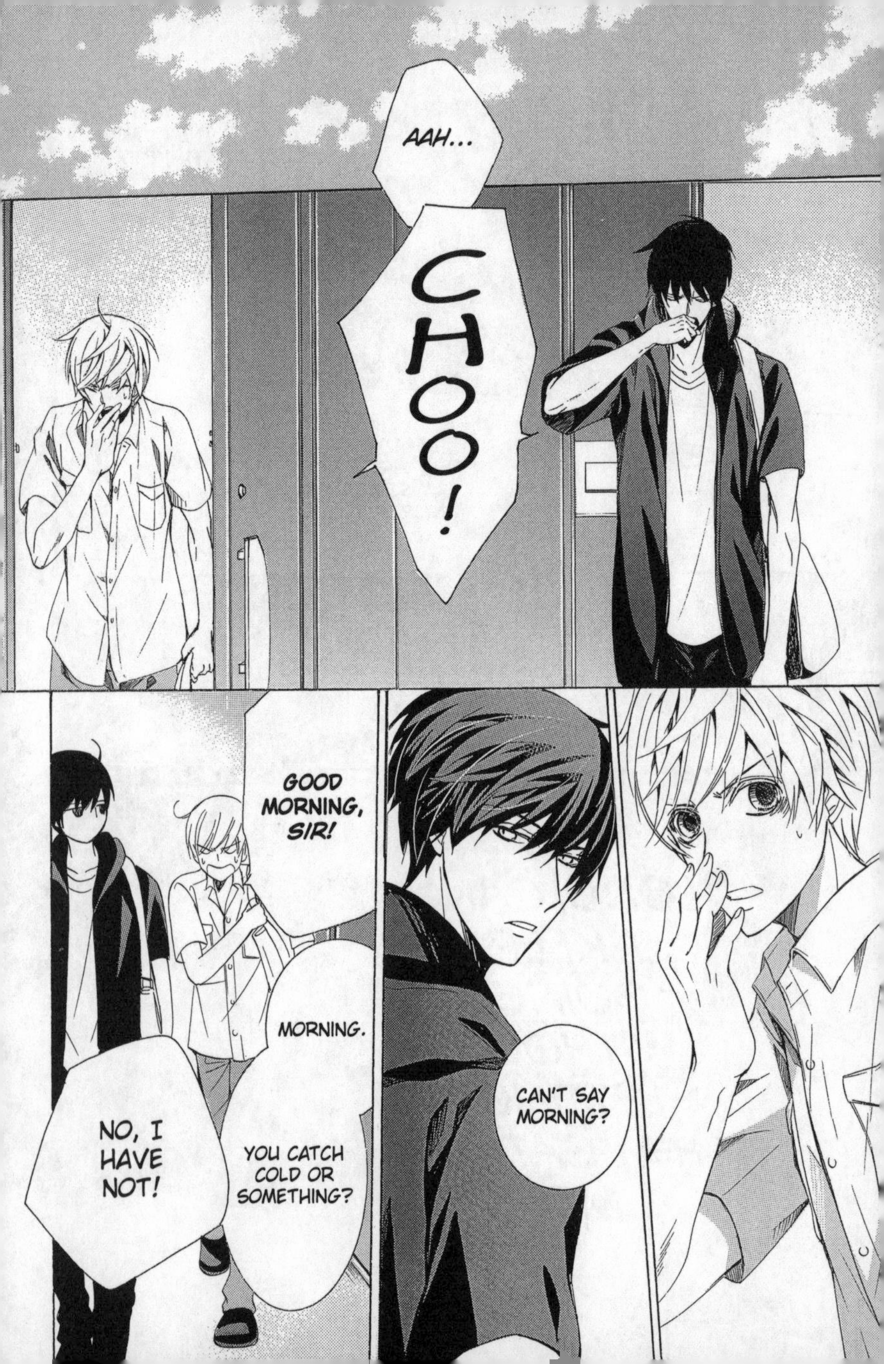
AAH...
CHOO!
CAN'T SAY MORNING?
GOOD MORNING, SIR!
MORNING.
YOU CATCH COLD OR SOMETHING?
NO, I HAVE NOT!

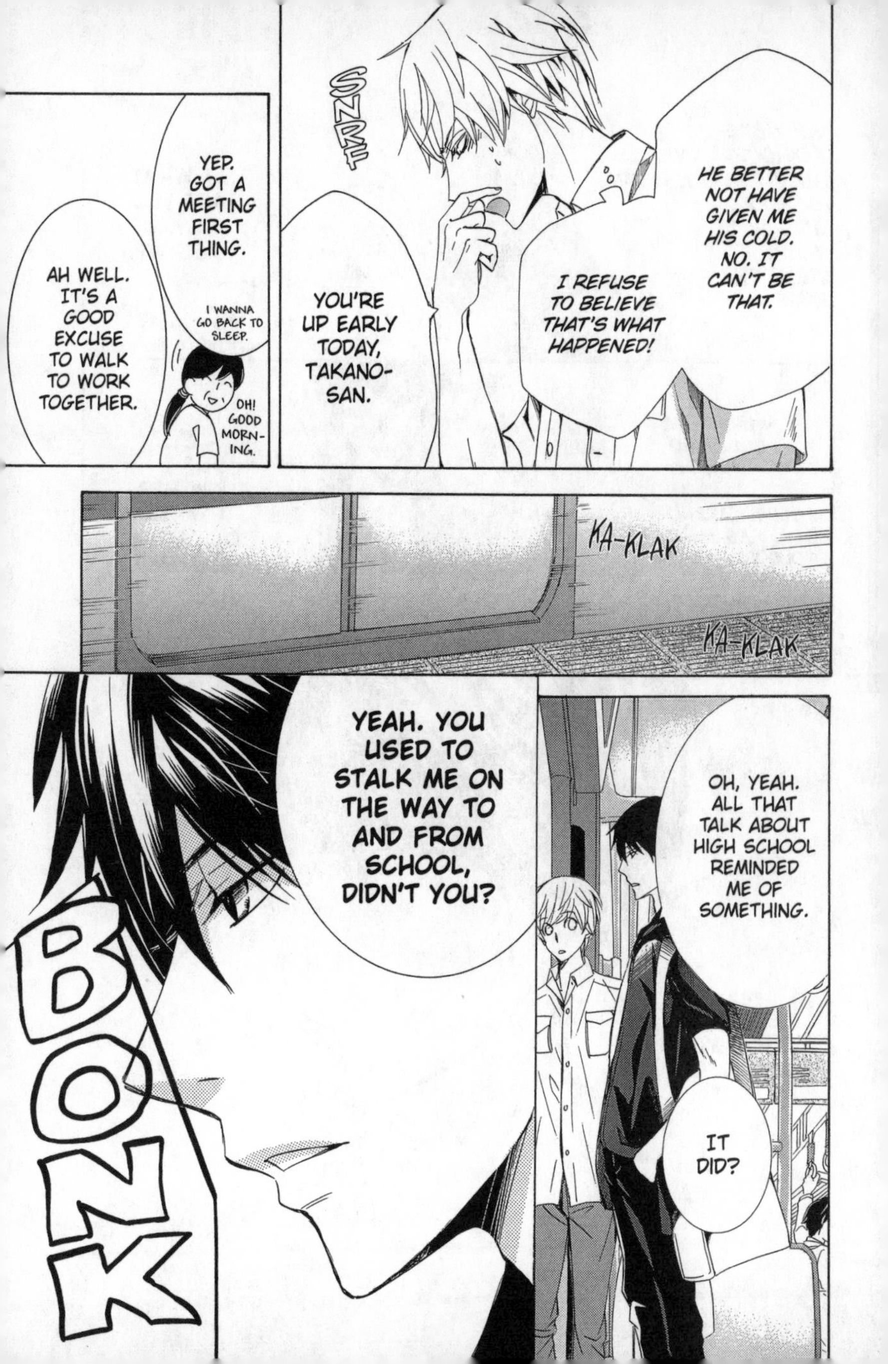
SNRF
HE BETTER NOT HAVE GIVEN ME HIS COLD. NO. IT CAN'T BE THAT.
I REFUSE TO BELIEVE THAT'S WHAT HAPPENED!
YOU'RE UP EARLY TODAY, TAKANO-SAN.
YEP. GOT A MEETING FIRST THING.
I WANNA GO BACK TO SLEEP.
OH! GOOD MORN-ING.
AH WELL. IT'S A GOOD EXCUSE TO WALK TO WORK TOGETHER.
KA-KLAK
KA-KLAK
OH, YEAH. ALL THAT TALK ABOUT HIGH SCHOOL REMINDED ME OF SOMETHING.
IT DID?
YEAH. YOU USED TO STALK ME ON THE WAY TO AND FROM SCHOOL, DIDN'T YOU?
BONK

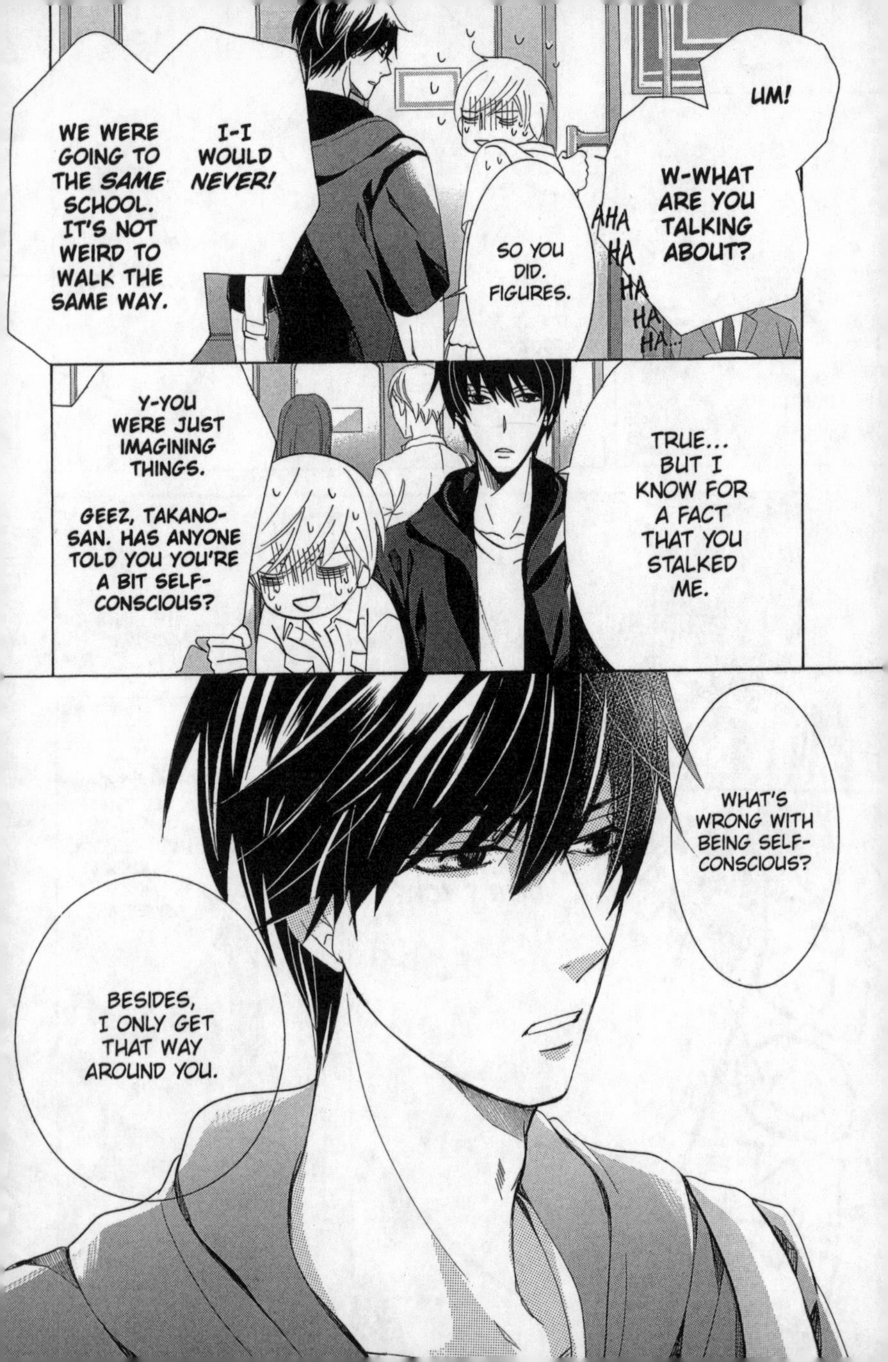
UM!
W-WHAT ARE YOU TALKING ABOUT?
AHA HA HA HA HA...
SO YOU DID. FIGURES.
I-I WOULD NEVER!
WE WERE GOING TO THE SAME SCHOOL. IT'S NOT WEIRD TO WALK THE SAME WAY.
TRUE... BUT I KNOW FOR A FACT THAT YOU STALKED ME.
Y-YOU WERE JUST IMAGINING THINGS.
GEEZ, TAKANO-SAN. HAS ANYONE TOLD YOU YOU'RE A BIT SELF-CONSCIOUS?
WHAT'S WRONG WITH BEING SELF-CONSCIOUS?
BESIDES, I ONLY GET THAT WAY AROUND YOU.

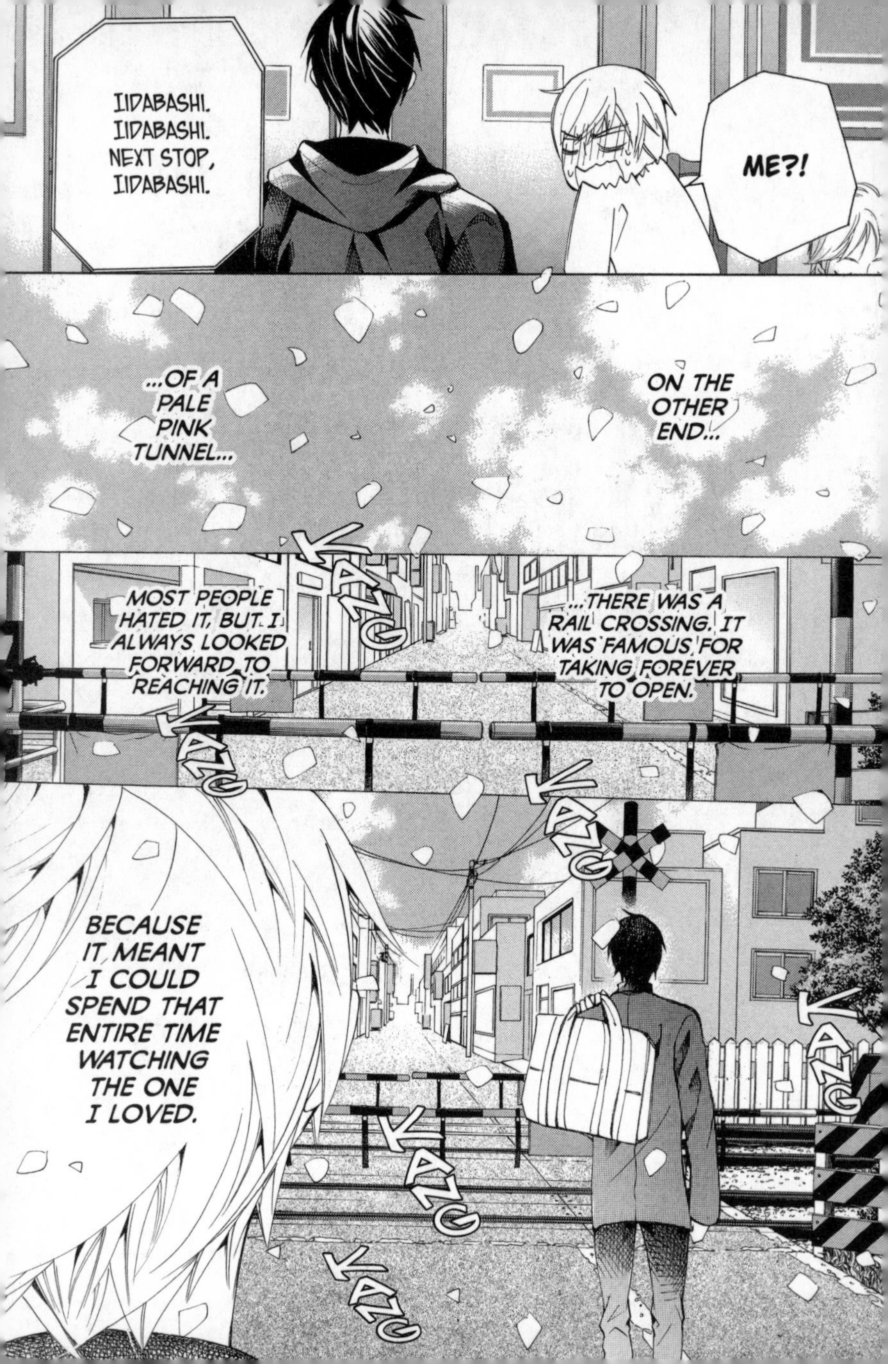
ME?!
IIDABASHI. IIDABASHI. NEXT STOP, IIDABASHI.
ON THE OTHER END...
...OF A PALE PINK TUNNEL...
KANG
...THERE WAS A RAIL CROSSING. IT WAS FAMOUS FOR TAKING FOREVER TO OPEN.
MOST PEOPLE HATED IT, BUT I ALWAYS LOOKED FORWARD TO REACHING IT.
KANG
KANG
KANG
BECAUSE IT MEANT I COULD SPEND THAT ENTIRE TIME WATCHING THE ONE I LOVED.
KANG
KANG

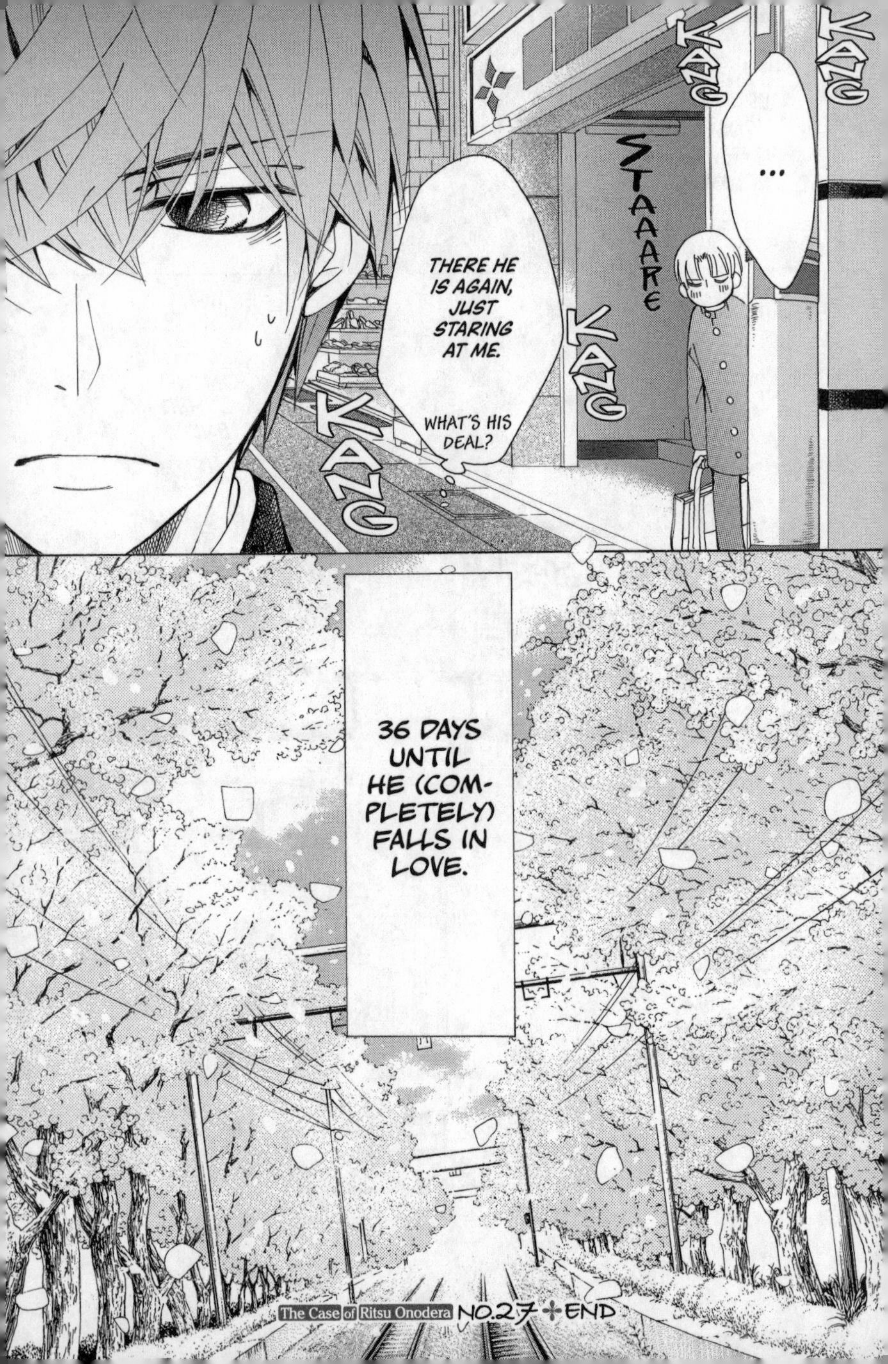
KANG
KANG
...
STAAARE
KANG
THERE HE IS AGAIN, JUST STARING AT ME.
WHAT'S HIS DEAL?
KANG
36 DAYS UNTIL HE (COMPLETELY) FALLS IN LOVE.
The Case of Ritsu Onodera NO.27 END

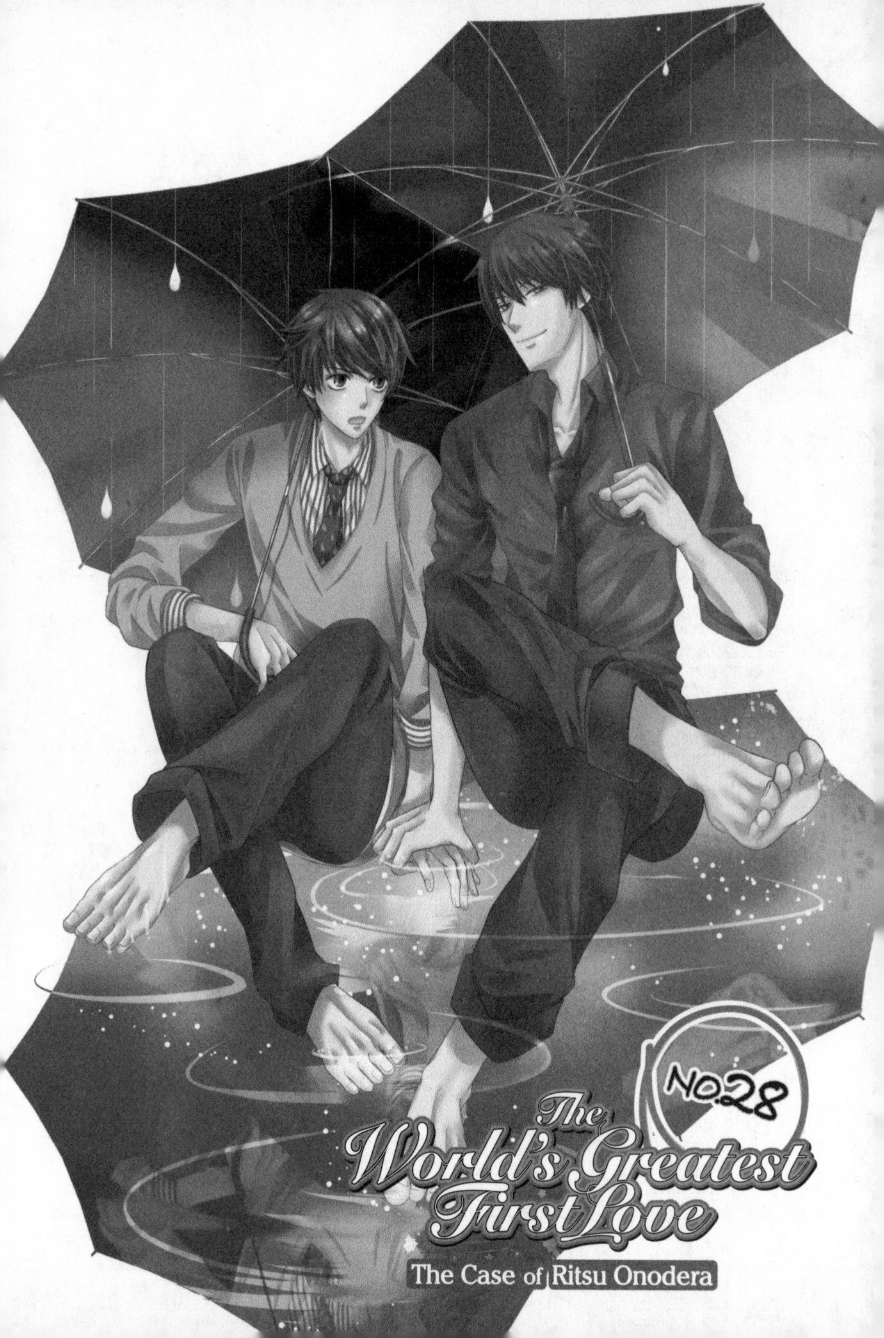
NO.28
The World's Greatest First Love
The Case of Ritsu Onodera

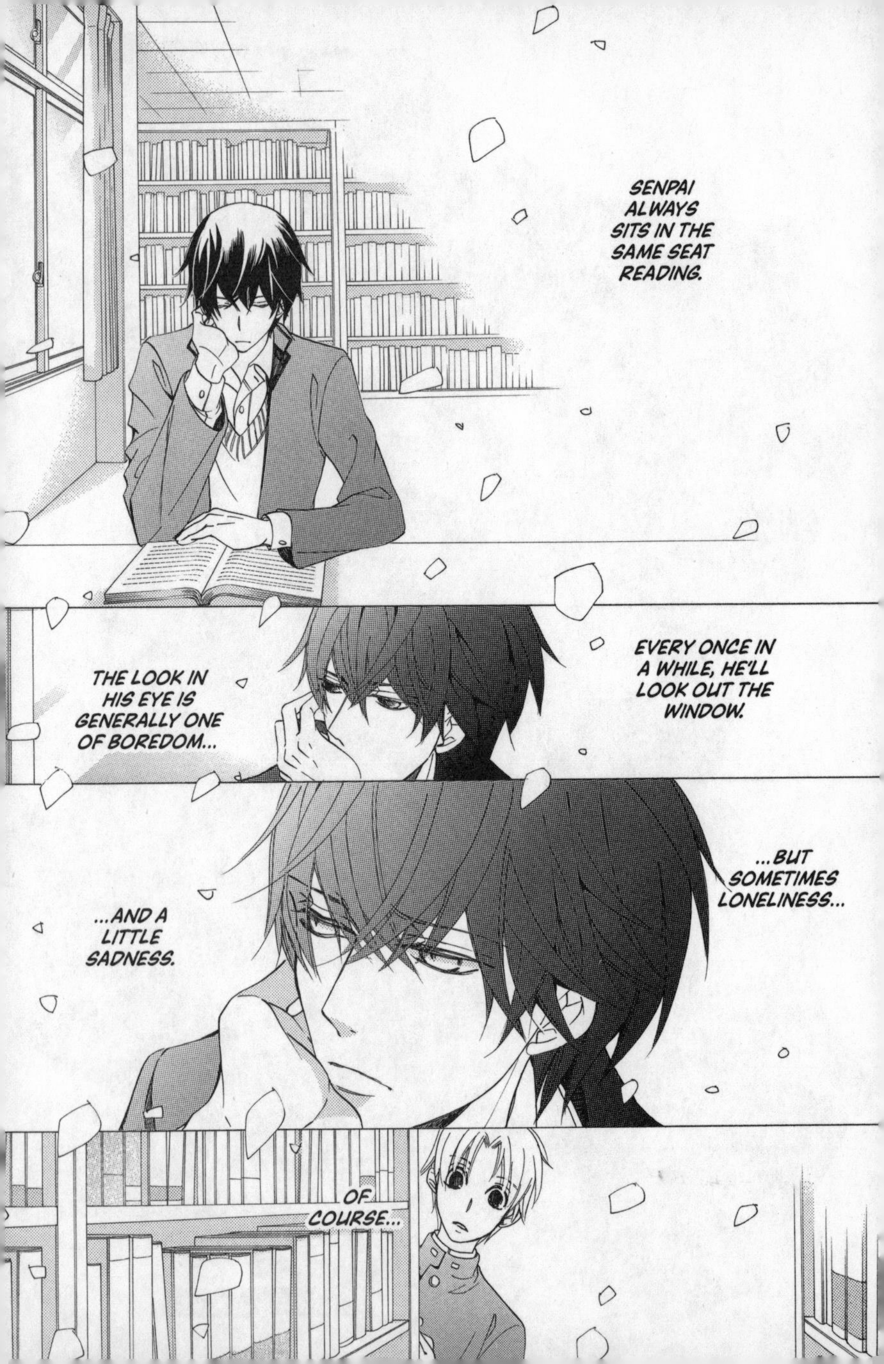
SENPAI ALWAYS SITS IN THE SAME SEAT READING.
EVERY ONCE IN A WHILE, HE'LL LOOK OUT THE WINDOW.
THE LOOK IN HIS EYE IS GENERALLY ONE OF BOREDOM...
...BUT SOMETIMES LONELINESS...
...AND A LITTLE SADNESS.
OF COURSE...

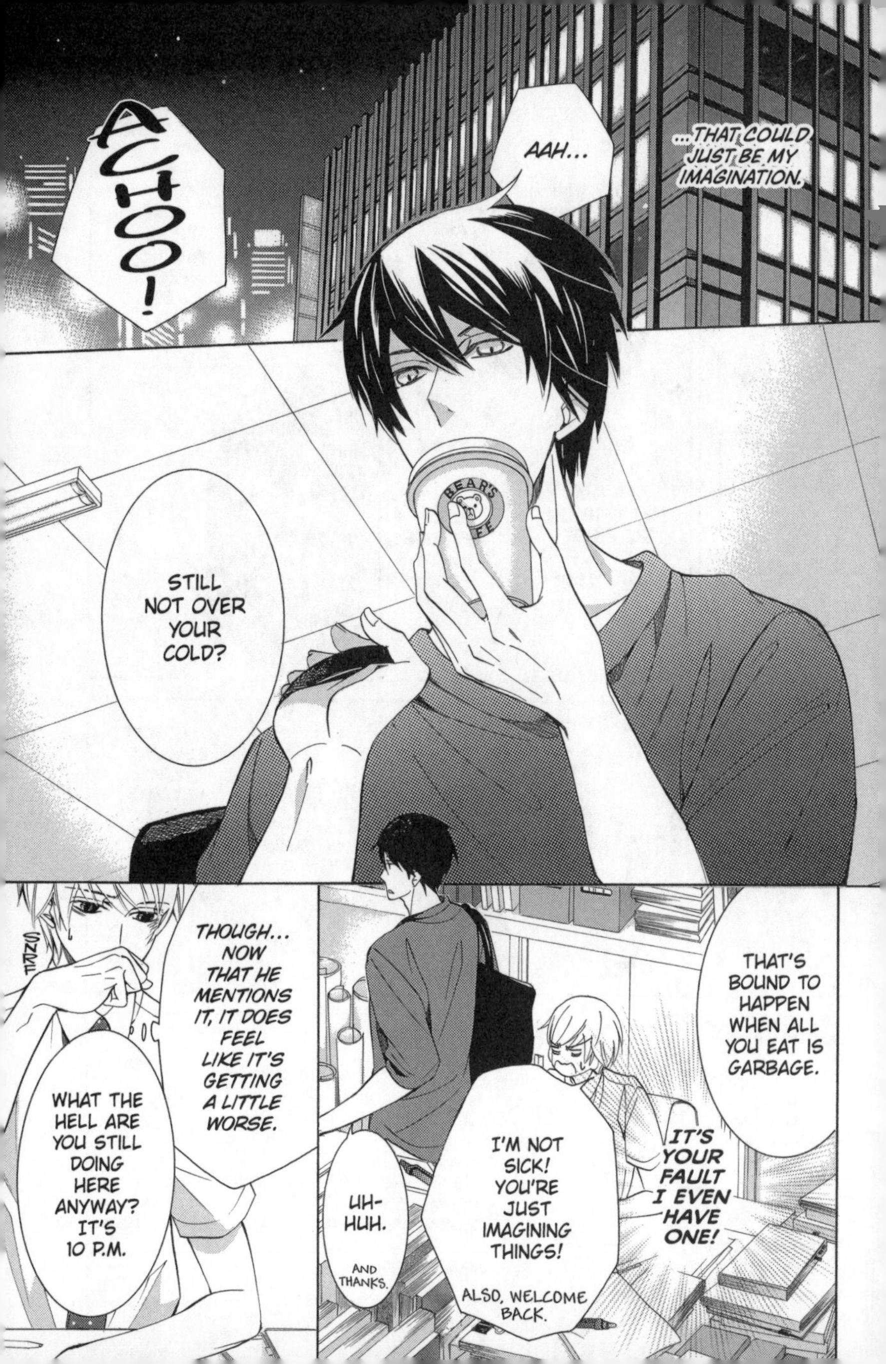
...THAT COULD JUST BE MY IMAGINATION.
AAH...
ACHOO!
STILL NOT OVER YOUR COLD?
THAT'S BOUND TO HAPPEN WHEN ALL YOU EAT IS GARBAGE.
IT'S YOUR FAULT I EVEN HAVE ONE!
I'M NOT SICK! YOU'RE JUST IMAGINING THINGS!
ALSO, WELCOME BACK.
UH-HUH.
AND THANKS.
THOUGH... NOW THAT HE MENTIONS IT, IT DOES FEEL LIKE IT'S GETTING A LITTLE WORSE.
SNRF
WHAT THE HELL ARE YOU STILL DOING HERE ANYWAY? IT'S 10 P.M.

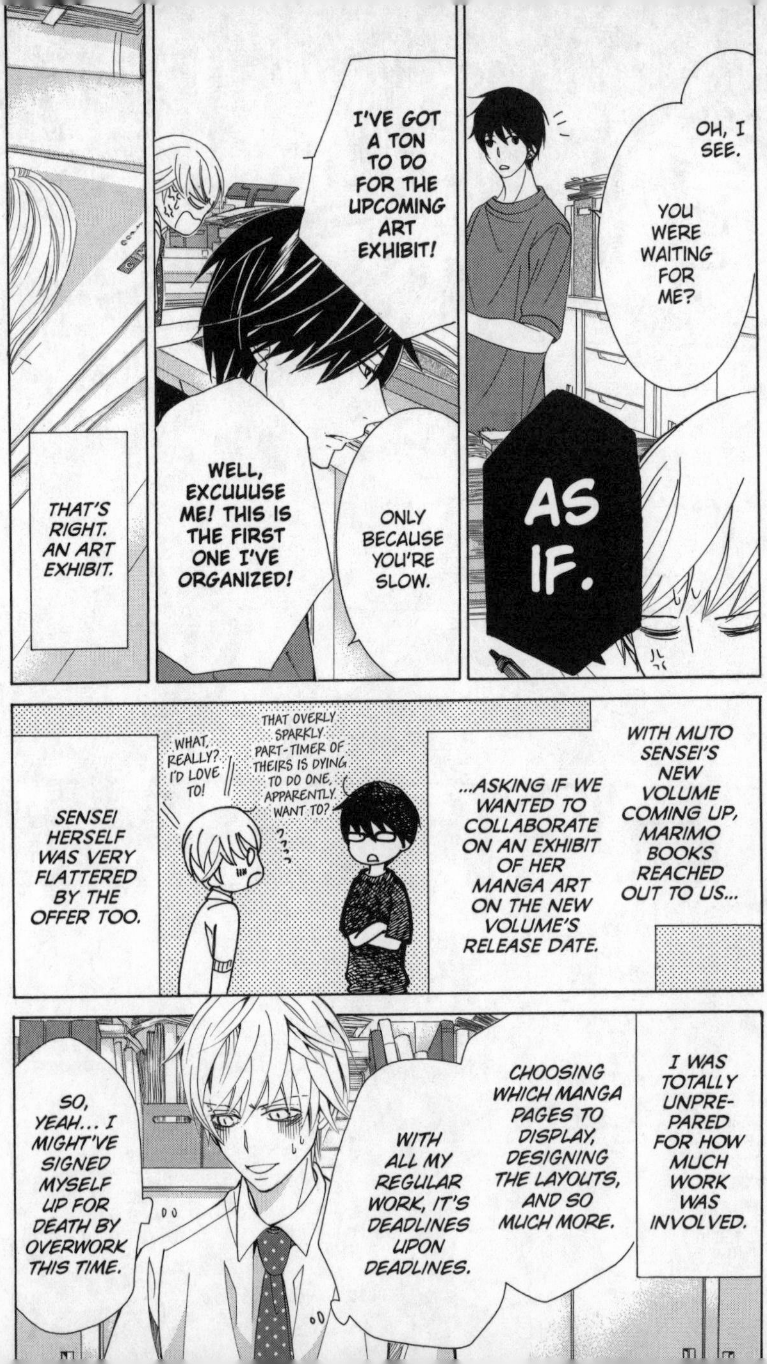
OH, I SEE.
YOU WERE WAITING FOR ME?
AS IF.
I'VE GOT A TON TO DO FOR THE UPCOMING ART EXHIBIT!
ONLY BECAUSE YOU'RE SLOW.
WELL, EXCUUUSE ME! THIS IS THE FIRST ONE I'VE ORGANIZED!
THAT'S RIGHT. AN ART EXHIBIT.
WITH MUTO SENSEI'S NEW VOLUME COMING UP, MARIMO BOOKS REACHED OUT TO US...
...ASKING IF WE WANTED TO COLLABORATE ON AN EXHIBIT OF HER MANGA ART ON THE NEW VOLUME'S RELEASE DATE.
THAT OVERLY SPARKLY PART-TIMER OF THEIRS IS DYING TO DO ONE, APPARENTLY. WANT TO?
WHAT, REALLY? I'D LOVE TO!
SENSEI HERSELF WAS VERY FLATTERED BY THE OFFER TOO.
I WAS TOTALLY UNPREPARED FOR HOW MUCH WORK WAS INVOLVED.
CHOOSING WHICH MANGA PAGES TO DISPLAY, DESIGNING THE LAYOUTS, AND SO MUCH MORE.
WITH ALL MY REGULAR WORK, IT'S DEADLINES UPON DEADLINES.
SO, YEAH... I MIGHT'VE SIGNED MYSELF UP FOR DEATH BY OVERWORK THIS TIME.

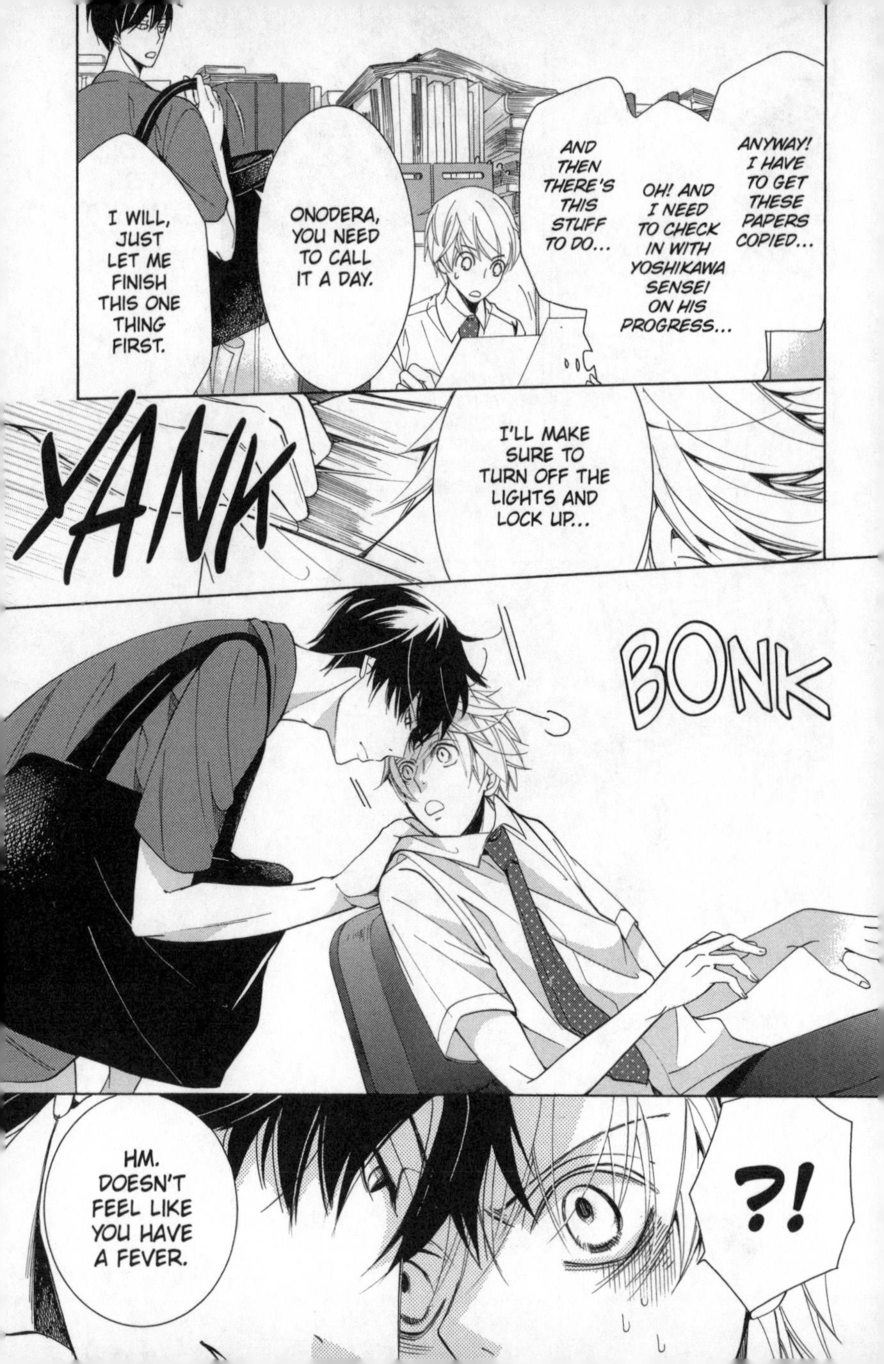
ANYWAY! I HAVE TO GET THESE PAPERS COPIED...
OH! AND I NEED TO CHECK IN WITH YOSHIKAWA SENSEI ON HIS PROGRESS...
AND THEN THERE'S THIS STUFF TO DO...
ONODERA, YOU NEED TO CALL IT A DAY.
I WILL, JUST LET ME FINISH THIS ONE THING FIRST.
I'LL MAKE SURE TO TURN OFF THE LIGHTS AND LOCK UP...
YANK
BONK
?!
HM. DOESN'T FEEL LIKE YOU HAVE A FEVER.

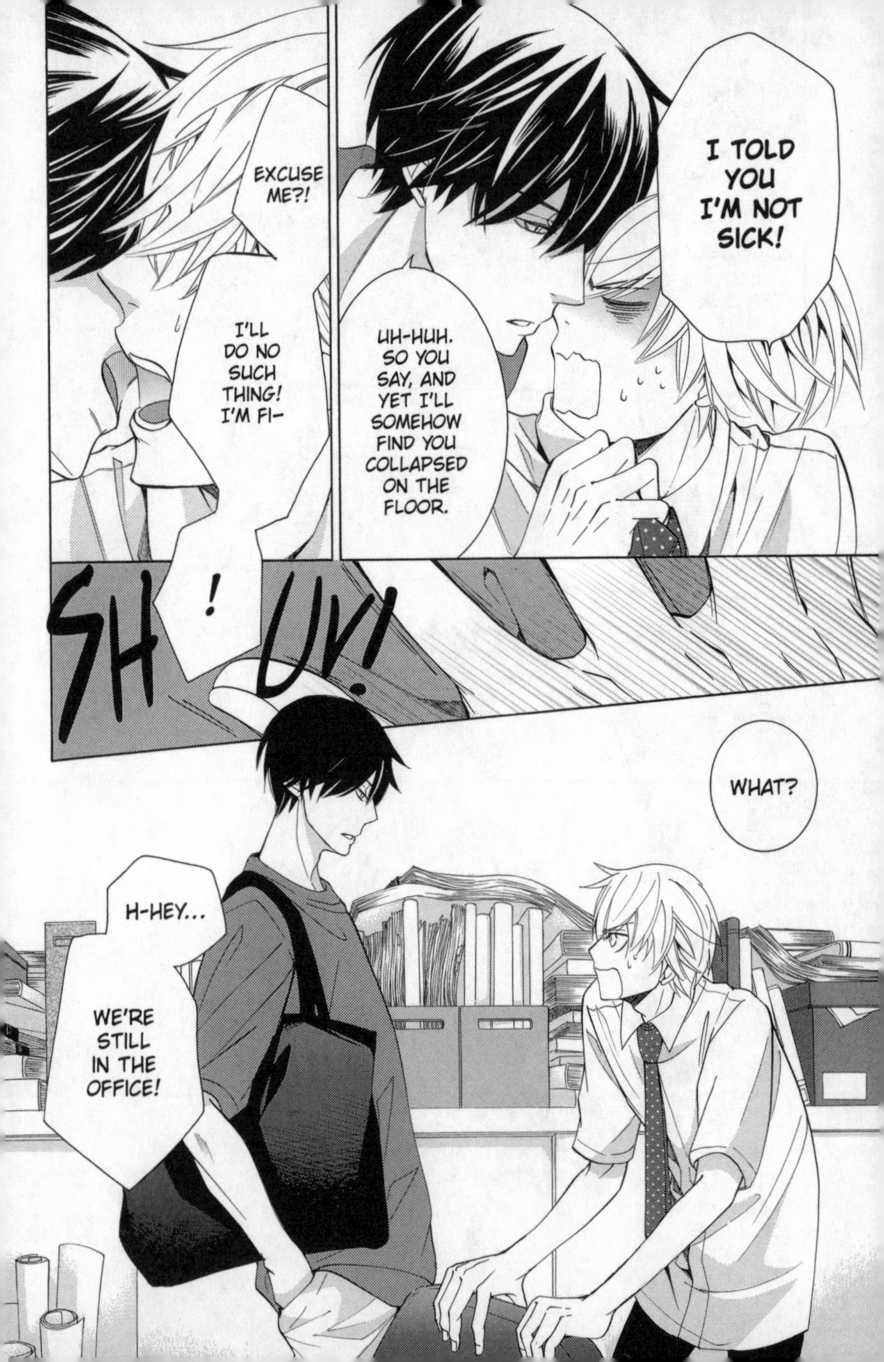
I TOLD YOU I'M NOT SICK!
UH-HUH. SO YOU SAY, AND YET I'LL SOMEHOW FIND YOU COLLAPSED ON THE FLOOR.
EXCUSE ME?!
I'LL DO NO SUCH THING! I'M FI-
SHUV!
WHAT?
H-HEY...
WE'RE STILL IN THE OFFICE!

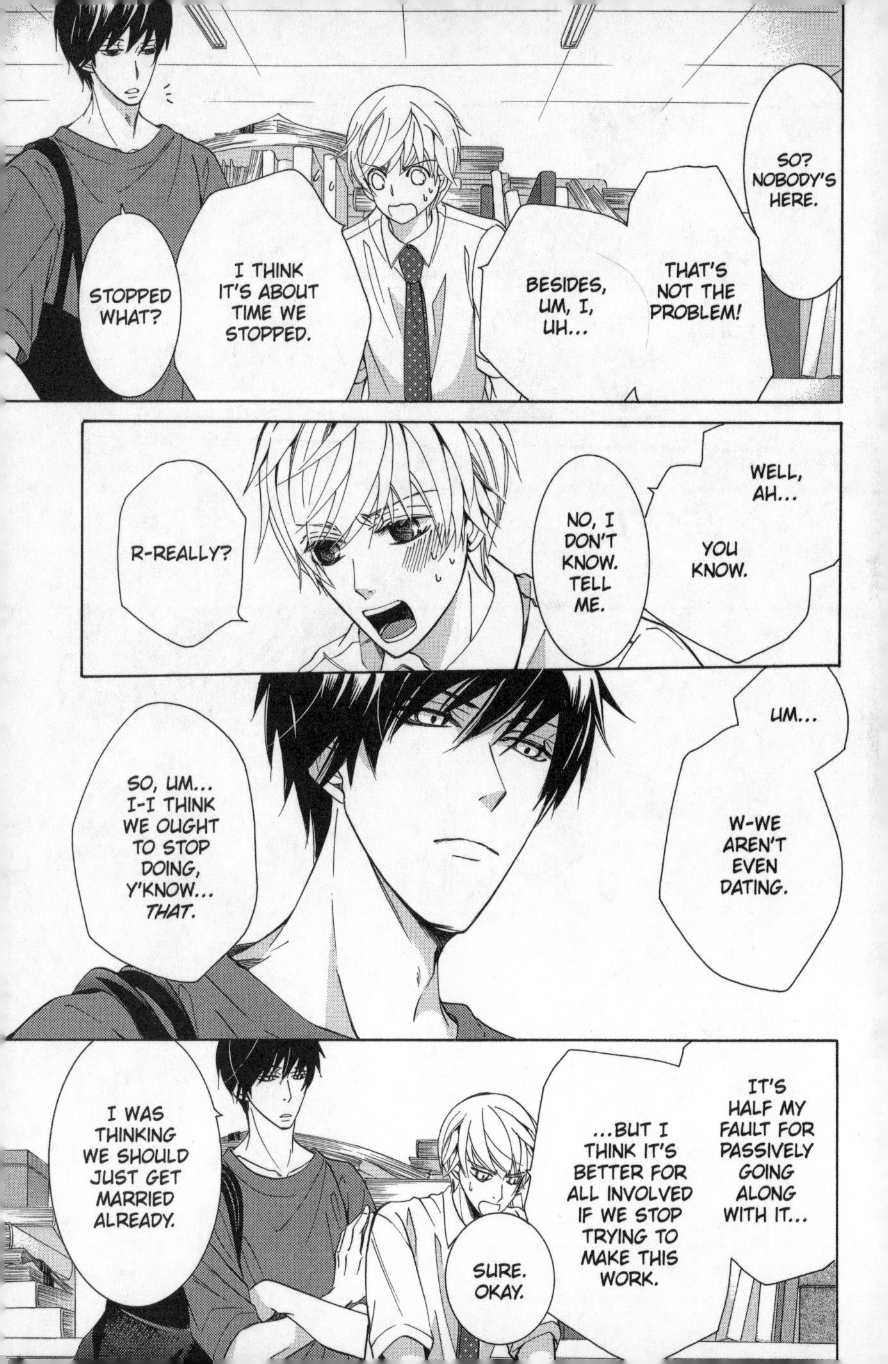
SO? NOBODY'S HERE.
THAT'S NOT THE PROBLEM!
BESIDES, UM, I, UH...
I THINK IT'S ABOUT TIME WE STOPPED.
STOPPED WHAT?
WELL, AH...
YOU KNOW.
NO, I DON'T KNOW. TELL ME.
R-REALLY?
UM...
W-WE AREN'T EVEN DATING.
SO, UM... I-I THINK WE OUGHT TO STOP DOING, Y'KNOW... *THAT.*
IT'S HALF MY FAULT FOR PASSIVELY GOING ALONG WITH IT...
...BUT I THINK IT'S BETTER FOR ALL INVOLVED IF WE STOP TRYING TO MAKE THIS WORK.
SURE. OKAY.
I WAS THINKING WE SHOULD JUST GET MARRIED ALREADY.

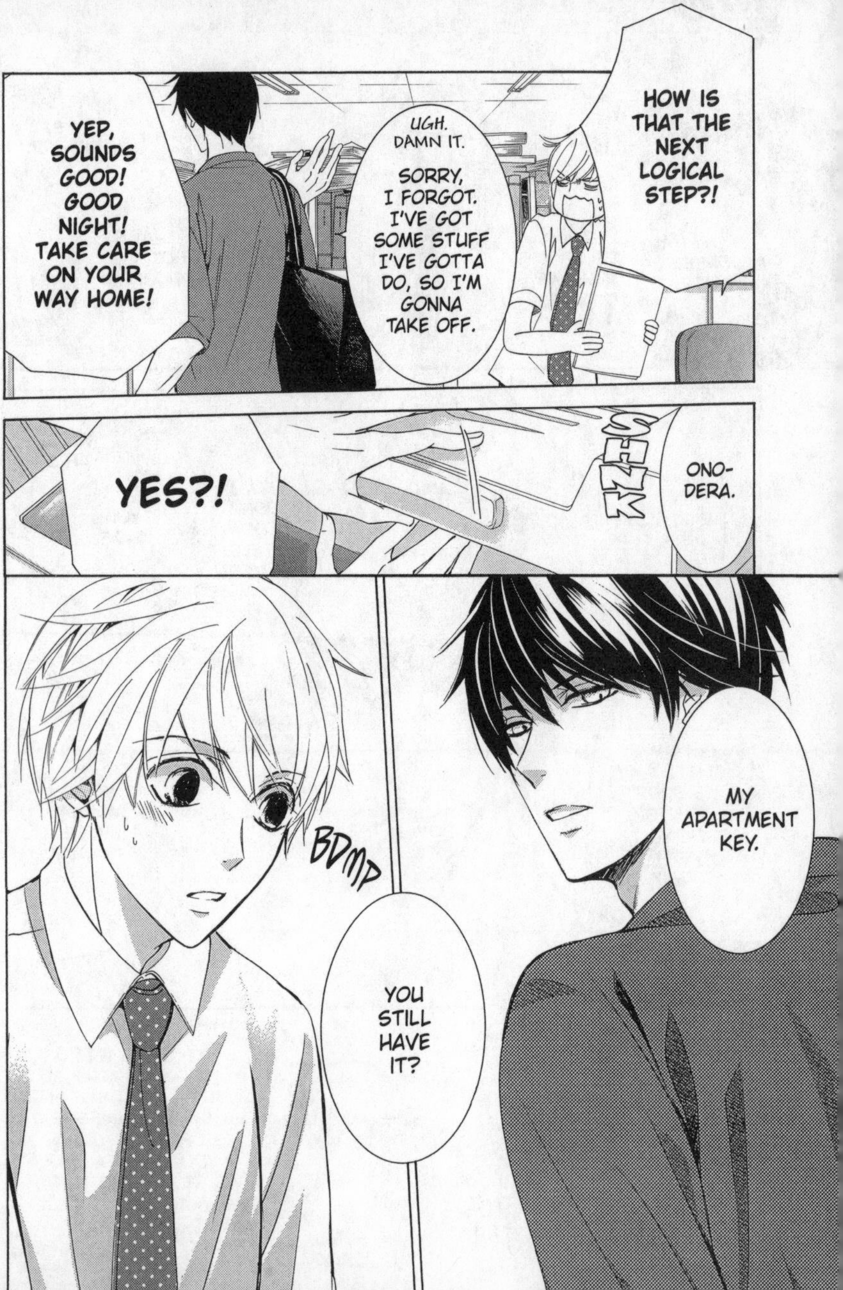
HOW IS THAT THE NEXT LOGICAL STEP?!
UGH. DAMN IT.
SORRY, I FORGOT. I'VE GOT SOME STUFF I'VE GOTTA DO, SO I'M GONNA TAKE OFF.
YEP, SOUNDS GOOD! GOOD NIGHT! TAKE CARE ON YOUR WAY HOME!
ONO-DERA.
SHNK
YES?!
MY APARTMENT KEY.
YOU STILL HAVE IT?
BDMP

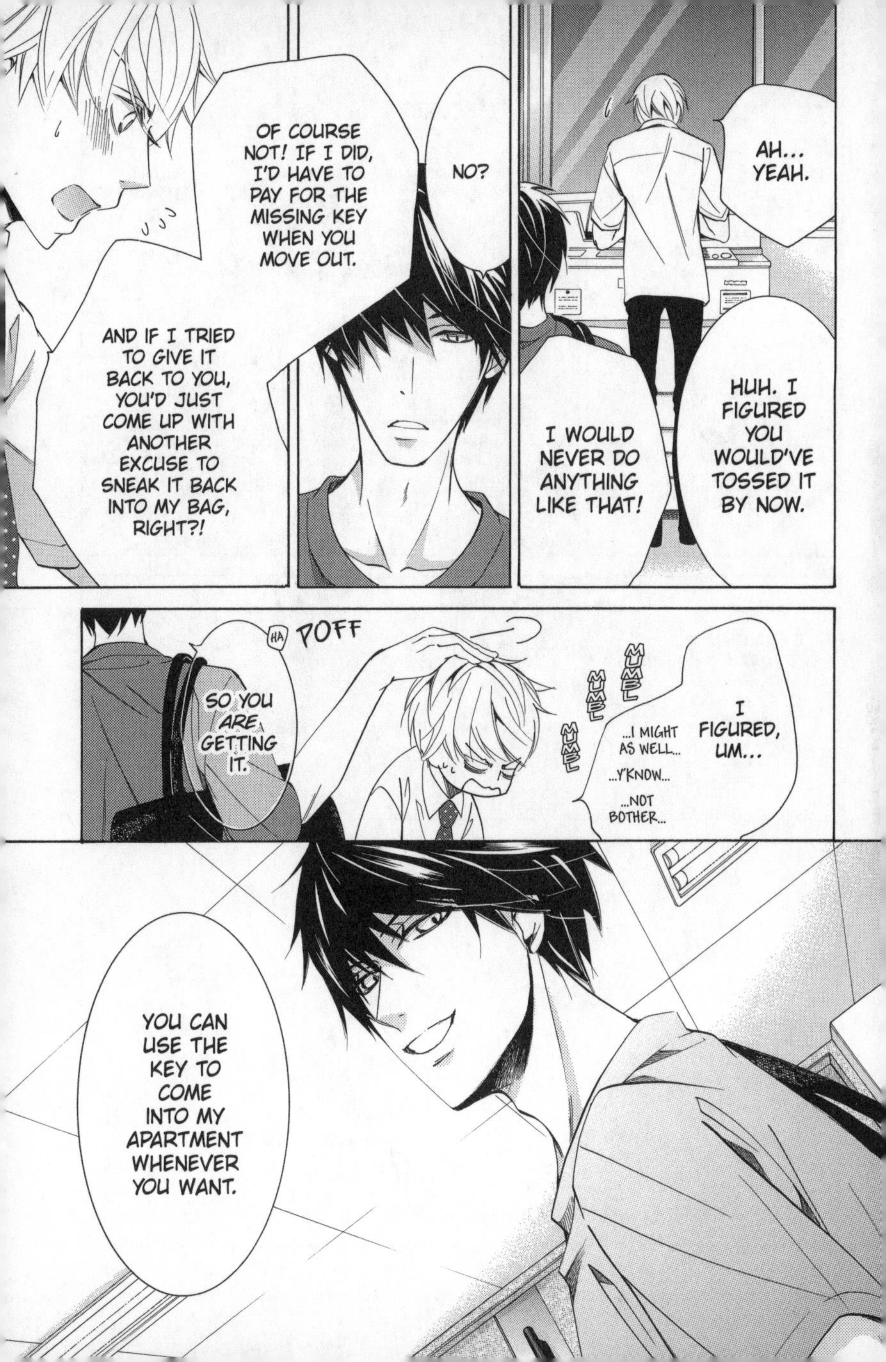
AH... YEAH.
HUH. I FIGURED YOU WOULD'VE TOSSED IT BY NOW.
I WOULD NEVER DO ANYTHING LIKE THAT!
NO?
OF COURSE NOT! IF I DID, I'D HAVE TO PAY FOR THE MISSING KEY WHEN YOU MOVE OUT.
AND IF I TRIED TO GIVE IT BACK TO YOU, YOU'D JUST COME UP WITH ANOTHER EXCUSE TO SNEAK IT BACK INTO MY BAG, RIGHT?!
I FIGURED, UM...
...I MIGHT AS WELL...
...Y'KNOW...
...NOT BOTHER...
MUMBL
MUMBL
MUMBL
POFF
HA
SO YOU ARE GETTING IT.
YOU CAN USE THE KEY TO COME INTO MY APARTMENT WHENEVER YOU WANT.

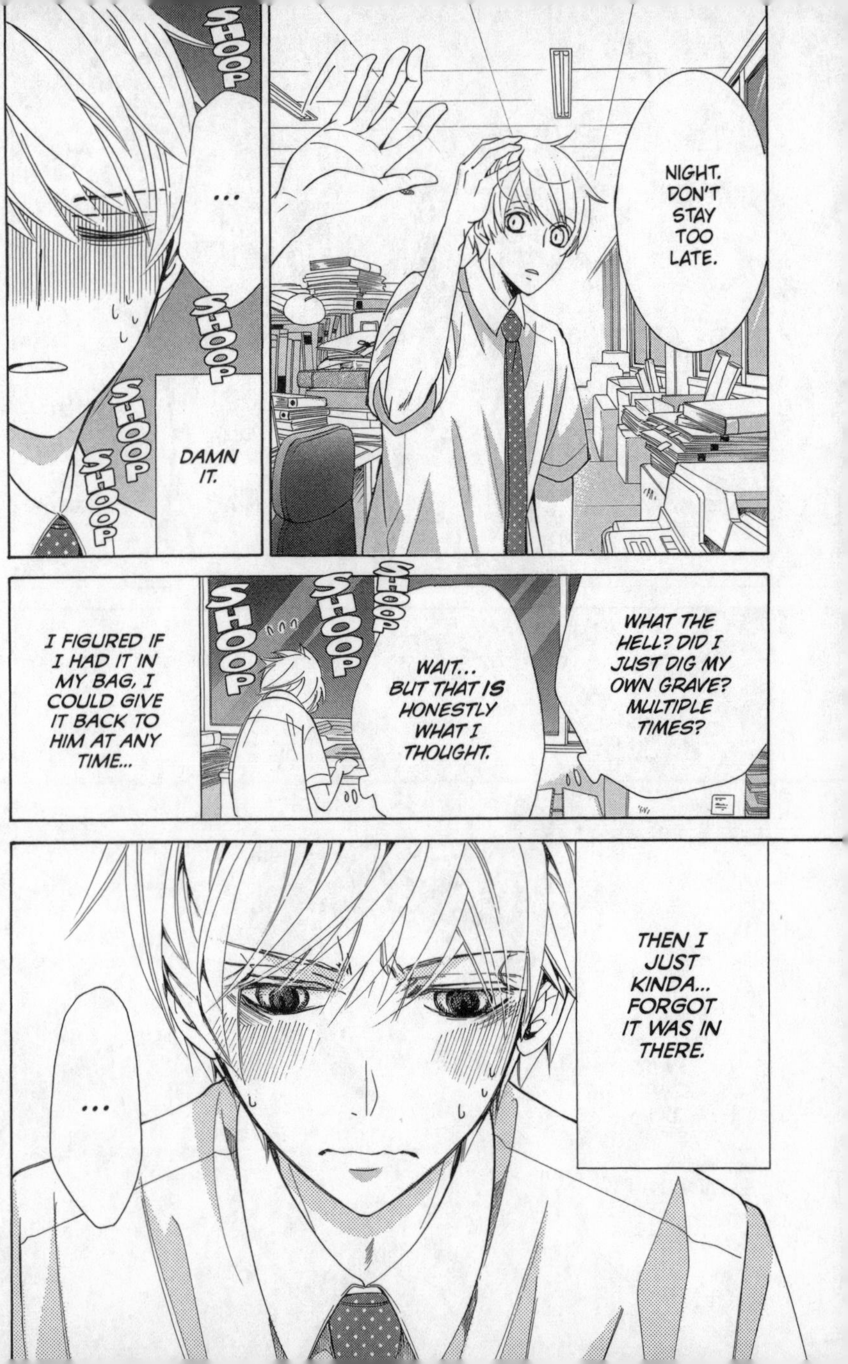
NIGHT. DON'T STAY TOO LATE.
SHOOP
...
SHOOP
SHOOP
SHOOP
DAMN IT.
WHAT THE HELL? DID I JUST DIG MY OWN GRAVE? MULTIPLE TIMES?
WAIT... BUT THAT IS HONESTLY WHAT I THOUGHT.
SHOOP
SHOOP
SHOOP
I FIGURED IF I HAD IT IN MY BAG, I COULD GIVE IT BACK TO HIM AT ANY TIME...
THEN I JUST KINDA... FORGOT IT WAS IN THERE.
...

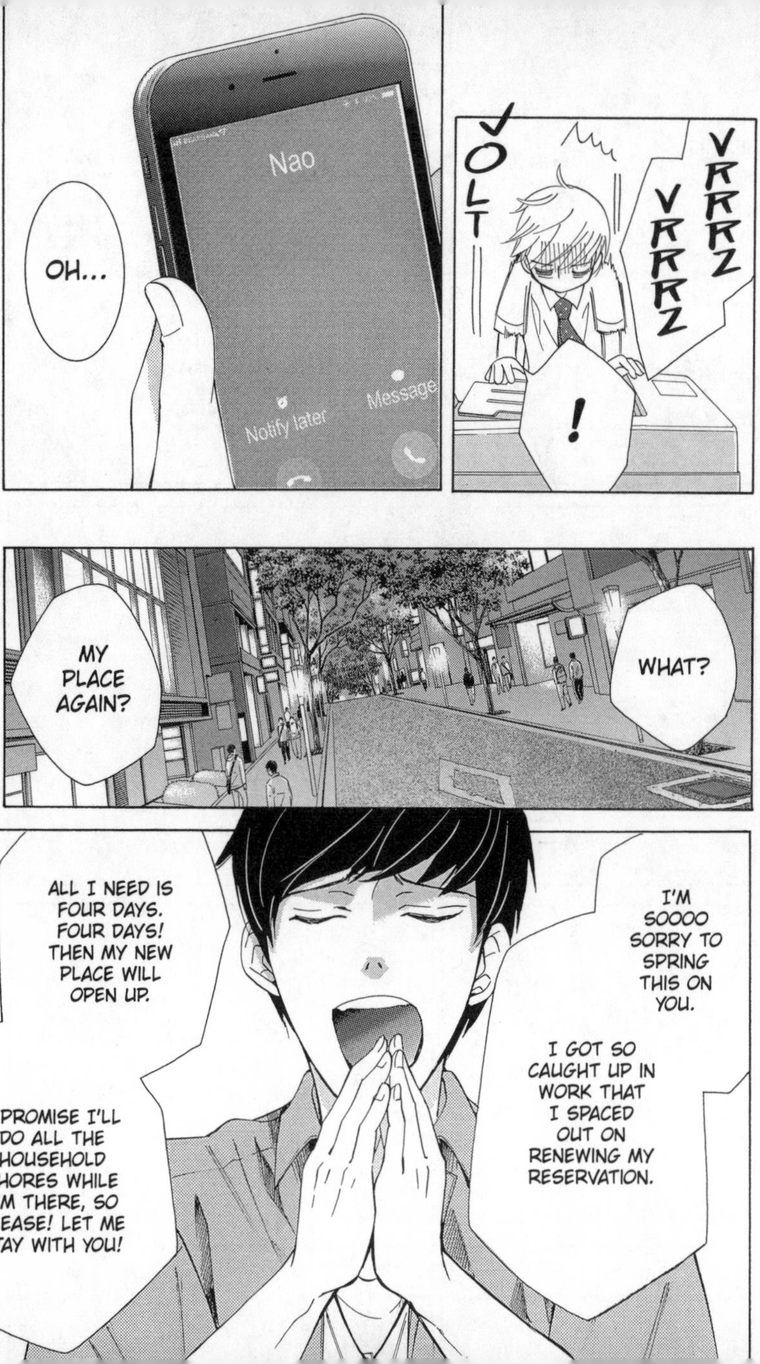
VRRRZ
VRRRZ
VOLT
!
Nao
Message
Notify later
OH...
WHAT?
MY PLACE AGAIN?
I'M SOOOO SORRY TO SPRING THIS ON YOU.
I GOT SO CAUGHT UP IN WORK THAT I SPACED OUT ON RENEWING MY RESERVATION.
ALL I NEED IS FOUR DAYS. FOUR DAYS! THEN MY NEW PLACE WILL OPEN UP.
I PROMISE I'LL DO ALL THE HOUSEHOLD CHORES WHILE I'M THERE, SO PLEASE! LET ME STAY WITH YOU!

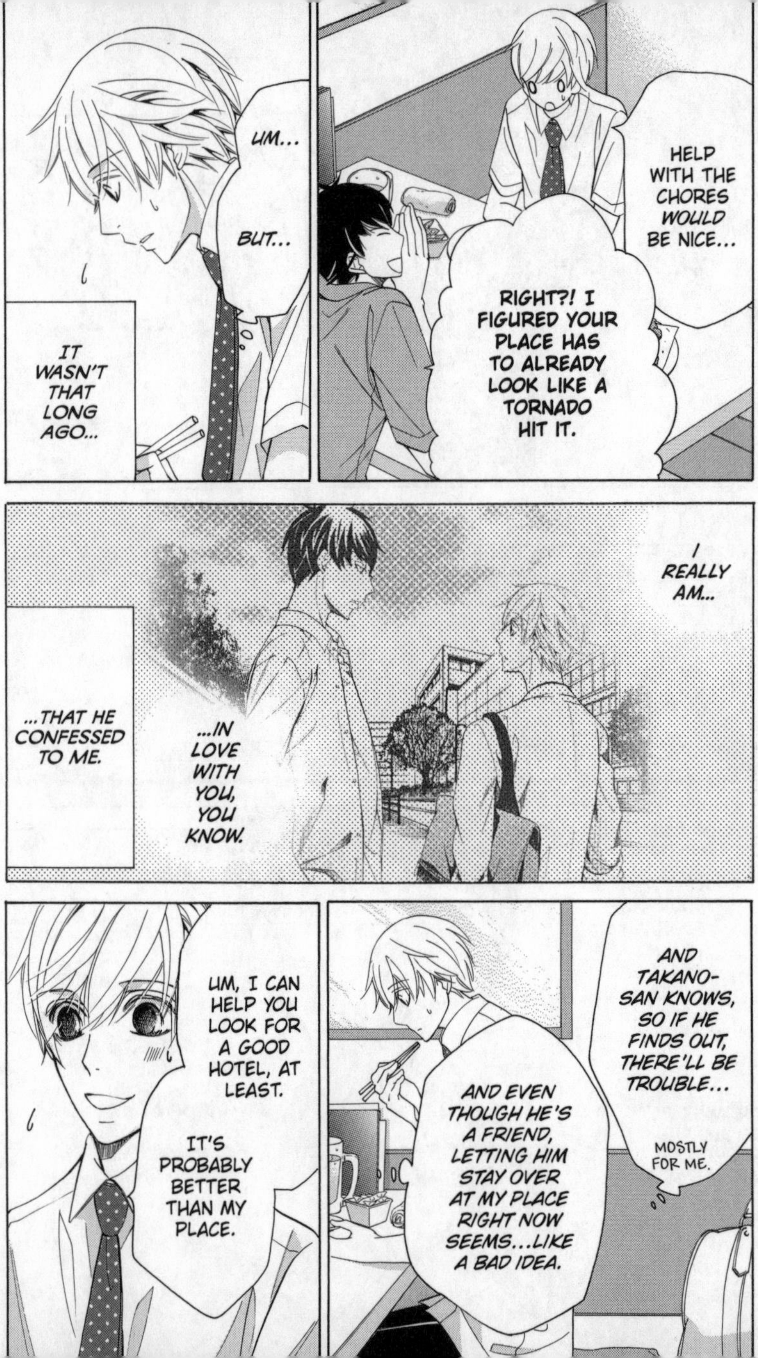
HELP WITH THE CHORES WOULD BE NICE...
RIGHT?! I FIGURED YOUR PLACE HAS TO ALREADY LOOK LIKE A TORNADO HIT IT.
UM...
BUT...
IT WASN'T THAT LONG AGO...
I REALLY AM...
...IN LOVE WITH YOU, YOU KNOW.
...THAT HE CONFESSED TO ME.
AND TAKANO-SAN KNOWS, SO IF HE FINDS OUT, THERE'LL BE TROUBLE...
MOSTLY FOR ME.
AND EVEN THOUGH HE'S A FRIEND, LETTING HIM STAY OVER AT MY PLACE RIGHT NOW SEEMS...LIKE A BAD IDEA.
UM, I CAN HELP YOU LOOK FOR A GOOD HOTEL, AT LEAST.
IT'S PROBABLY BETTER THAN MY PLACE.

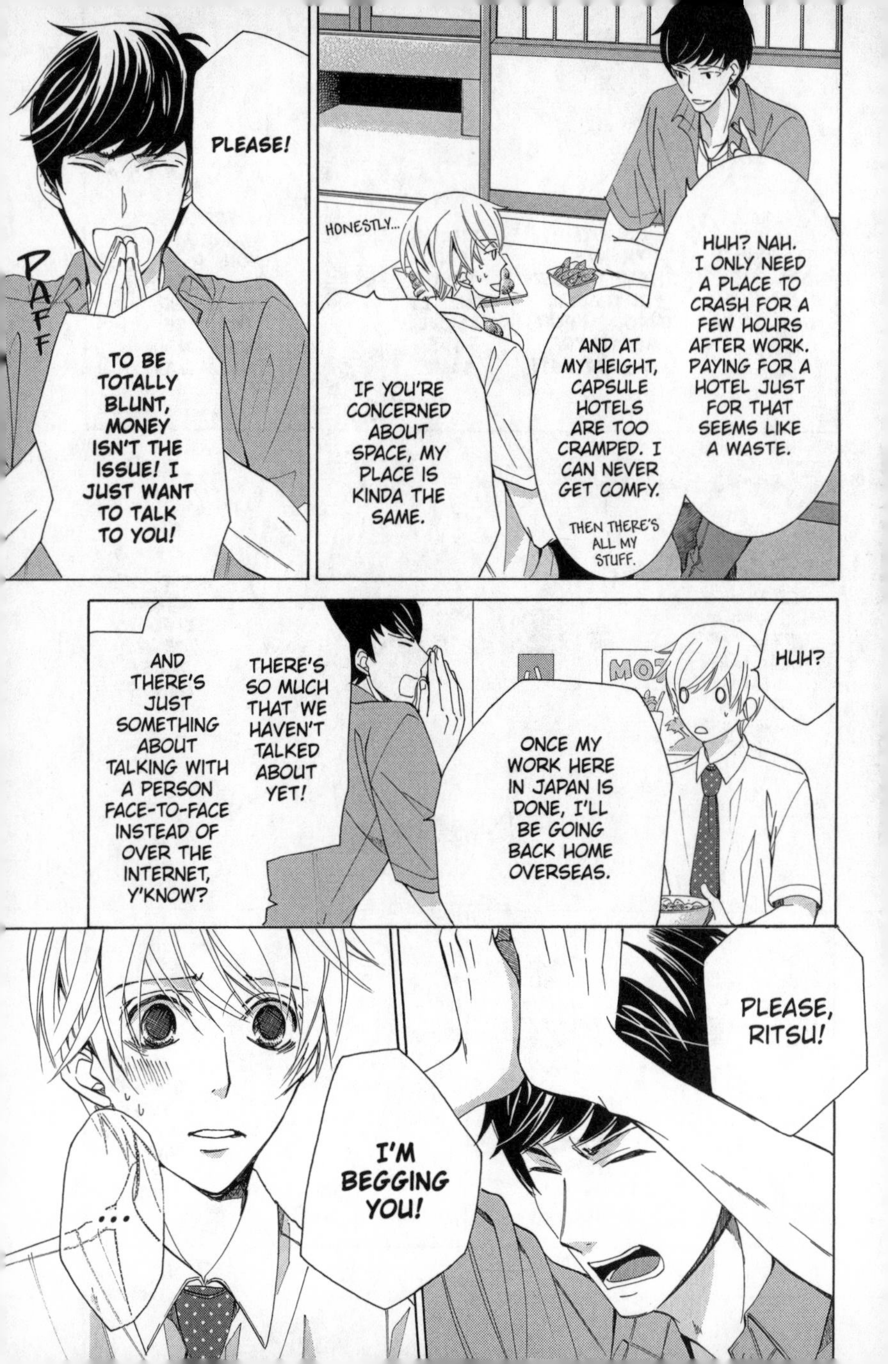
HUH? NAH. I ONLY NEED A PLACE TO CRASH FOR A FEW HOURS AFTER WORK. PAYING FOR A HOTEL JUST FOR THAT SEEMS LIKE A WASTE.
AND AT MY HEIGHT, CAPSULE HOTELS ARE TOO CRAMPED. I CAN NEVER GET COMFY.
THEN THERE'S ALL MY STUFF.
HONESTLY...
IF YOU'RE CONCERNED ABOUT SPACE, MY PLACE IS KINDA THE SAME.
PLEASE!
PAFF
TO BE TOTALLY BLUNT, MONEY ISN'T THE ISSUE! I JUST WANT TO TALK TO YOU!
HUH?
ONCE MY WORK HERE IN JAPAN IS DONE, I'LL BE GOING BACK HOME OVERSEAS.
THERE'S SO MUCH THAT WE HAVEN'T TALKED ABOUT YET!
AND THERE'S JUST SOMETHING ABOUT TALKING WITH A PERSON FACE-TO-FACE INSTEAD OF OVER THE INTERNET, Y'KNOW?
PLEASE, RITSU!
I'M BEGGING YOU!
...

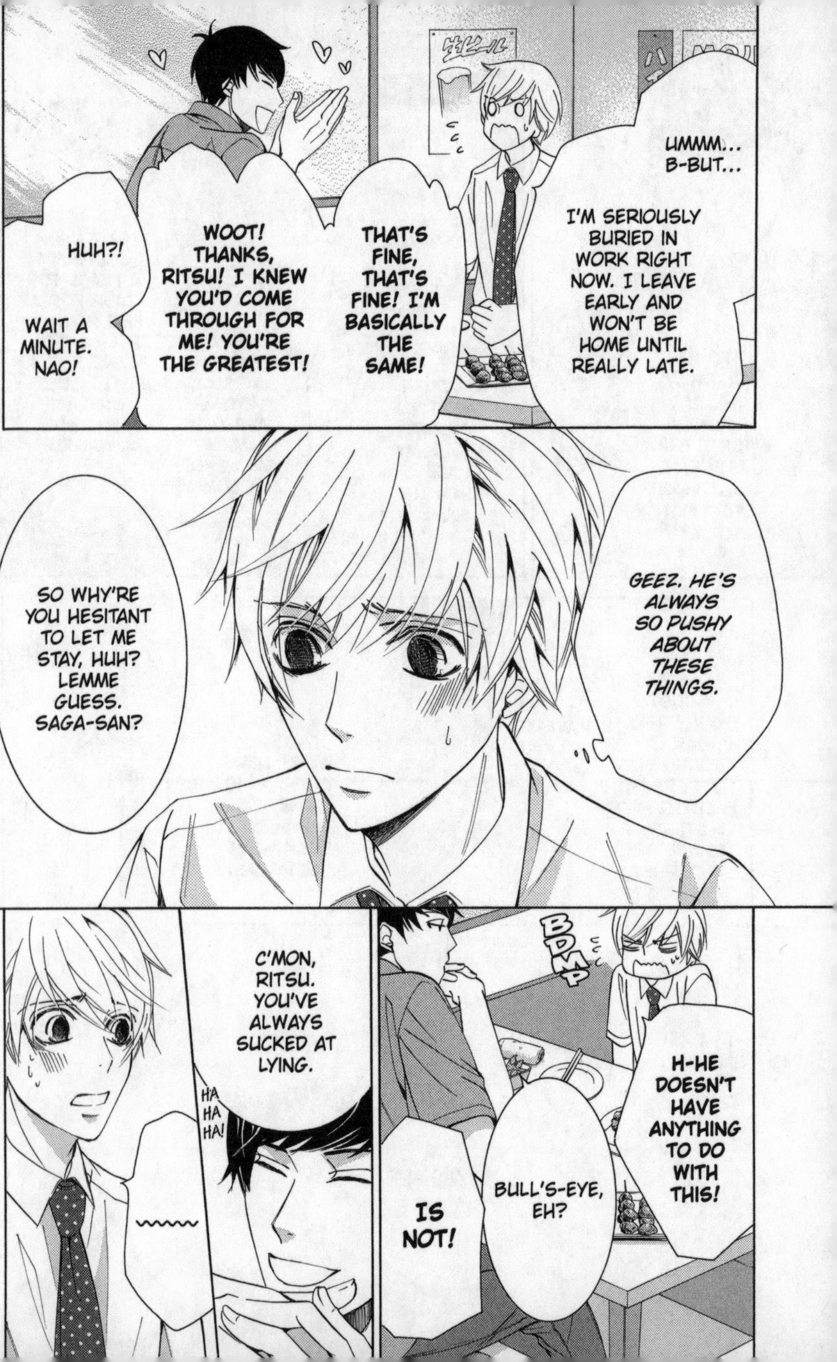
UMMM... B-BUT...
I'M SERIOUSLY BURIED IN WORK RIGHT NOW. I LEAVE EARLY AND WON'T BE HOME UNTIL REALLY LATE.
THAT'S FINE, THAT'S FINE! I'M BASICALLY THE SAME!
WOOT! THANKS, RITSU! I KNEW YOU'D COME THROUGH FOR ME! YOU'RE THE GREATEST!
HUH?!
WAIT A MINUTE. NAO!
GEEZ. HE'S ALWAYS SO PUSHY ABOUT THESE THINGS.
SO WHY'RE YOU HESITANT TO LET ME STAY, HUH? LEMME GUESS. SAGA-SAN?
BDMP
H-HE DOESN'T HAVE ANYTHING TO DO WITH THIS!
BULL'S-EYE, EH?
IS NOT!
C'MON, RITSU. YOU'VE ALWAYS SUCKED AT LYING.
HA HA HA!
~~~~~
~~~~~

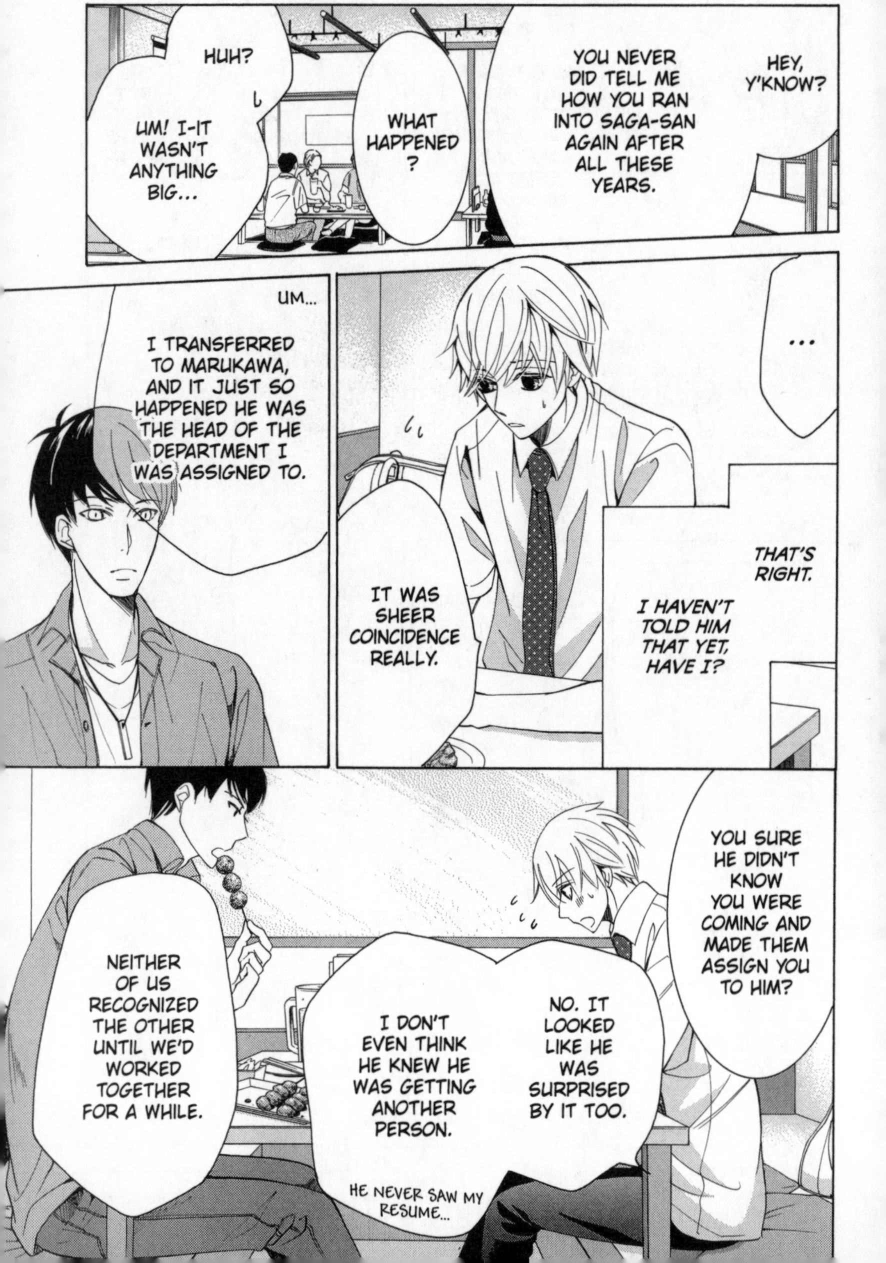
HEY, Y'KNOW?
YOU NEVER DID TELL ME HOW YOU RAN INTO SAGA-SAN AGAIN AFTER ALL THESE YEARS.
WHAT HAPPENED?
HUH?
UM! I-IT WASN'T ANYTHING BIG...
...
THAT'S RIGHT.
I HAVEN'T TOLD HIM THAT YET, HAVE I?
IT WAS SHEER COINCIDENCE REALLY.
UM...
I TRANSFERRED TO MARUKAWA, AND IT JUST SO HAPPENED HE WAS THE HEAD OF THE DEPARTMENT I WAS ASSIGNED TO.
YOU SURE HE DIDN'T KNOW YOU WERE COMING AND MADE THEM ASSIGN YOU TO HIM?
NO. IT LOOKED LIKE HE WAS SURPRISED BY IT TOO.
I DON'T EVEN THINK HE KNEW HE WAS GETTING ANOTHER PERSON.
HE NEVER SAW MY RESUME...
NEITHER OF US RECOGNIZED THE OTHER UNTIL WE'D WORKED TOGETHER FOR A WHILE.

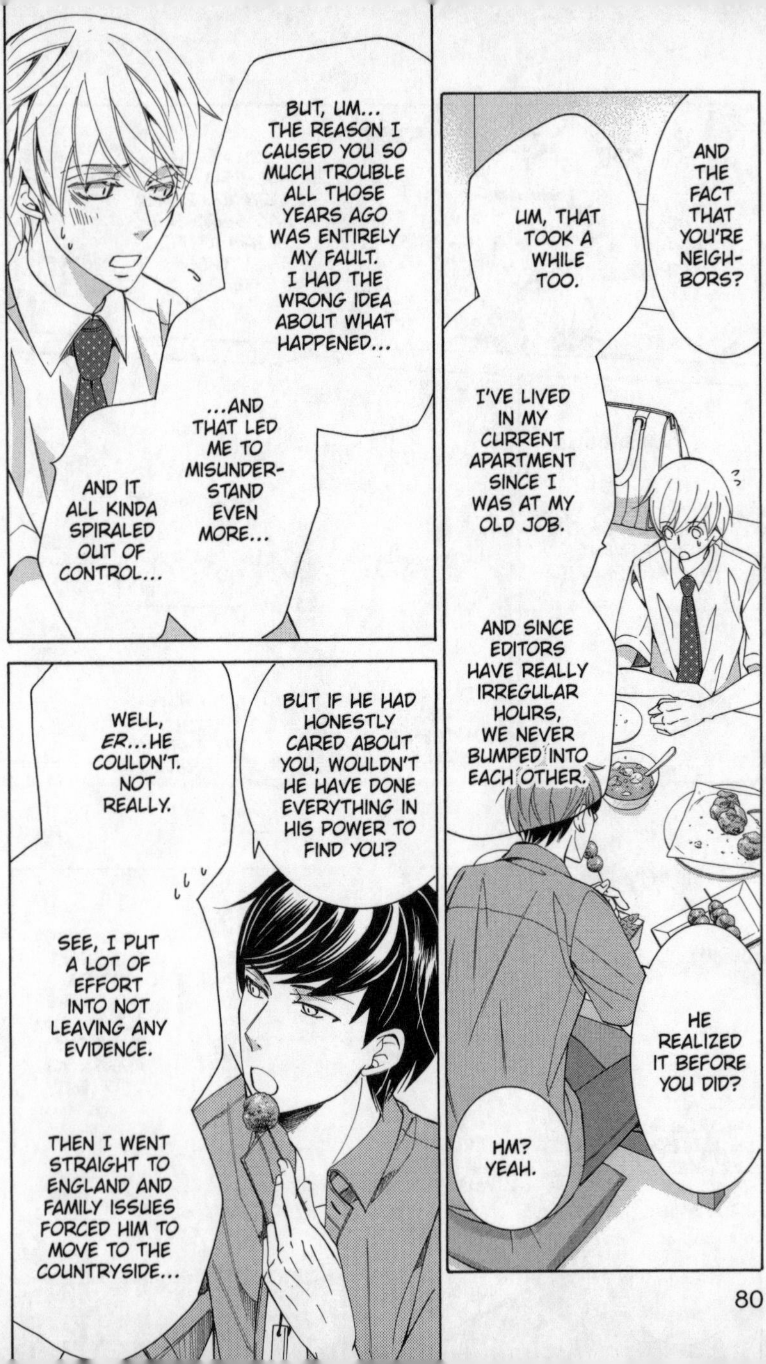
AND THE FACT THAT YOU'RE NEIGH-BORS?
UM, THAT TOOK A WHILE TOO.
I'VE LIVED IN MY CURRENT APARTMENT SINCE I WAS AT MY OLD JOB.
AND SINCE EDITORS HAVE REALLY IRREGULAR HOURS, WE NEVER BUMPED INTO EACH OTHER.
HE REALIZED IT BEFORE YOU DID?
HM? YEAH.
BUT, UM... THE REASON I CAUSED YOU SO MUCH TROUBLE ALL THOSE YEARS AGO WAS ENTIRELY MY FAULT. I HAD THE WRONG IDEA ABOUT WHAT HAPPENED...
...AND THAT LED ME TO MISUNDER-STAND EVEN MORE...
AND IT ALL KINDA SPIRALED OUT OF CONTROL...
BUT IF HE HAD HONESTLY CARED ABOUT YOU, WOULDN'T HE HAVE DONE EVERYTHING IN HIS POWER TO FIND YOU?
WELL, *ER*...HE COULDN'T. NOT REALLY.
SEE, I PUT A LOT OF EFFORT INTO NOT LEAVING ANY EVIDENCE.
THEN I WENT STRAIGHT TO ENGLAND AND FAMILY ISSUES FORCED HIM TO MOVE TO THE COUNTRYSIDE...

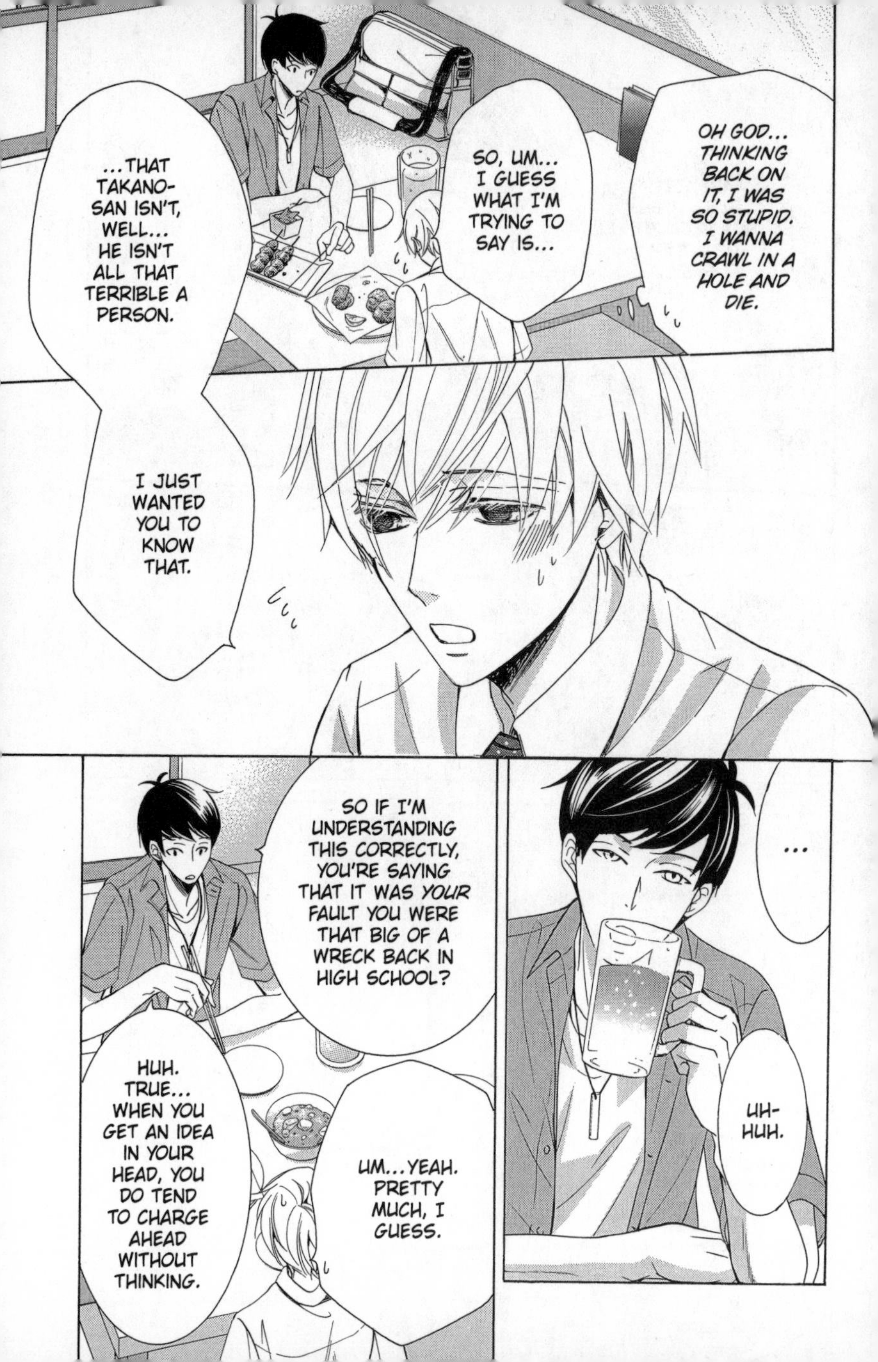
OH GOD... THINKING BACK ON IT, I WAS SO STUPID. I WANNA CRAWL IN A HOLE AND DIE.
SO, UM... I GUESS WHAT I'M TRYING TO SAY IS...
...THAT TAKANO-SAN ISN'T, WELL... HE ISN'T ALL THAT TERRIBLE A PERSON.
I JUST WANTED YOU TO KNOW THAT.
...
UH-HUH.
SO IF I'M UNDERSTANDING THIS CORRECTLY, YOU'RE SAYING THAT IT WAS *YOUR* FAULT YOU WERE THAT BIG OF A WRECK BACK IN HIGH SCHOOL?
UM...YEAH. PRETTY MUCH, I GUESS.
HUH. TRUE... WHEN YOU GET AN IDEA IN YOUR HEAD, YOU DO TEND TO CHARGE AHEAD WITHOUT THINKING.

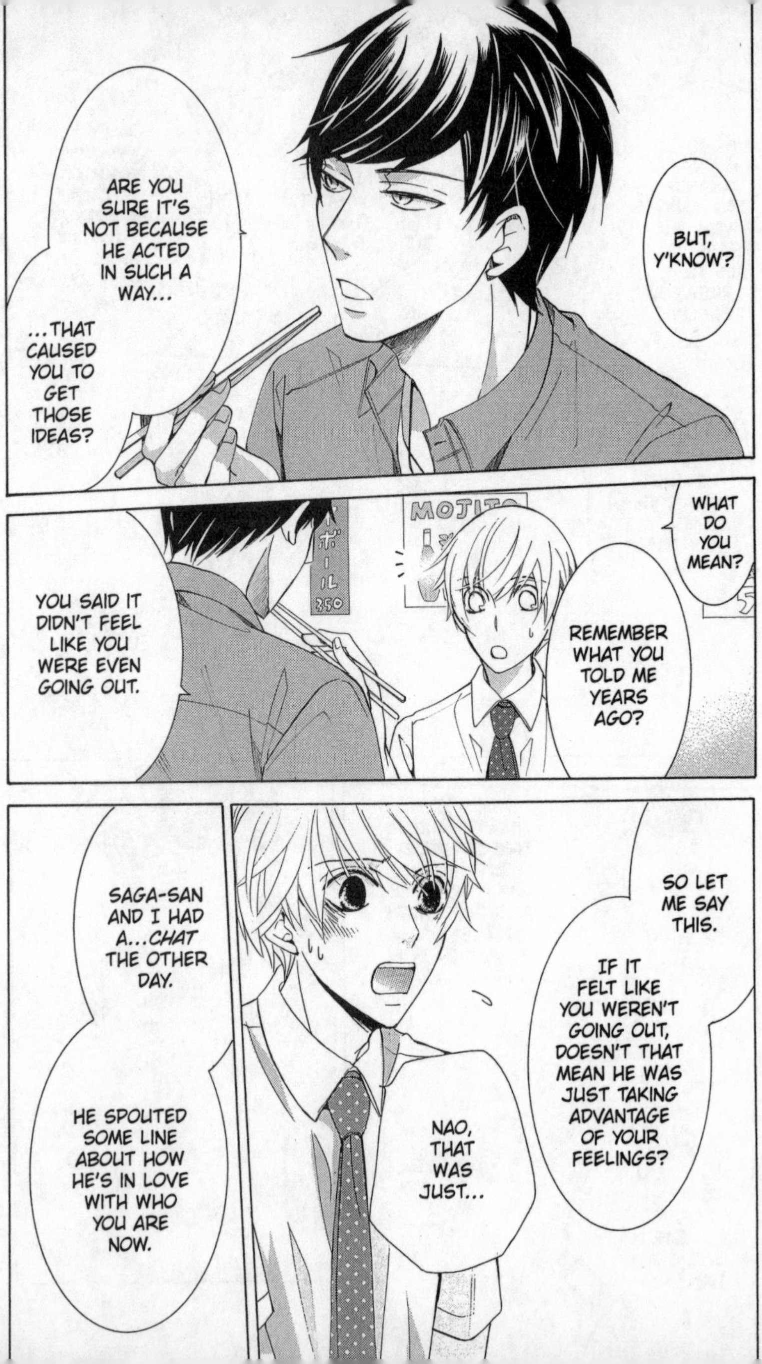
BUT, Y'KNOW?
ARE YOU SURE IT'S NOT BECAUSE HE ACTED IN SUCH A WAY...
...THAT CAUSED YOU TO GET THOSE IDEAS?
WHAT DO YOU MEAN?
REMEMBER WHAT YOU TOLD ME YEARS AGO?
YOU SAID IT DIDN'T FEEL LIKE YOU WERE EVEN GOING OUT.
SO LET ME SAY THIS.
IF IT FELT LIKE YOU WEREN'T GOING OUT, DOESN'T THAT MEAN HE WAS JUST TAKING ADVANTAGE OF YOUR FEELINGS?
NAO, THAT WAS JUST...
SAGA-SAN AND I HAD A...*CHAT* THE OTHER DAY.
HE SPOUTED SOME LINE ABOUT HOW HE'S IN LOVE WITH WHO YOU ARE NOW.

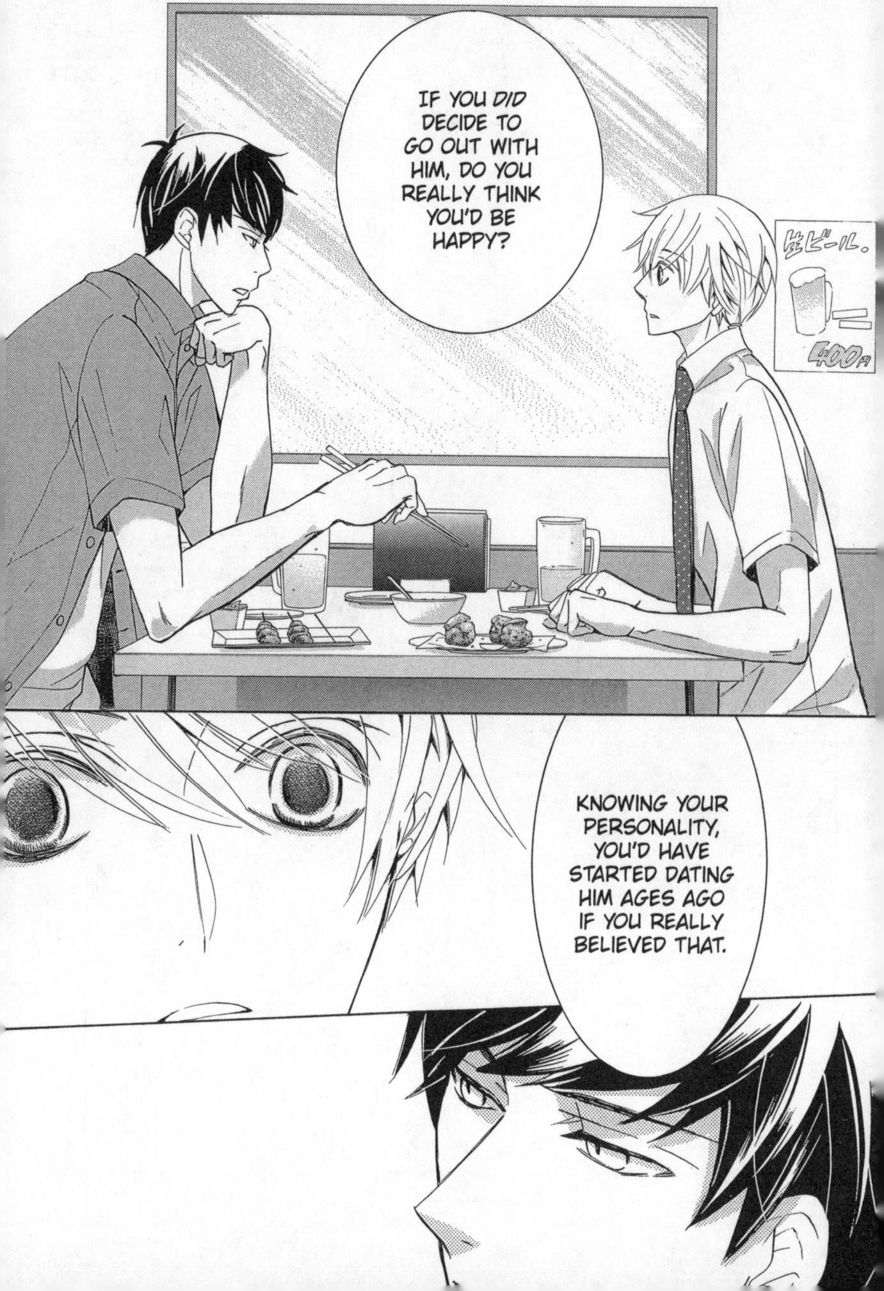
IF YOU *DID* DECIDE TO GO OUT WITH HIM, DO YOU REALLY THINK YOU'D BE HAPPY?
生ビール。
400円
KNOWING YOUR PERSONALITY, YOU'D HAVE STARTED DATING HIM AGES AGO IF YOU REALLY BELIEVED THAT.

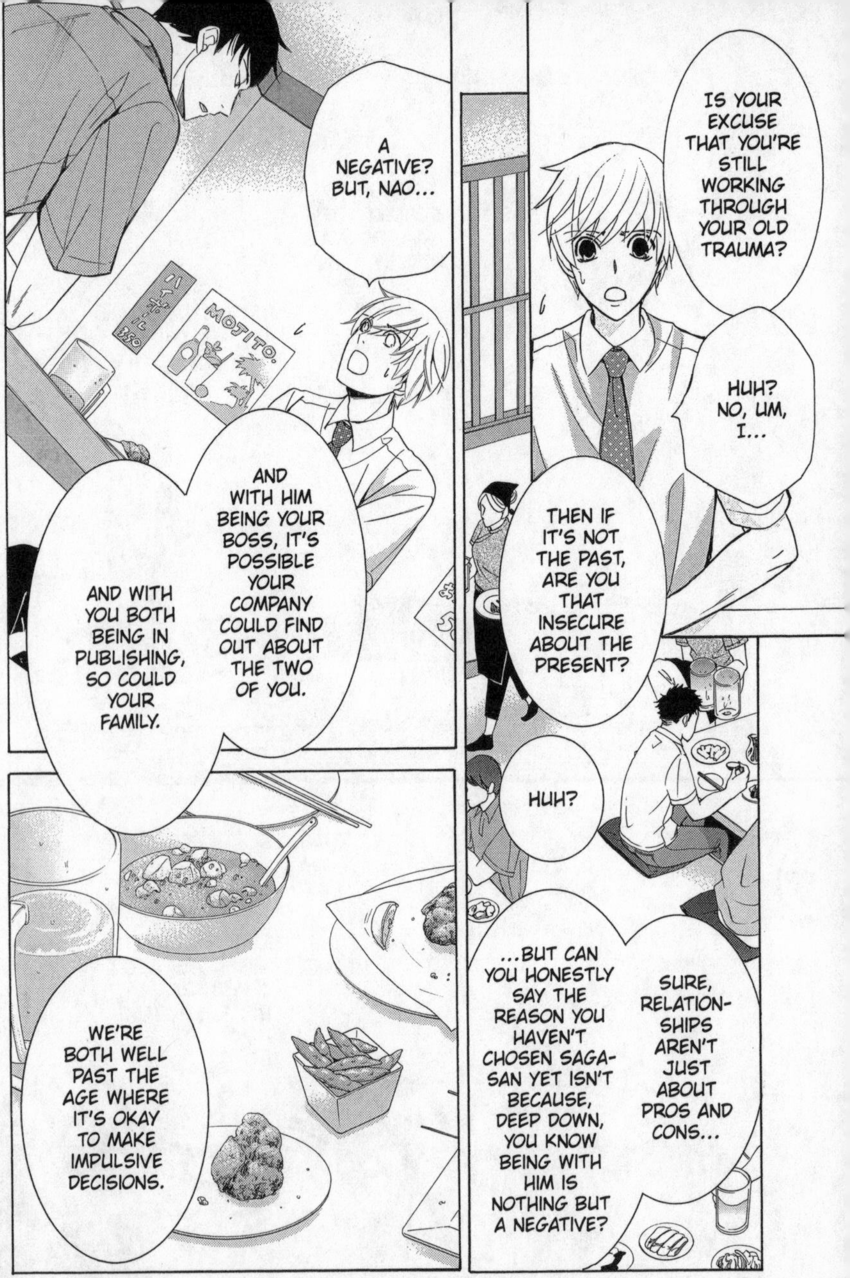
IS YOUR EXCUSE THAT YOU'RE STILL WORKING THROUGH YOUR OLD TRAUMA?
HUH? NO, UM, I...
THEN IF IT'S NOT THE PAST, ARE YOU THAT INSECURE ABOUT THE PRESENT?
HUH?
SURE, RELATIONSHIPS AREN'T JUST ABOUT PROS AND CONS...
...BUT CAN YOU HONESTLY SAY THE REASON YOU HAVEN'T CHOSEN SAGA-SAN YET ISN'T BECAUSE, DEEP DOWN, YOU KNOW BEING WITH HIM IS NOTHING BUT A NEGATIVE?
A NEGATIVE? BUT, NAO...
AND WITH HIM BEING YOUR BOSS, IT'S POSSIBLE YOUR COMPANY COULD FIND OUT ABOUT THE TWO OF YOU.
AND WITH YOU BOTH BEING IN PUBLISHING, SO COULD YOUR FAMILY.
WE'RE BOTH WELL PAST THE AGE WHERE IT'S OKAY TO MAKE IMPULSIVE DECISIONS.
MOJITO.

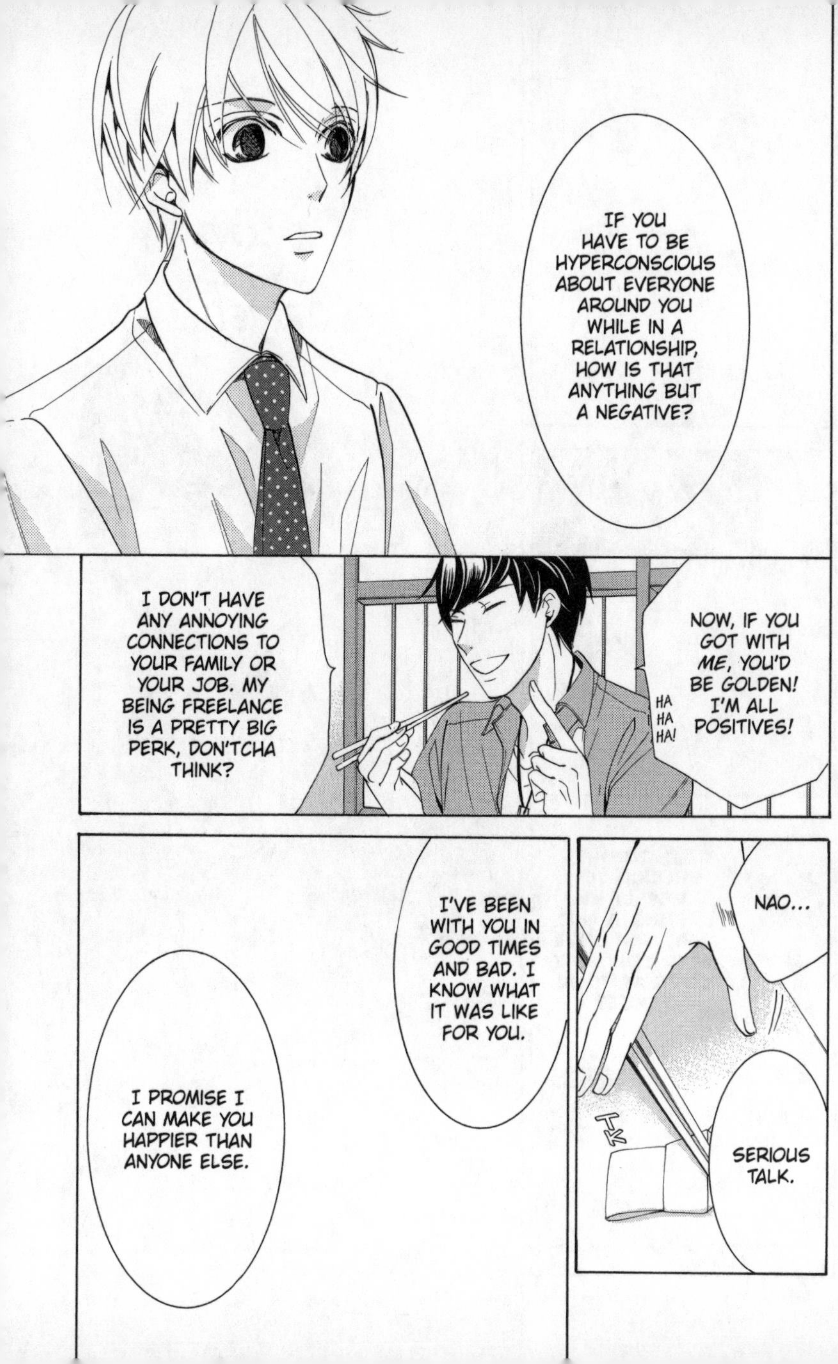
IF YOU HAVE TO BE HYPERCONSCIOUS ABOUT EVERYONE AROUND YOU WHILE IN A RELATIONSHIP, HOW IS THAT ANYTHING BUT A NEGATIVE?
NOW, IF YOU GOT WITH *ME*, YOU'D BE GOLDEN! I'M ALL POSITIVES!
HA HA HA!
I DON'T HAVE ANY ANNOYING CONNECTIONS TO YOUR FAMILY OR YOUR JOB. MY BEING FREELANCE IS A PRETTY BIG PERK, DON'TCHA THINK?
NAO...
TK
SERIOUS TALK.
I'VE BEEN WITH YOU IN GOOD TIMES AND BAD. I KNOW WHAT IT WAS LIKE FOR YOU.
I PROMISE I CAN MAKE YOU HAPPIER THAN ANYONE ELSE.

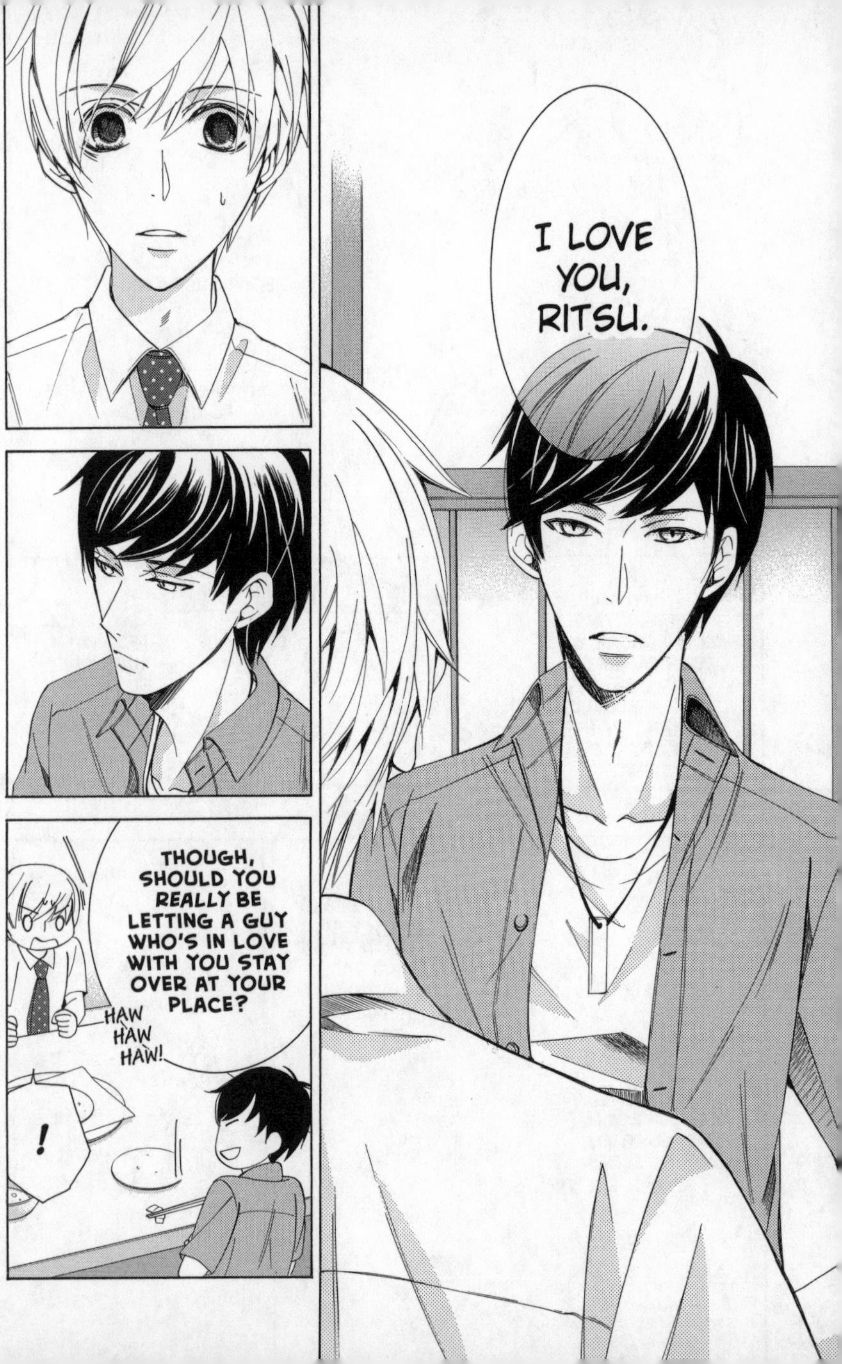
I LOVE YOU, RITSU.
THOUGH, SHOULD YOU REALLY BE LETTING A GUY WHO'S IN LOVE WITH YOU STAY OVER AT YOUR PLACE?
HAW HAW HAW!
!

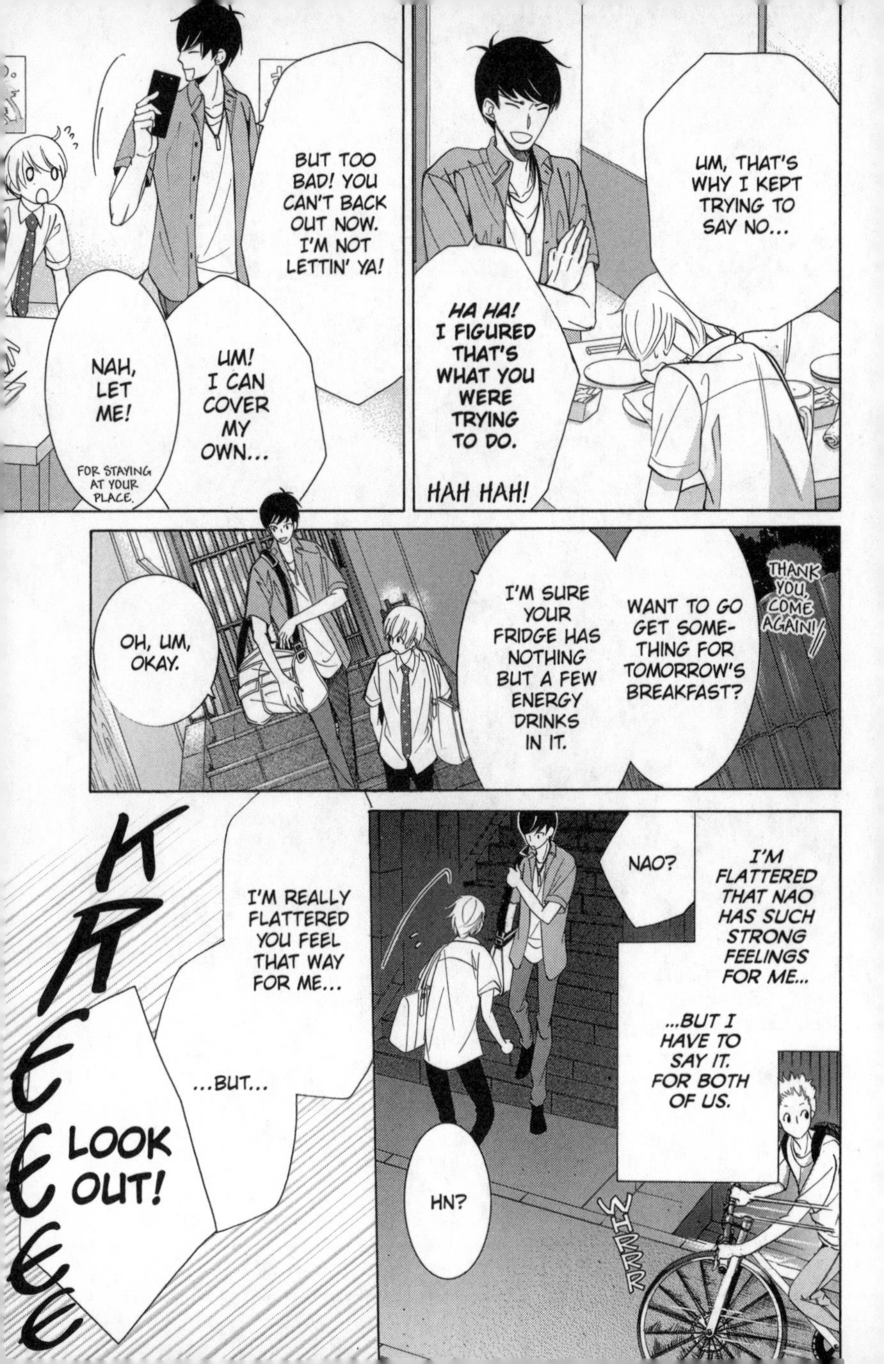
UM, THAT'S WHY I KEPT TRYING TO SAY NO...
HA HA! I FIGURED THAT'S WHAT YOU WERE TRYING TO DO.
HAH HAH!
BUT TOO BAD! YOU CAN'T BACK OUT NOW. I'M NOT LETTIN' YA!
UM! I CAN COVER MY OWN...
NAH, LET ME!
FOR STAYING AT YOUR PLACE.
THANK YOU, COME AGAIN!
WANT TO GO GET SOME-THING FOR TOMORROW'S BREAKFAST?
I'M SURE YOUR FRIDGE HAS NOTHING BUT A FEW ENERGY DRINKS IN IT.
OH, UM, OKAY.
I'M FLATTERED THAT NAO HAS SUCH STRONG FEELINGS FOR ME...
NAO?
...BUT I HAVE TO SAY IT. FOR BOTH OF US.
WHRRR
HN?
I'M REALLY FLATTERED YOU FEEL THAT WAY FOR ME...
...BUT...
KREEEEEE
LOOK OUT!

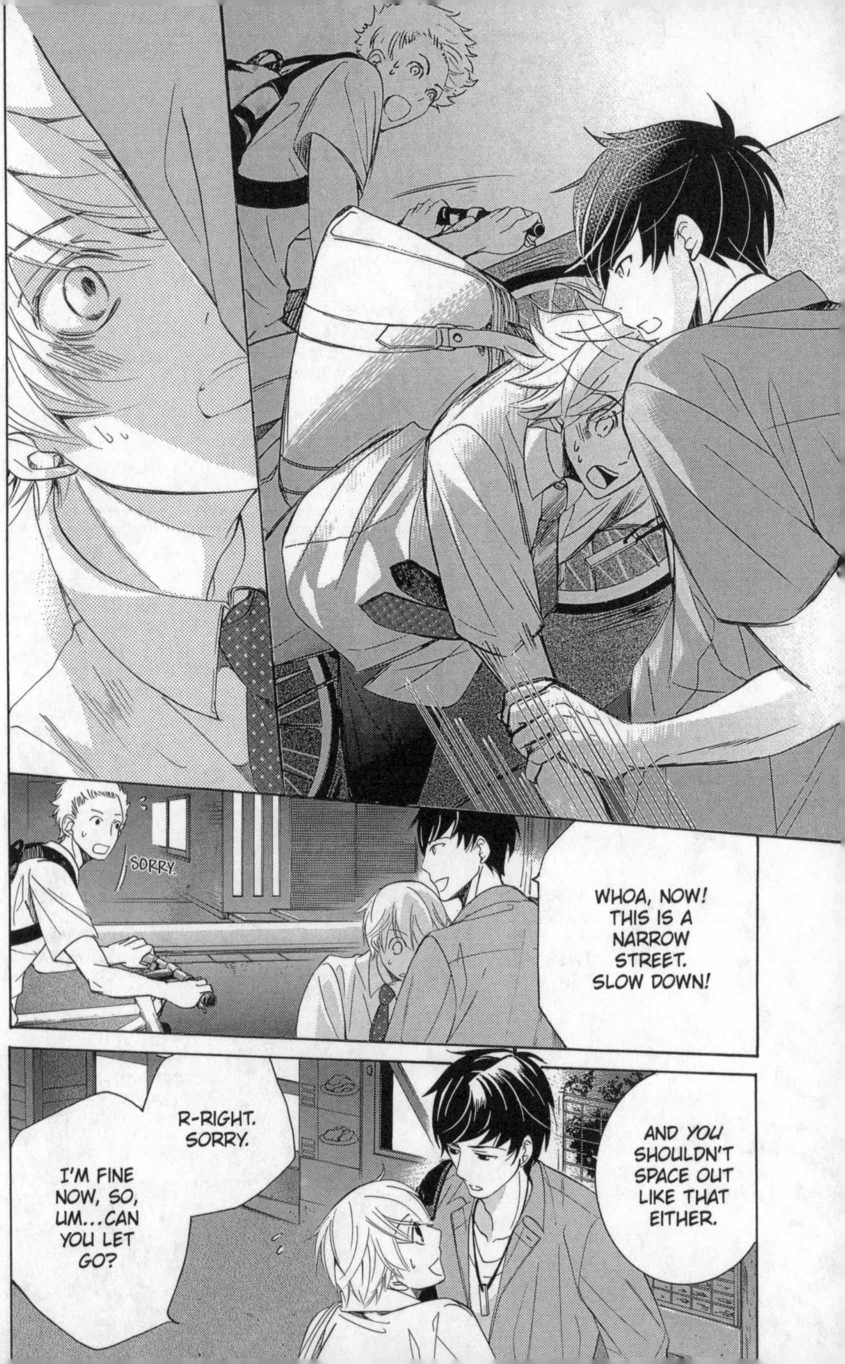
WHOA, NOW! THIS IS A NARROW STREET. SLOW DOWN!
SORRY.
AND YOU SHOULDN'T SPACE OUT LIKE THAT EITHER.
R-RIGHT. SORRY.
I'M FINE NOW, SO, UM...CAN YOU LET GO?

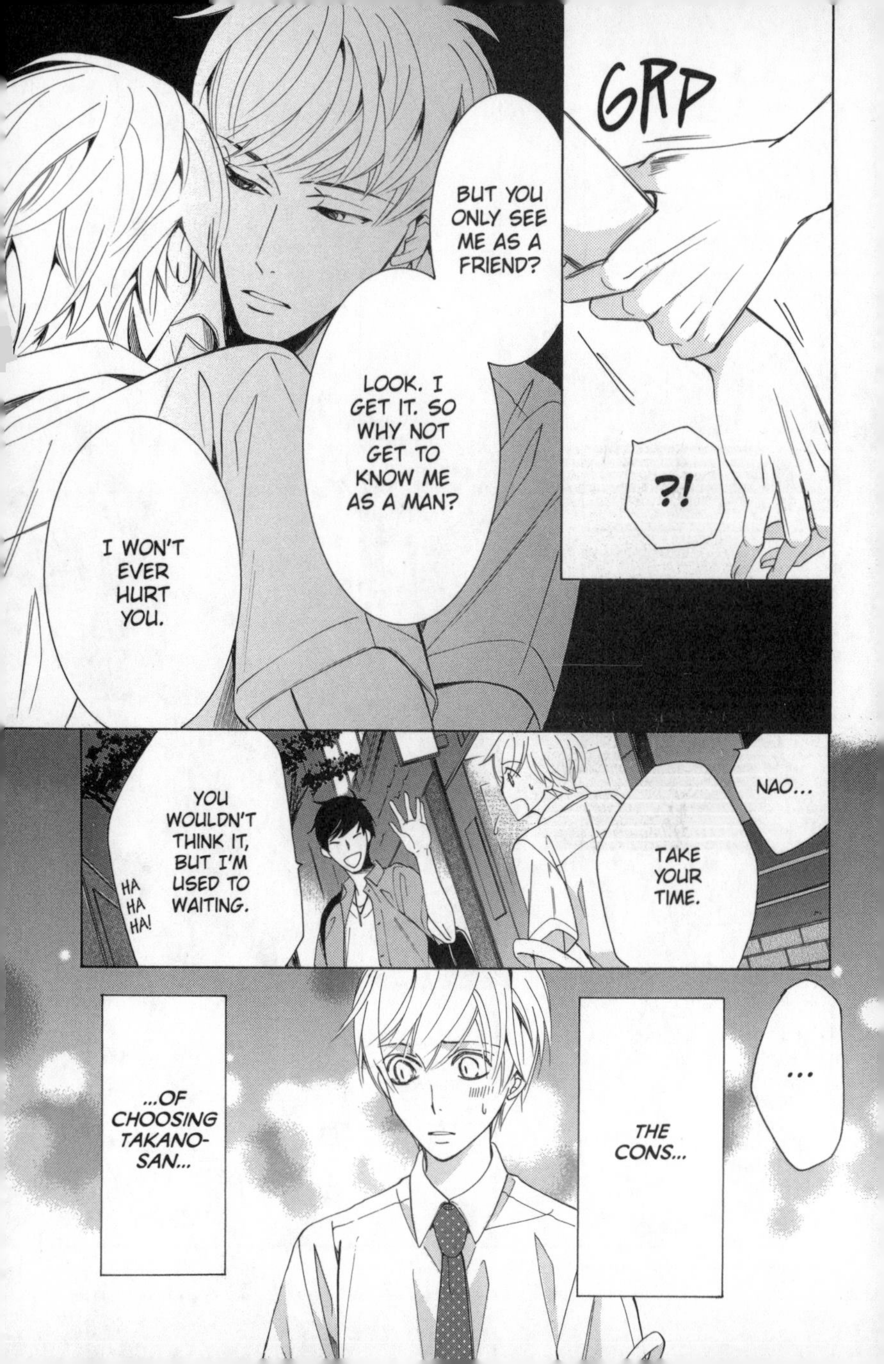
GRP
?!
BUT YOU ONLY SEE ME AS A FRIEND?
LOOK. I GET IT. SO WHY NOT GET TO KNOW ME AS A MAN?
I WON'T EVER HURT YOU.
NAO...
TAKE YOUR TIME.
YOU WOULDN'T THINK IT, BUT I'M USED TO WAITING.
HA HA HA!
...
THE CONS...
...OF CHOOSING TAKANO-SAN...

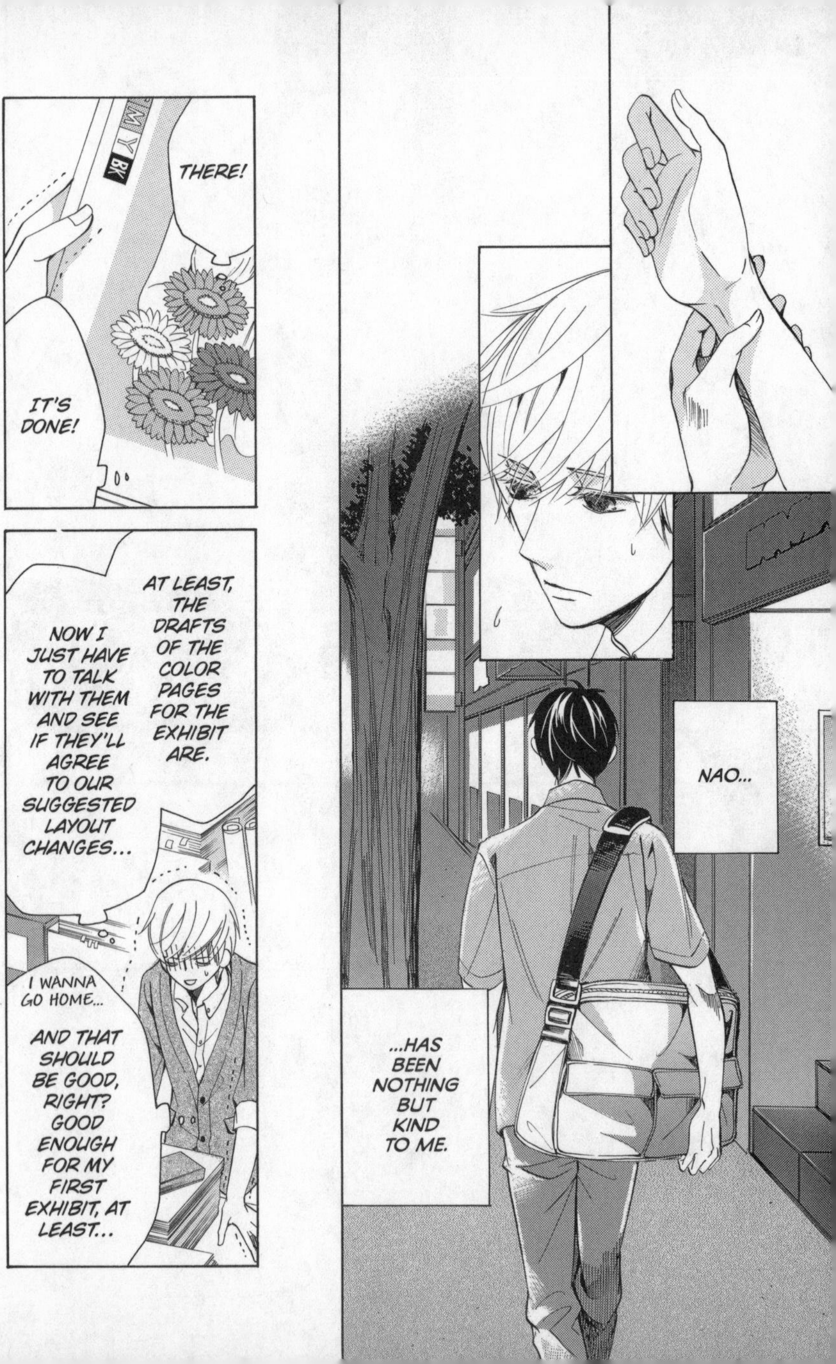
NAO...
...HAS BEEN NOTHING BUT KIND TO ME.
THERE!
IT'S DONE!
AT LEAST, THE DRAFTS OF THE COLOR PAGES FOR THE EXHIBIT ARE.
NOW I JUST HAVE TO TALK WITH THEM AND SEE IF THEY'LL AGREE TO OUR SUGGESTED LAYOUT CHANGES...
I WANNA GO HOME...
AND THAT SHOULD BE GOOD, RIGHT? GOOD ENOUGH FOR MY FIRST EXHIBIT, AT LEAST...

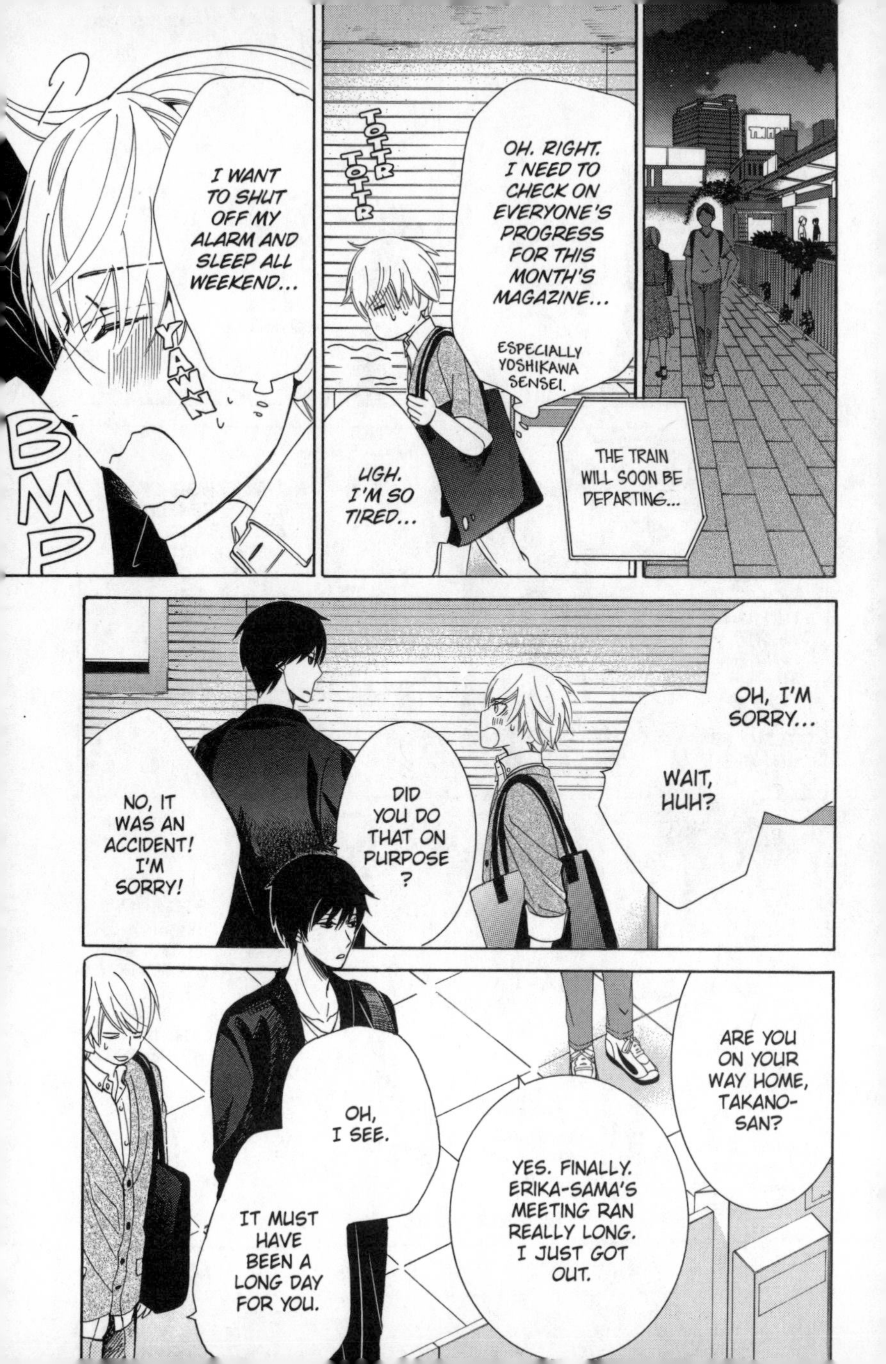
THE TRAIN WILL SOON BE DEPARTING...
OH. RIGHT. I NEED TO CHECK ON EVERYONE'S PROGRESS FOR THIS MONTH'S MAGAZINE...
ESPECIALLY YOSHIKAWA SENSEI.
TOTTR TOTTR
UGH. I'M SO TIRED...
I WANT TO SHUT OFF MY ALARM AND SLEEP ALL WEEKEND...
YAWN
BMP
OH, I'M SORRY...
WAIT, HUH?
DID YOU DO THAT ON PURPOSE?
NO, IT WAS AN ACCIDENT! I'M SORRY!
ARE YOU ON YOUR WAY HOME, TAKANO-SAN?
YES. FINALLY. ERIKA-SAMA'S MEETING RAN REALLY LONG. I JUST GOT OUT.
OH, I SEE.
IT MUST HAVE BEEN A LONG DAY FOR YOU.

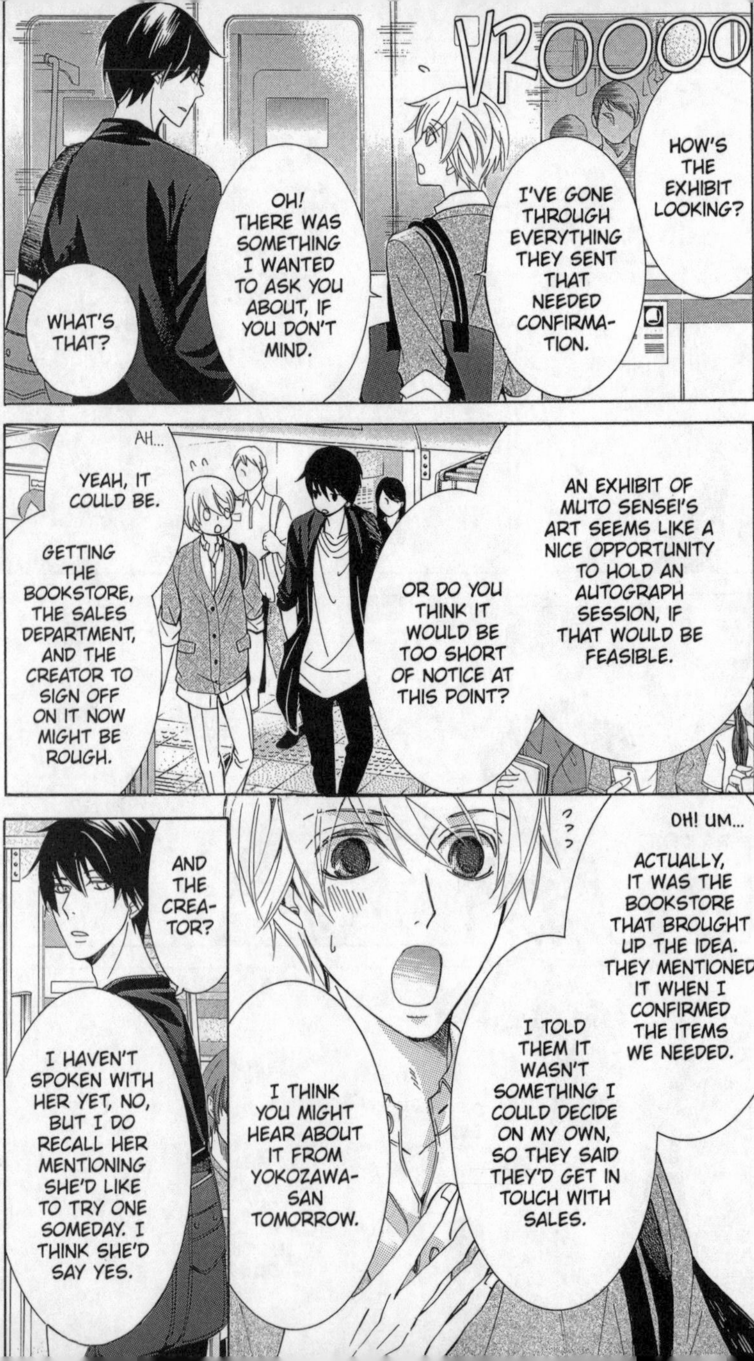
VROOOO
HOW'S THE EXHIBIT LOOKING?
I'VE GONE THROUGH EVERYTHING THEY SENT THAT NEEDED CONFIRMATION.
OH! THERE WAS SOMETHING I WANTED TO ASK YOU ABOUT, IF YOU DON'T MIND.
WHAT'S THAT?
AN EXHIBIT OF MUTO SENSEI'S ART SEEMS LIKE A NICE OPPORTUNITY TO HOLD AN AUTOGRAPH SESSION, IF THAT WOULD BE FEASIBLE.
OR DO YOU THINK IT WOULD BE TOO SHORT OF NOTICE AT THIS POINT?
AH... YEAH, IT COULD BE.
GETTING THE BOOKSTORE, THE SALES DEPARTMENT, AND THE CREATOR TO SIGN OFF ON IT NOW MIGHT BE ROUGH.
OH! UM... ACTUALLY, IT WAS THE BOOKSTORE THAT BROUGHT UP THE IDEA. THEY MENTIONED IT WHEN I CONFIRMED THE ITEMS WE NEEDED.
I TOLD THEM IT WASN'T SOMETHING I COULD DECIDE ON MY OWN, SO THEY SAID THEY'D GET IN TOUCH WITH SALES.
I THINK YOU MIGHT HEAR ABOUT IT FROM YOKOZAWA-SAN TOMORROW.
AND THE CREATOR?
I HAVEN'T SPOKEN WITH HER YET, NO, BUT I DO RECALL HER MENTIONING SHE'D LIKE TO TRY ONE SOMEDAY. I THINK SHE'D SAY YES.

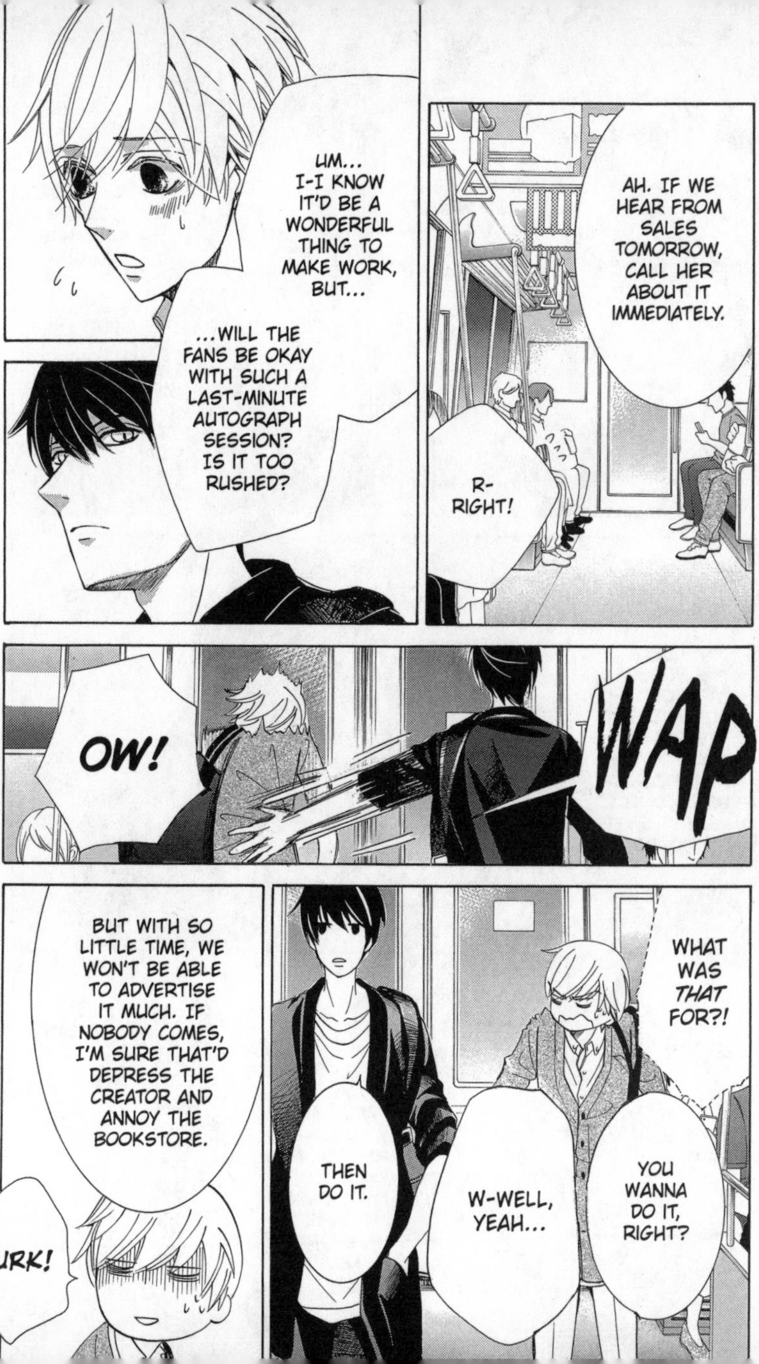
AH. IF WE HEAR FROM SALES TOMORROW, CALL HER ABOUT IT IMMEDIATELY.
R-RIGHT!
UM... I-I KNOW IT'D BE A WONDERFUL THING TO MAKE WORK, BUT...
...WILL THE FANS BE OKAY WITH SUCH A LAST-MINUTE AUTOGRAPH SESSION? IS IT TOO RUSHED?
WAP
OW!
WHAT WAS *THAT* FOR?!
YOU WANNA DO IT, RIGHT?
W-WELL, YEAH...
THEN DO IT.
BUT WITH SO LITTLE TIME, WE WON'T BE ABLE TO ADVERTISE IT MUCH. IF NOBODY COMES, I'M SURE THAT'D DEPRESS THE CREATOR AND ANNOY THE BOOKSTORE.
URK!

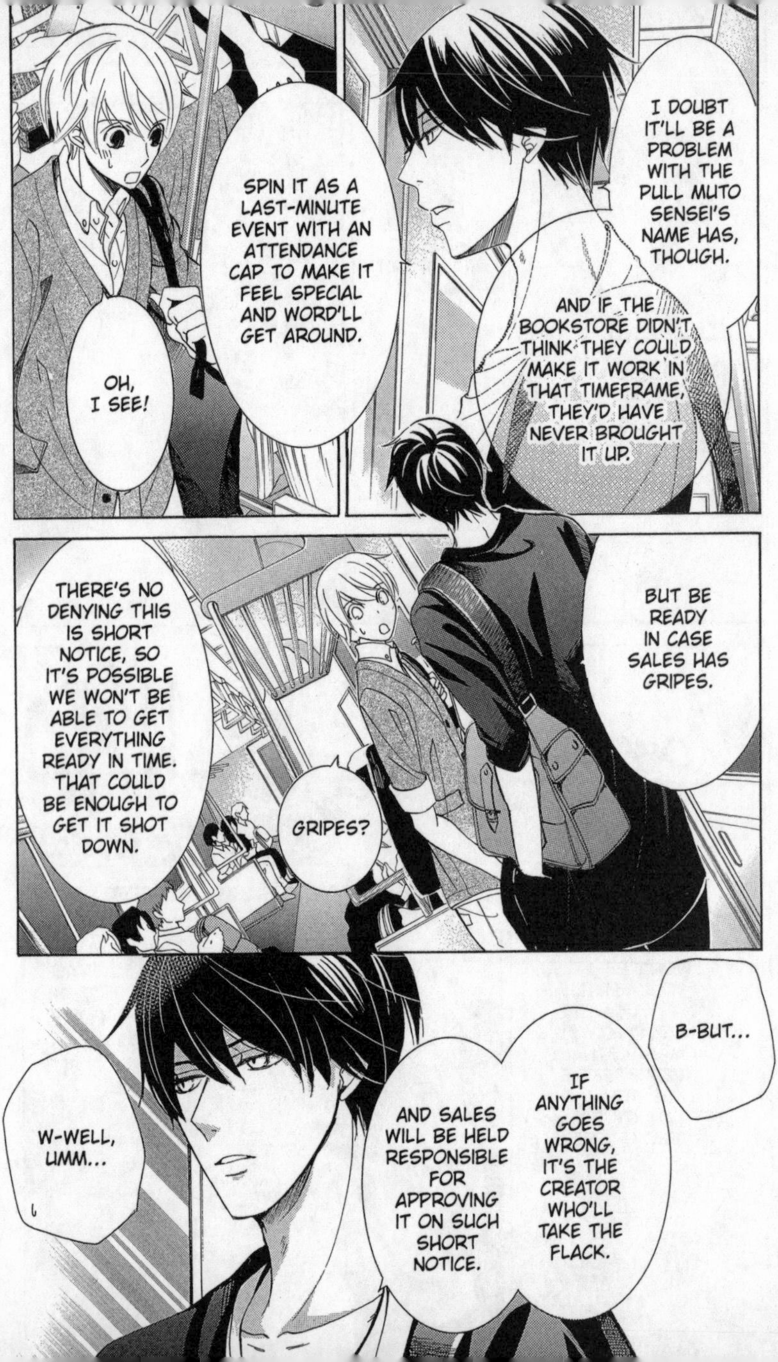
I DOUBT IT'LL BE A PROBLEM WITH THE PULL MUTO SENSEI'S NAME HAS, THOUGH.
AND IF THE BOOKSTORE DIDN'T THINK THEY COULD MAKE IT WORK IN THAT TIMEFRAME, THEY'D HAVE NEVER BROUGHT IT UP.
SPIN IT AS A LAST-MINUTE EVENT WITH AN ATTENDANCE CAP TO MAKE IT FEEL SPECIAL AND WORD'LL GET AROUND.
OH, I SEE!
BUT BE READY IN CASE SALES HAS GRIPES.
GRIPES?
THERE'S NO DENYING THIS IS SHORT NOTICE, SO IT'S POSSIBLE WE WON'T BE ABLE TO GET EVERYTHING READY IN TIME. THAT COULD BE ENOUGH TO GET IT SHOT DOWN.
B-BUT...
IF ANYTHING GOES WRONG, IT'S THE CREATOR WHO'LL TAKE THE FLACK.
AND SALES WILL BE HELD RESPONSIBLE FOR APPROVING IT ON SUCH SHORT NOTICE.
W-WELL, UMM...

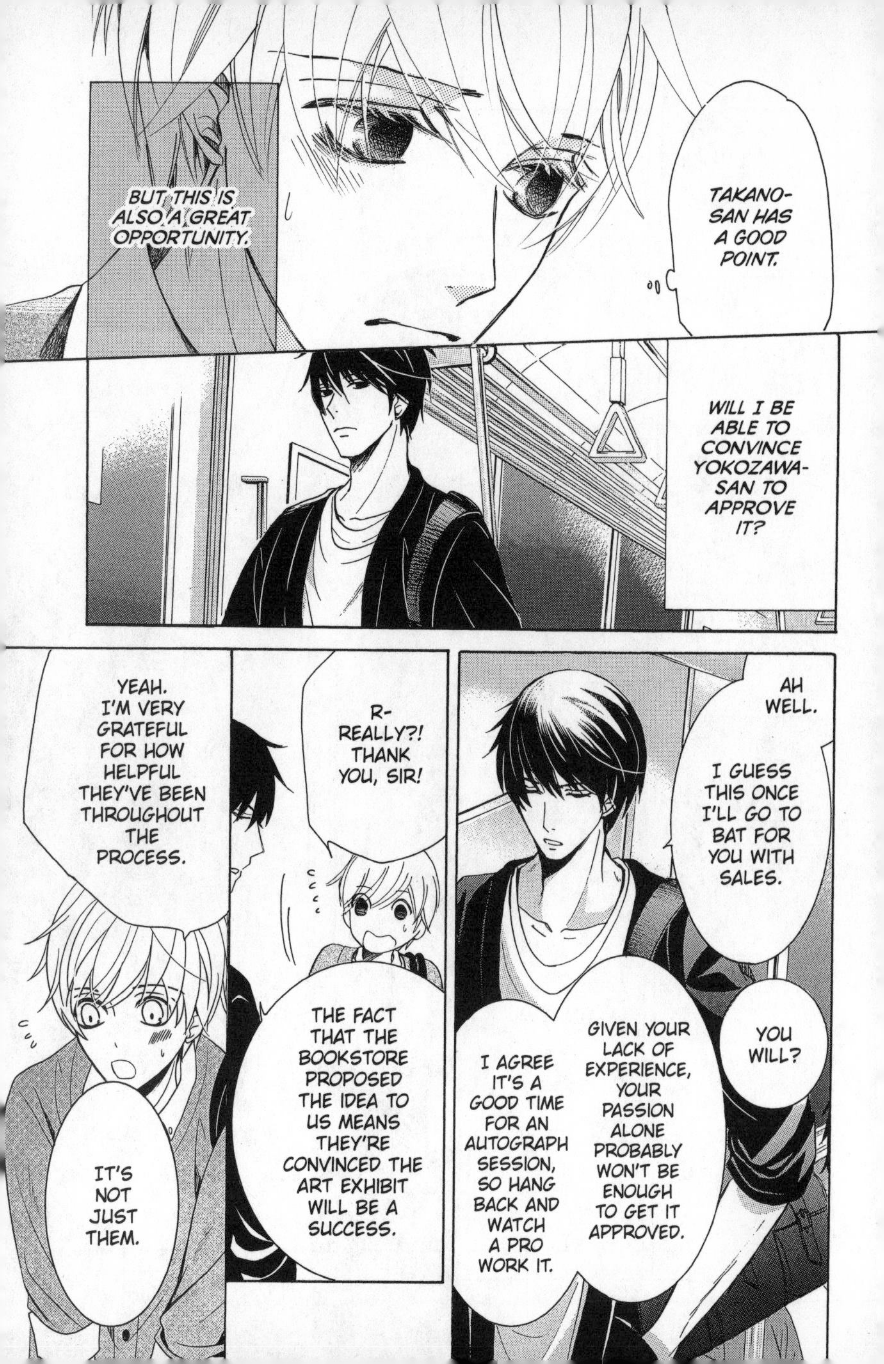
TAKANO-SAN HAS A GOOD POINT.
BUT THIS IS ALSO A GREAT OPPORTUNITY.
WILL I BE ABLE TO CONVINCE YOKOZAWA-SAN TO APPROVE IT?
AH WELL.
I GUESS THIS ONCE I'LL GO TO BAT FOR YOU WITH SALES.
YOU WILL?
GIVEN YOUR LACK OF EXPERIENCE, YOUR PASSION ALONE PROBABLY WON'T BE ENOUGH TO GET IT APPROVED.
I AGREE IT'S A GOOD TIME FOR AN AUTOGRAPH SESSION, SO HANG BACK AND WATCH A PRO WORK IT.
R-REALLY?! THANK YOU, SIR!
THE FACT THAT THE BOOKSTORE PROPOSED THE IDEA TO US MEANS THEY'RE CONVINCED THE ART EXHIBIT WILL BE A SUCCESS.
YEAH. I'M VERY GRATEFUL FOR HOW HELPFUL THEY'VE BEEN THROUGHOUT THE PROCESS.
IT'S NOT JUST THEM.

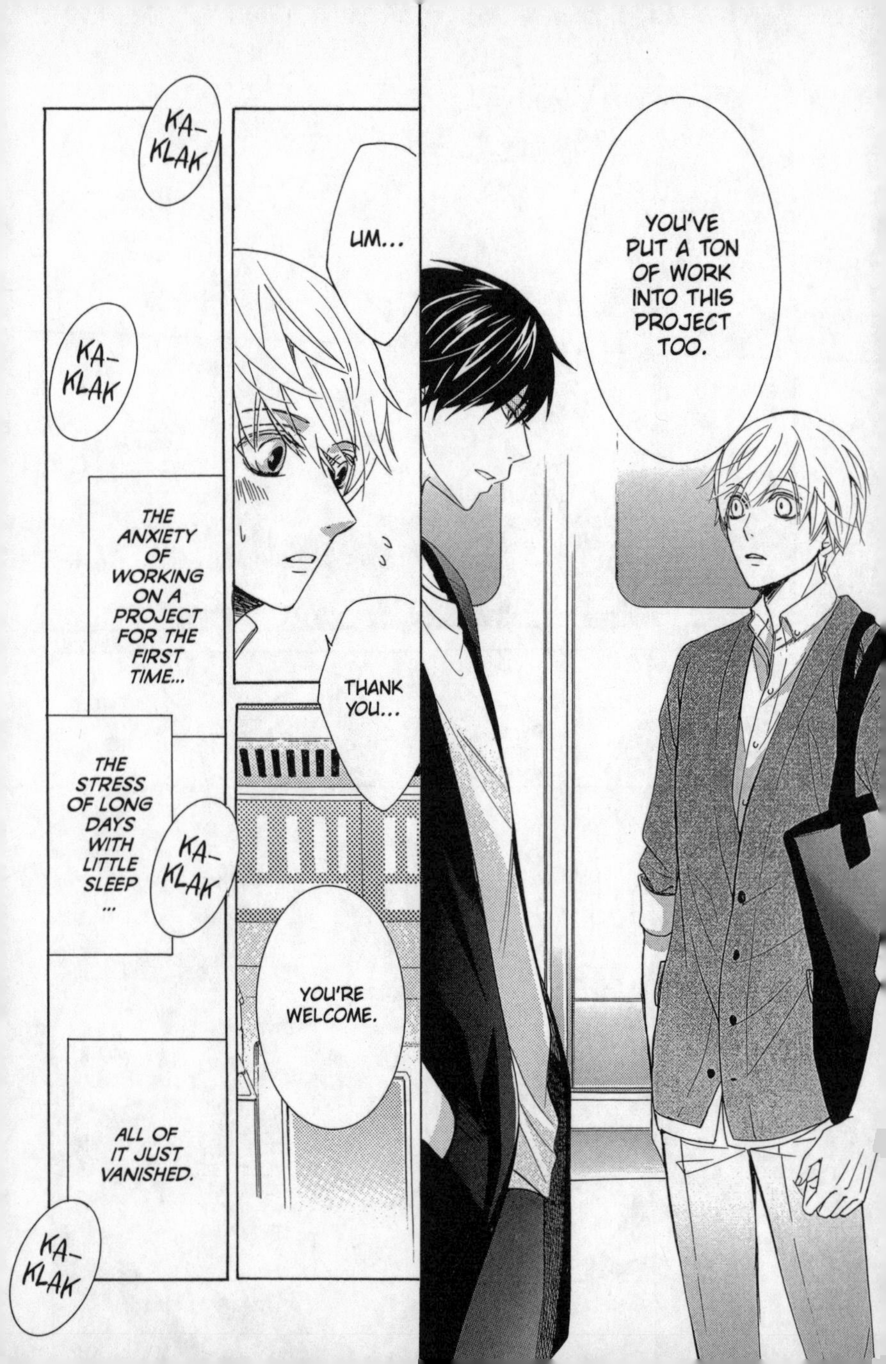
YOU'VE PUT A TON OF WORK INTO THIS PROJECT TOO.
UM...
THANK YOU...
YOU'RE WELCOME.
KA-KLAK
KA-KLAK
THE ANXIETY OF WORKING ON A PROJECT FOR THE FIRST TIME...
THE STRESS OF LONG DAYS WITH LITTLE SLEEP ...
KA-KLAK
ALL OF IT JUST VANISHED.
KA-KLAK

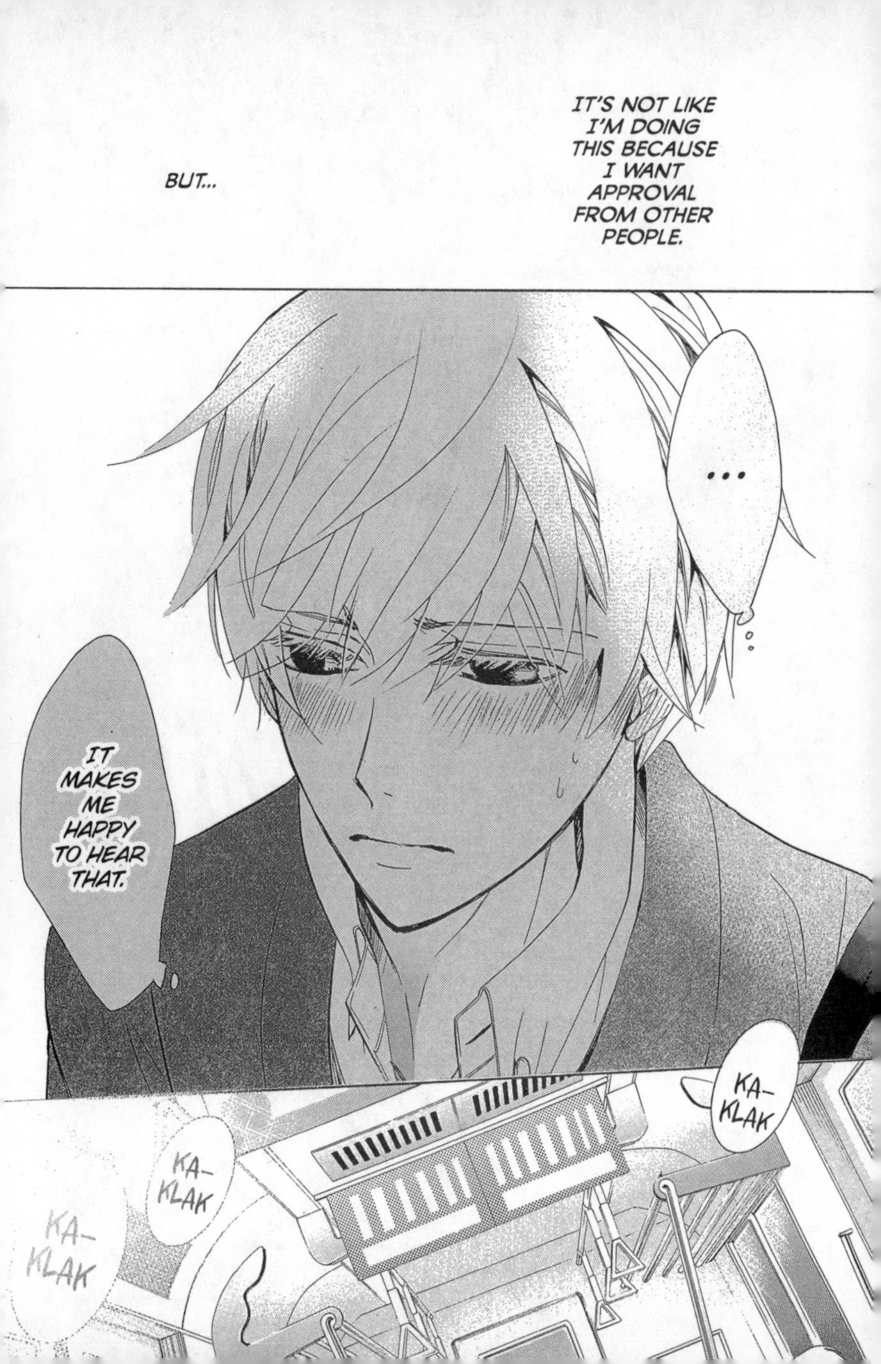
IT'S NOT LIKE I'M DOING THIS BECAUSE I WANT APPROVAL FROM OTHER PEOPLE.
BUT...
...
IT MAKES ME HAPPY TO HEAR THAT.
KA-KLAK
KA-KLAK
KA-KLAK

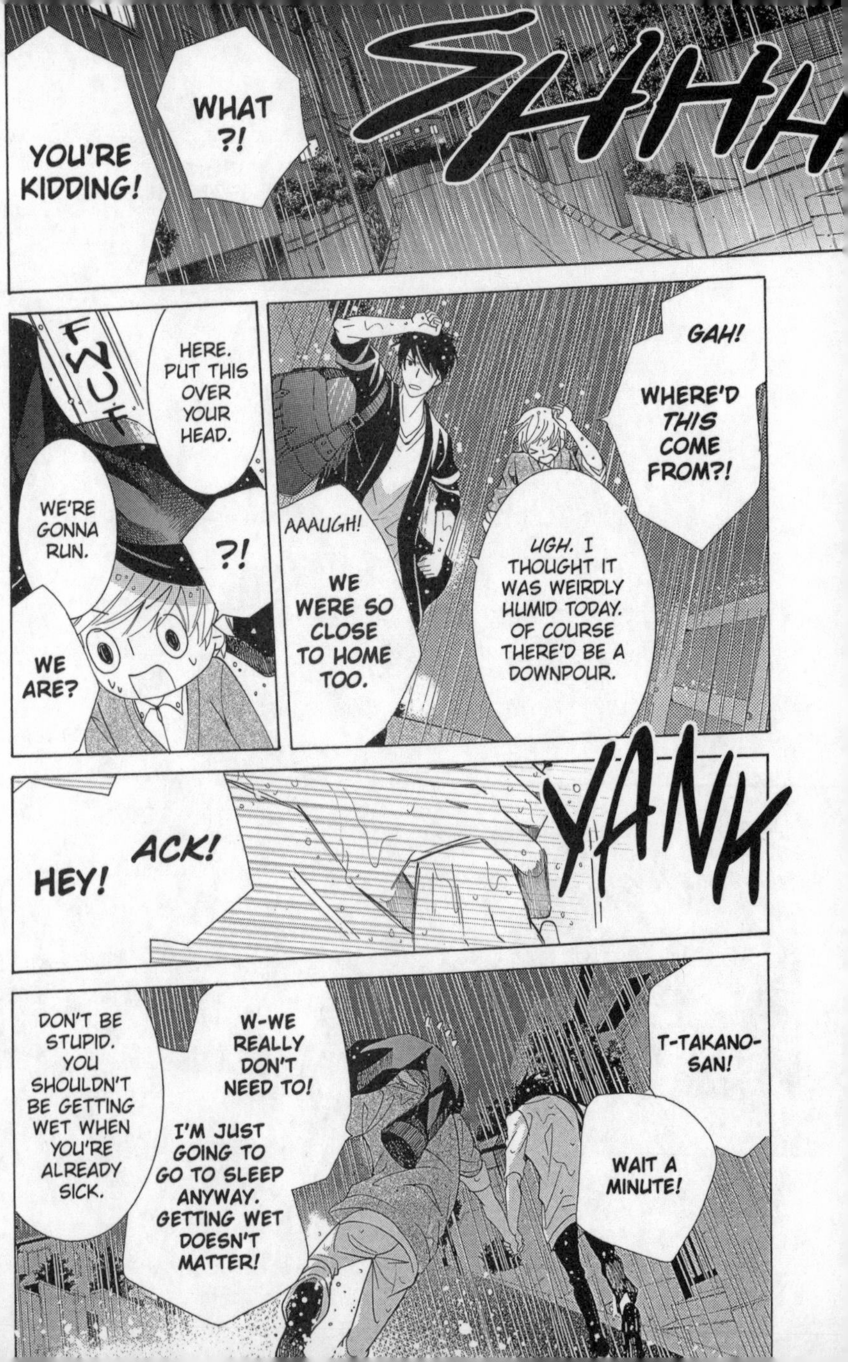
SHHHH
WHAT ?!
YOU'RE KIDDING!
GAH!
WHERE'D *THIS* COME FROM?!
UGH. I THOUGHT IT WAS WEIRDLY HUMID TODAY. OF COURSE THERE'D BE A DOWNPOUR.
AAAUGH!
WE WERE SO CLOSE TO HOME TOO.
FWUF
HERE. PUT THIS OVER YOUR HEAD.
?!
WE'RE GONNA RUN.
WE ARE?
YANK
ACK!
HEY!
T-TAKANO-SAN!
WAIT A MINUTE!
W-WE REALLY DON'T NEED TO!
I'M JUST GOING TO GO TO SLEEP ANYWAY. GETTING WET DOESN'T MATTER!
DON'T BE STUPID. YOU SHOULDN'T BE GETTING WET WHEN YOU'RE ALREADY SICK.

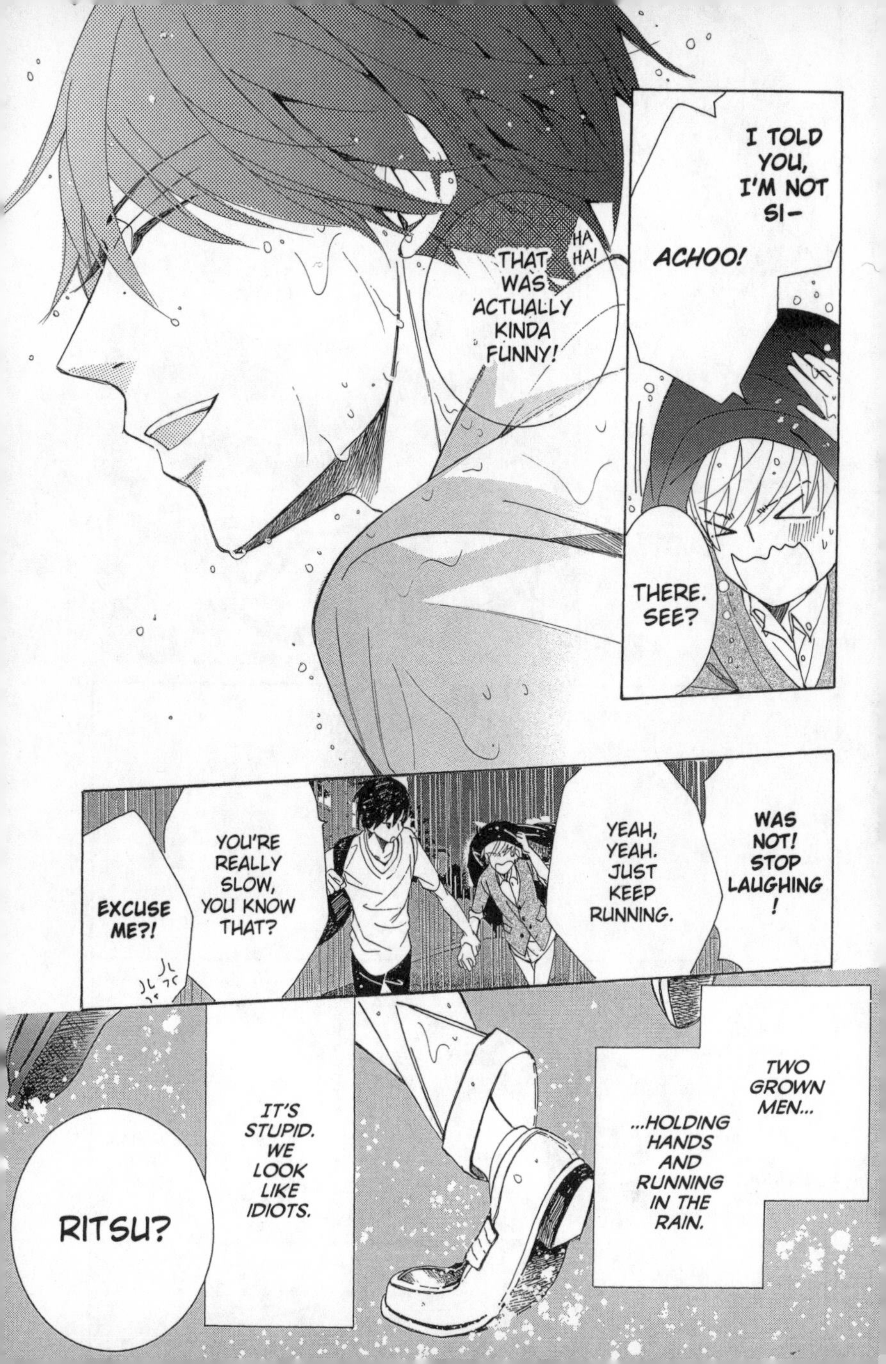
I TOLD YOU, I'M NOT SI—
ACHOO!
THERE. SEE?
HA HA!
THAT WAS ACTUALLY KINDA FUNNY!
WAS NOT! STOP LAUGHING!
YEAH, YEAH. JUST KEEP RUNNING.
YOU'RE REALLY SLOW, YOU KNOW THAT?
EXCUSE ME?!
TWO GROWN MEN...
...HOLDING HANDS AND RUNNING IN THE RAIN.
IT'S STUPID. WE LOOK LIKE IDIOTS.
RITSU?

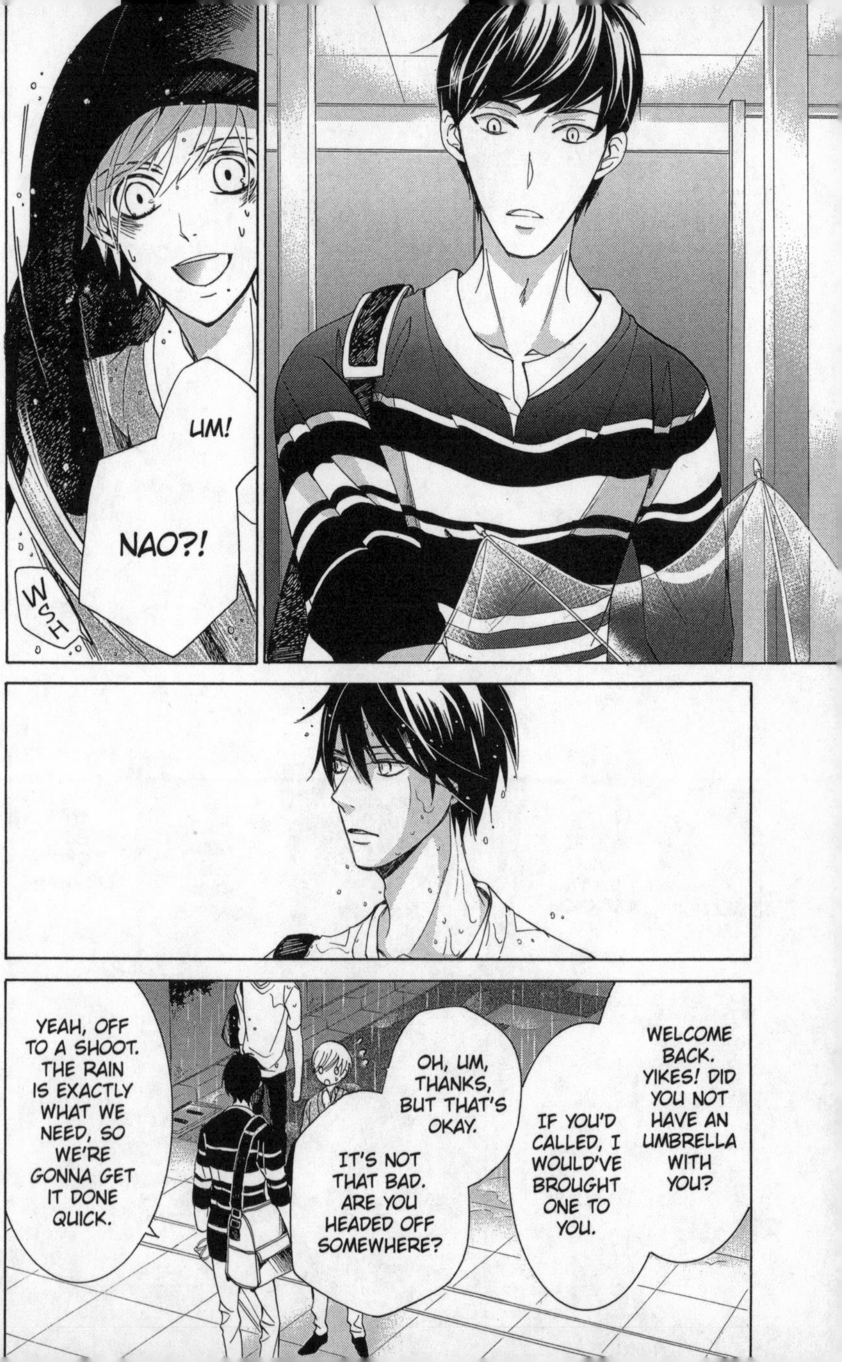
UM!
NAO?!
WSH
WELCOME BACK. YIKES! DID YOU NOT HAVE AN UMBRELLA WITH YOU?
IF YOU'D CALLED, I WOULD'VE BROUGHT ONE TO YOU.
OH, UM, THANKS, BUT THAT'S OKAY.
IT'S NOT THAT BAD. ARE YOU HEADED OFF SOMEWHERE?
YEAH, OFF TO A SHOOT. THE RAIN IS EXACTLY WHAT WE NEED, SO WE'RE GONNA GET IT DONE QUICK.

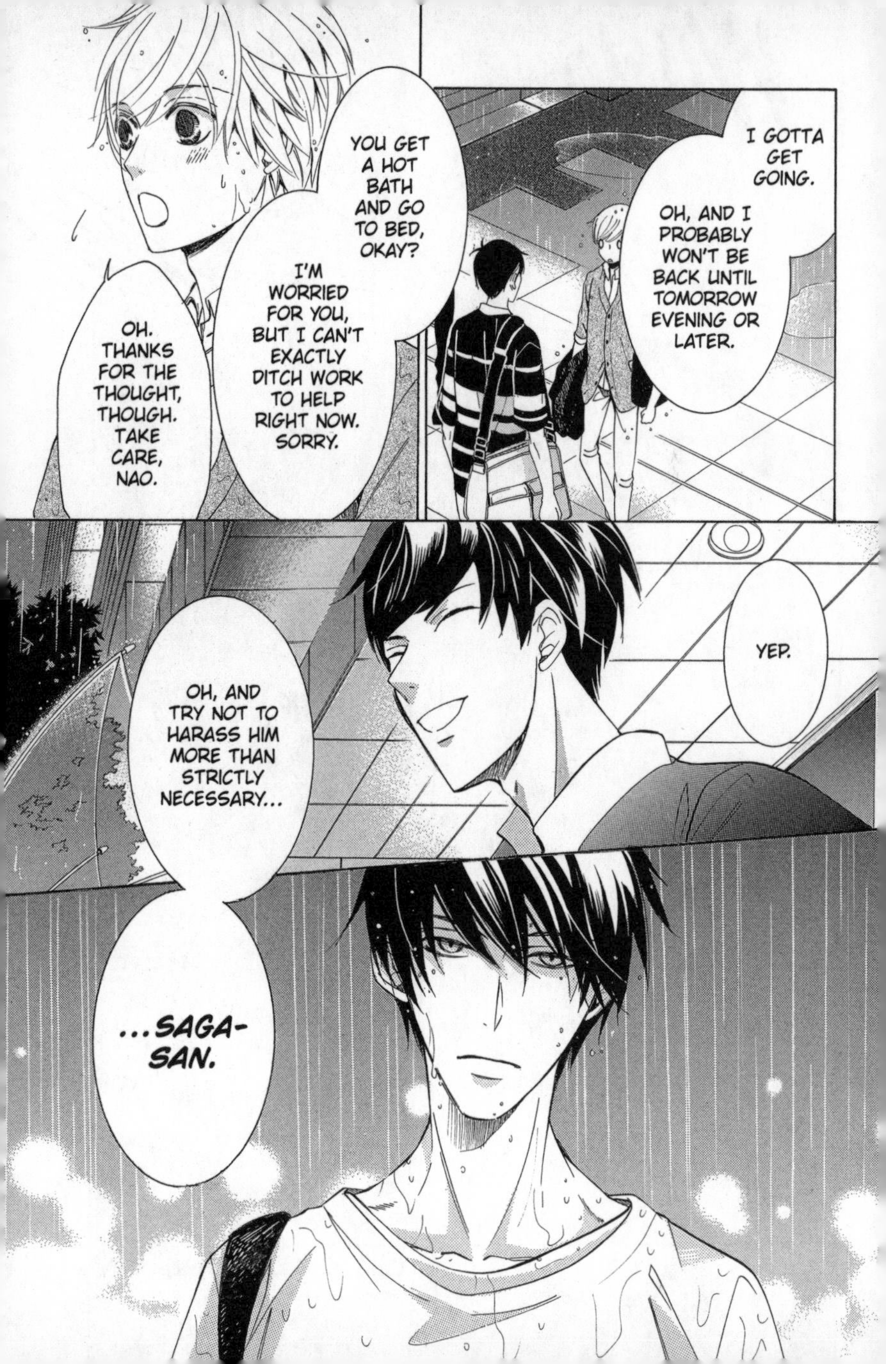
I GOTTA GET GOING.
OH, AND I PROBABLY WON'T BE BACK UNTIL TOMORROW EVENING OR LATER.
YOU GET A HOT BATH AND GO TO BED, OKAY?
I'M WORRIED FOR YOU, BUT I CAN'T EXACTLY DITCH WORK TO HELP RIGHT NOW. SORRY.
OH. THANKS FOR THE THOUGHT, THOUGH. TAKE CARE, NAO.
YEP.
OH, AND TRY NOT TO HARASS HIM MORE THAN STRICTLY NECESSARY...
...SAGA-SAN.

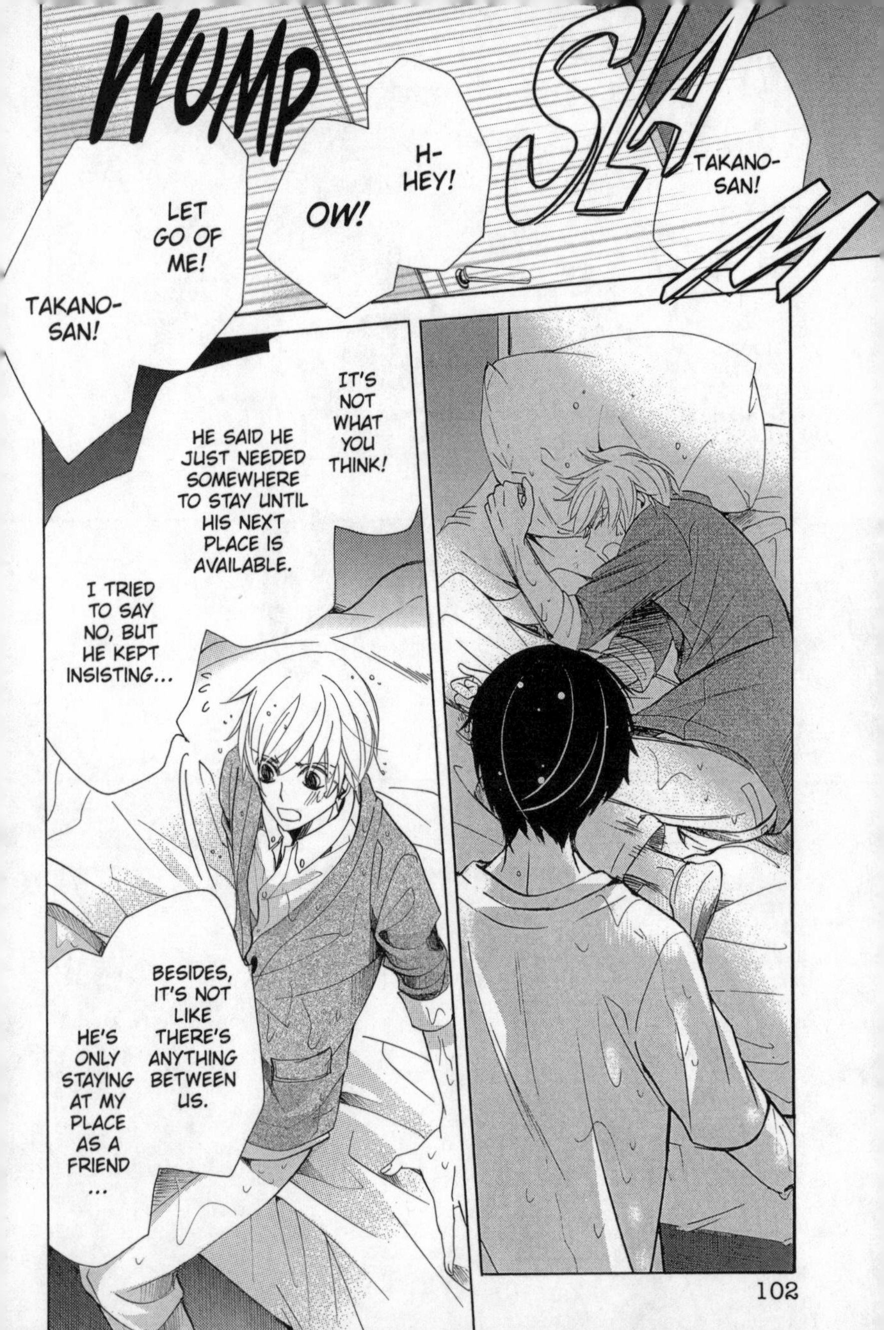
SLAM
TAKANO-SAN!
H-HEY!
OW!
WUMP
LET GO OF ME!
TAKANO-SAN!
IT'S NOT WHAT YOU THINK!
HE SAID HE JUST NEEDED SOMEWHERE TO STAY UNTIL HIS NEXT PLACE IS AVAILABLE.
I TRIED TO SAY NO, BUT HE KEPT INSISTING...
BESIDES, IT'S NOT LIKE THERE'S ANYTHING BETWEEN US.
HE'S ONLY STAYING AT MY PLACE AS A FRIEND...

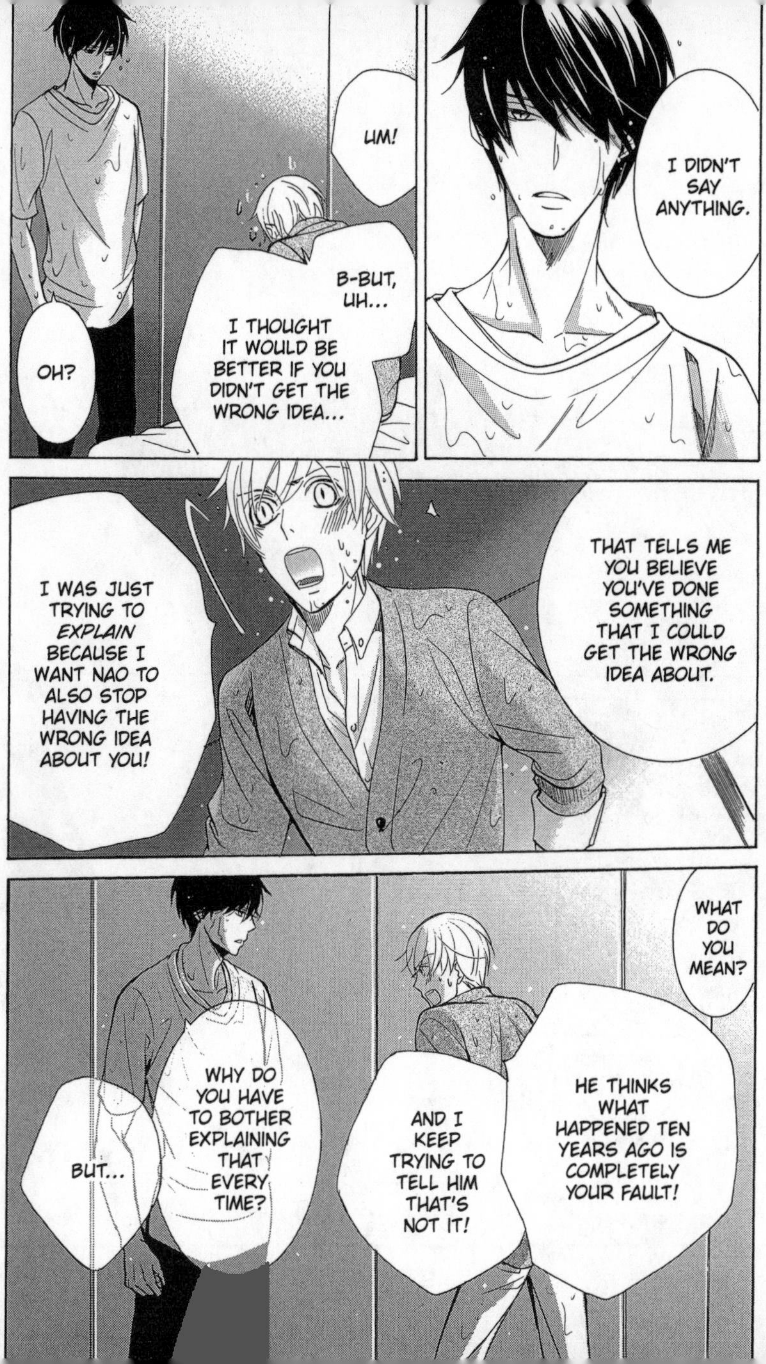
I DIDN'T SAY ANYTHING.
UM!
B-BUT, UH...
I THOUGHT IT WOULD BE BETTER IF YOU DIDN'T GET THE WRONG IDEA...
OH?
THAT TELLS ME YOU BELIEVE YOU'VE DONE SOMETHING THAT I COULD GET THE WRONG IDEA ABOUT.
I WAS JUST TRYING TO *EXPLAIN* BECAUSE I WANT NAO TO ALSO STOP HAVING THE WRONG IDEA ABOUT YOU!
WHAT DO YOU MEAN?
HE THINKS WHAT HAPPENED TEN YEARS AGO IS COMPLETELY YOUR FAULT!
AND I KEEP TRYING TO TELL HIM THAT'S NOT IT!
WHY DO YOU HAVE TO BOTHER EXPLAINING THAT EVERY TIME?
BUT...

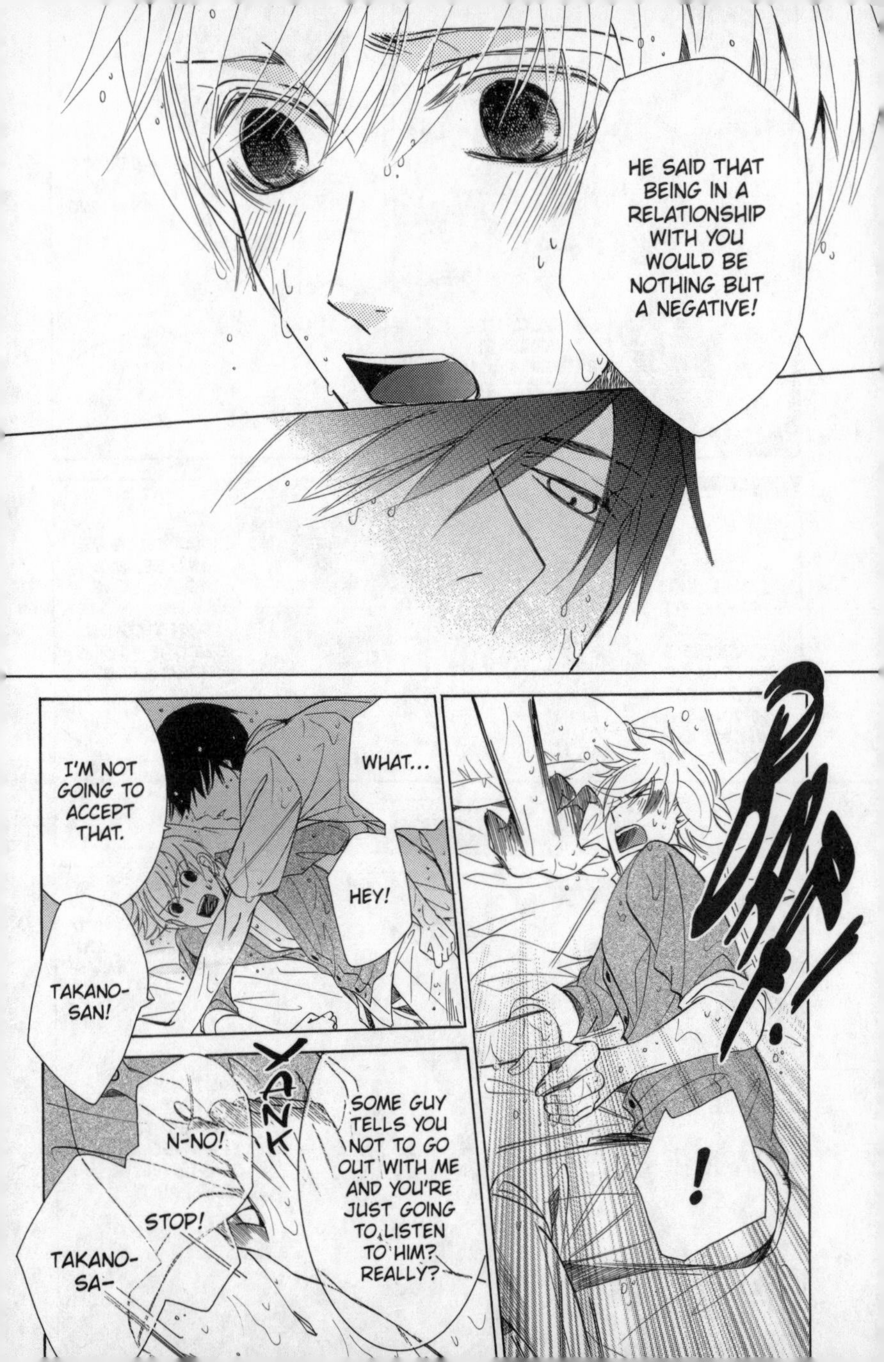
HE SAID THAT BEING IN A RELATIONSHIP WITH YOU WOULD BE NOTHING BUT A NEGATIVE!
DAP!
!
WHAT...
I'M NOT GOING TO ACCEPT THAT.
HEY!
TAKANO-SAN!
SOME GUY TELLS YOU NOT TO GO OUT WITH ME AND YOU'RE JUST GOING TO LISTEN TO HIM? REALLY?
YANK
N-NO!
STOP!
TAKANO-SA-

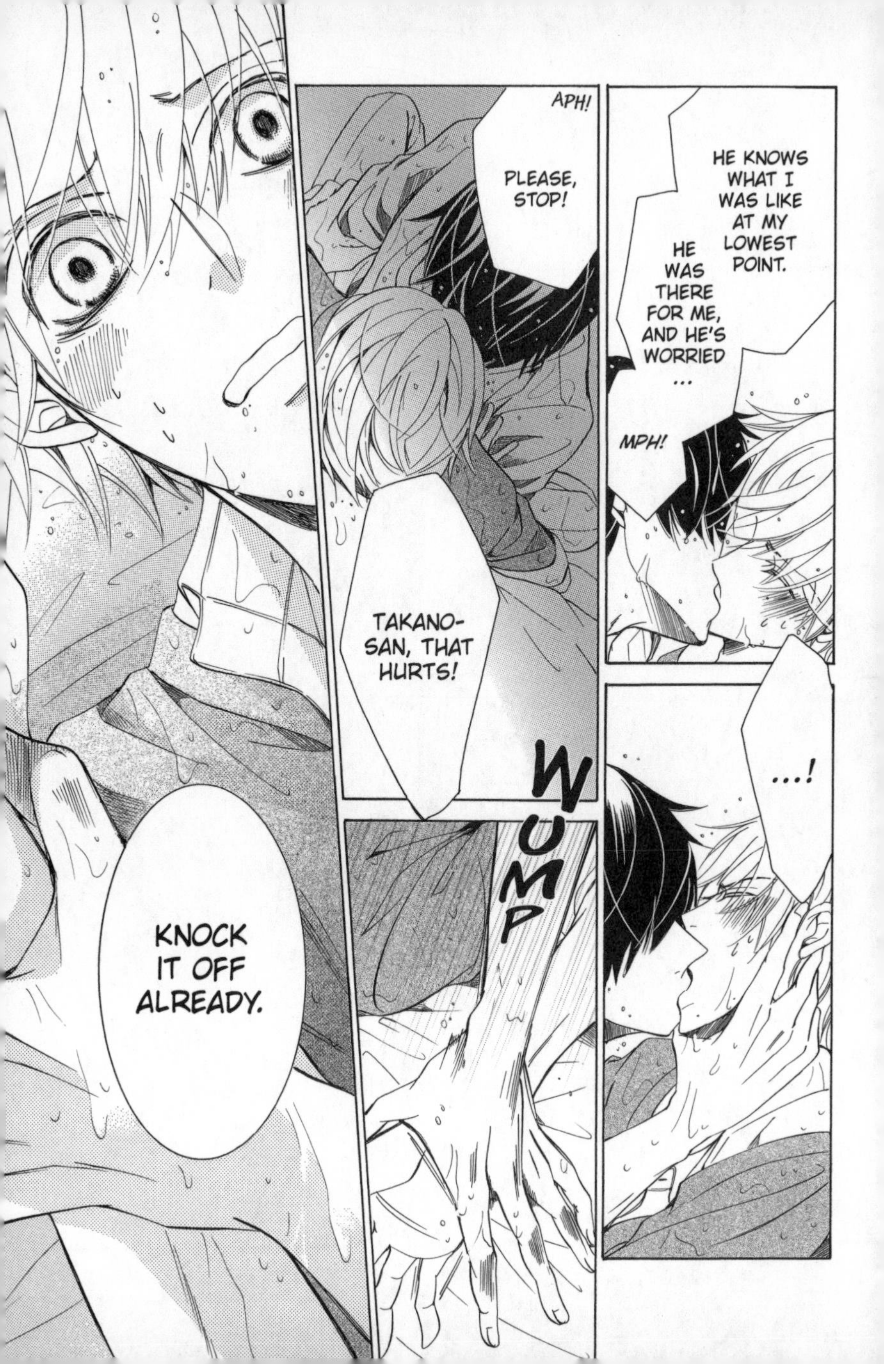
HE KNOWS WHAT I WAS LIKE AT MY LOWEST POINT.
HE WAS THERE FOR ME, AND HE'S WORRIED ...
MPH!
APH!
PLEASE, STOP!
TAKANO-SAN, THAT HURTS!
...!
WUMP
KNOCK IT OFF ALREADY.

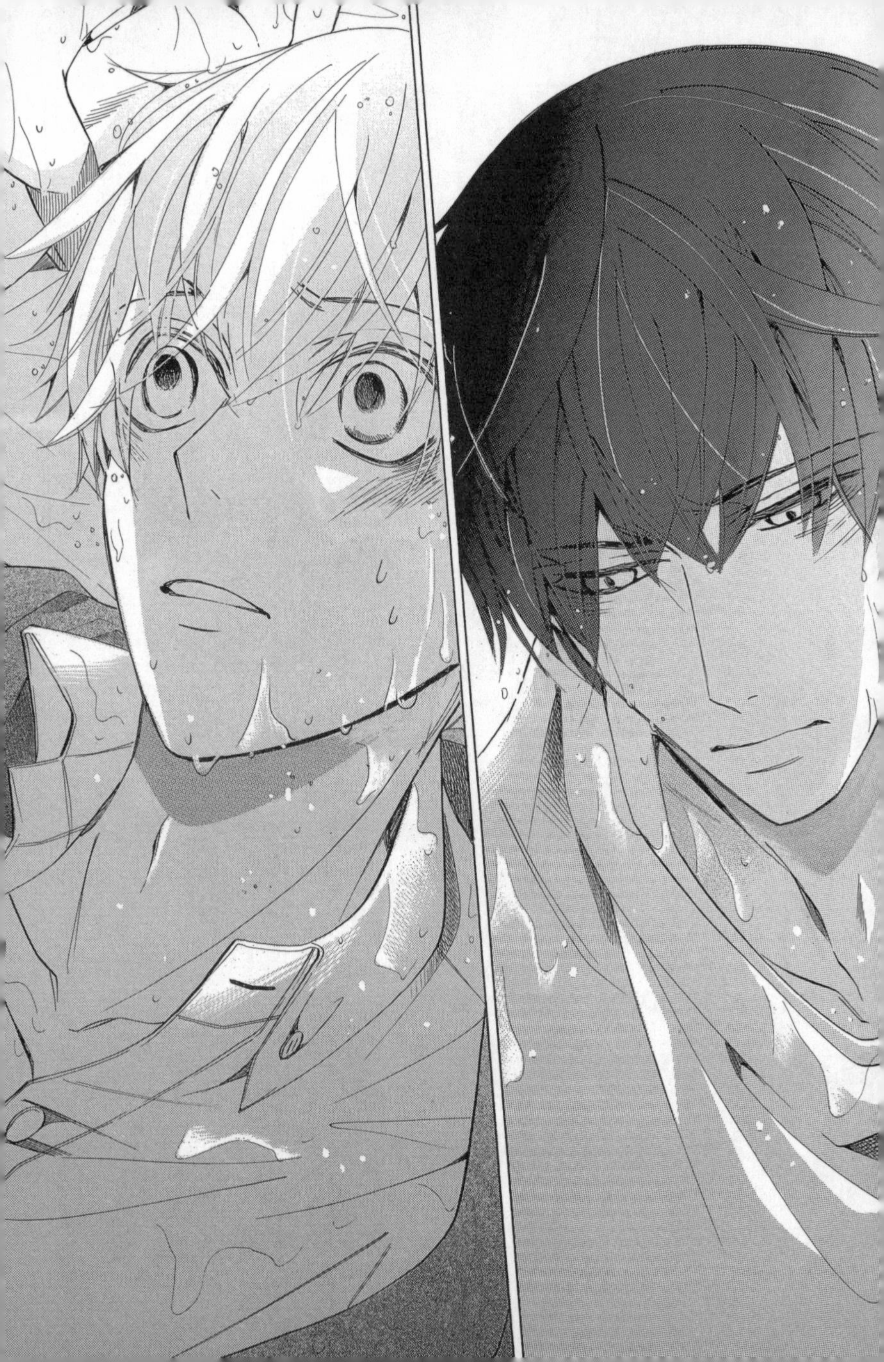

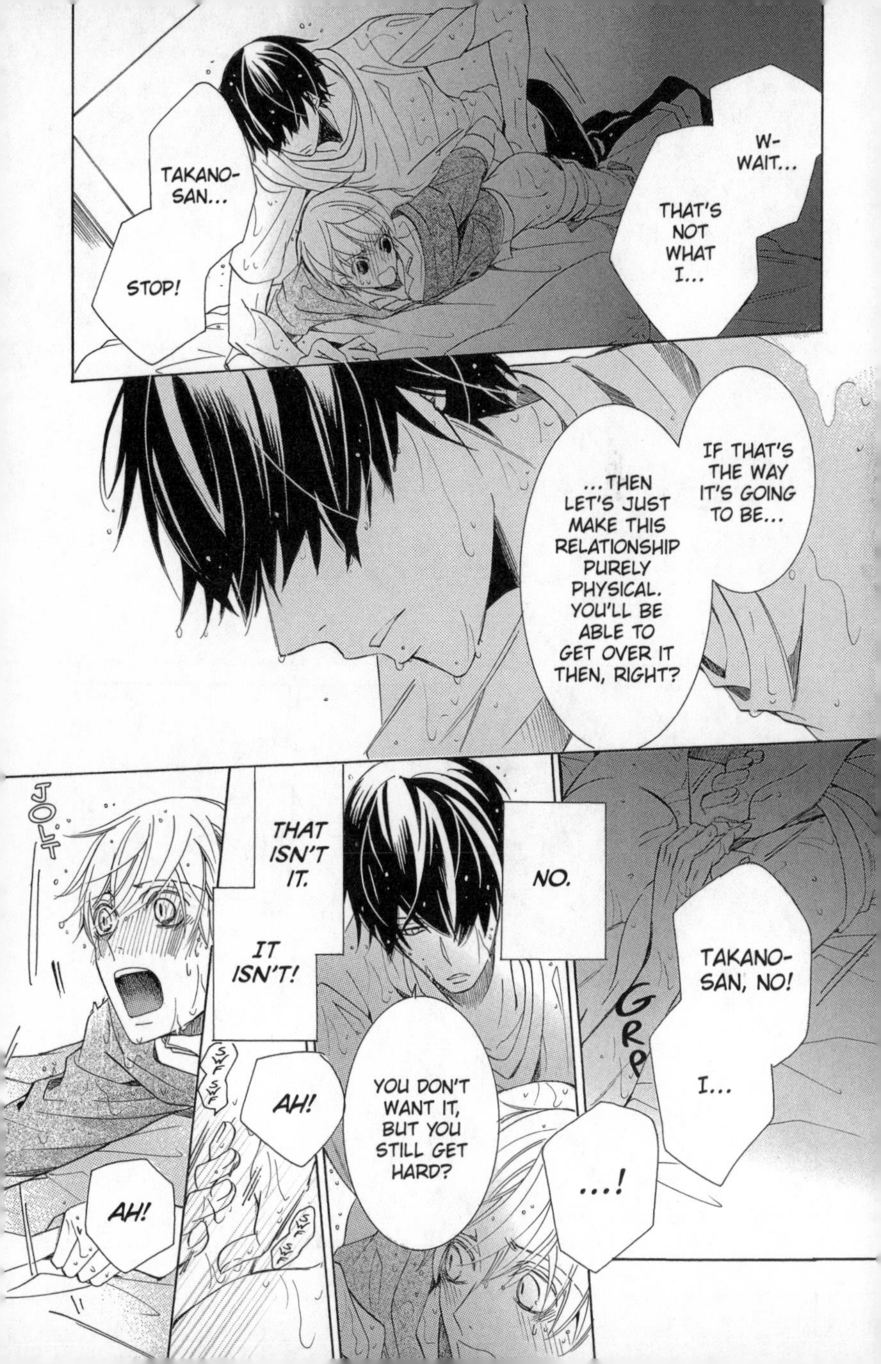
W-
WAIT...
THAT'S NOT WHAT I...
TAKANO-SAN...
STOP!
IF THAT'S THE WAY IT'S GOING TO BE...
...THEN LET'S JUST MAKE THIS RELATIONSHIP PURELY PHYSICAL. YOU'LL BE ABLE TO GET OVER IT THEN, RIGHT?
TAKANO-SAN, NO!
GRP
I...
...!
NO.
YOU DON'T WANT IT, BUT YOU STILL GET HARD?
THAT ISN'T IT.
IT ISN'T!
JOLT
SWF SWF
AH!
AH!

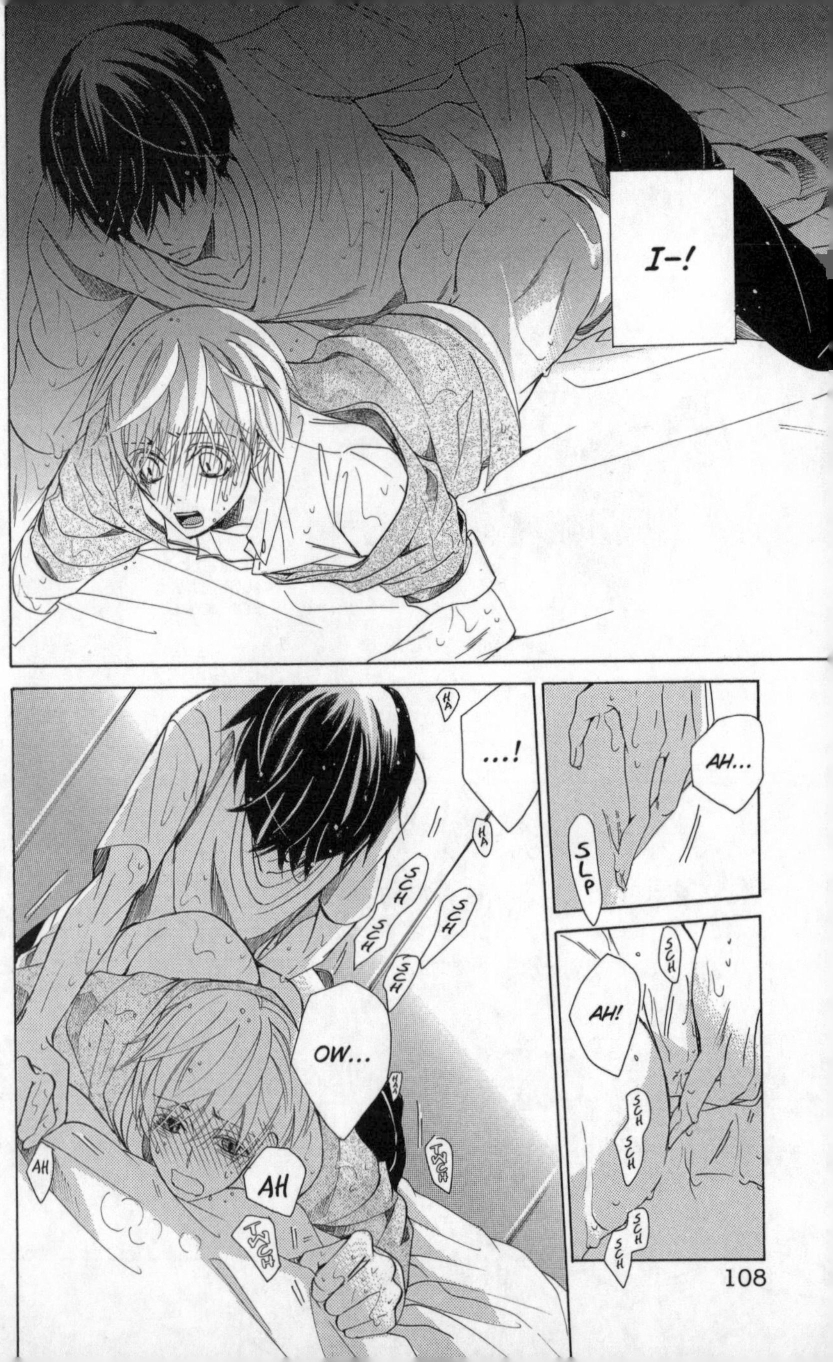
I-!
AH...
SLP
SCH
AH!
SCH
SCH
SCH
SCH
HA
...!
HA
SCH
SCH SCH
SCH
OW...
HA
TSCH
AH
TSCH
AH

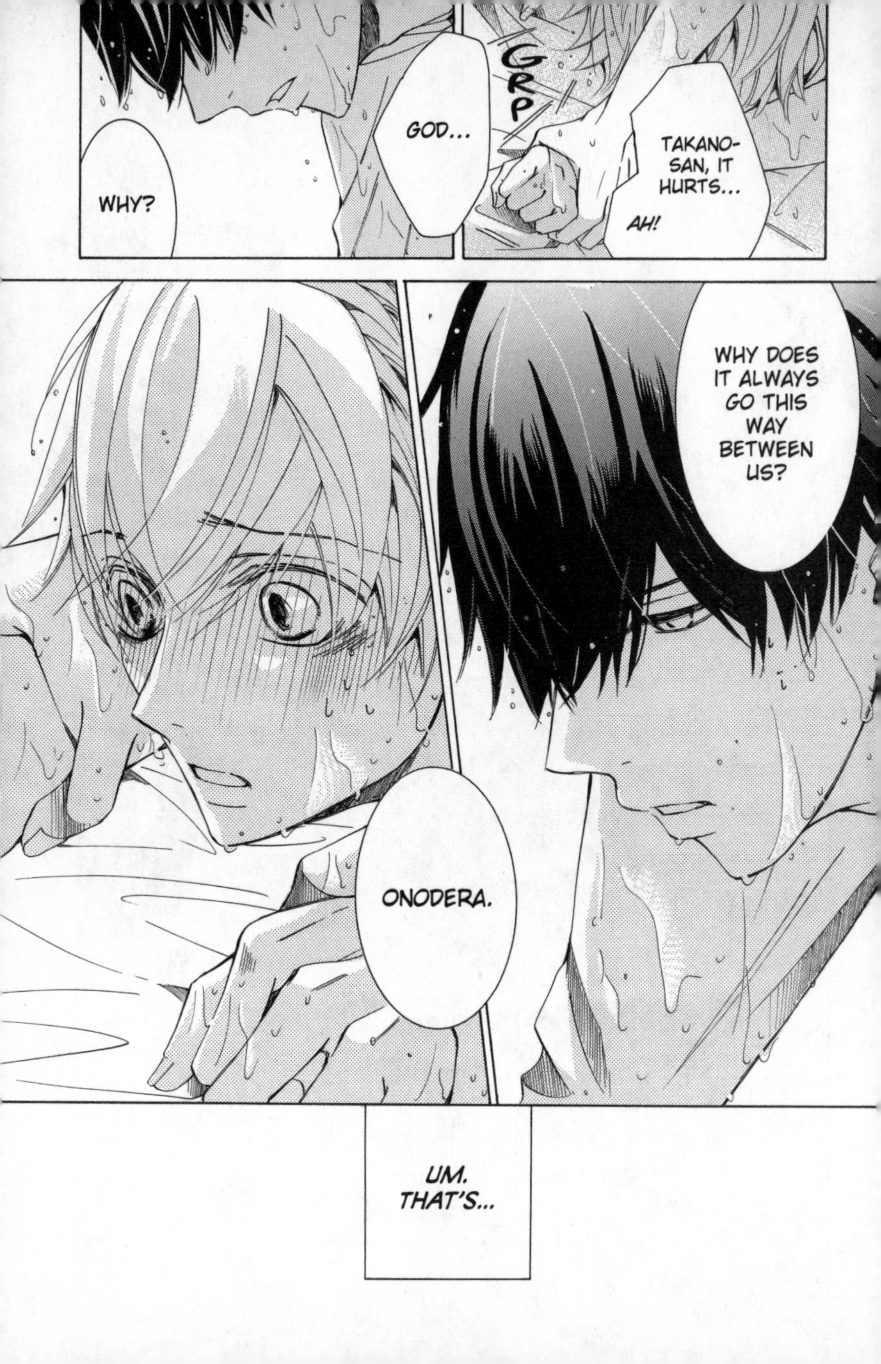

GRP
TAKANO-SAN, IT HURTS...
AH!
GOD...
WHY?
WHY DOES IT ALWAYS GO THIS WAY BETWEEN US?
ONODERA.
UM. THAT'S...

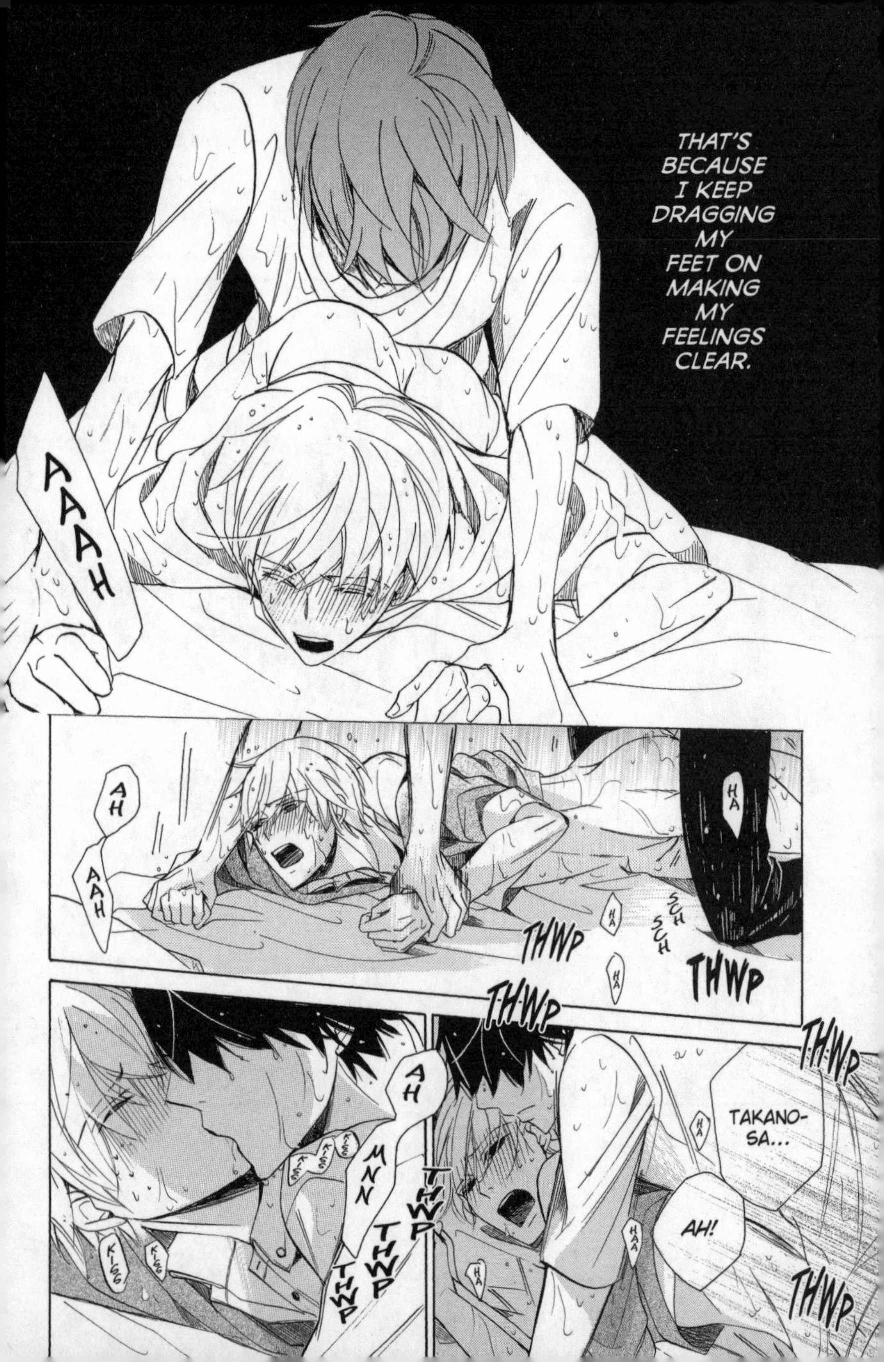
THAT'S BECAUSE I KEEP DRAGGING MY FEET ON MAKING MY FEELINGS CLEAR.
AAAH
HA
SCH SCH
THWP
HA
HA
THWP
AAH
AH
THWP
THWP
TAKANO-SA...
HA
AH!
HAA
HA
THWP
THWP
AH
MNN
KISS
KISS
KISS
KISS
THWP
THWP
THWP

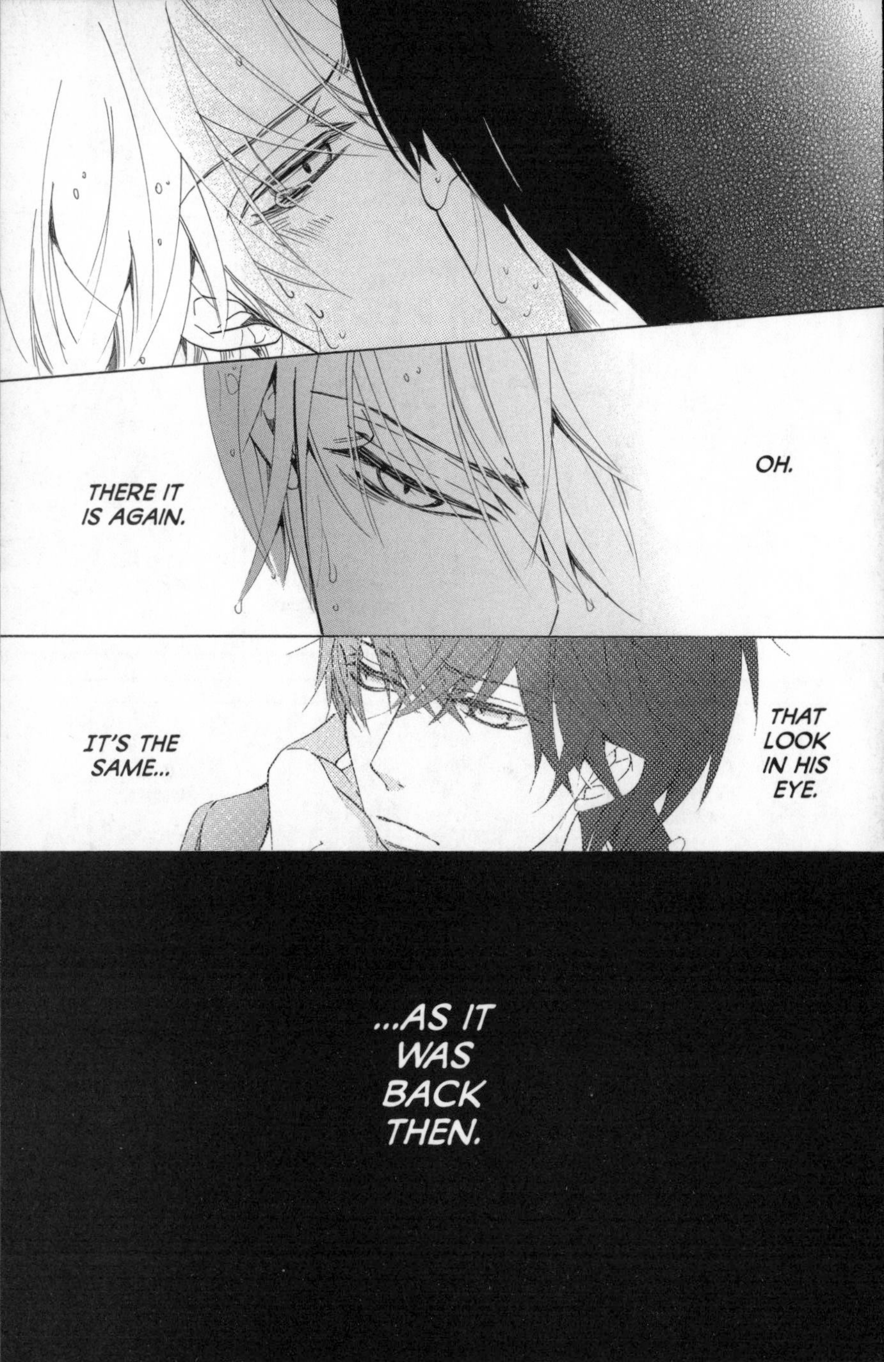
OH.
THERE IT IS AGAIN.
THAT LOOK IN HIS EYE.
IT'S THE SAME...
...AS IT WAS BACK THEN.

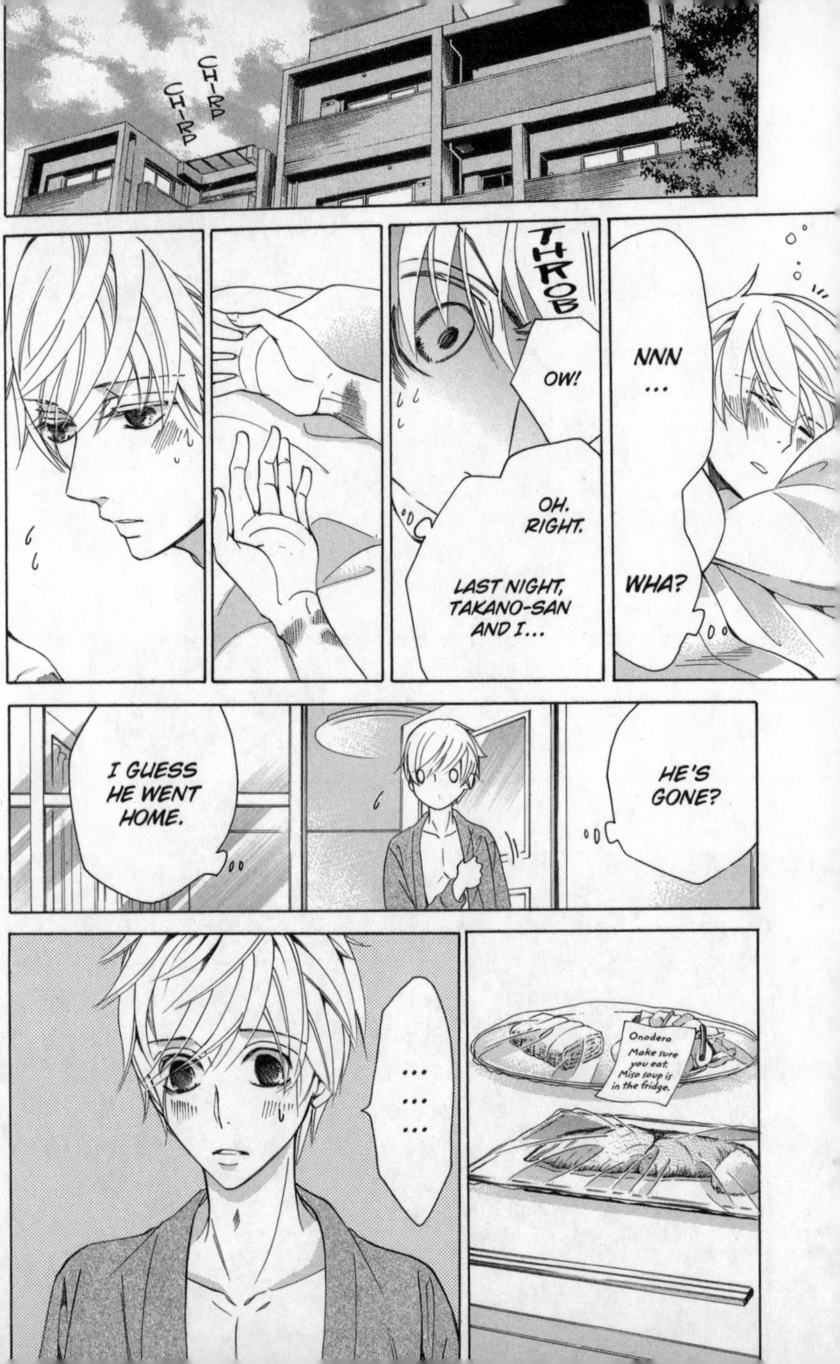
CHIRP
CHIRP
NNN ...
WHA?
THROB
OW!
OH. RIGHT.
LAST NIGHT, TAKANO-SAN AND I...
HE'S GONE?
I GUESS HE WENT HOME.
Onodera
Make sure you eat. Miso soup is in the fridge.
...
...
...

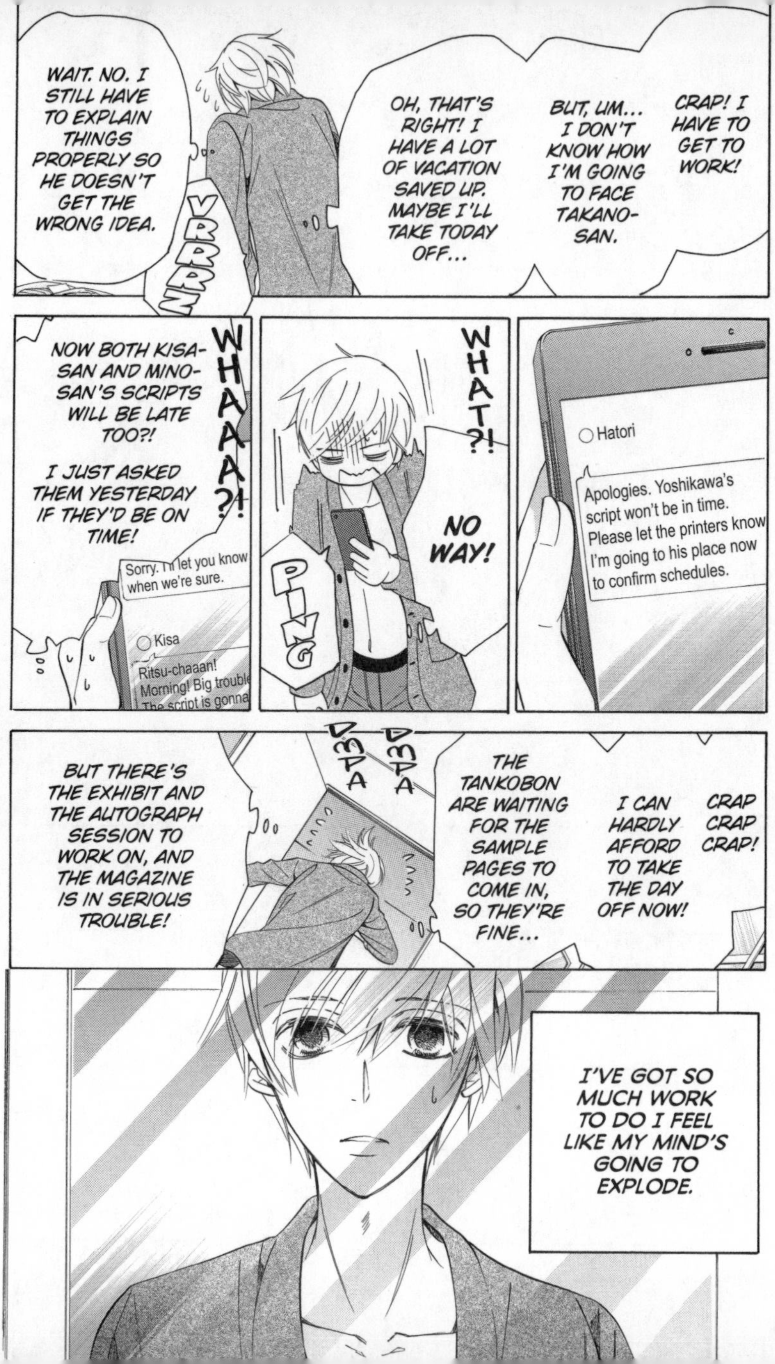
CRAP! I HAVE TO GET TO WORK!
BUT, UM... I DON'T KNOW HOW I'M GOING TO FACE TAKANO-SAN.
OH, THAT'S RIGHT! I HAVE A LOT OF VACATION SAVED UP. MAYBE I'LL TAKE TODAY OFF...
VRRRZ
WAIT. NO. I STILL HAVE TO EXPLAIN THINGS PROPERLY SO HE DOESN'T GET THE WRONG IDEA.
Hatori
Apologies. Yoshikawa's script won't be in time. Please let the printers know I'm going to his place now to confirm schedules.
WHAT?!
NO WAY!
PING
WHAAAA?!
NOW BOTH KISA-SAN AND MINO-SAN'S SCRIPTS WILL BE LATE TOO?!
I JUST ASKED THEM YESTERDAY IF THEY'D BE ON TIME!
Sorry. I'll let you know when we're sure.
Kisa
Ritsu-chaaan!
CRAP CRAP CRAP!
I CAN HARDLY AFFORD TO TAKE THE DAY OFF NOW!
THE TANKOBON ARE WAITING FOR THE SAMPLE PAGES TO COME IN, SO THEY'RE FINE...
DMPA
DMPA
BUT THERE'S THE EXHIBIT AND THE AUTOGRAPH SESSION TO WORK ON, AND THE MAGAZINE IS IN SERIOUS TROUBLE!
I'VE GOT SO MUCH WORK TO DO I FEEL LIKE MY MIND'S GOING TO EXPLODE.

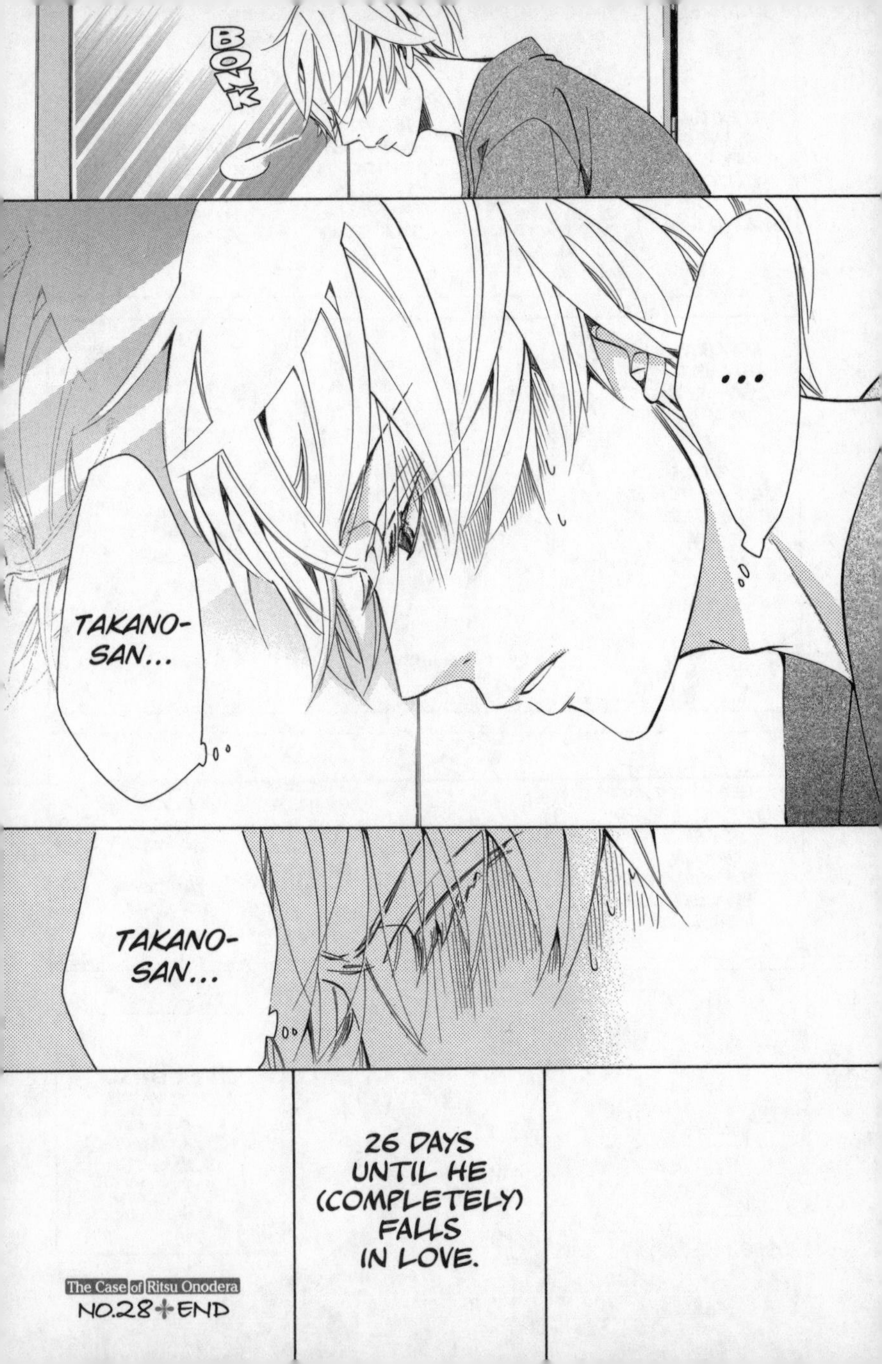
BONK
...
TAKANO-SAN...
TAKANO-SAN...
26 DAYS UNTIL HE (COMPLETELY) FALLS IN LOVE.
The Case of Ritsu Onodera
NO.28 END

The World's Greatest First Love

The Case of Ritsu Onodera

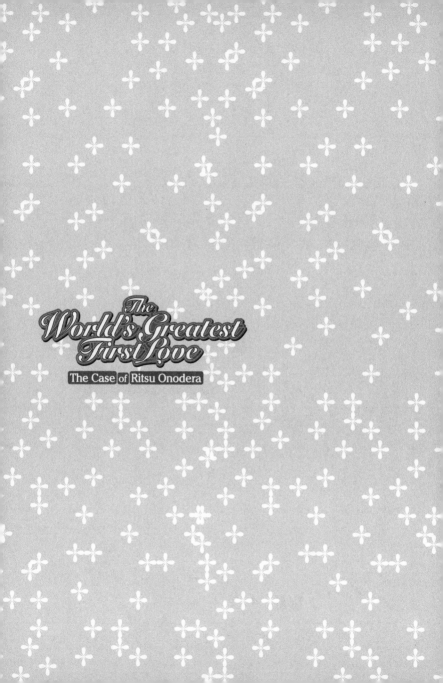

The World's Greatest First Love

The Case of Ritsu Onodera

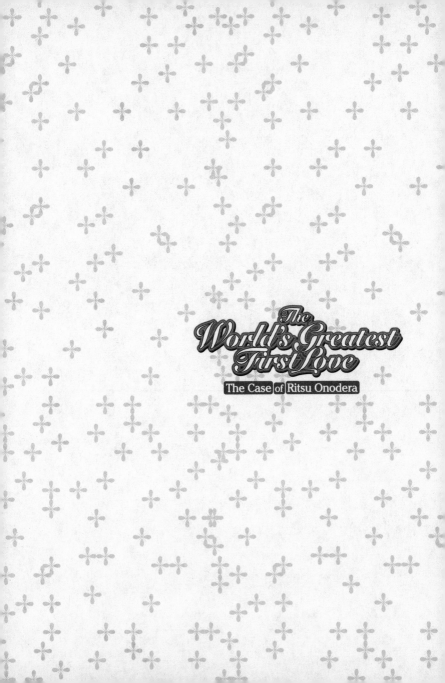

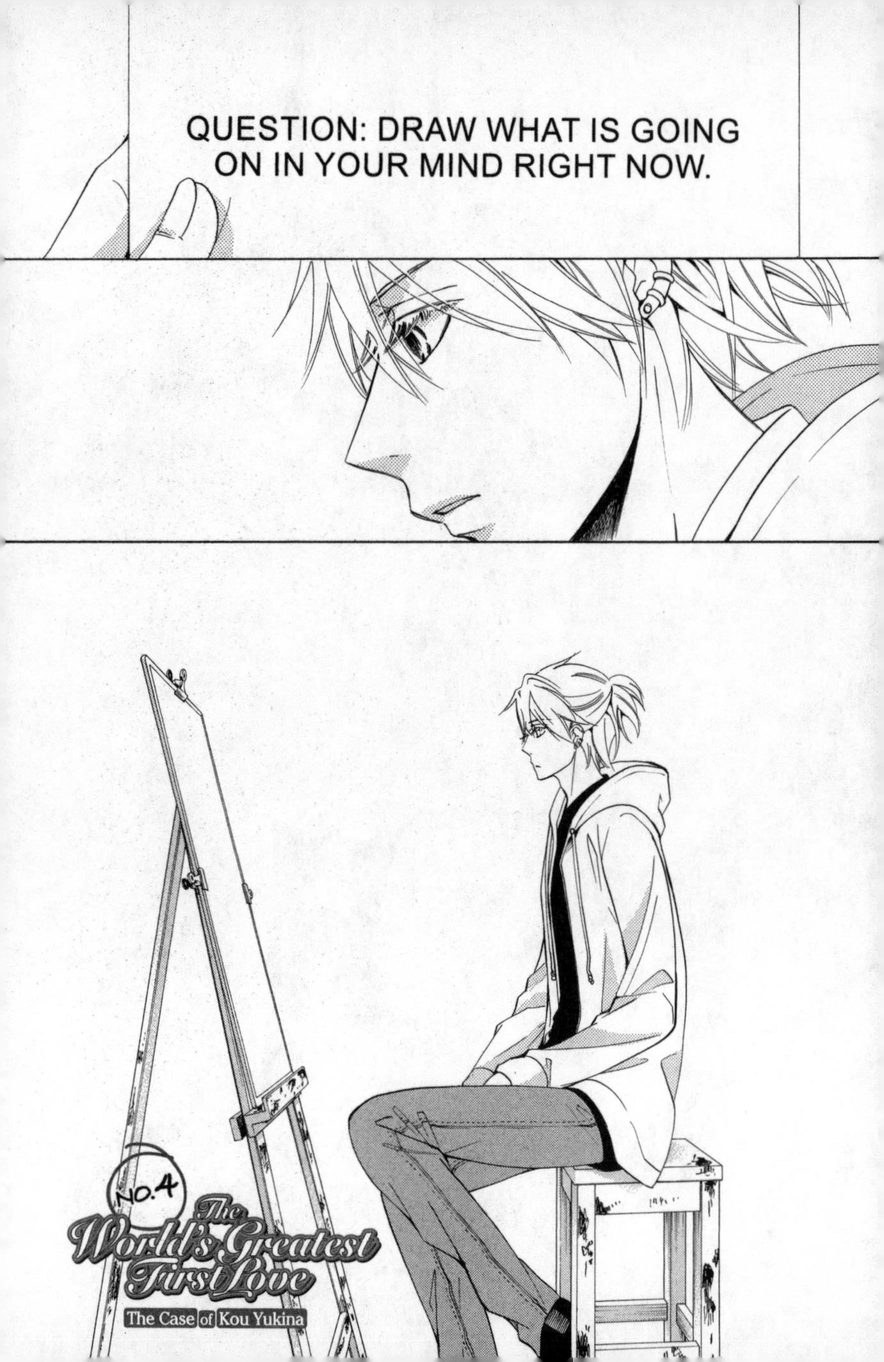
QUESTION: DRAW WHAT IS GOING ON IN YOUR MIND RIGHT NOW.
NO.4
The World's Greatest First Love
The Case of Kou Yukina

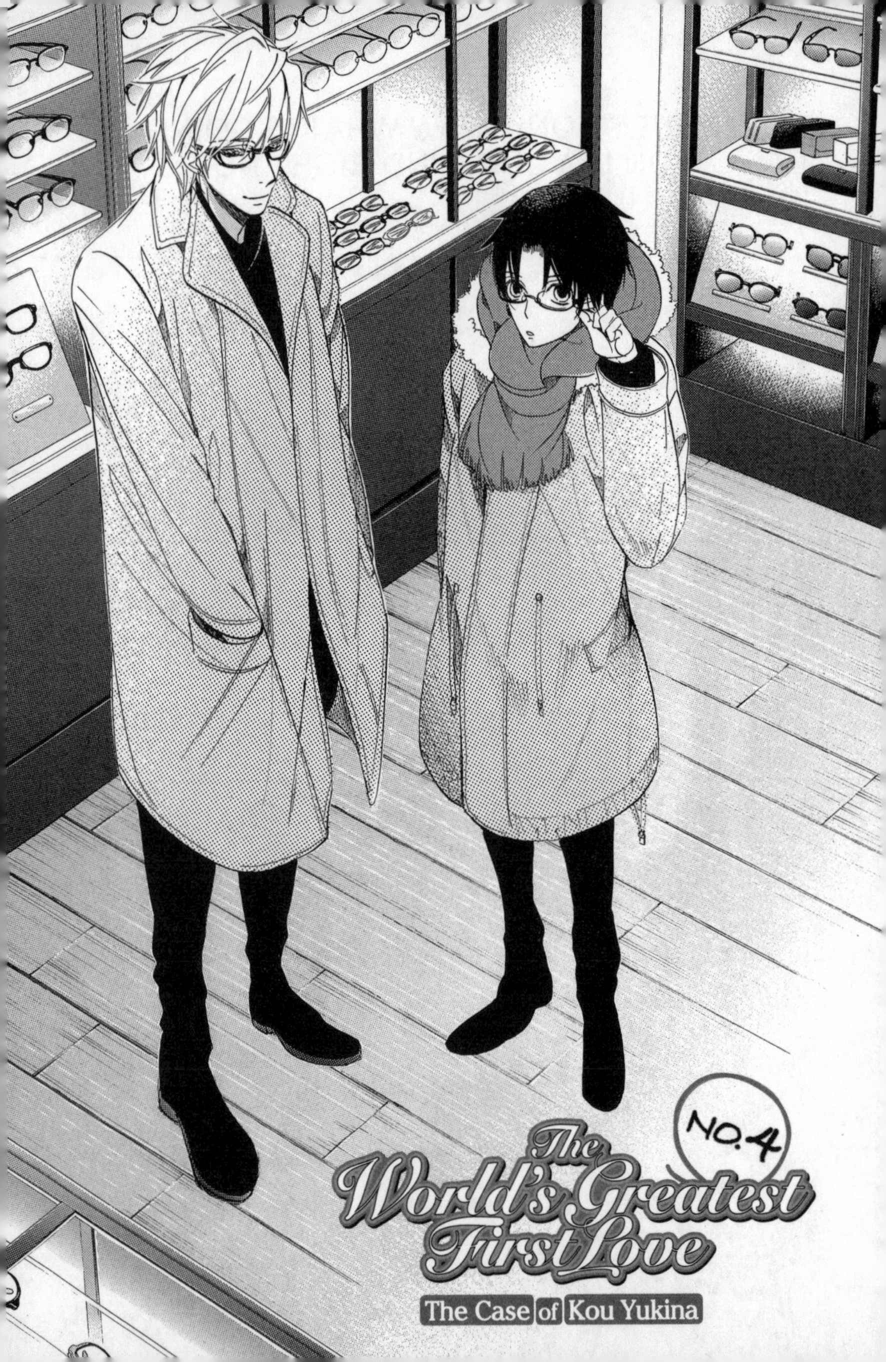
NO.4
The World's Greatest First Love
The Case of Kou Yukina

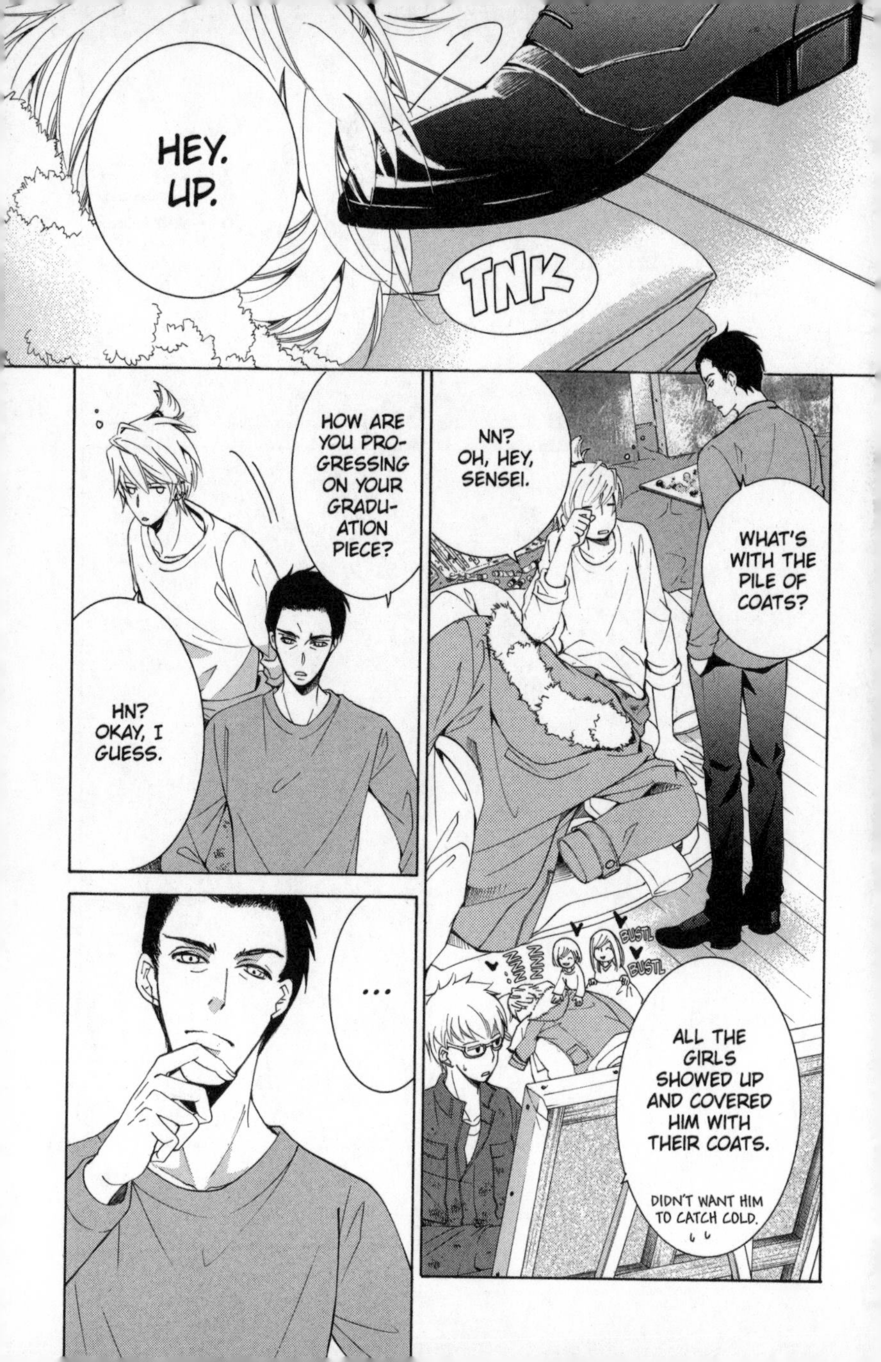
HEY. UP.
TNK
NN? OH, HEY, SENSEI.
WHAT'S WITH THE PILE OF COATS?
BUSTL
BUSTL
NNN
NNN
ALL THE GIRLS SHOWED UP AND COVERED HIM WITH THEIR COATS.
DIDN'T WANT HIM TO CATCH COLD.
HOW ARE YOU PRO-GRESSING ON YOUR GRADU-ATION PIECE?
HN? OKAY, I GUESS.
...

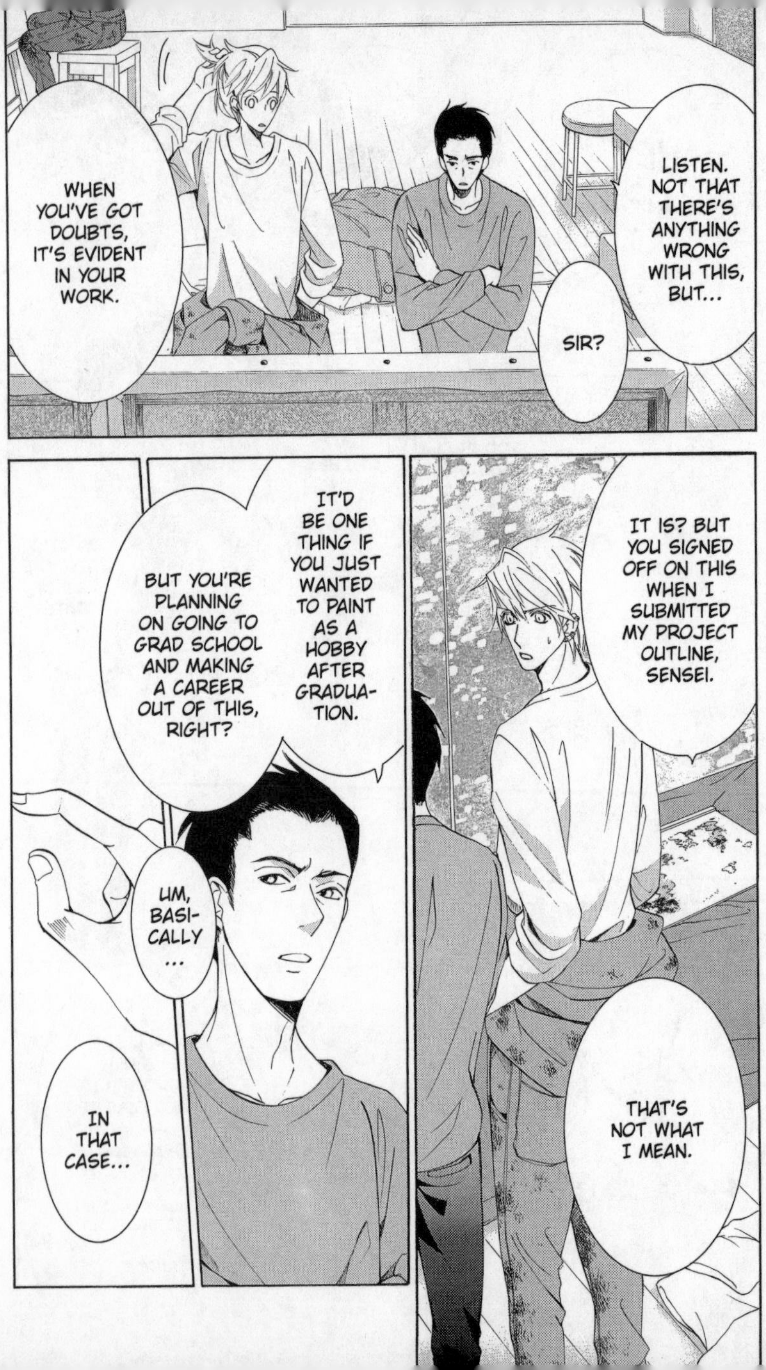
LISTEN. NOT THAT THERE'S ANYTHING WRONG WITH THIS, BUT...
SIR?
WHEN YOU'VE GOT DOUBTS, IT'S EVIDENT IN YOUR WORK.
IT IS? BUT YOU SIGNED OFF ON THIS WHEN I SUBMITTED MY PROJECT OUTLINE, SENSEI.
THAT'S NOT WHAT I MEAN.
IT'D BE ONE THING IF YOU JUST WANTED TO PAINT AS A HOBBY AFTER GRADUA-TION.
BUT YOU'RE PLANNING ON GOING TO GRAD SCHOOL AND MAKING A CAREER OUT OF THIS, RIGHT?
UM, BASI-CALLY...
IN THAT CASE...

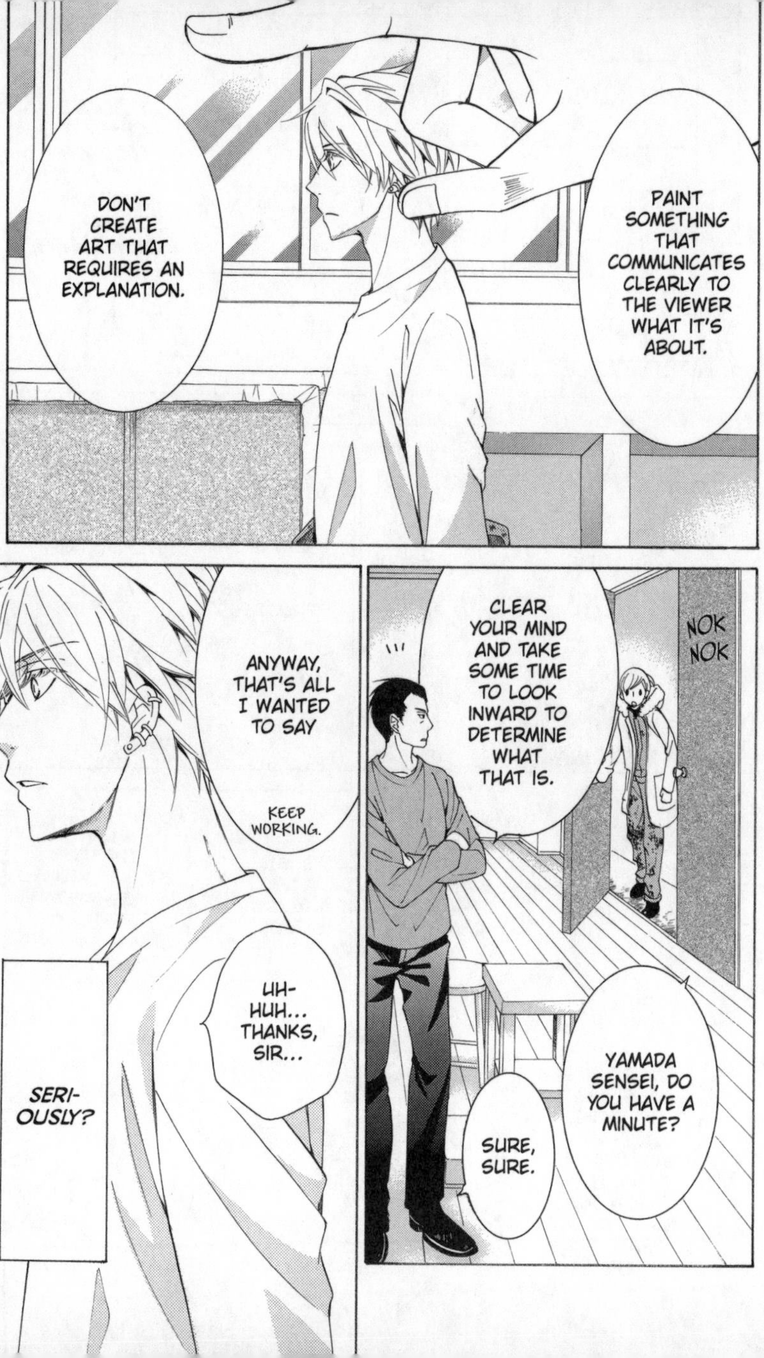
PAINT SOMETHING THAT COMMUNICATES CLEARLY TO THE VIEWER WHAT IT'S ABOUT.
DON'T CREATE ART THAT REQUIRES AN EXPLANATION.
CLEAR YOUR MIND AND TAKE SOME TIME TO LOOK INWARD TO DETERMINE WHAT THAT IS.
NOK NOK
YAMADA SENSEI, DO YOU HAVE A MINUTE?
SURE, SURE.
ANYWAY, THAT'S ALL I WANTED TO SAY
KEEP WORKING.
UH-HUH... THANKS, SIR...
SERI-OUSLY?

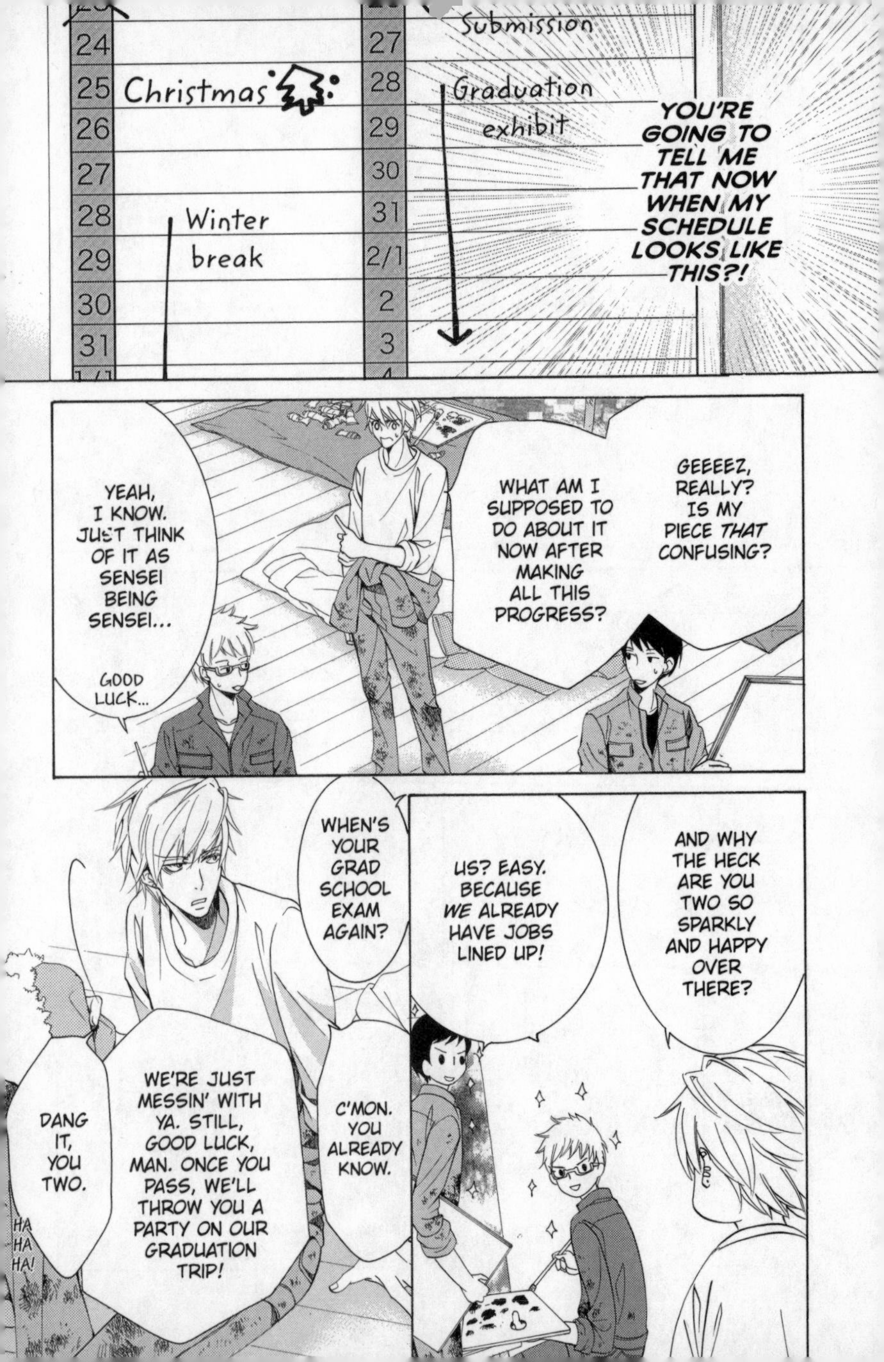
Submission
Graduation exhibit
YOU'RE GOING TO TELL ME THAT NOW WHEN MY SCHEDULE LOOKS LIKE THIS?!
Christmas
Winter break
GEEEEZ, REALLY? IS MY PIECE *THAT* CONFUSING?
WHAT AM I SUPPOSED TO DO ABOUT IT NOW AFTER MAKING ALL THIS PROGRESS?
YEAH, I KNOW. JUST THINK OF IT AS SENSEI BEING SENSEI...
GOOD LUCK...
AND WHY THE HECK ARE YOU TWO SO SPARKLY AND HAPPY OVER THERE?
US? EASY. BECAUSE *WE* ALREADY HAVE JOBS LINED UP!
WHEN'S YOUR GRAD SCHOOL EXAM AGAIN?
C'MON. YOU ALREADY KNOW.
WE'RE JUST MESSIN' WITH YA. STILL, GOOD LUCK, MAN. ONCE YOU PASS, WE'LL THROW YOU A PARTY ON OUR GRADUATION TRIP!
DANG IT, YOU TWO.
HA HA HA!

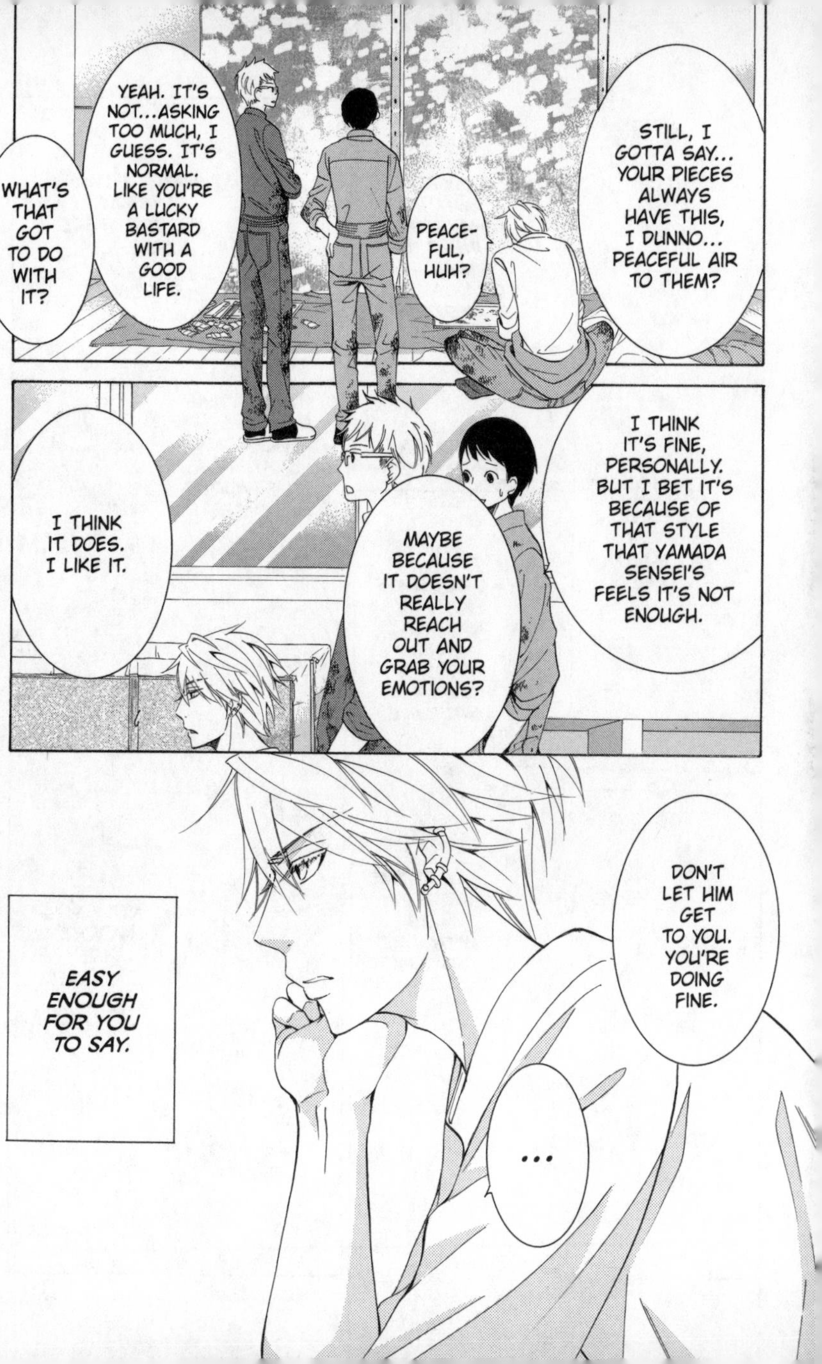
STILL, I GOTTA SAY... YOUR PIECES ALWAYS HAVE THIS, I DUNNO... PEACEFUL AIR TO THEM?
PEACE-FUL, HUH?
YEAH. IT'S NOT...ASKING TOO MUCH, I GUESS. IT'S NORMAL. LIKE YOU'RE A LUCKY BASTARD WITH A GOOD LIFE.
WHAT'S THAT GOT TO DO WITH IT?
I THINK IT'S FINE, PERSONALLY. BUT I BET IT'S BECAUSE OF THAT STYLE THAT YAMADA SENSEI'S FEELS IT'S NOT ENOUGH.
MAYBE BECAUSE IT DOESN'T REALLY REACH OUT AND GRAB YOUR EMOTIONS?
I THINK IT DOES. I LIKE IT.
DON'T LET HIM GET TO YOU. YOU'RE DOING FINE.
...
EASY ENOUGH FOR YOU TO SAY.

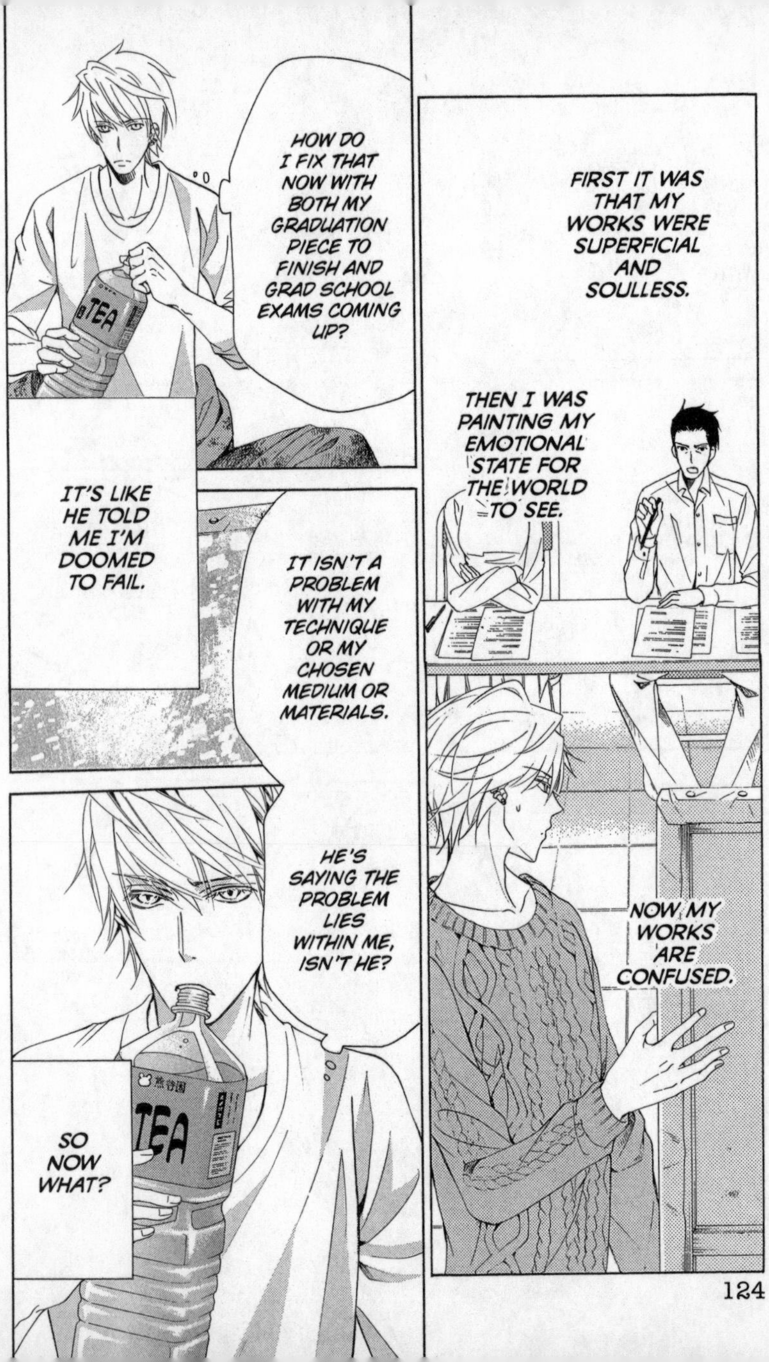
FIRST IT WAS THAT MY WORKS WERE SUPERFICIAL AND SOULLESS.
THEN I WAS PAINTING MY EMOTIONAL STATE FOR THE WORLD TO SEE.
NOW MY WORKS ARE CONFUSED.
HOW DO I FIX THAT NOW WITH BOTH MY GRADUATION PIECE TO FINISH AND GRAD SCHOOL EXAMS COMING UP?
IT ISN'T A PROBLEM WITH MY TECHNIQUE OR MY CHOSEN MEDIUM OR MATERIALS.
IT'S LIKE HE TOLD ME I'M DOOMED TO FAIL.
HE'S SAYING THE PROBLEM LIES WITHIN ME, ISN'T HE?
SO NOW WHAT?

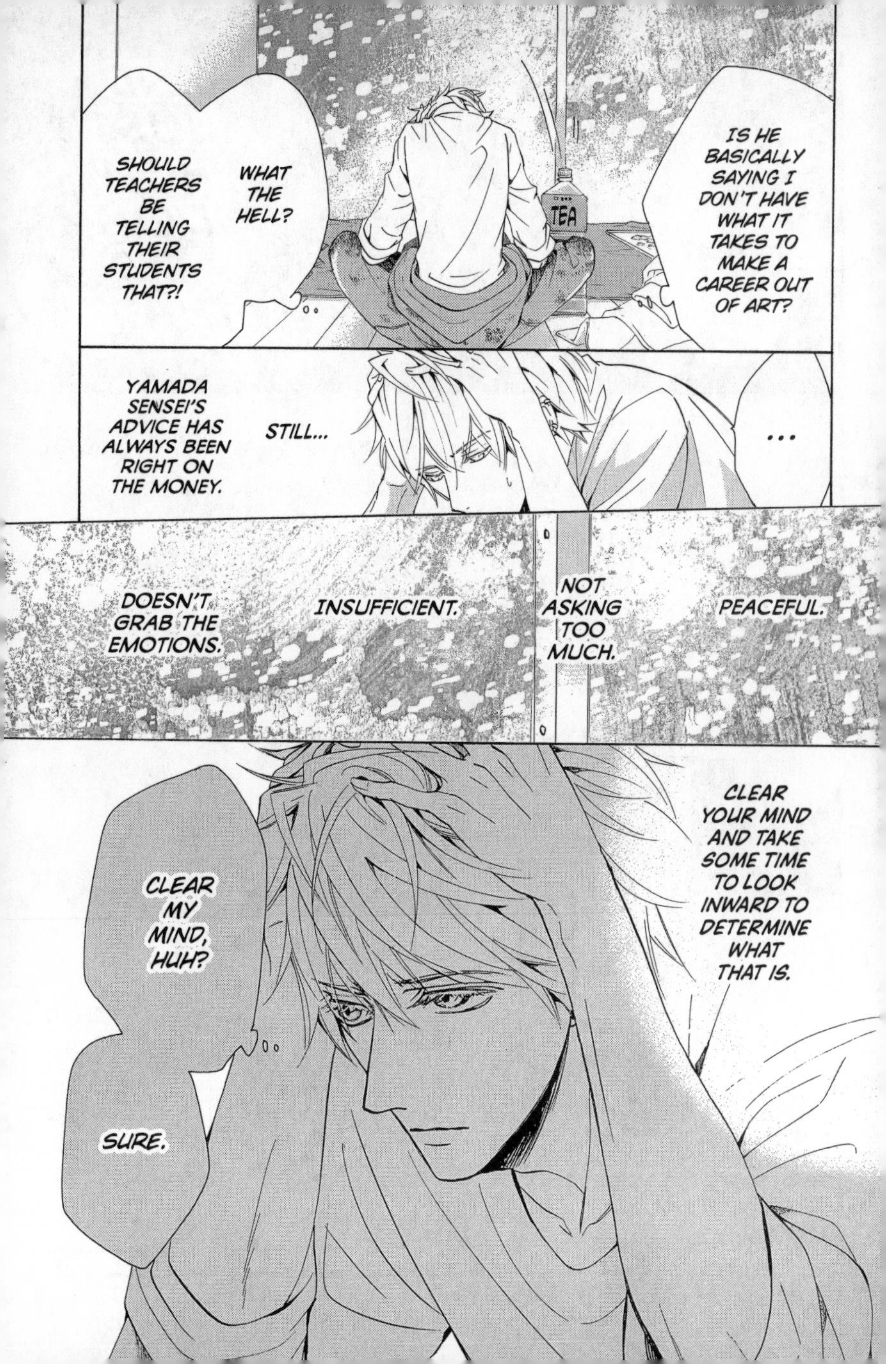
IS HE BASICALLY SAYING I DON'T HAVE WHAT IT TAKES TO MAKE A CAREER OUT OF ART?
TEA
WHAT THE HELL?
SHOULD TEACHERS BE TELLING THEIR STUDENTS THAT?!
...
STILL...
YAMADA SENSEI'S ADVICE HAS ALWAYS BEEN RIGHT ON THE MONEY.
PEACEFUL.
NOT ASKING TOO MUCH.
INSUFFICIENT.
DOESN'T GRAB THE EMOTIONS.
CLEAR YOUR MIND AND TAKE SOME TIME TO LOOK INWARD TO DETERMINE WHAT THAT IS.
CLEAR MY MIND, HUH?
SURE.

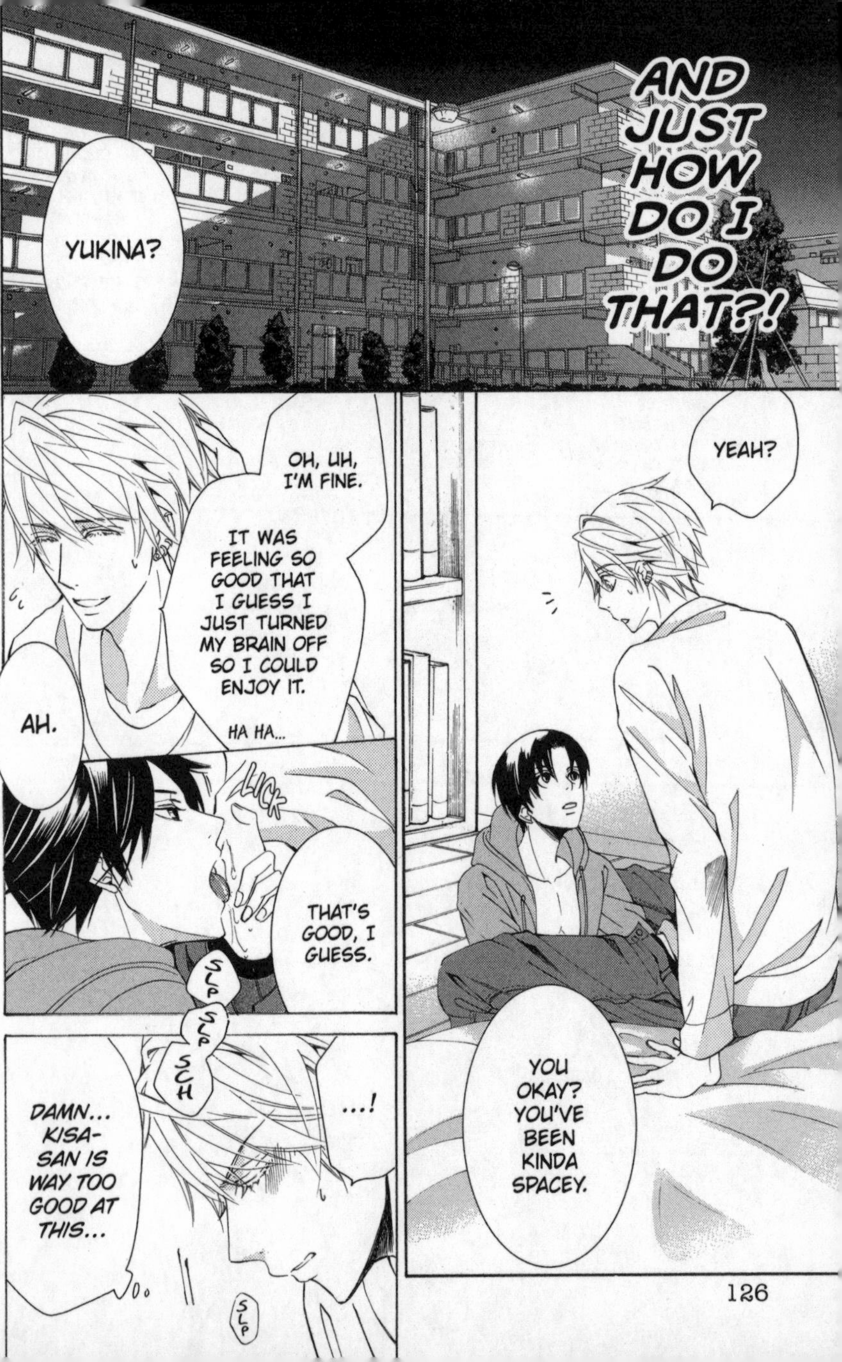
AND JUST HOW DO I DO THAT?!
YUKINA?
YEAH?
YOU OKAY? YOU'VE BEEN KINDA SPACEY.
OH, UH, I'M FINE.
IT WAS FEELING SO GOOD THAT I GUESS I JUST TURNED MY BRAIN OFF SO I COULD ENJOY IT.
HA HA...
AH.
LICK
THAT'S GOOD, I GUESS.
SLP
SLP
SCH
...!
DAMN... KISA-SAN IS WAY TOO GOOD AT THIS...
SLP

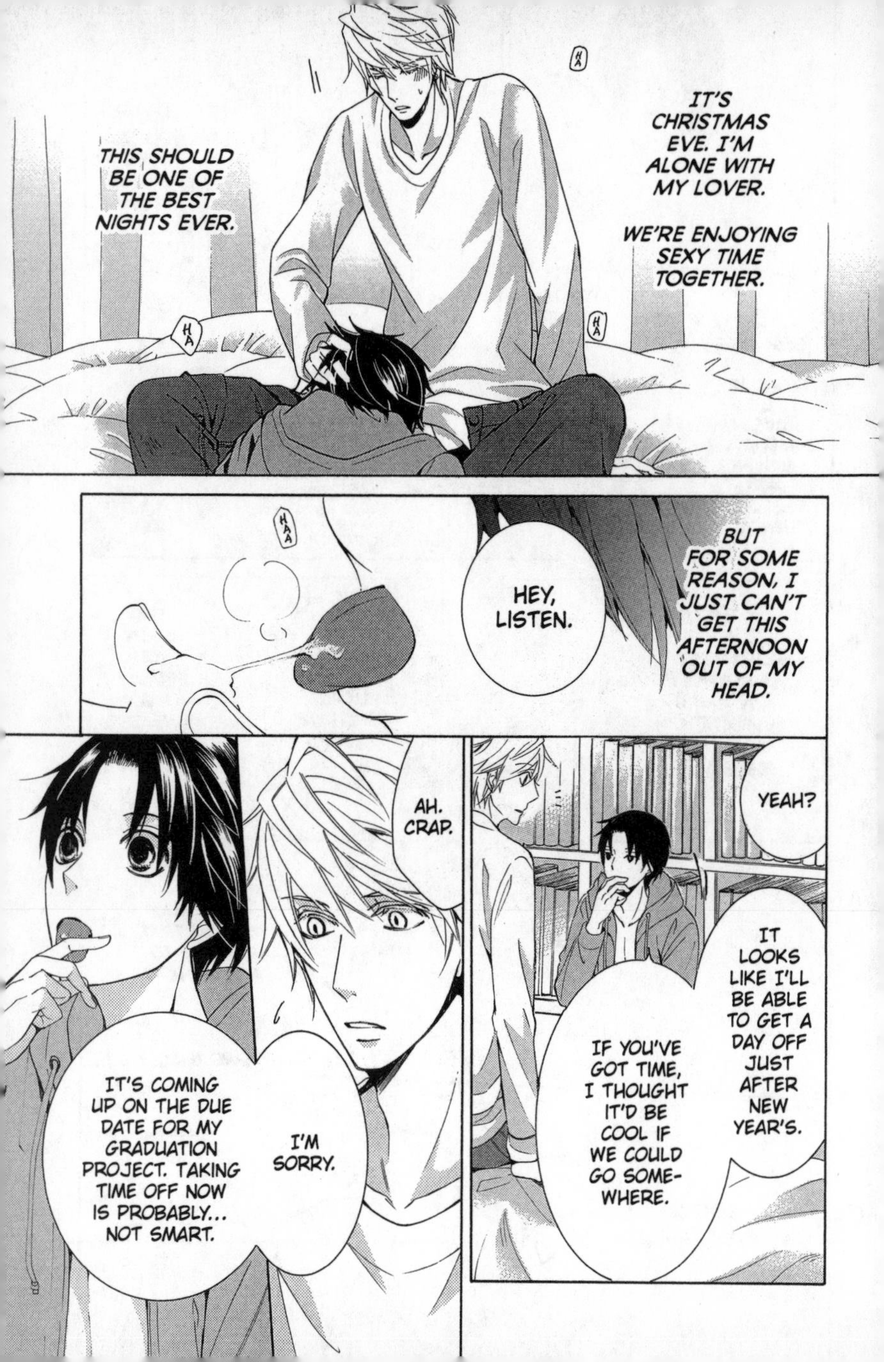
HA
IT'S CHRISTMAS EVE. I'M ALONE WITH MY LOVER.
WE'RE ENJOYING SEXY TIME TOGETHER.
HA
THIS SHOULD BE ONE OF THE BEST NIGHTS EVER.
HA
BUT FOR SOME REASON, I JUST CAN'T GET THIS AFTERNOON OUT OF MY HEAD.
HEY, LISTEN.
HAA
YEAH?
IT LOOKS LIKE I'LL BE ABLE TO GET A DAY OFF JUST AFTER NEW YEAR'S.
IF YOU'VE GOT TIME, I THOUGHT IT'D BE COOL IF WE COULD GO SOME-WHERE.
AH. CRAP.
I'M SORRY.
IT'S COMING UP ON THE DUE DATE FOR MY GRADUATION PROJECT. TAKING TIME OFF NOW IS PROBABLY... NOT SMART.

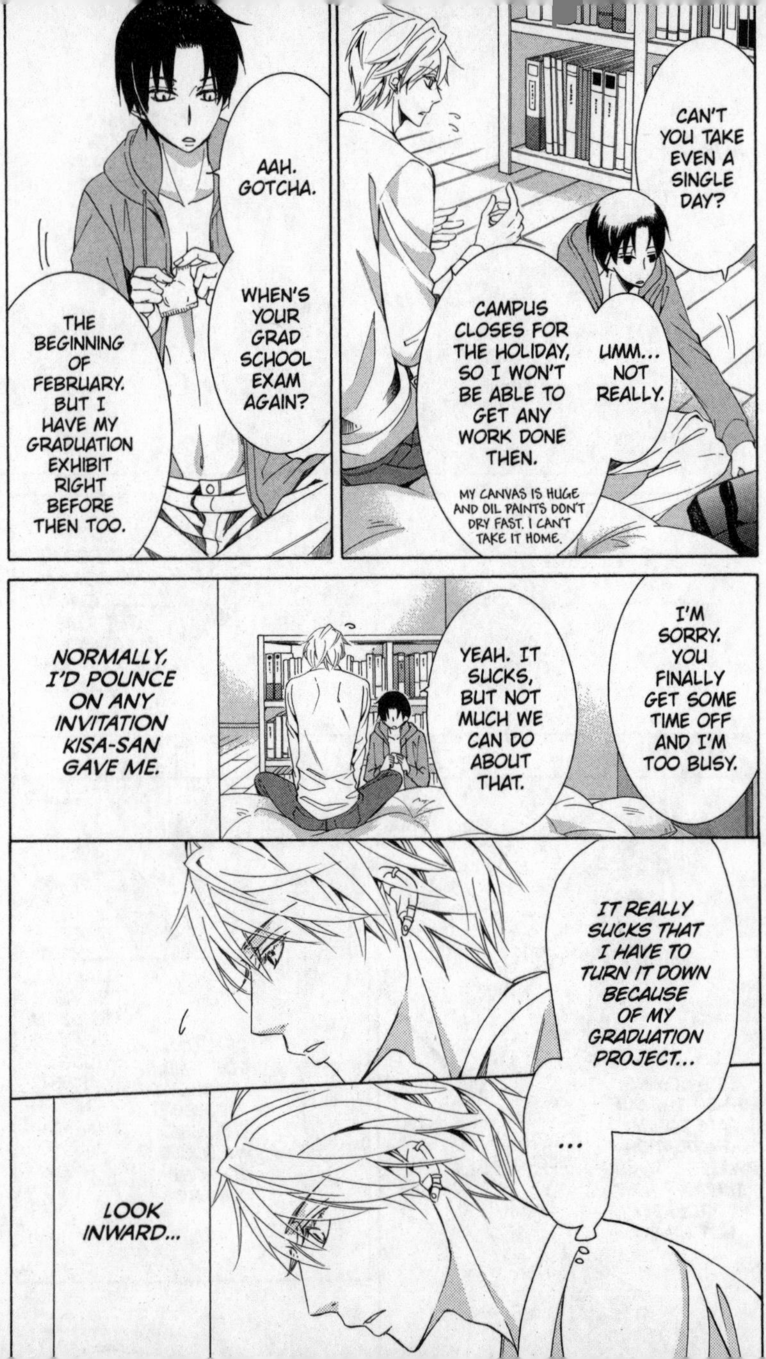
CAN'T YOU TAKE EVEN A SINGLE DAY?
UMM... NOT REALLY.
CAMPUS CLOSES FOR THE HOLIDAY, SO I WON'T BE ABLE TO GET ANY WORK DONE THEN.
MY CANVAS IS HUGE AND OIL PAINTS DON'T DRY FAST. I CAN'T TAKE IT HOME.
AAH. GOTCHA.
WHEN'S YOUR GRAD SCHOOL EXAM AGAIN?
THE BEGINNING OF FEBRUARY. BUT I HAVE MY GRADUATION EXHIBIT RIGHT BEFORE THEN TOO.
I'M SORRY. YOU FINALLY GET SOME TIME OFF AND I'M TOO BUSY.
YEAH. IT SUCKS, BUT NOT MUCH WE CAN DO ABOUT THAT.
NORMALLY, I'D POUNCE ON ANY INVITATION KISA-SAN GAVE ME.
IT REALLY SUCKS THAT I HAVE TO TURN IT DOWN BECAUSE OF MY GRADUATION PROJECT...
...
LOOK INWARD...

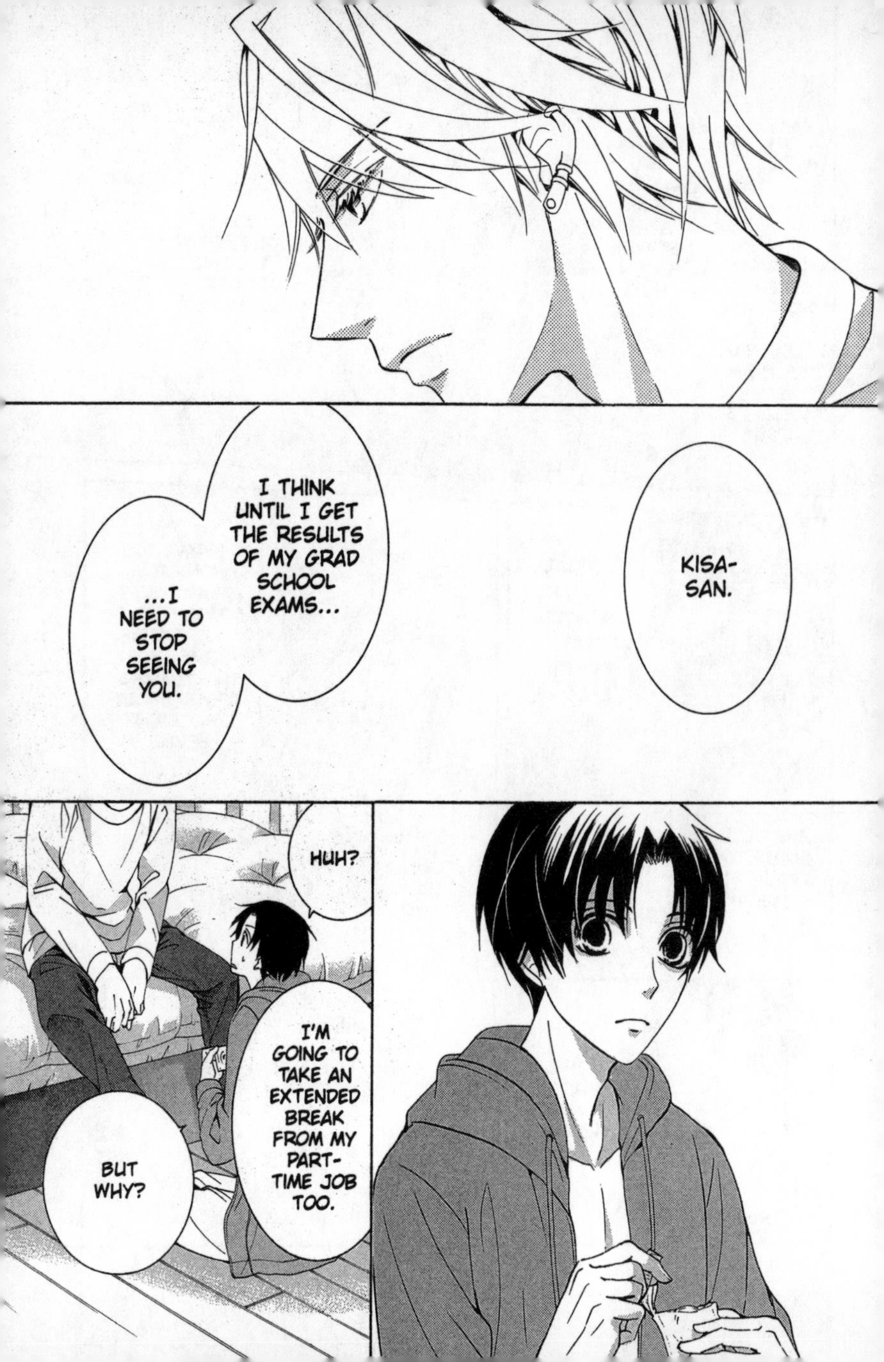
KISA-SAN.
I THINK UNTIL I GET THE RESULTS OF MY GRAD SCHOOL EXAMS...
...I NEED TO STOP SEEING YOU.
HUH?
I'M GOING TO TAKE AN EXTENDED BREAK FROM MY PART-TIME JOB TOO.
BUT WHY?

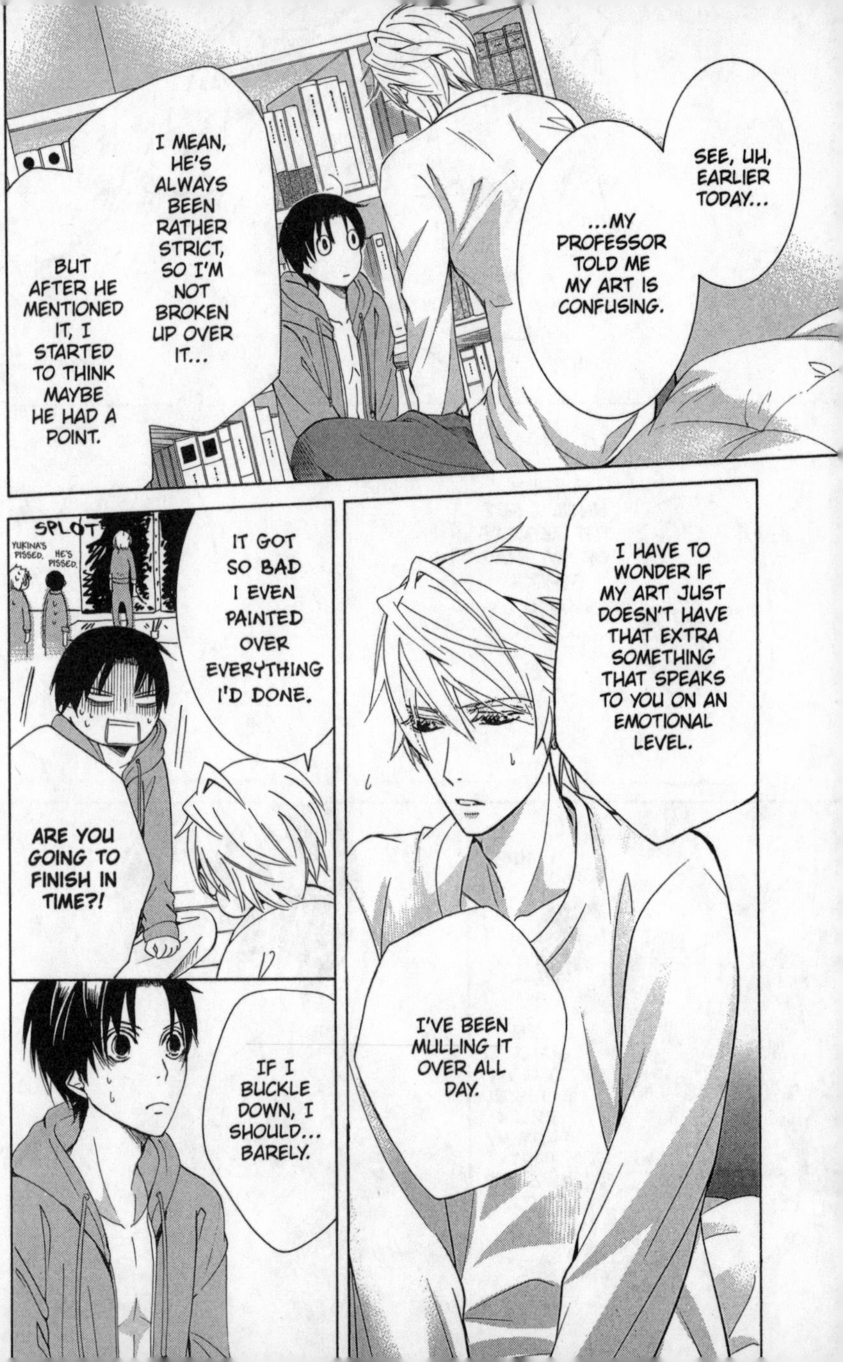
SEE, UH, EARLIER TODAY...
...MY PROFESSOR TOLD ME MY ART IS CONFUSING.
I MEAN, HE'S ALWAYS BEEN RATHER STRICT, SO I'M NOT BROKEN UP OVER IT...
BUT AFTER HE MENTIONED IT, I STARTED TO THINK MAYBE HE HAD A POINT.
I HAVE TO WONDER IF MY ART JUST DOESN'T HAVE THAT EXTRA SOMETHING THAT SPEAKS TO YOU ON AN EMOTIONAL LEVEL.
I'VE BEEN MULLING IT OVER ALL DAY.
IT GOT SO BAD I EVEN PAINTED OVER EVERYTHING I'D DONE.
SPLOT
HE'S PISSED.
YUKINA'S PISSED.
ARE YOU GOING TO FINISH IN TIME?!
IF I BUCKLE DOWN, I SHOULD... BARELY.

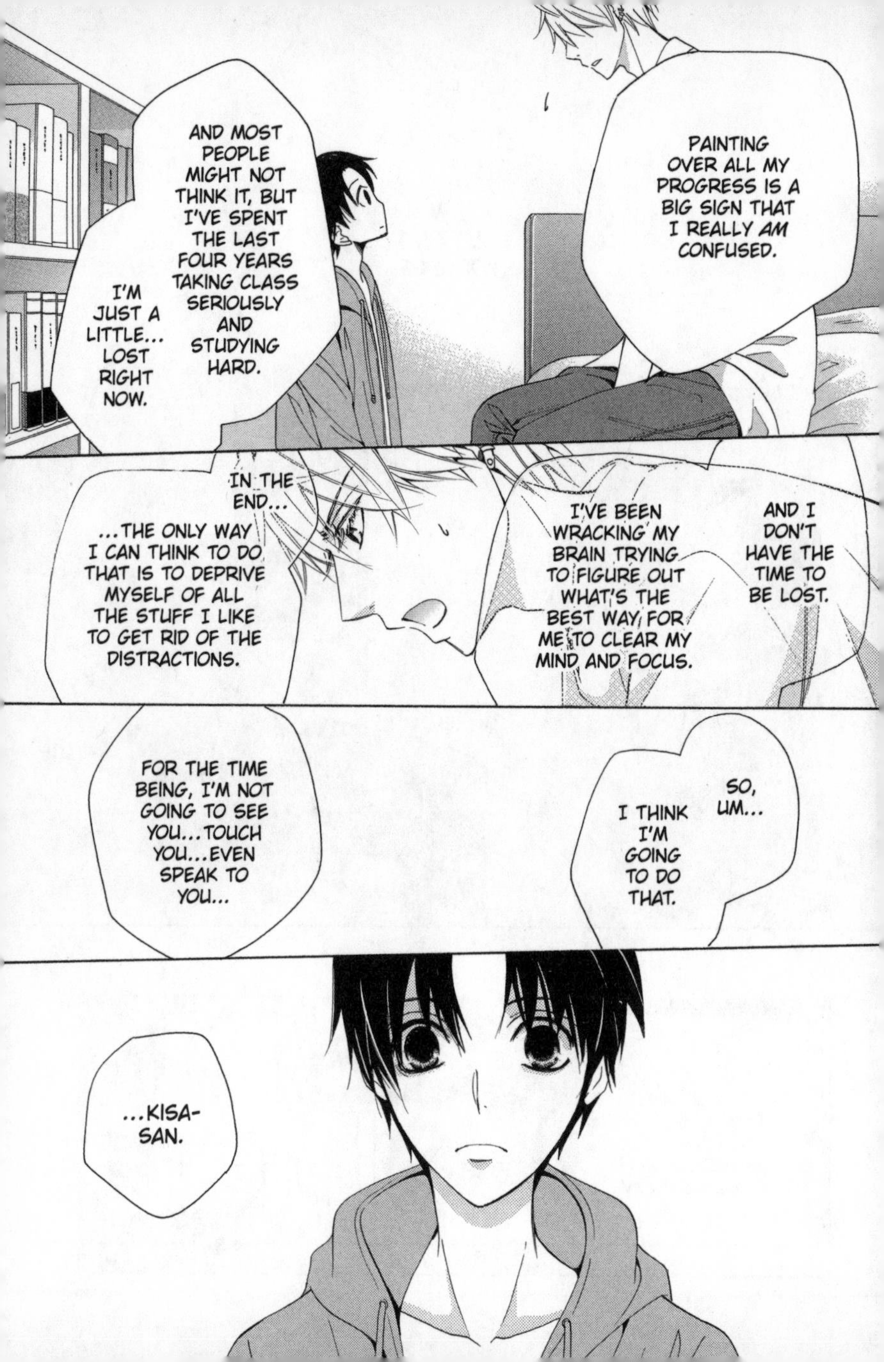
PAINTING OVER ALL MY PROGRESS IS A BIG SIGN THAT I REALLY *AM* CONFUSED.
AND MOST PEOPLE MIGHT NOT THINK IT, BUT I'VE SPENT THE LAST FOUR YEARS TAKING CLASS SERIOUSLY AND STUDYING HARD.
I'M JUST A LITTLE... LOST RIGHT NOW.
AND I DON'T HAVE THE TIME TO BE LOST.
I'VE BEEN WRACKING MY BRAIN TRYING TO FIGURE OUT WHAT'S THE BEST WAY FOR ME TO CLEAR MY MIND AND FOCUS.
IN THE END...
...THE ONLY WAY I CAN THINK TO DO THAT IS TO DEPRIVE MYSELF OF ALL THE STUFF I LIKE TO GET RID OF THE DISTRACTIONS.
SO, UM...
I THINK I'M GOING TO DO THAT.
FOR THE TIME BEING, I'M NOT GOING TO SEE YOU...TOUCH YOU...EVEN SPEAK TO YOU...
...KISA-SAN.

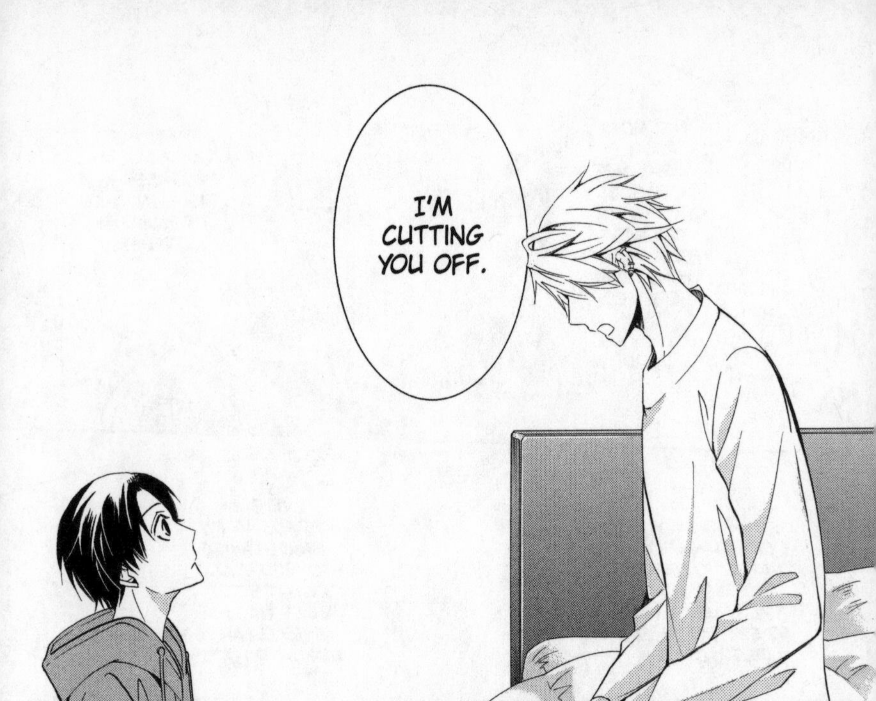
I'M CUTTING YOU OFF.
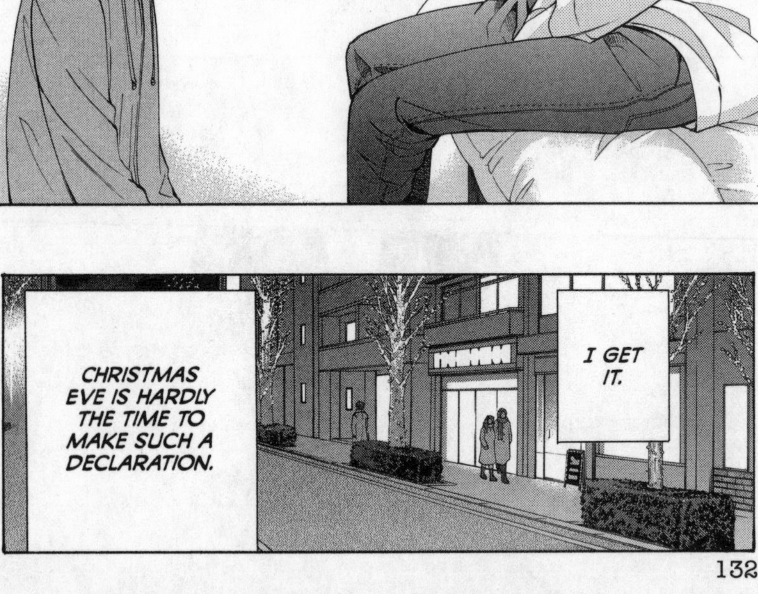
I GET IT.
CHRISTMAS EVE IS HARDLY THE TIME TO MAKE SUCH A DECLARATION.

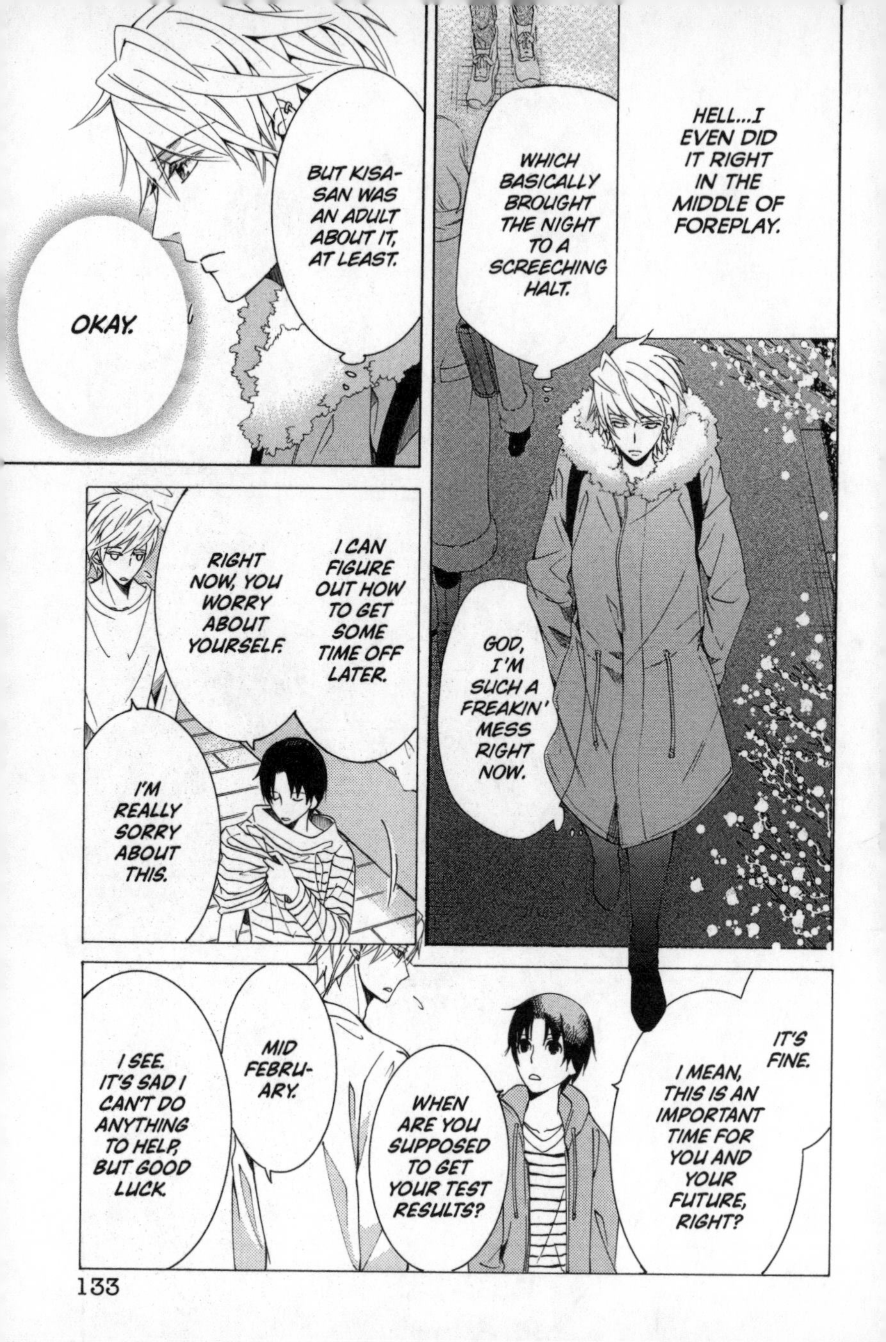
HELL...I EVEN DID IT RIGHT IN THE MIDDLE OF FOREPLAY.
WHICH BASICALLY BROUGHT THE NIGHT TO A SCREECHING HALT.
GOD, I'M SUCH A FREAKIN' MESS RIGHT NOW.
BUT KISA-SAN WAS AN ADULT ABOUT IT, AT LEAST.
OKAY.
I CAN FIGURE OUT HOW TO GET SOME TIME OFF LATER.
RIGHT NOW, YOU WORRY ABOUT YOURSELF.
I'M REALLY SORRY ABOUT THIS.
IT'S FINE.
I MEAN, THIS IS AN IMPORTANT TIME FOR YOU AND YOUR FUTURE, RIGHT?
WHEN ARE YOU SUPPOSED TO GET YOUR TEST RESULTS?
MID FEBRU-ARY.
I SEE. IT'S SAD I CAN'T DO ANYTHING TO HELP, BUT GOOD LUCK.

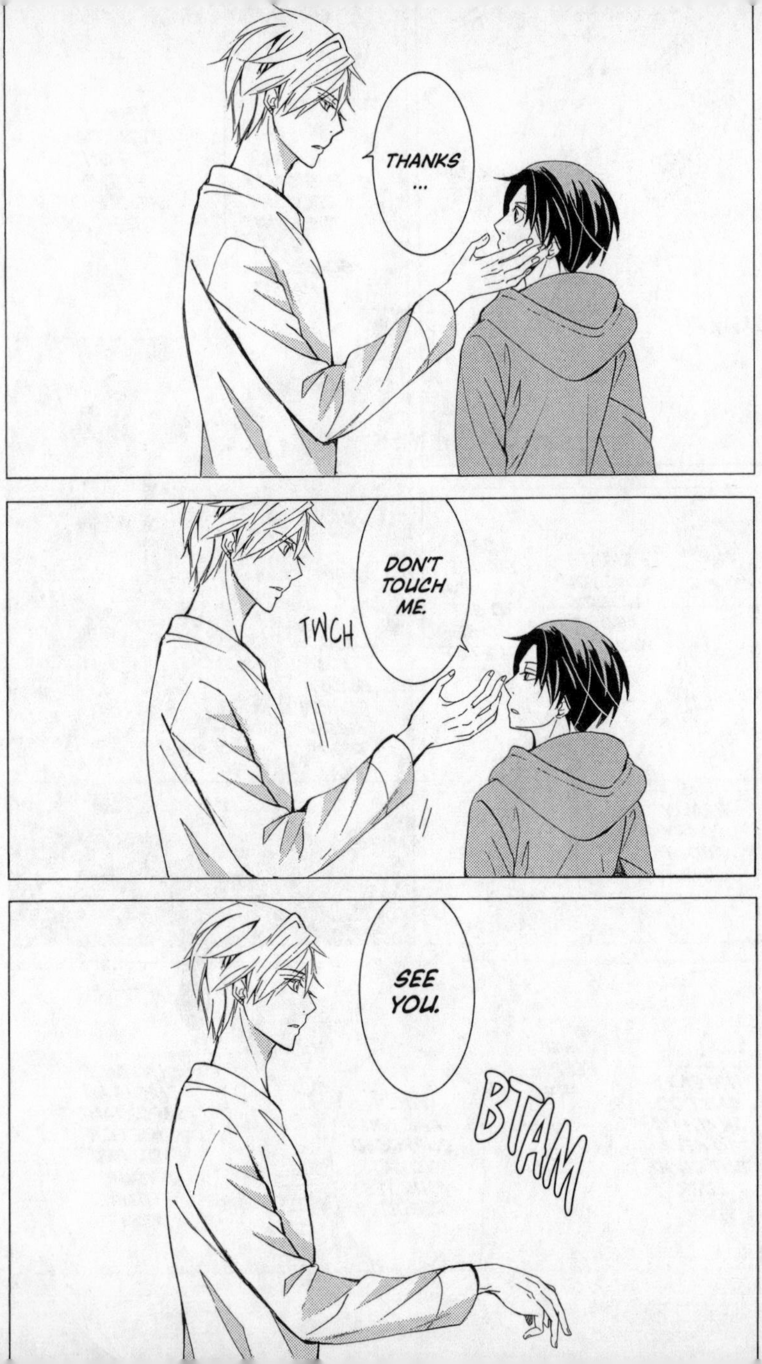
THANKS ...
DON'T TOUCH ME.
TWCH
SEE YOU.
BTAM

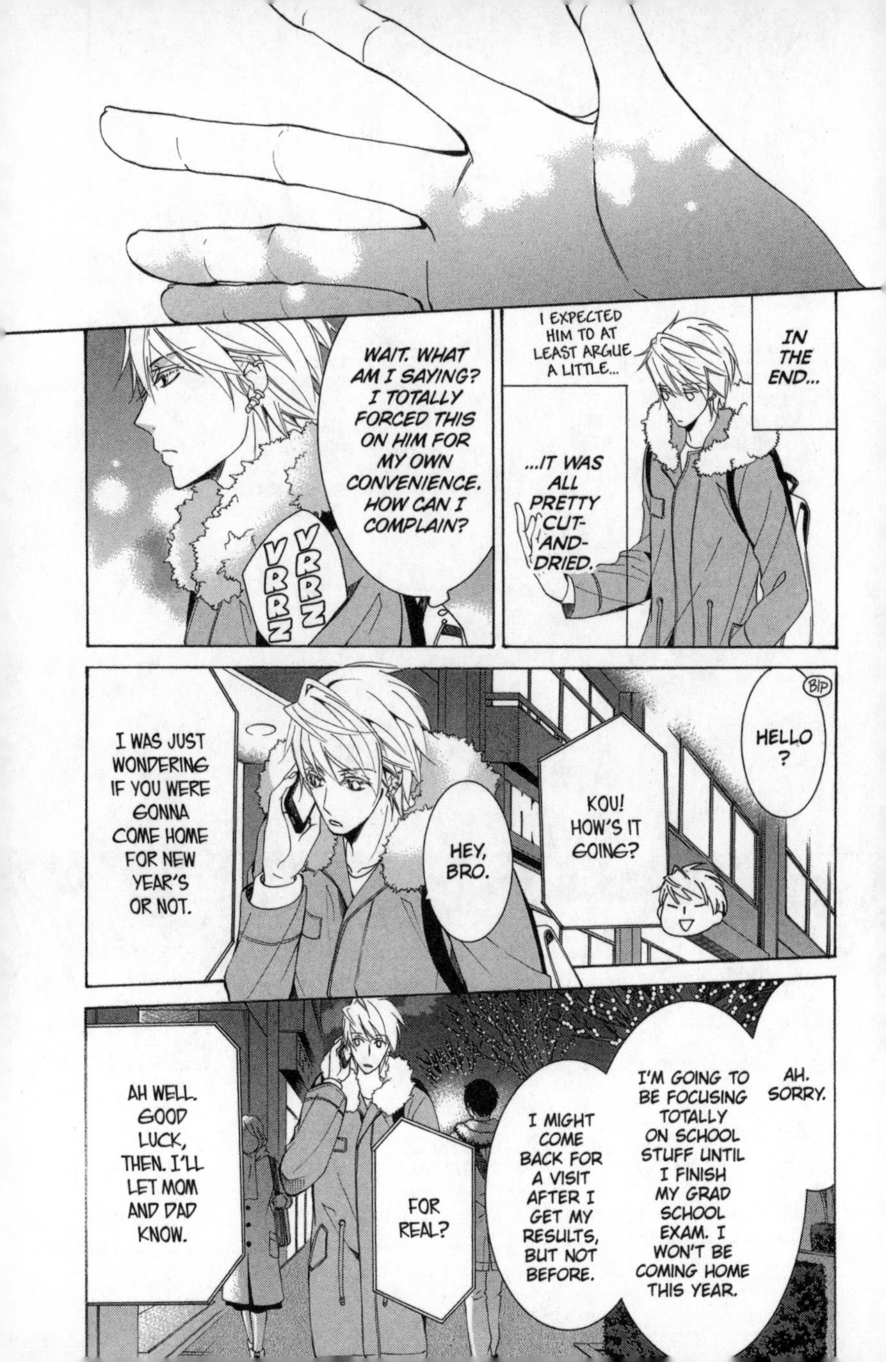

IN THE END...
I EXPECTED HIM TO AT LEAST ARGUE A LITTLE...
...IT WAS ALL PRETTY CUT-AND-DRIED.
WAIT. WHAT AM I SAYING? I TOTALLY FORCED THIS ON HIM FOR MY OWN CONVENIENCE. HOW CAN I COMPLAIN?
VRRZ VRRZ
BIP
HELLO?
KOU! HOW'S IT GOING?
HEY, BRO.
I WAS JUST WONDERING IF YOU WERE GONNA COME HOME FOR NEW YEAR'S OR NOT.
AH. SORRY.
I'M GOING TO BE FOCUSING TOTALLY ON SCHOOL STUFF UNTIL I FINISH MY GRAD SCHOOL EXAM. I WON'T BE COMING HOME THIS YEAR.
I MIGHT COME BACK FOR A VISIT AFTER I GET MY RESULTS, BUT NOT BEFORE.
FOR REAL?
AH WELL. GOOD LUCK, THEN. I'LL LET MOM AND DAD KNOW.

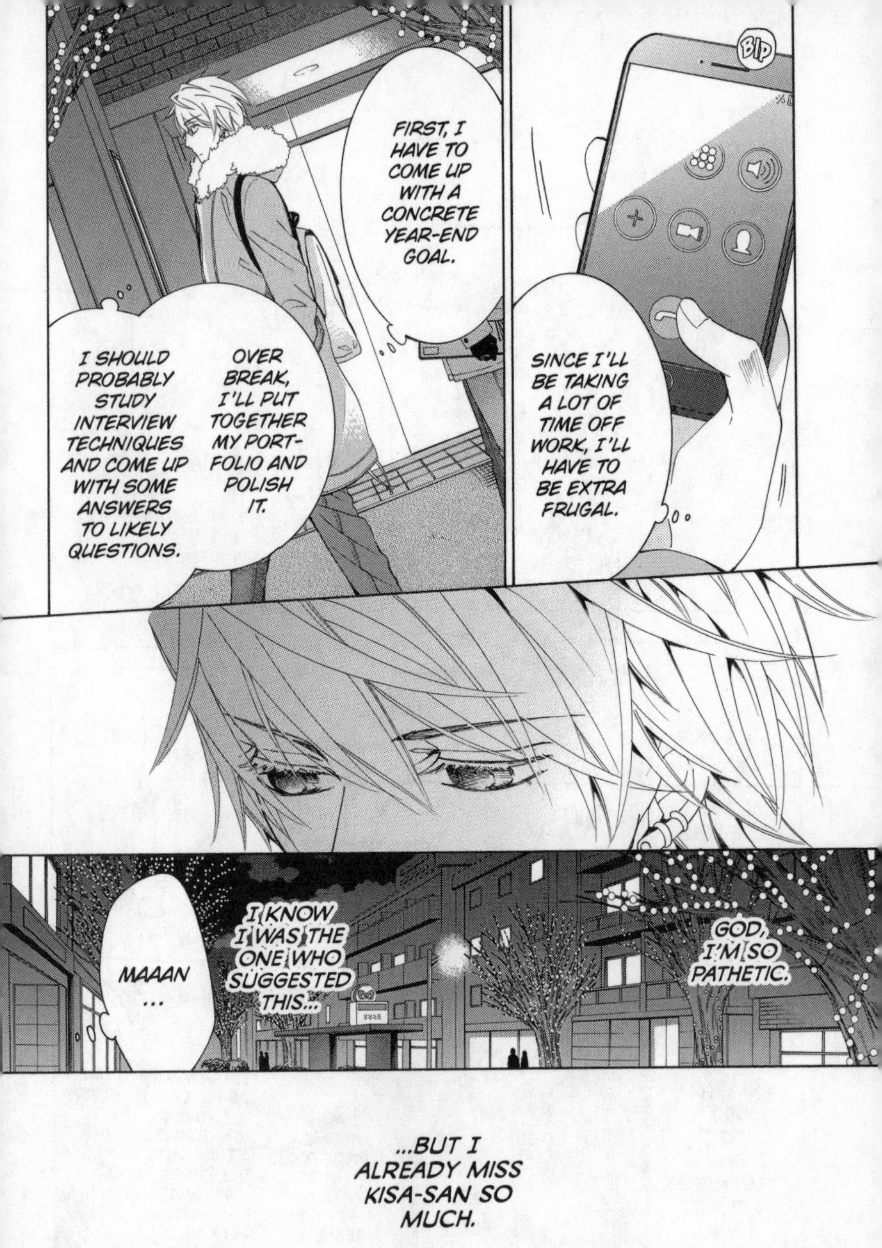
BIP
SINCE I'LL BE TAKING A LOT OF TIME OFF WORK, I'LL HAVE TO BE EXTRA FRUGAL.
FIRST, I HAVE TO COME UP WITH A CONCRETE YEAR-END GOAL.
OVER BREAK, I'LL PUT TOGETHER MY PORT-FOLIO AND POLISH IT.
I SHOULD PROBABLY STUDY INTERVIEW TECHNIQUES AND COME UP WITH SOME ANSWERS TO LIKELY QUESTIONS.
GOD, I'M SO PATHETIC.
I KNOW I WAS THE ONE WHO SUGGESTED THIS...
MAAAN ...
...BUT I ALREADY MISS KISA-SAN SO MUCH.

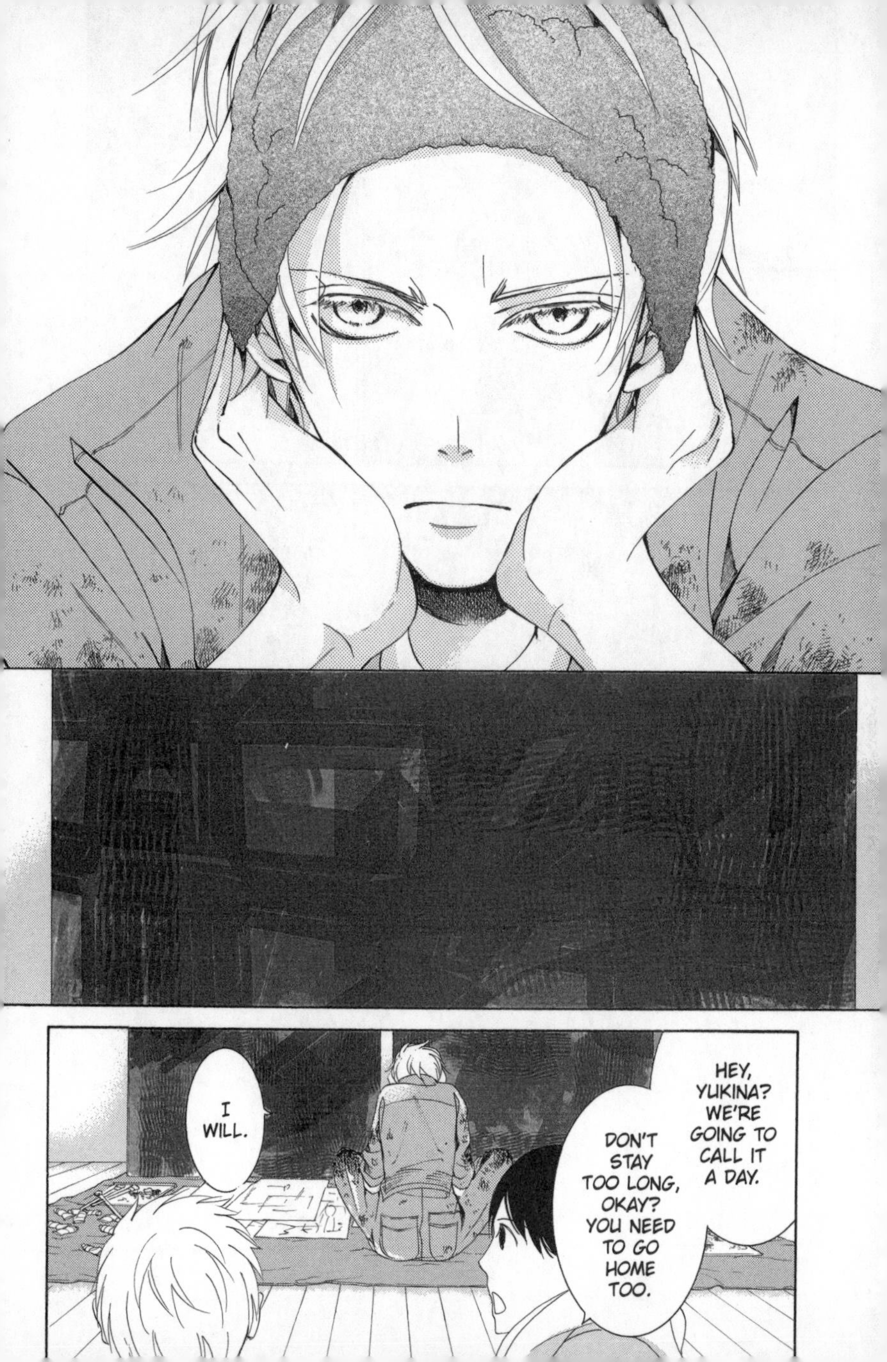
HEY, YUKINA? WE'RE GOING TO CALL IT A DAY.
DON'T STAY TOO LONG, OKAY? YOU NEED TO GO HOME TOO.
I WILL.

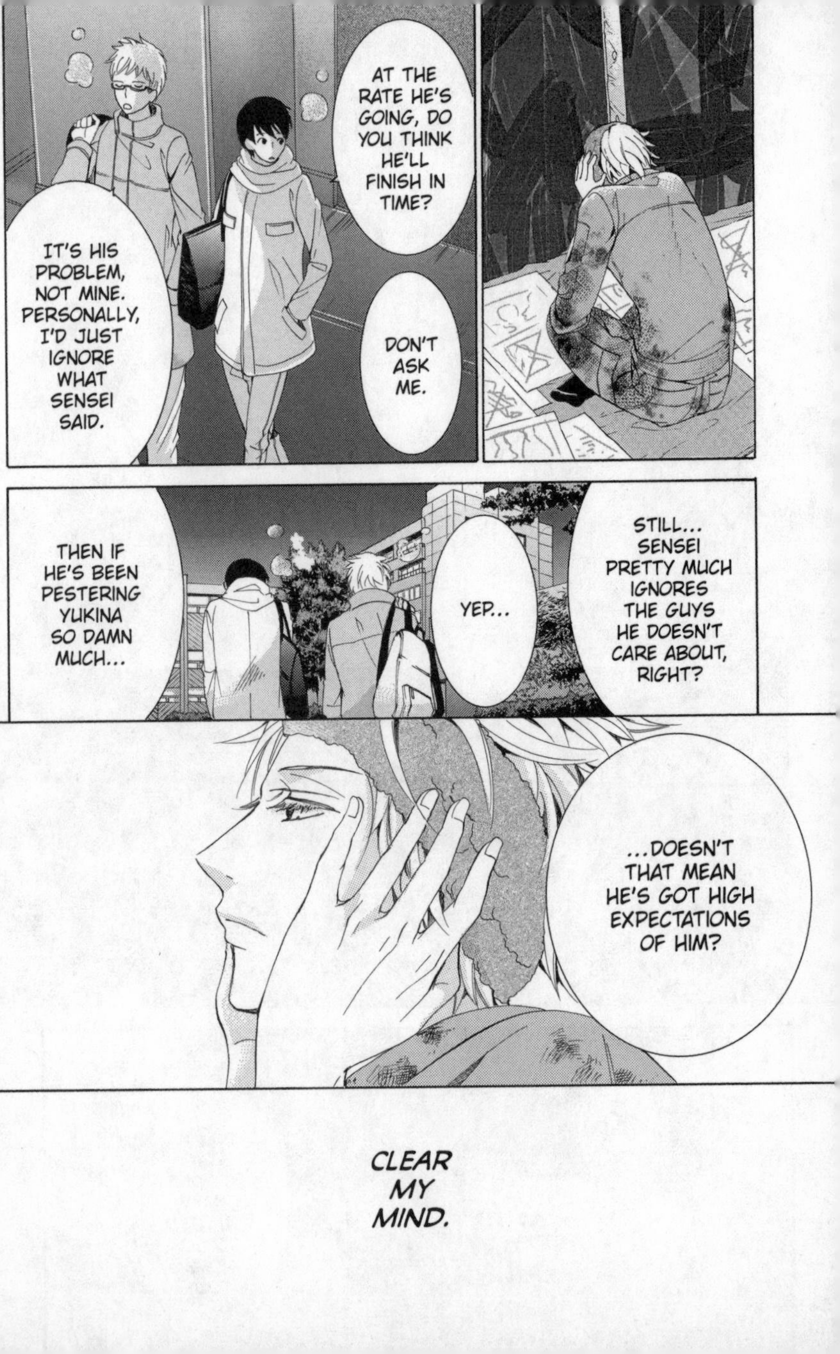
AT THE RATE HE'S GOING, DO YOU THINK HE'LL FINISH IN TIME?
DON'T ASK ME.
IT'S HIS PROBLEM, NOT MINE. PERSONALLY, I'D JUST IGNORE WHAT SENSEI SAID.
STILL... SENSEI PRETTY MUCH IGNORES THE GUYS HE DOESN'T CARE ABOUT, RIGHT?
YEP...
THEN IF HE'S BEEN PESTERING YUKINA SO DAMN MUCH...
...DOESN'T THAT MEAN HE'S GOT HIGH EXPECTATIONS OF HIM?
CLEAR MY MIND.

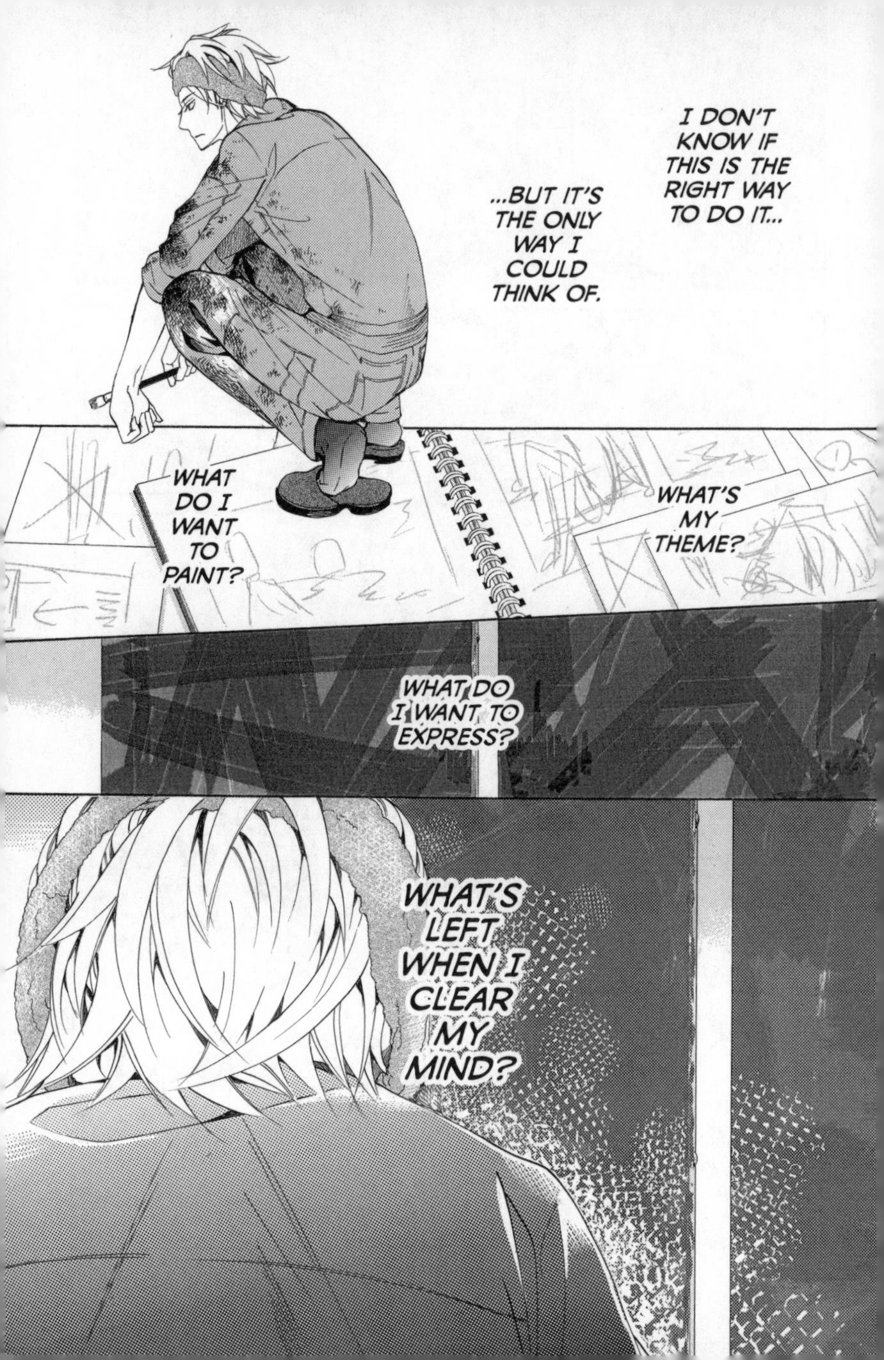
I DON'T KNOW IF THIS IS THE RIGHT WAY TO DO IT...
...BUT IT'S THE ONLY WAY I COULD THINK OF.
WHAT'S MY THEME?
WHAT DO I WANT TO PAINT?
WHAT DO I WANT TO EXPRESS?
WHAT'S LEFT WHEN I CLEAR MY MIND?

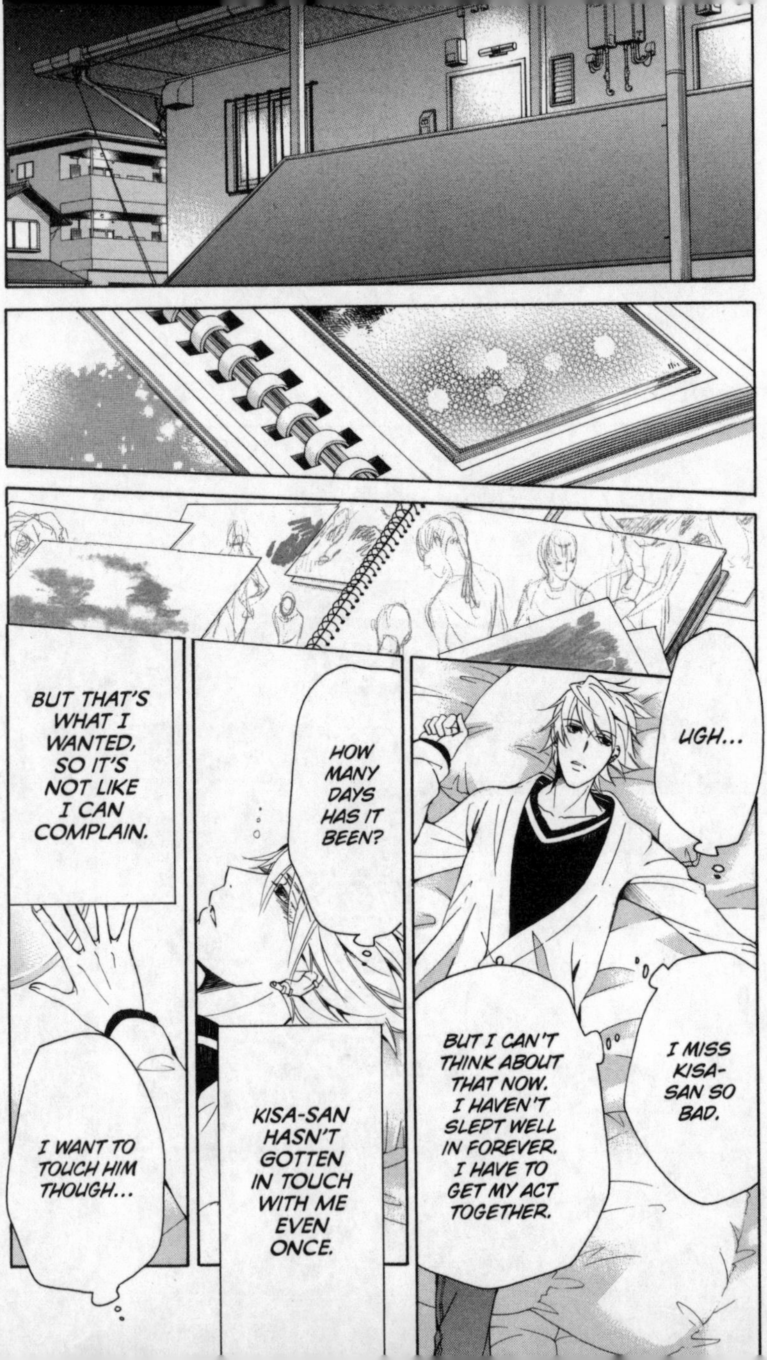
UGH...
I MISS KISA-SAN SO BAD.
BUT I CAN'T THINK ABOUT THAT NOW. I HAVEN'T SLEPT WELL IN FOREVER. I HAVE TO GET MY ACT TOGETHER.
HOW MANY DAYS HAS IT BEEN?
KISA-SAN HASN'T GOTTEN IN TOUCH WITH ME EVEN ONCE.
BUT THAT'S WHAT I WANTED, SO IT'S NOT LIKE I CAN COMPLAIN.
I WANT TO TOUCH HIM THOUGH...

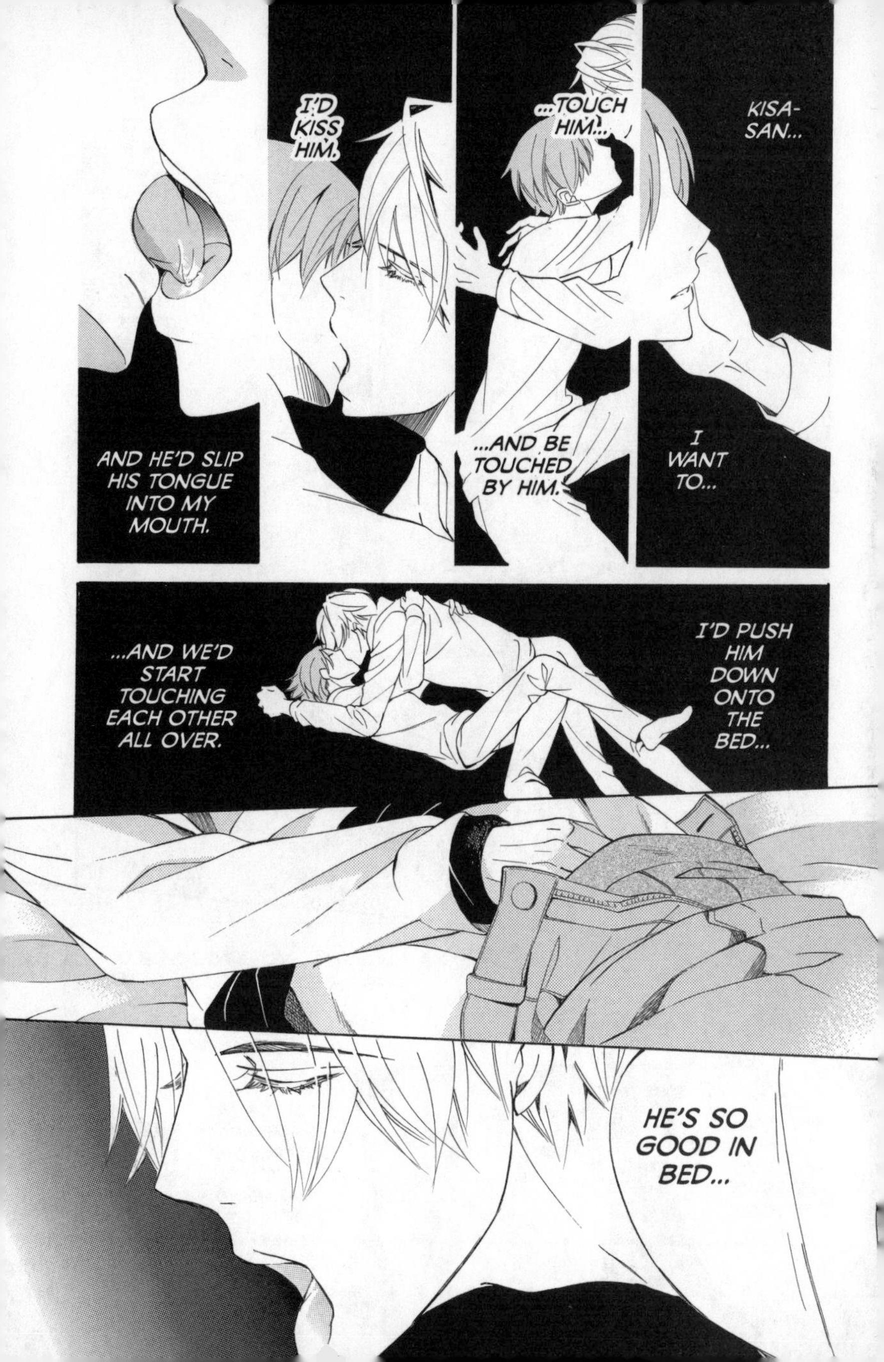
KISA-SAN...
I WANT TO...
...TOUCH HIM...
...AND BE TOUCHED BY HIM.
I'D KISS HIM.
AND HE'D SLIP HIS TONGUE INTO MY MOUTH.
I'D PUSH HIM DOWN ONTO THE BED...
...AND WE'D START TOUCHING EACH OTHER ALL OVER.
HE'S SO GOOD IN BED...

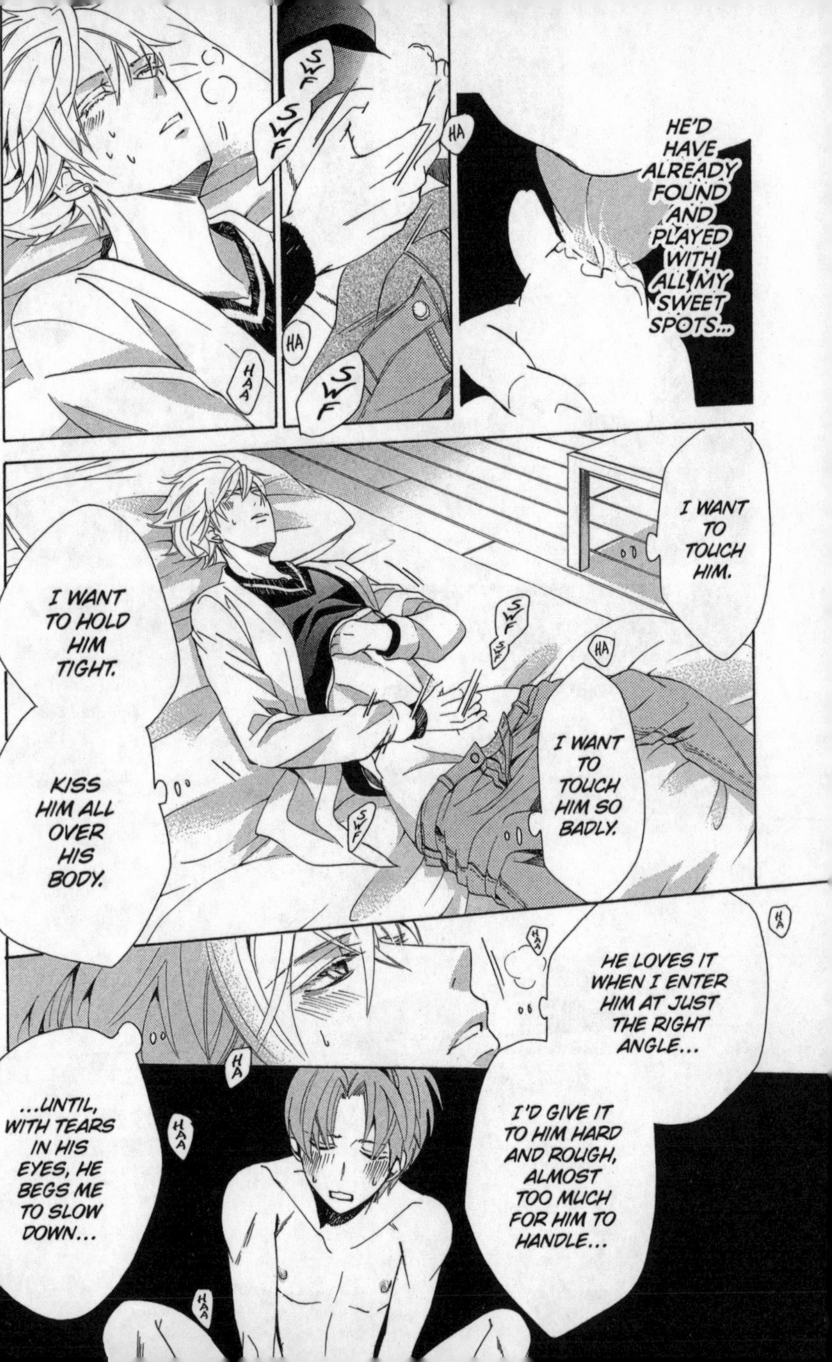
HE'D HAVE ALREADY FOUND AND PLAYED WITH ALL MY SWEET SPOTS...
SWF SWF
HA
HA
SWF
HAA
I WANT TO TOUCH HIM.
I WANT TO HOLD HIM TIGHT.
SWF SWF
HA
KISS HIM ALL OVER HIS BODY.
I WANT TO TOUCH HIM SO BADLY.
SWF
HA
HAA
HE LOVES IT WHEN I ENTER HIM AT JUST THE RIGHT ANGLE...
HA
I'D GIVE IT TO HIM HARD AND ROUGH, ALMOST TOO MUCH FOR HIM TO HANDLE...
...UNTIL, WITH TEARS IN HIS EYES, HE BEGS ME TO SLOW DOWN...
HAA
HAA

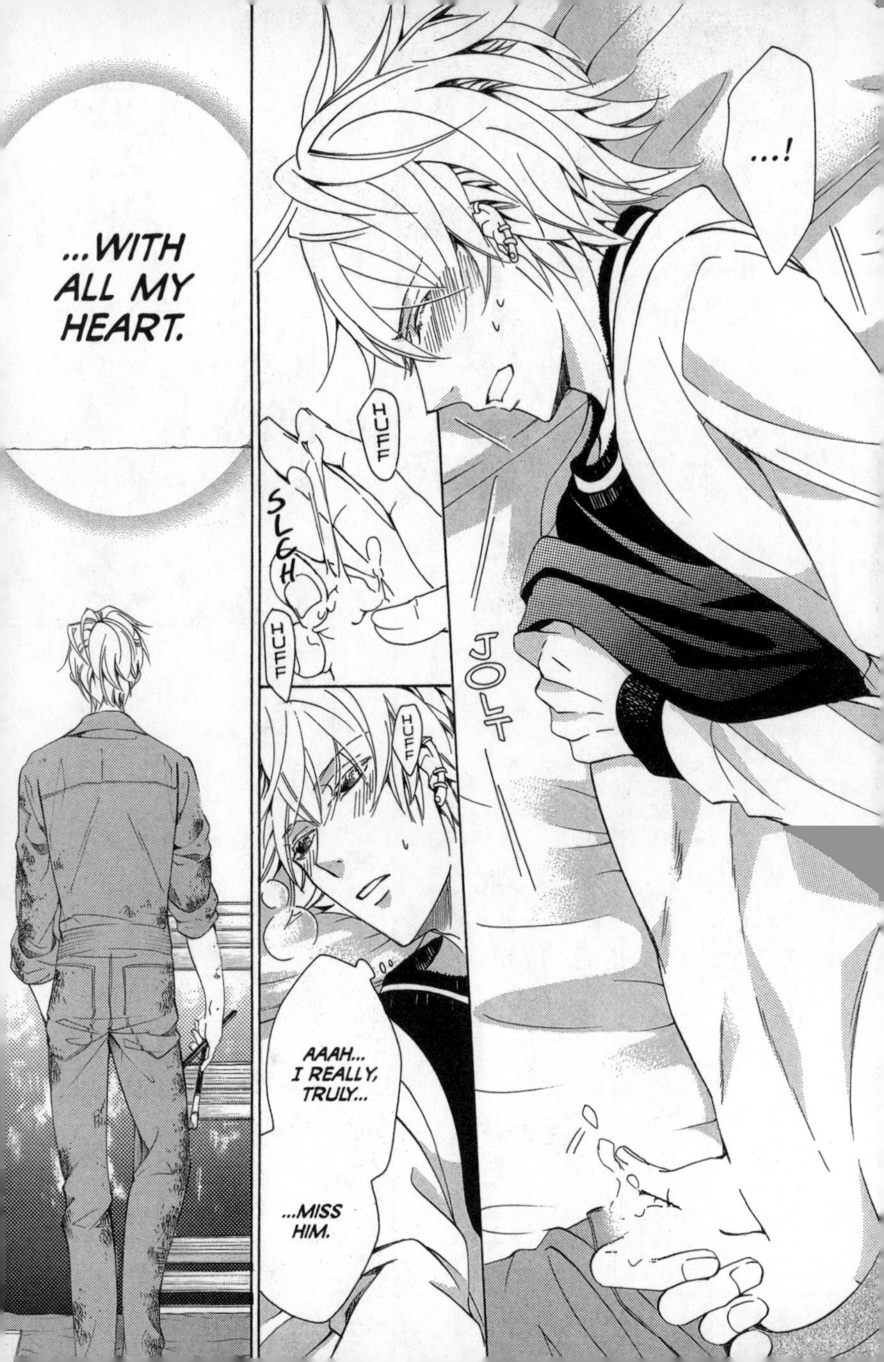
...!
HUFF
SLGH
HUFF
JOLT
HUFF
AAAH... I REALLY, TRULY...
...MISS HIM.
...WITH ALL MY HEART.

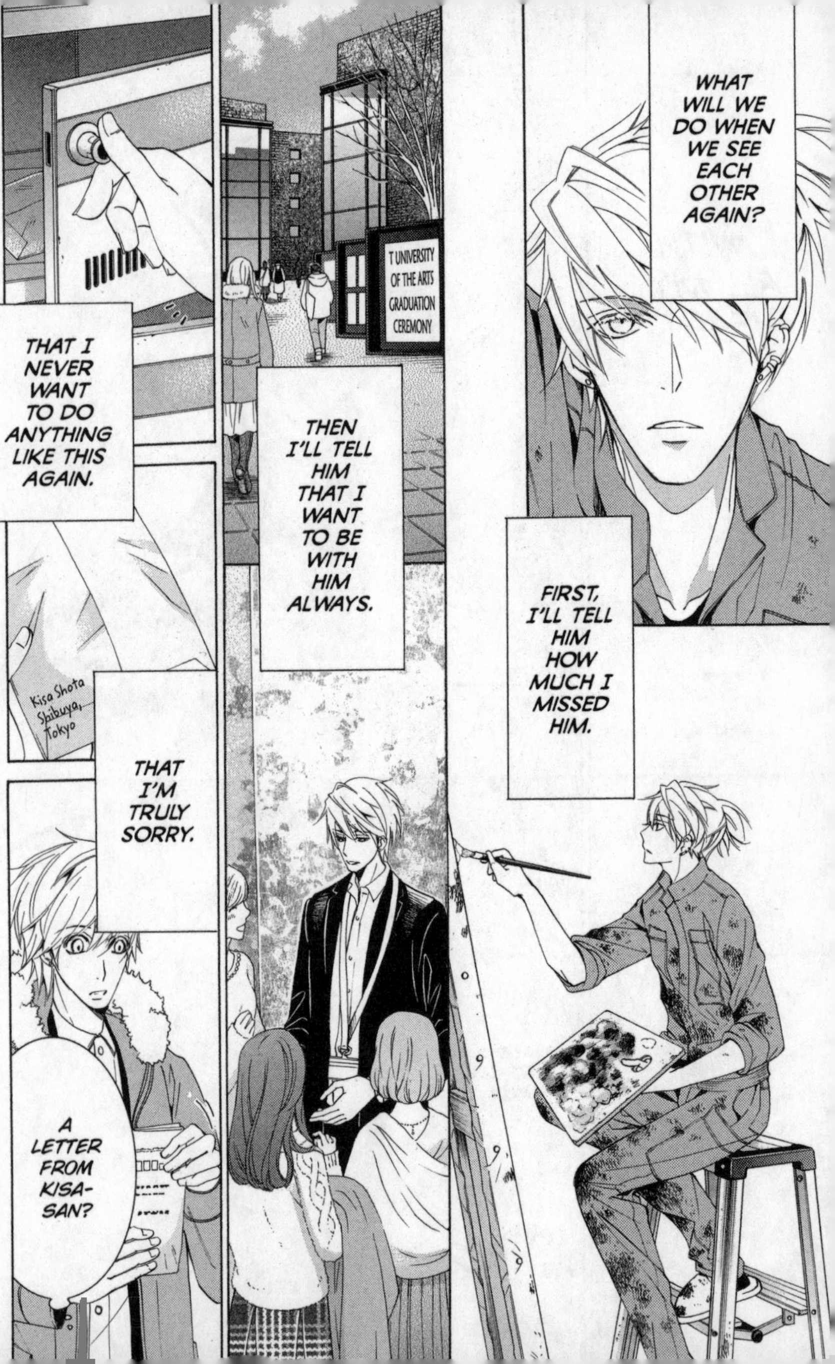
WHAT WILL WE DO WHEN WE SEE EACH OTHER AGAIN?
FIRST, I'LL TELL HIM HOW MUCH I MISSED HIM.
T UNIVERSITY OF THE ARTS GRADUATION CEREMONY
THEN I'LL TELL HIM THAT I WANT TO BE WITH HIM ALWAYS.
THAT I NEVER WANT TO DO ANYTHING LIKE THIS AGAIN.
Kisa Shota Shibuya, Tokyo
THAT I'M TRULY SORRY.
A LETTER FROM KISA-SAN?

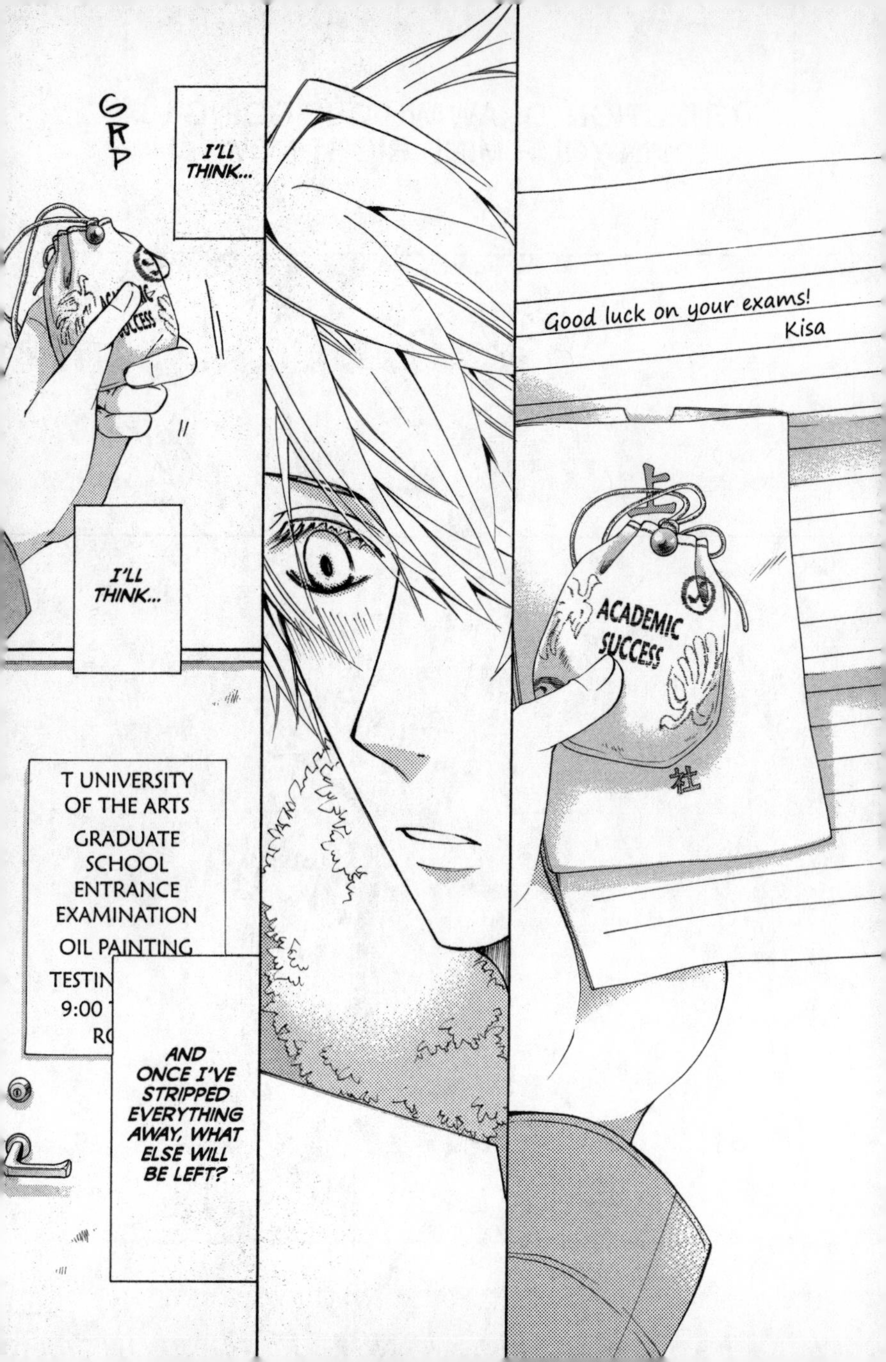
Good luck on your exams!
Kisa
ACADEMIC SUCCESS
I'LL THINK...
GRP
I'LL THINK...
T UNIVERSITY OF THE ARTS
GRADUATE SCHOOL ENTRANCE EXAMINATION
OIL PAINTING
AND ONCE I'VE STRIPPED EVERYTHING AWAY, WHAT ELSE WILL BE LEFT?

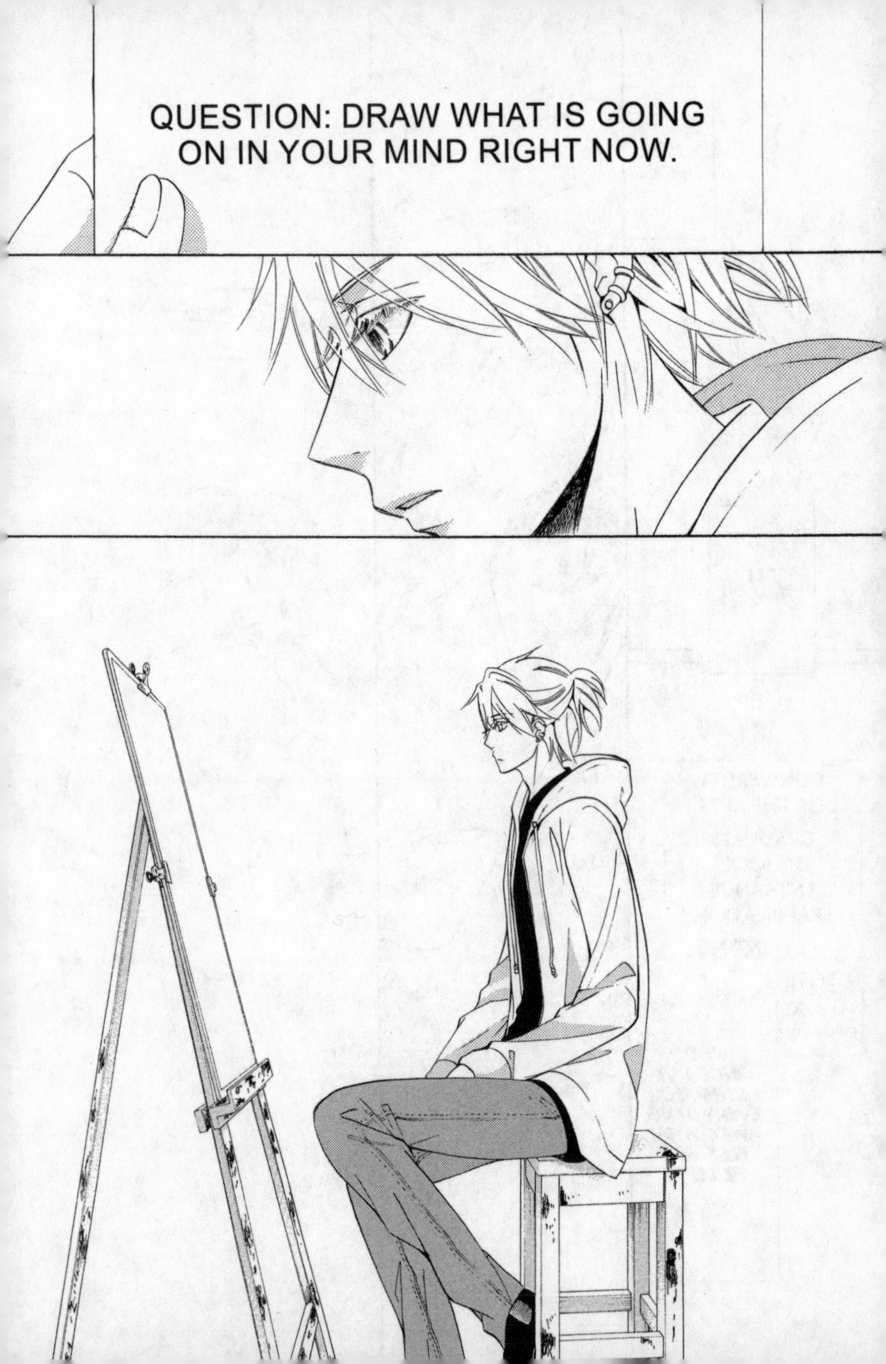
QUESTION: DRAW WHAT IS GOING ON IN YOUR MIND RIGHT NOW.

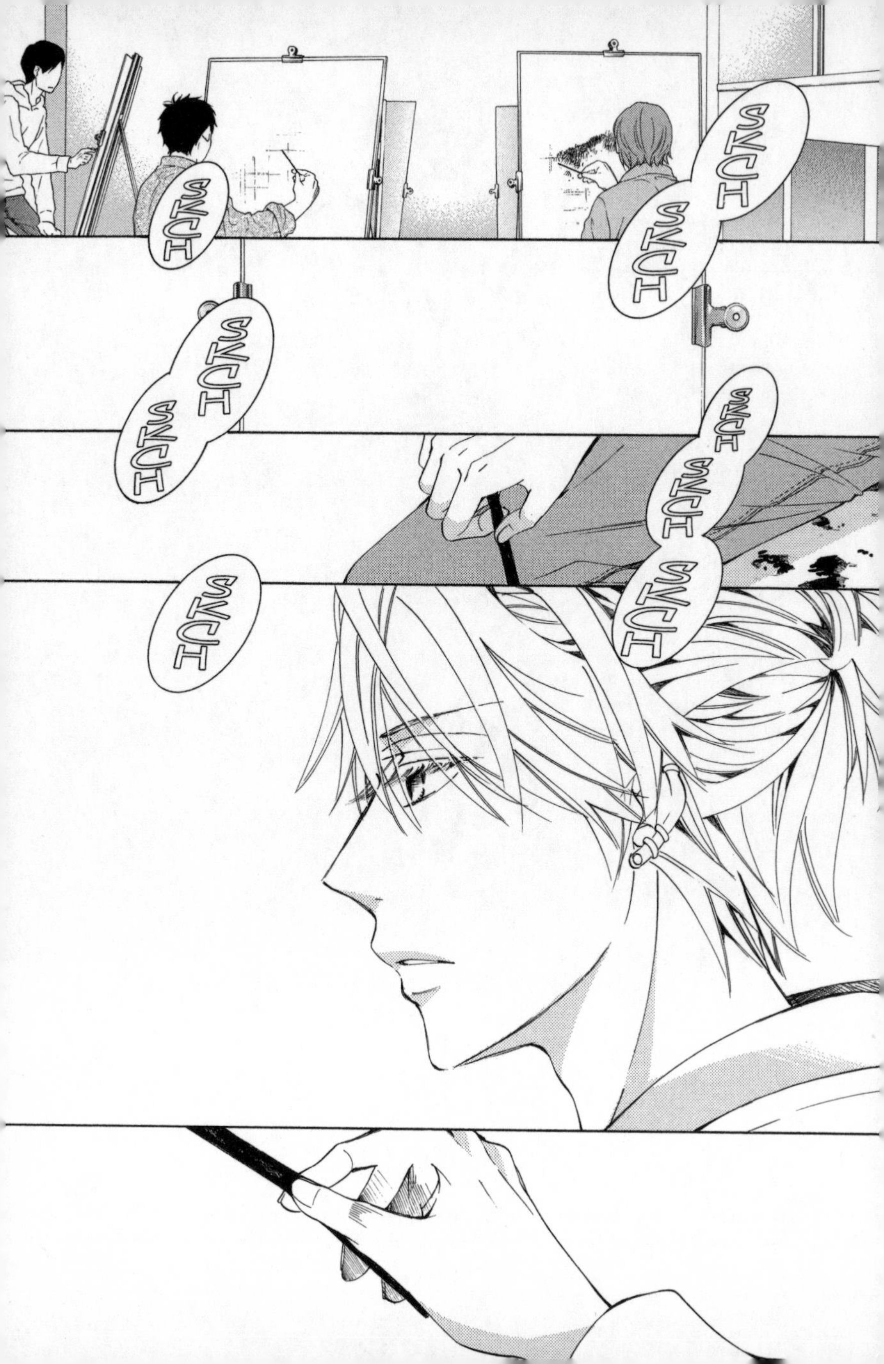
SKCH
SKCH
SKCH
SKCH
SKCH
SKCH
SKCH
SKCH
SKCH

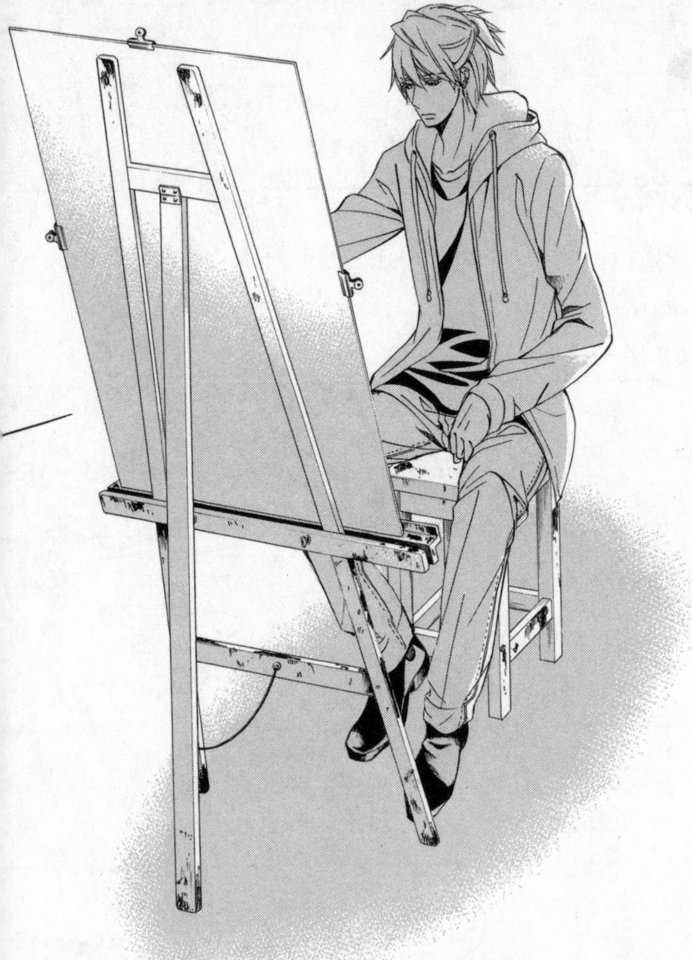

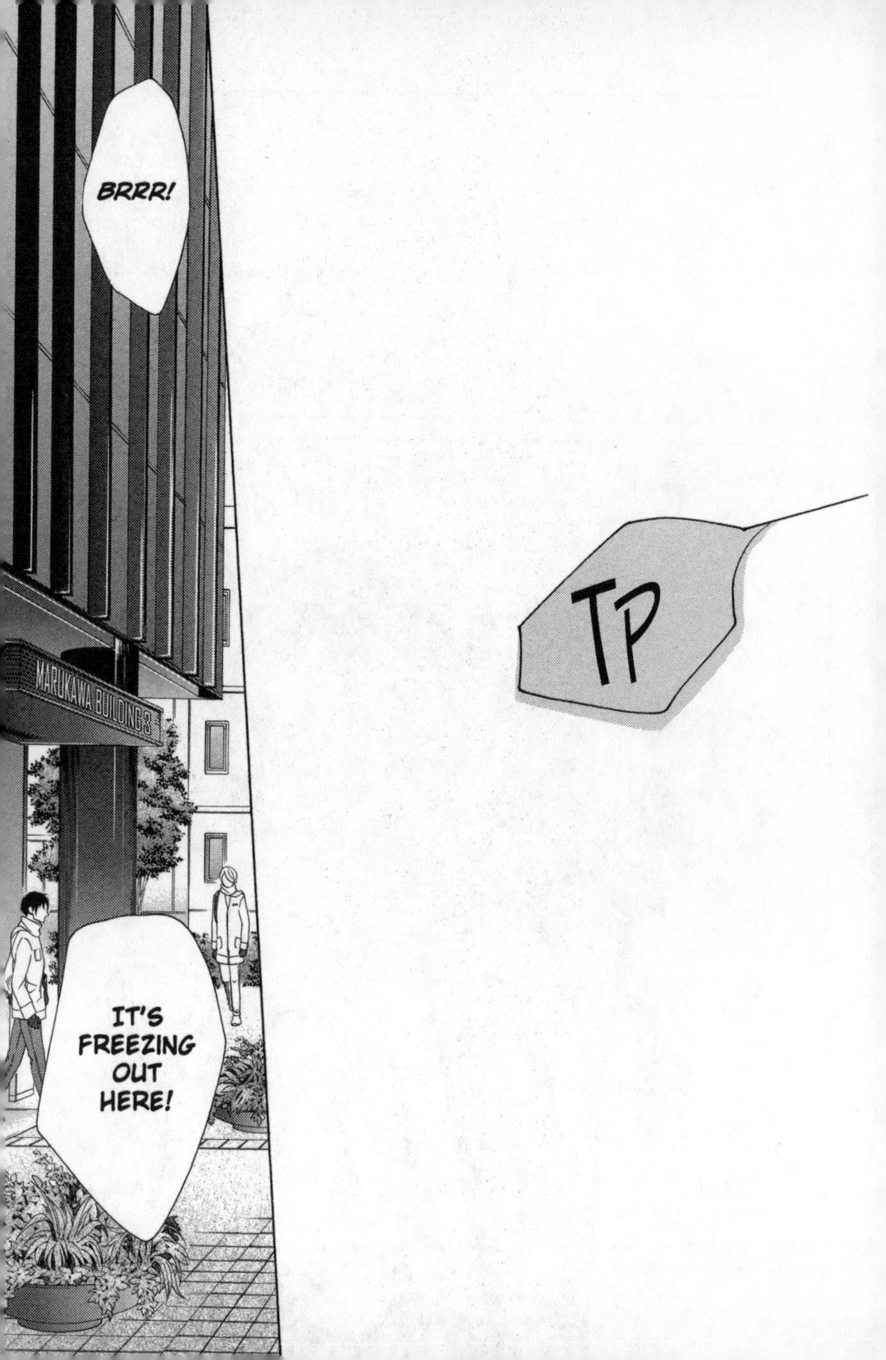
TP
BRRR!
MARUKAWA BUILDING 3
IT'S FREEZING OUT HERE!

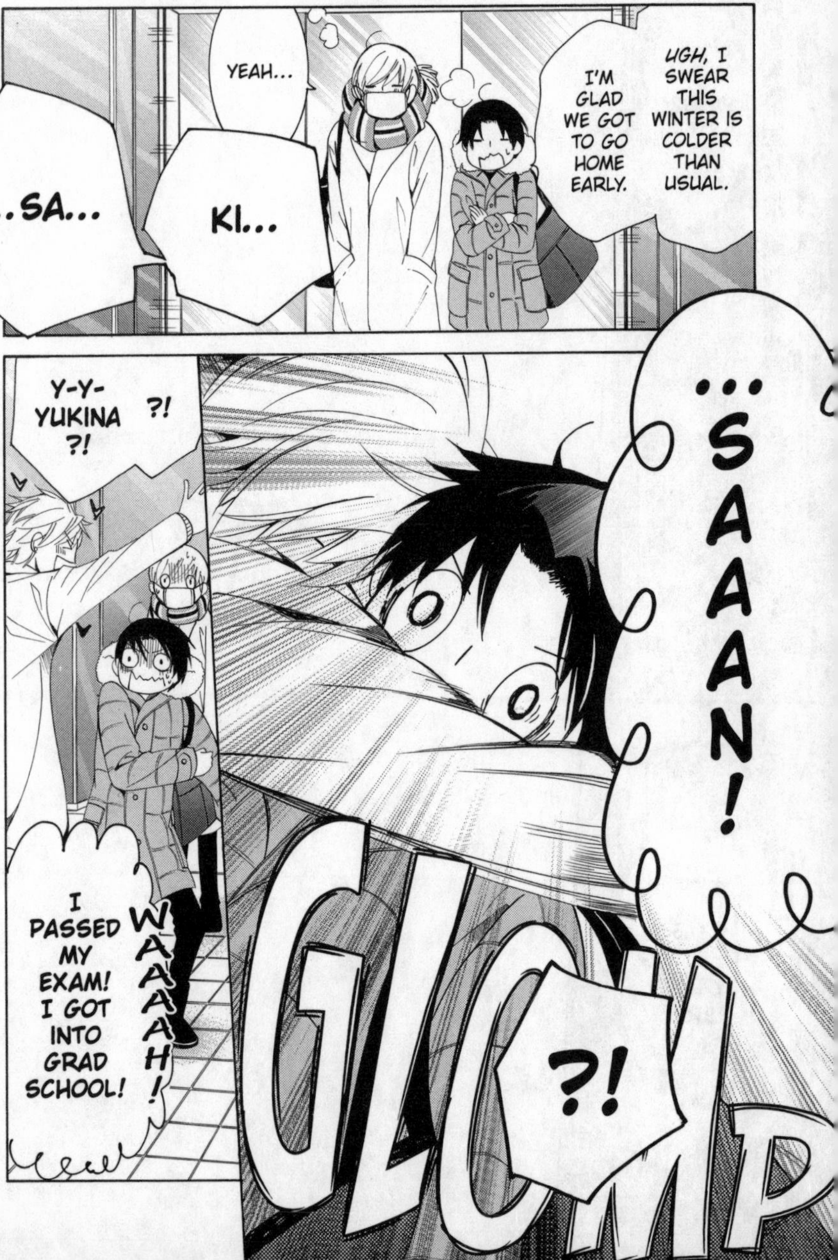
UGH, I SWEAR THIS WINTER IS COLDER THAN USUAL.
I'M GLAD WE GOT TO GO HOME EARLY.
YEAH...
...SA...
KI...
...SAAAN!
?!
GLOMP
Y-Y-YUKINA ?!
?!
I PASSED MY EXAM! I GOT INTO GRAD SCHOOL!
WAAAAH!

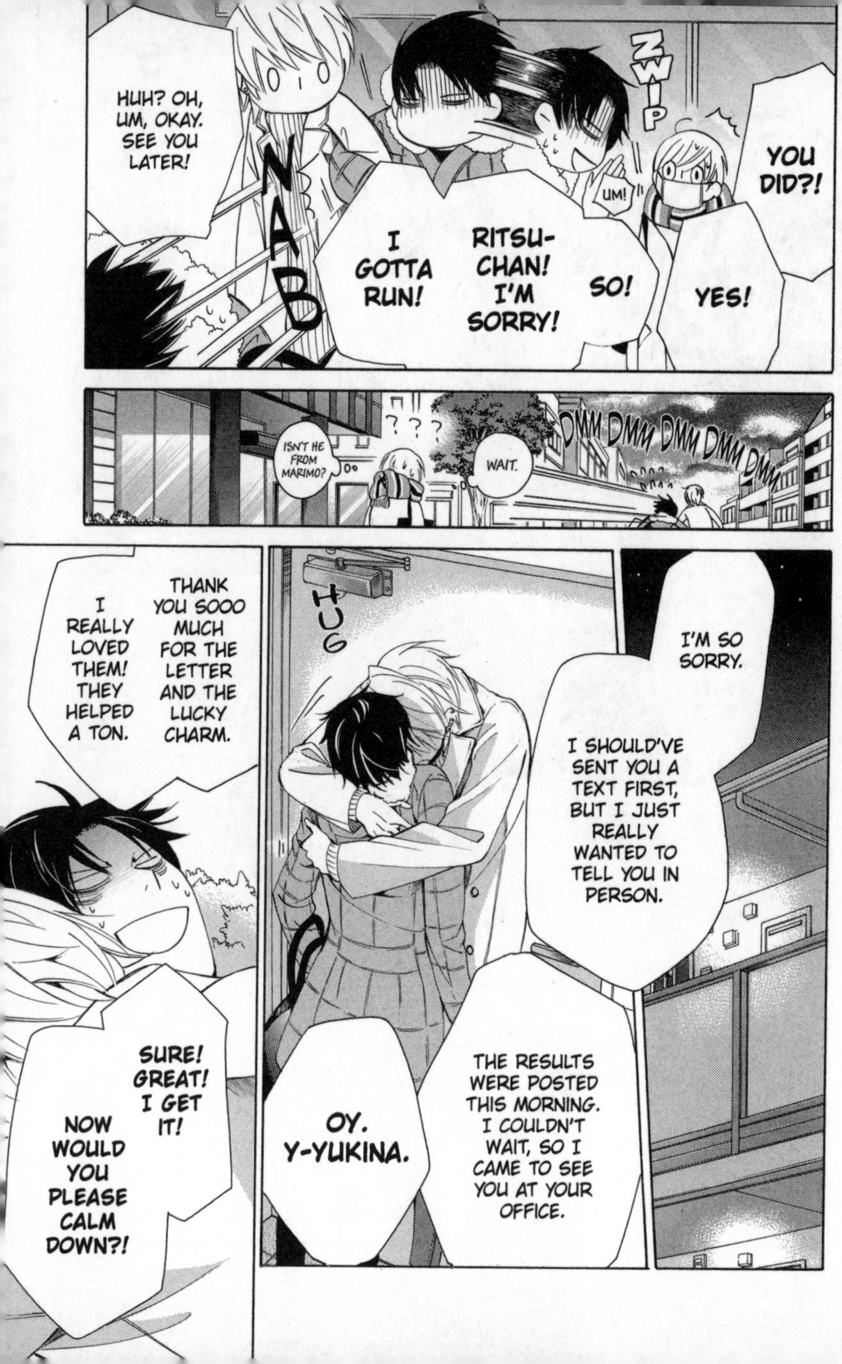
YOU DID?!
YES!
UM!
ZWIP
SO!
RITSU-CHAN! I'M SORRY!
I GOTTA RUN!
HUH? OH, UM, OKAY. SEE YOU LATER!
NAB
DMM DMM DMM DMM DMM
WAIT.
???
ISN'T HE FROM MARIMO?
I'M SO SORRY.
I SHOULD'VE SENT YOU A TEXT FIRST, BUT I JUST REALLY WANTED TO TELL YOU IN PERSON.
HUG
THE RESULTS WERE POSTED THIS MORNING. I COULDN'T WAIT, SO I CAME TO SEE YOU AT YOUR OFFICE.
OY. Y-YUKINA.
THANK YOU SOOO MUCH FOR THE LETTER AND THE LUCKY CHARM.
I REALLY LOVED THEM! THEY HELPED A TON.
SURE! GREAT! I GET IT!
NOW WOULD YOU PLEASE CALM DOWN?!

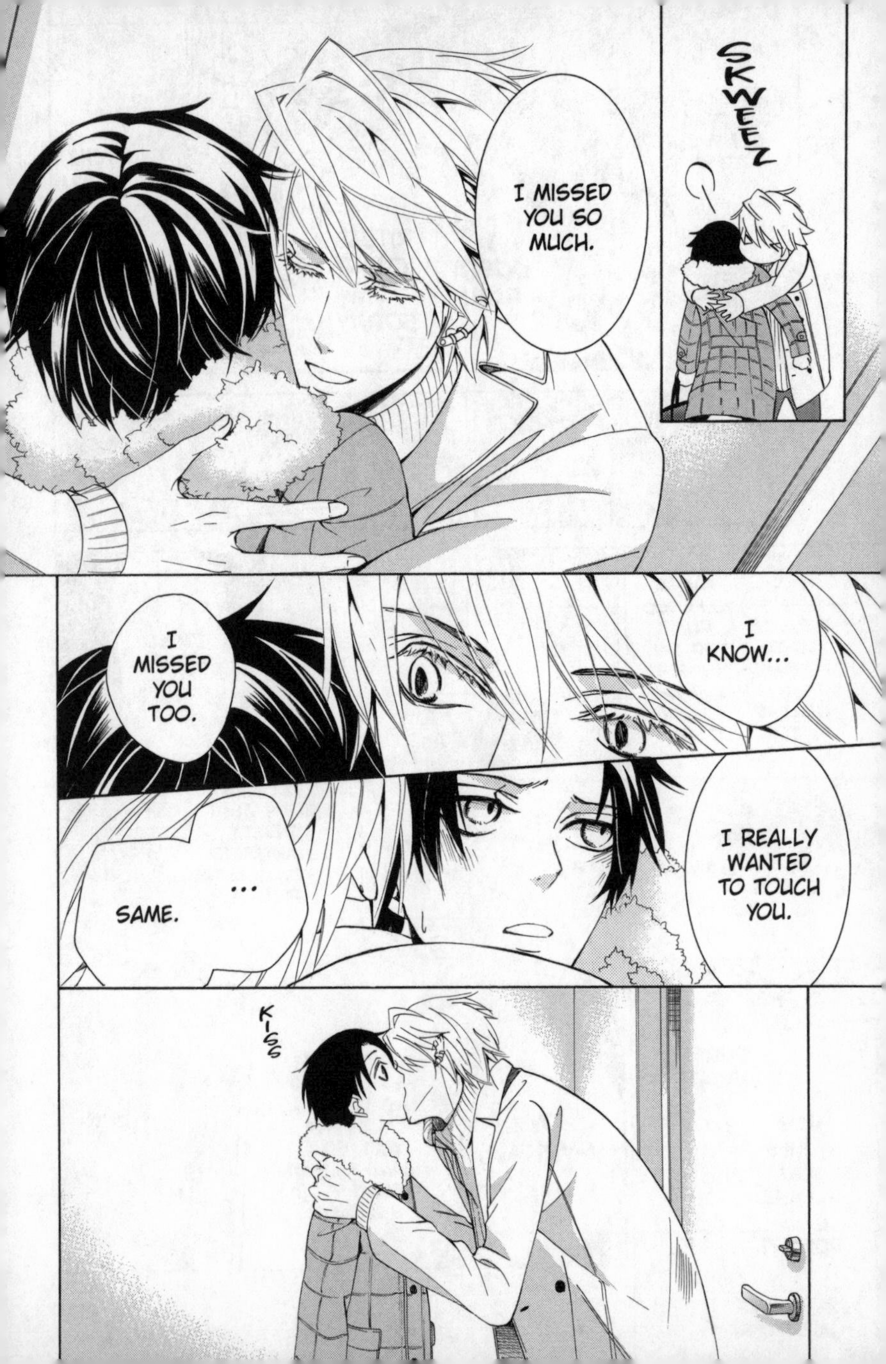
SKWEEZ
I MISSED YOU SO MUCH.
I KNOW...
I MISSED YOU TOO.
I REALLY WANTED TO TOUCH YOU.
...
SAME.
KISS

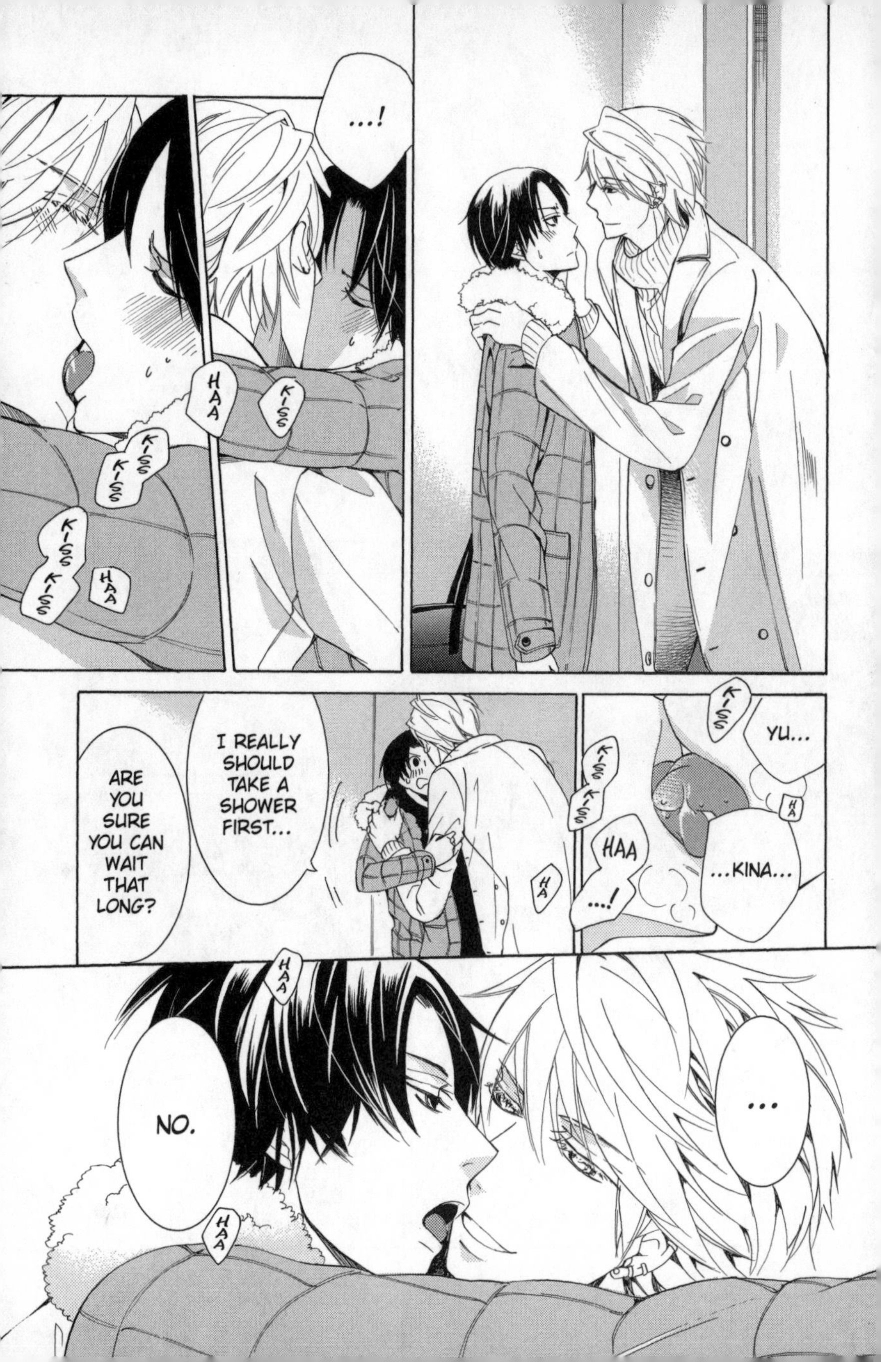
...!
HAA
KISS
KISS
KISS
KISS
KISS
HAA
KISS
YU...
HA
KISS
KISS
HAA
...KINA...
...!
I REALLY SHOULD TAKE A SHOWER FIRST...
HA
ARE YOU SURE YOU CAN WAIT THAT LONG?
...
HAA
NO.
HAA

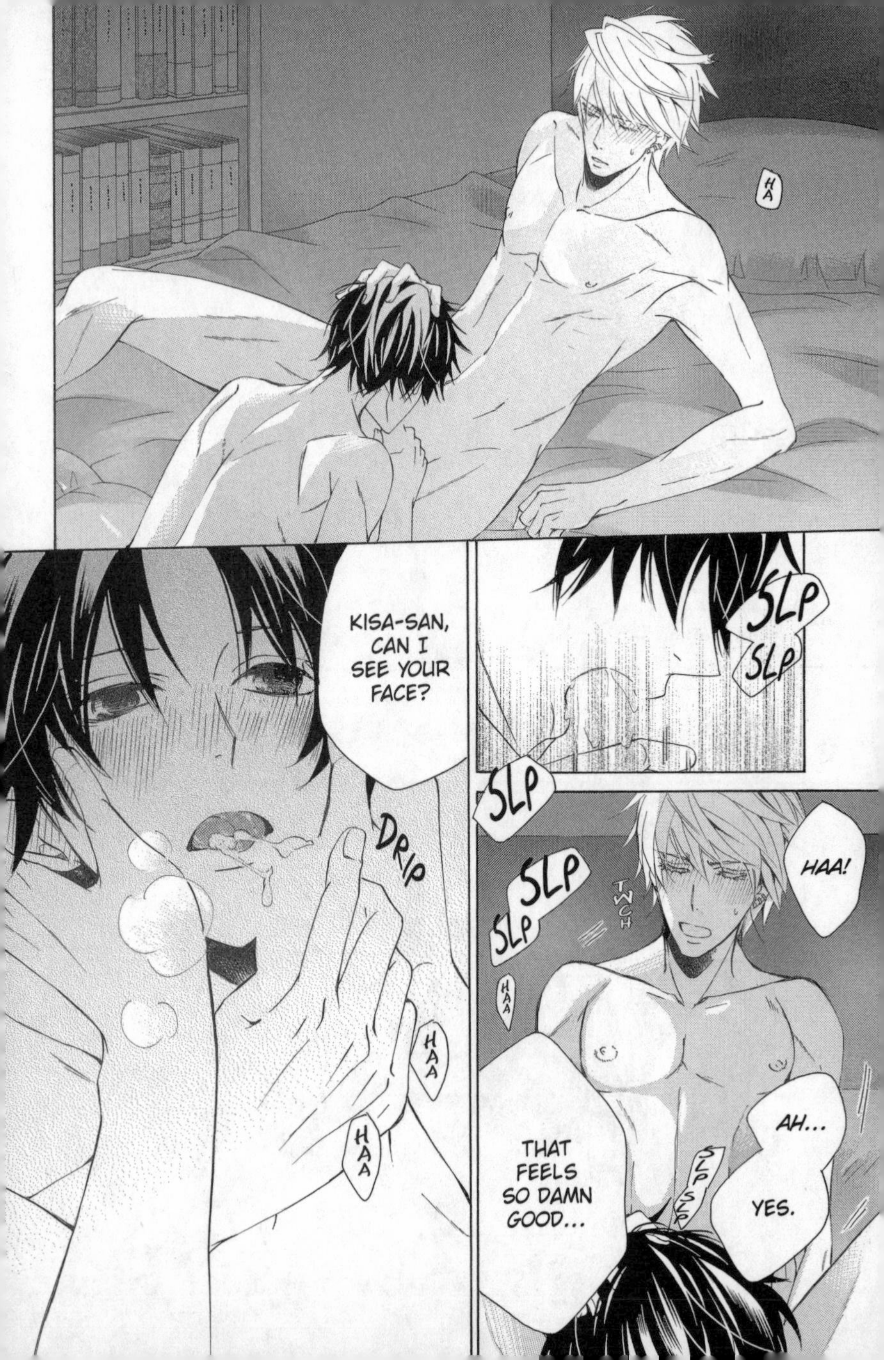
HA
SLP
SLP
SLP
HAA!
TWCH
SLP
SLP
HAA
AH...
YES.
SLP SLP
THAT FEELS SO DAMN GOOD...
KISA-SAN, CAN I SEE YOUR FACE?
DRIP
HAA
HAA

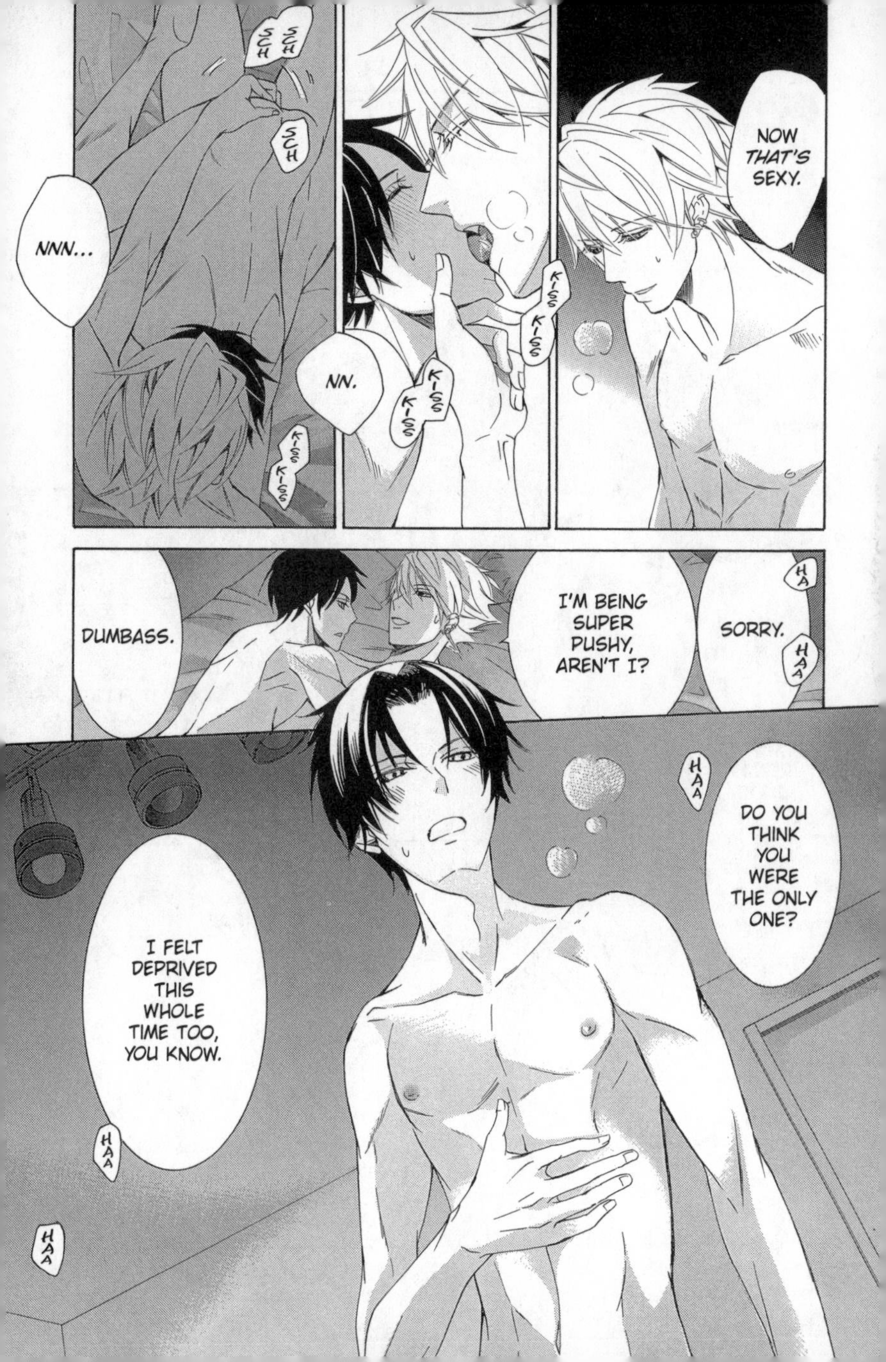
NOW THAT'S SEXY.
KISS KISS
NN.
KISS KISS
SCH SCH
SCH
NNN...
KISS KISS
HA
HAA
SORRY.
I'M BEING SUPER PUSHY, AREN'T I?
DUMBASS.
HAA
DO YOU THINK YOU WERE THE ONLY ONE?
I FELT DEPRIVED THIS WHOLE TIME TOO, YOU KNOW.
HAA
HAA

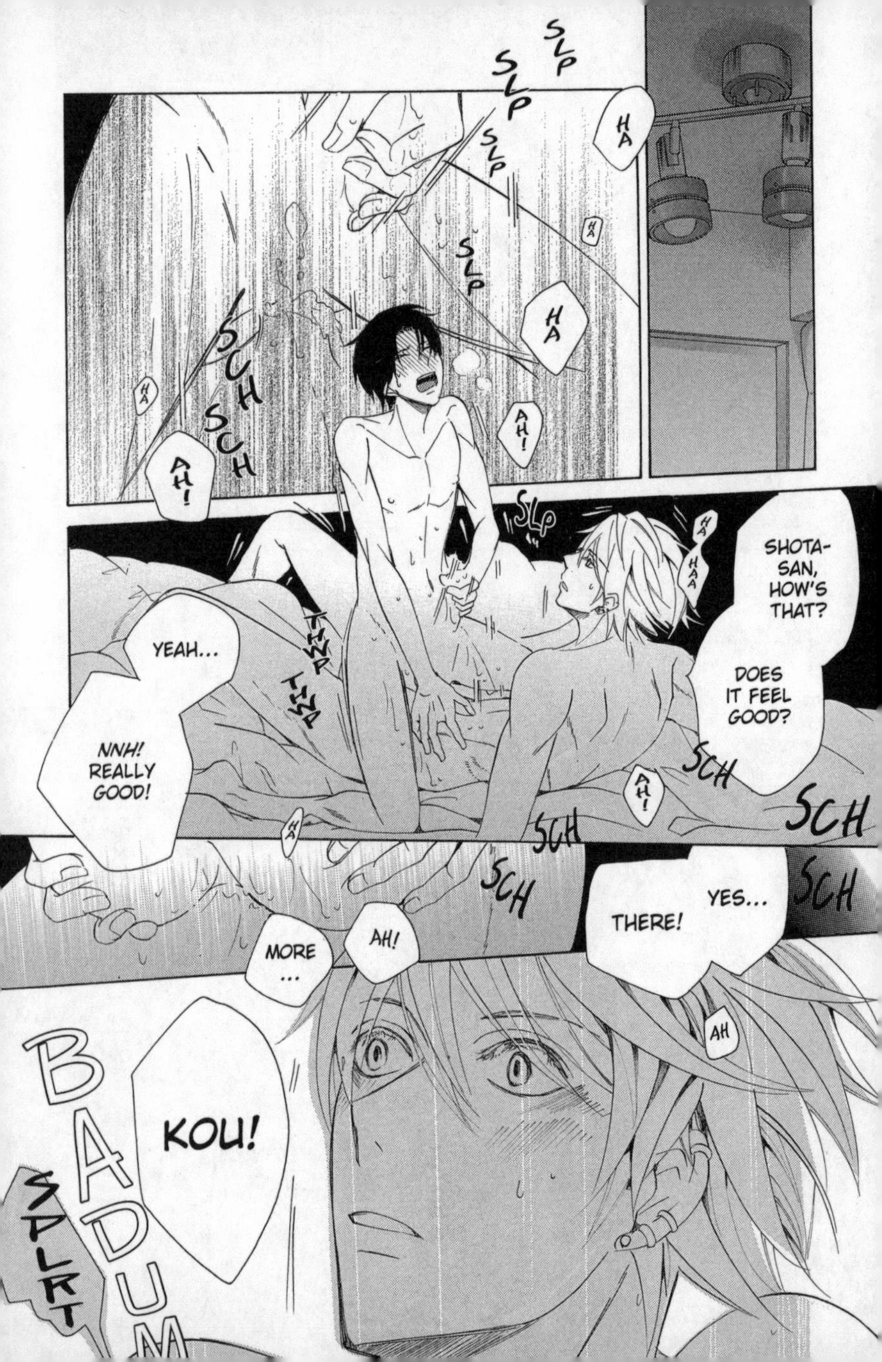
SLP
SLP
SLP
SLP
HA
HA
SLP
HA
AH!
HA
SCH
SCH
AH!
SLP
HA
HAA
SHOTA-SAN, HOW'S THAT?
DOES IT FEEL GOOD?
SCH
AH!
SCH
YEAH...
THWP
THWP
NNH! REALLY GOOD!
SCH
HA
SCH
YES...
THERE!
SCH
AH!
MORE...
AH
KOU!
BADUM
SPLRT

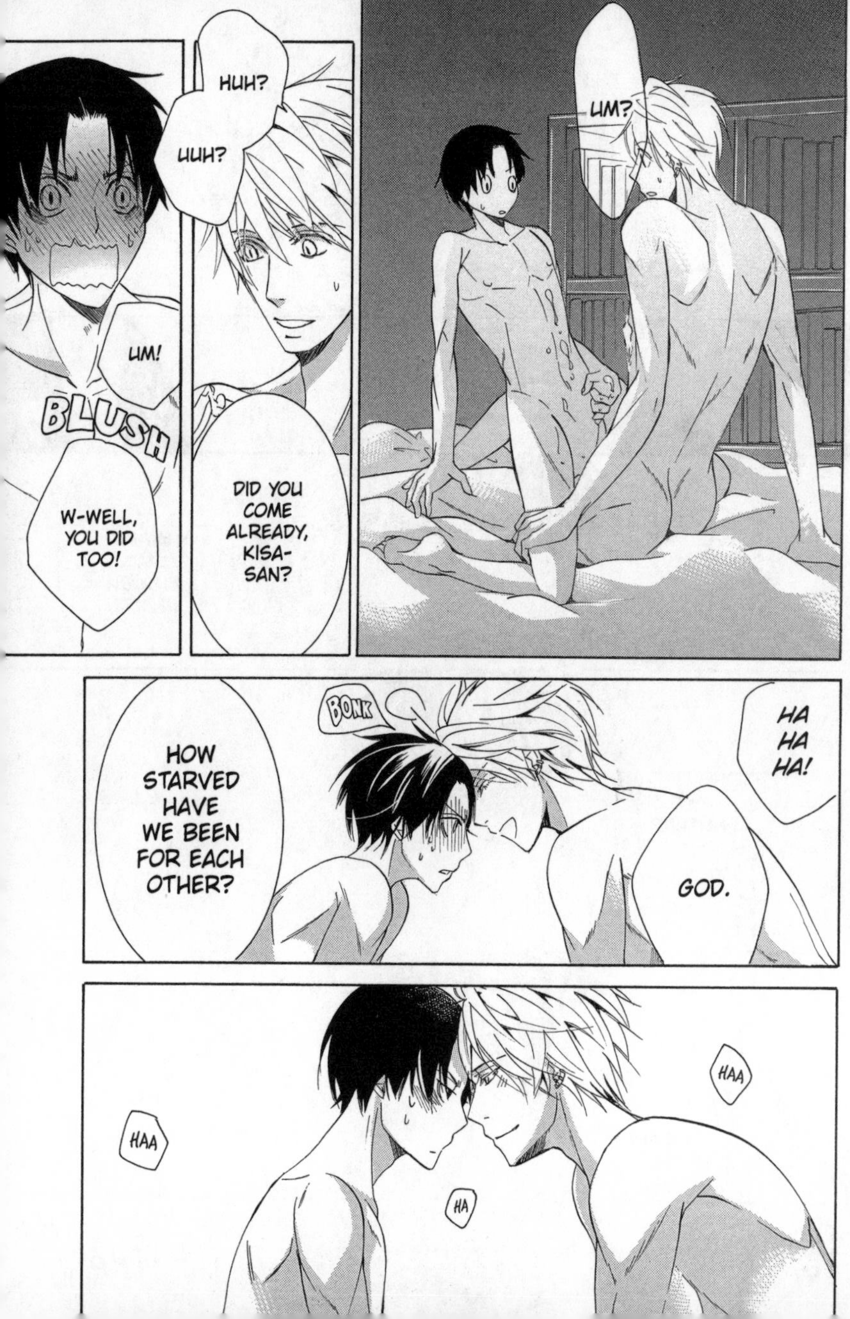
UM?
HUH?
UUH?
DID YOU COME ALREADY, KISA-SAN?
UM!
BLUSH
W-WELL, YOU DID TOO!
HA HA HA!
GOD.
BONK
HOW STARVED HAVE WE BEEN FOR EACH OTHER?
HAA
HA
HAA

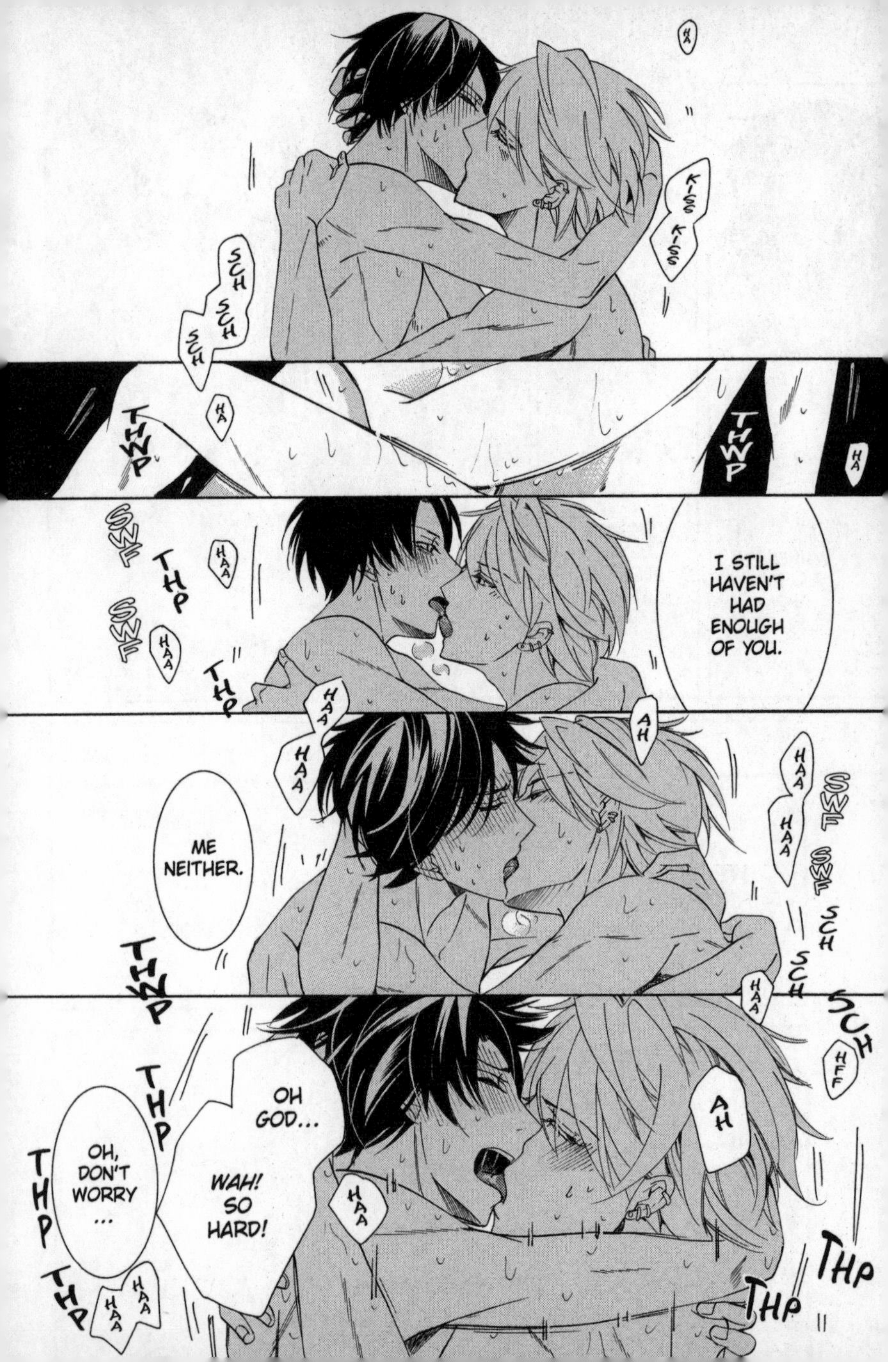
HA
KISS KISS
SCH SCH SCH
HA
THWP
HA
THWP
I STILL HAVEN'T HAD ENOUGH OF YOU.
HAA
THP
SWF
SWF
HAA
THP
AH
HAA HAA
SWF SWF
SCH SCH
HAA HAA
ME NEITHER.
THWP
HAA
SCH
HFF
AH
OH GOD...
WAH! SO HARD!
HAA
THP
OH, DON'T WORRY ...
THP
THP
THP
HAA HAA

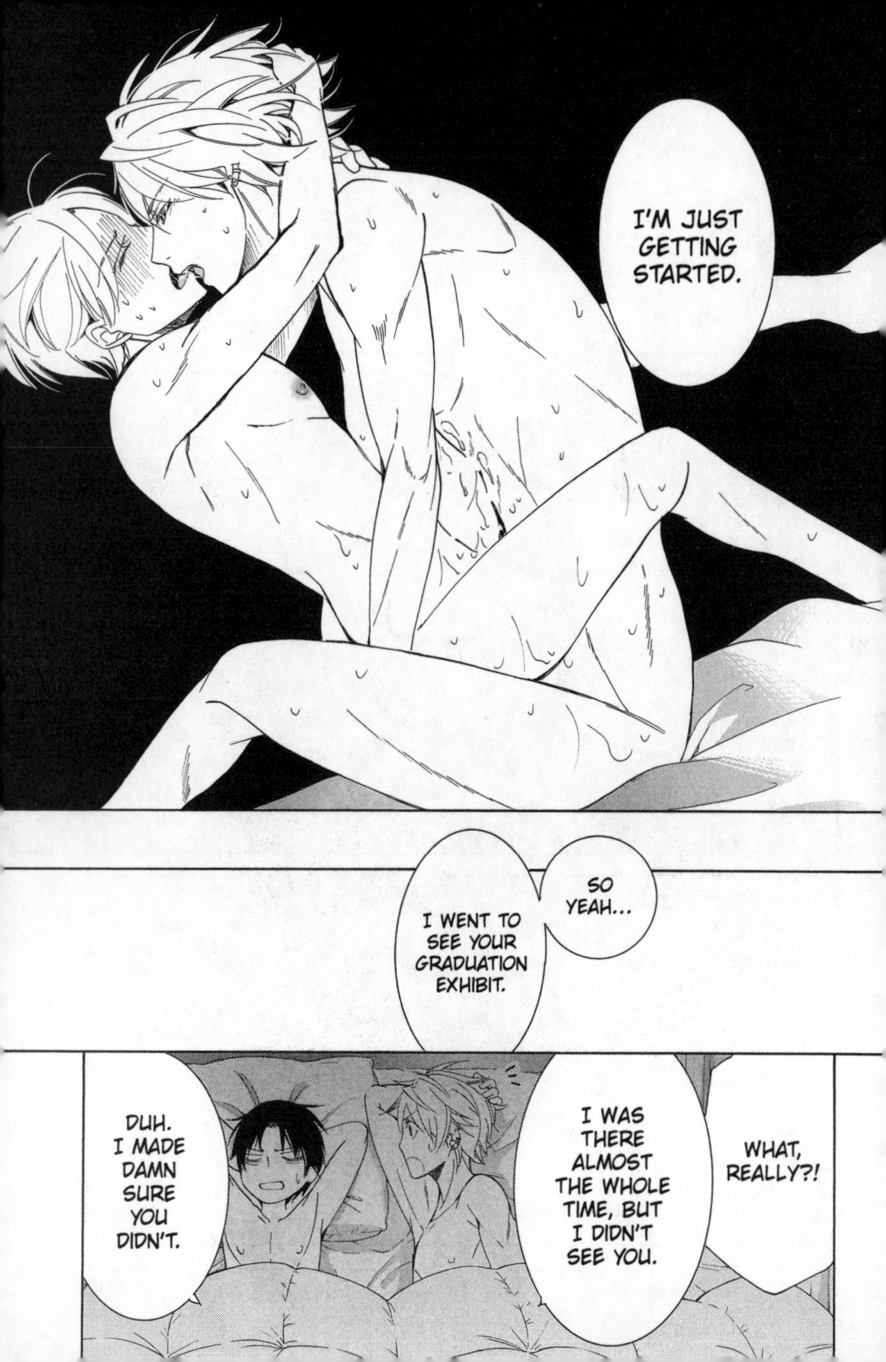
I'M JUST GETTING STARTED.
SO YEAH...
I WENT TO SEE YOUR GRADUATION EXHIBIT.
WHAT, REALLY?!
I WAS THERE ALMOST THE WHOLE TIME, BUT I DIDN'T SEE YOU.
DUH. I MADE DAMN SURE YOU DIDN'T.

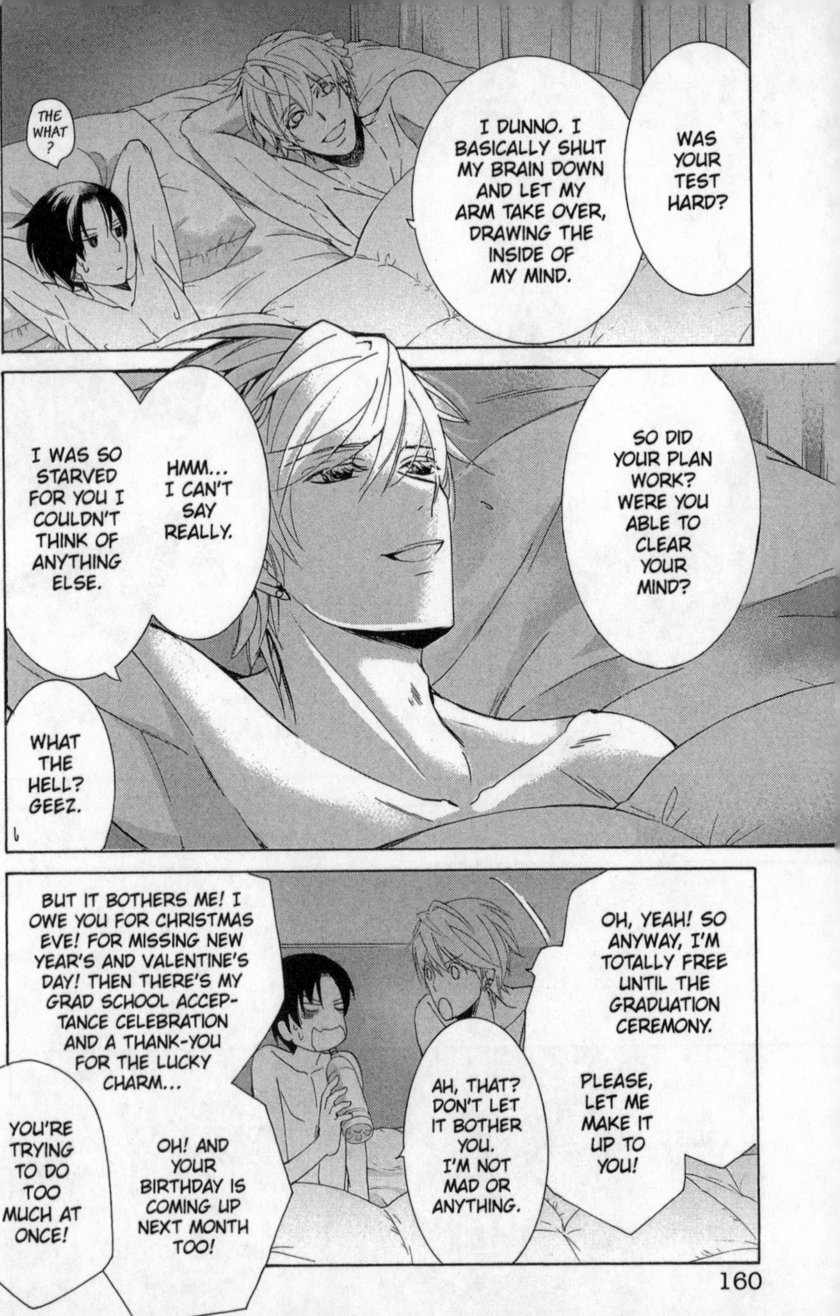
WAS YOUR TEST HARD?
I DUNNO. I BASICALLY SHUT MY BRAIN DOWN AND LET MY ARM TAKE OVER, DRAWING THE INSIDE OF MY MIND.
THE WHAT?
SO DID YOUR PLAN WORK? WERE YOU ABLE TO CLEAR YOUR MIND?
HMM... I CAN'T SAY REALLY.
I WAS SO STARVED FOR YOU I COULDN'T THINK OF ANYTHING ELSE.
WHAT THE HELL? GEEZ.
OH, YEAH! SO ANYWAY, I'M TOTALLY FREE UNTIL THE GRADUATION CEREMONY.
PLEASE, LET ME MAKE IT UP TO YOU!
AH, THAT? DON'T LET IT BOTHER YOU. I'M NOT MAD OR ANYTHING.
BUT IT BOTHERS ME! I OWE YOU FOR CHRISTMAS EVE! FOR MISSING NEW YEAR'S AND VALENTINE'S DAY! THEN THERE'S MY GRAD SCHOOL ACCEP-TANCE CELEBRATION AND A THANK-YOU FOR THE LUCKY CHARM...
OH! AND YOUR BIRTHDAY IS COMING UP NEXT MONTH TOO!
YOU'RE TRYING TO DO TOO MUCH AT ONCE!

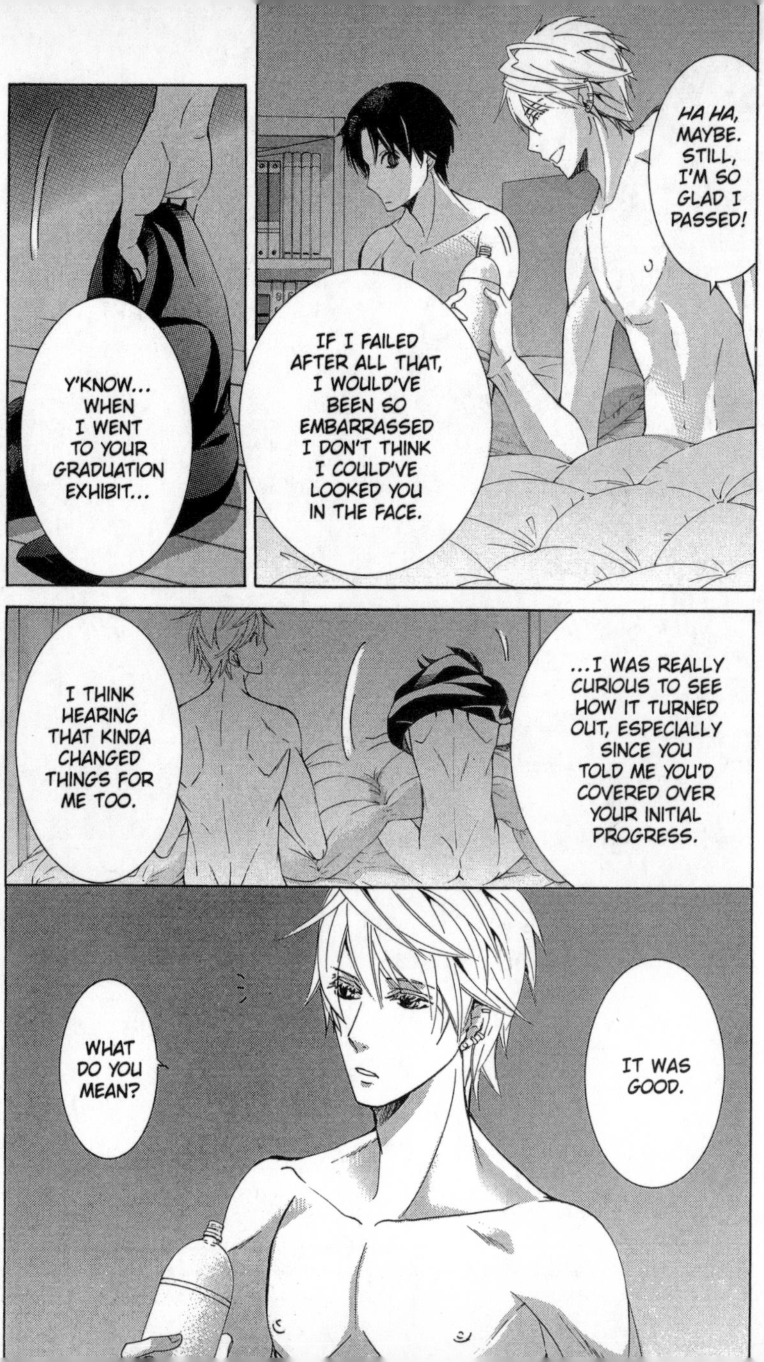
HA HA, MAYBE. STILL, I'M SO GLAD I PASSED!
IF I FAILED AFTER ALL THAT, I WOULD'VE BEEN SO EMBARRASSED I DON'T THINK I COULD'VE LOOKED YOU IN THE FACE.
Y'KNOW... WHEN I WENT TO YOUR GRADUATION EXHIBIT...
...I WAS REALLY CURIOUS TO SEE HOW IT TURNED OUT, ESPECIALLY SINCE YOU TOLD ME YOU'D COVERED OVER YOUR INITIAL PROGRESS.
I THINK HEARING THAT KINDA CHANGED THINGS FOR ME TOO.
IT WAS GOOD.
WHAT DO YOU MEAN?

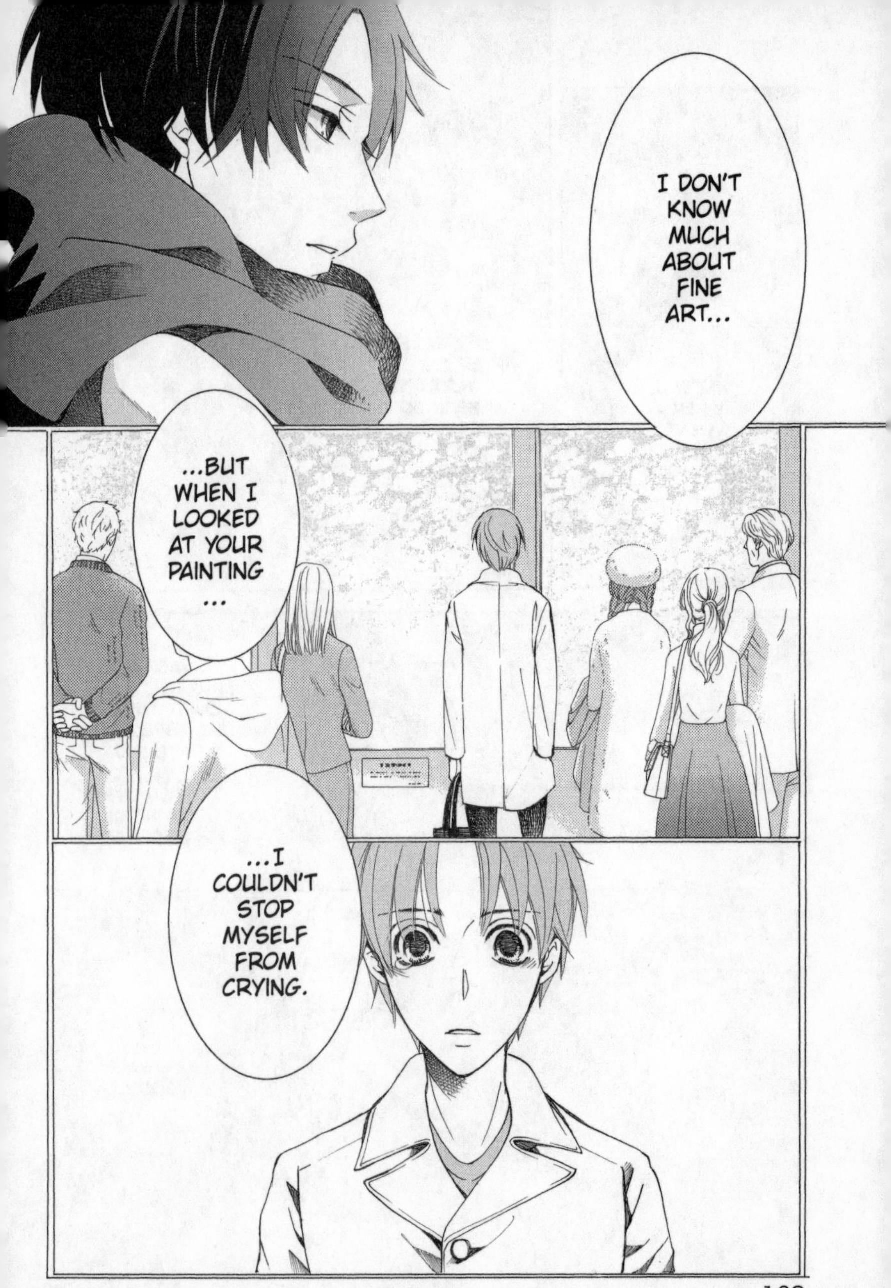
I DON'T KNOW MUCH ABOUT FINE ART...
...BUT WHEN I LOOKED AT YOUR PAINTING...
...I COULDN'T STOP MYSELF FROM CRYING.

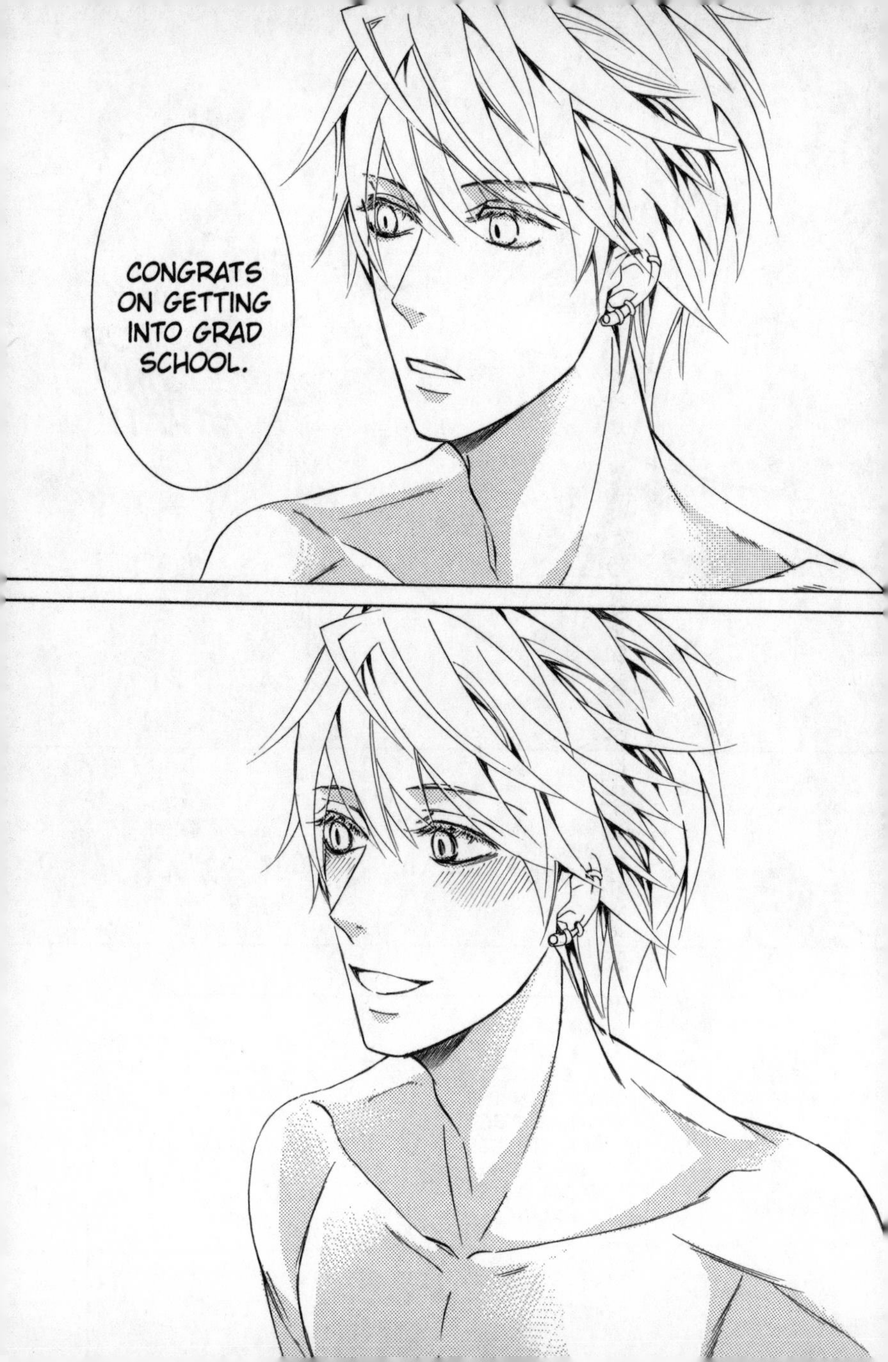
CONGRATS ON GETTING INTO GRAD SCHOOL.

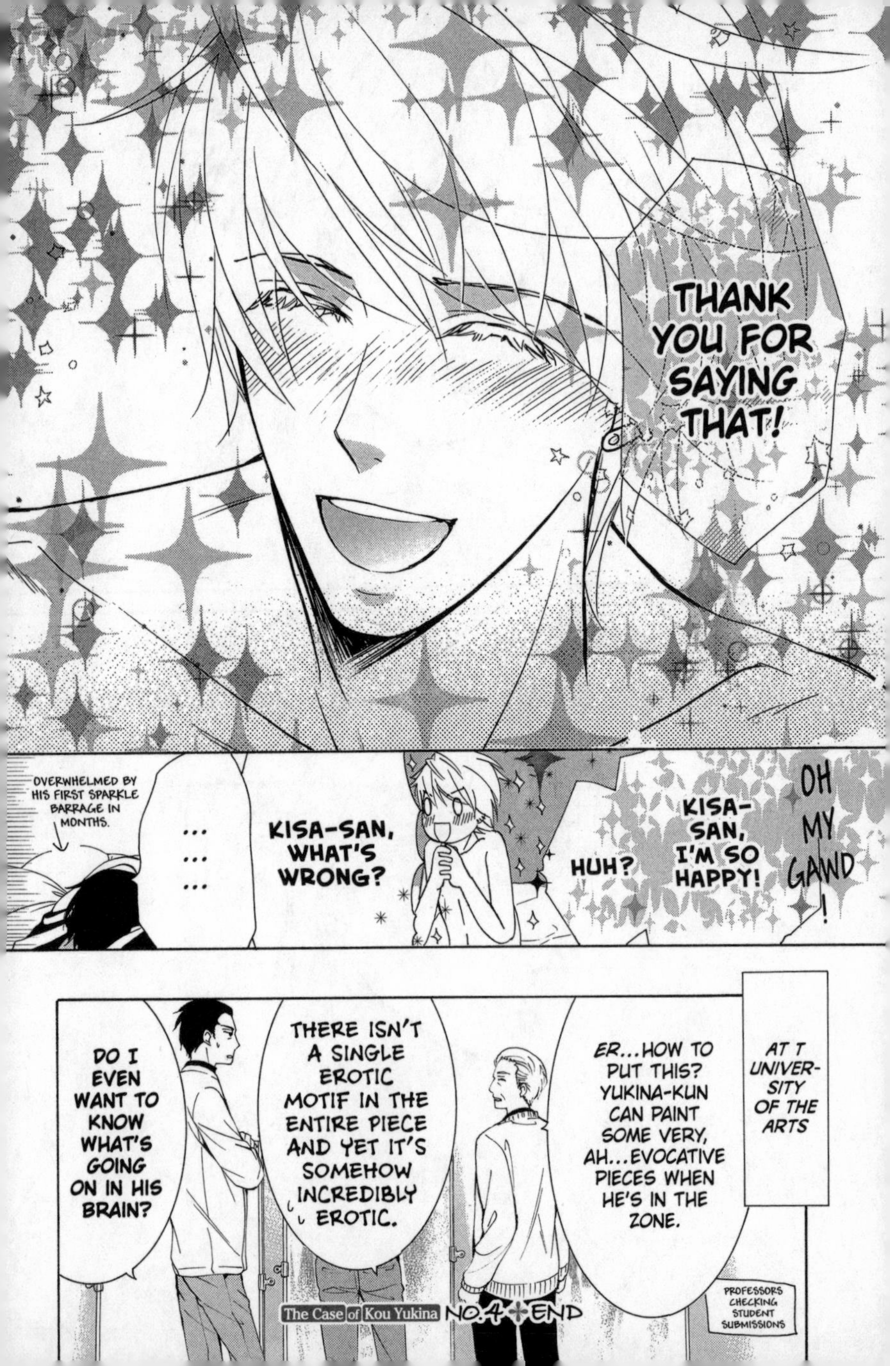
THANK YOU FOR SAYING THAT!
OH MY GAWD!
KISA-SAN, I'M SO HAPPY!
HUH?
KISA-SAN, WHAT'S WRONG?
... ...
OVERWHELMED BY HIS FIRST SPARKLE BARRAGE IN MONTHS.
AT T UNIVERSITY OF THE ARTS
ER...HOW TO PUT THIS? YUKINA-KUN CAN PAINT SOME VERY, AH...EVOCATIVE PIECES WHEN HE'S IN THE ZONE.
THERE ISN'T A SINGLE EROTIC MOTIF IN THE ENTIRE PIECE AND YET IT'S SOMEHOW INCREDIBLY EROTIC.
DO I EVEN WANT TO KNOW WHAT'S GOING ON IN HIS BRAIN?
PROFESSORS CHECKING STUDENT SUBMISSIONS
The Case of Kou Yukina NO.4 END

The World's Greatest First Love

The Case of Ritsu Onodera

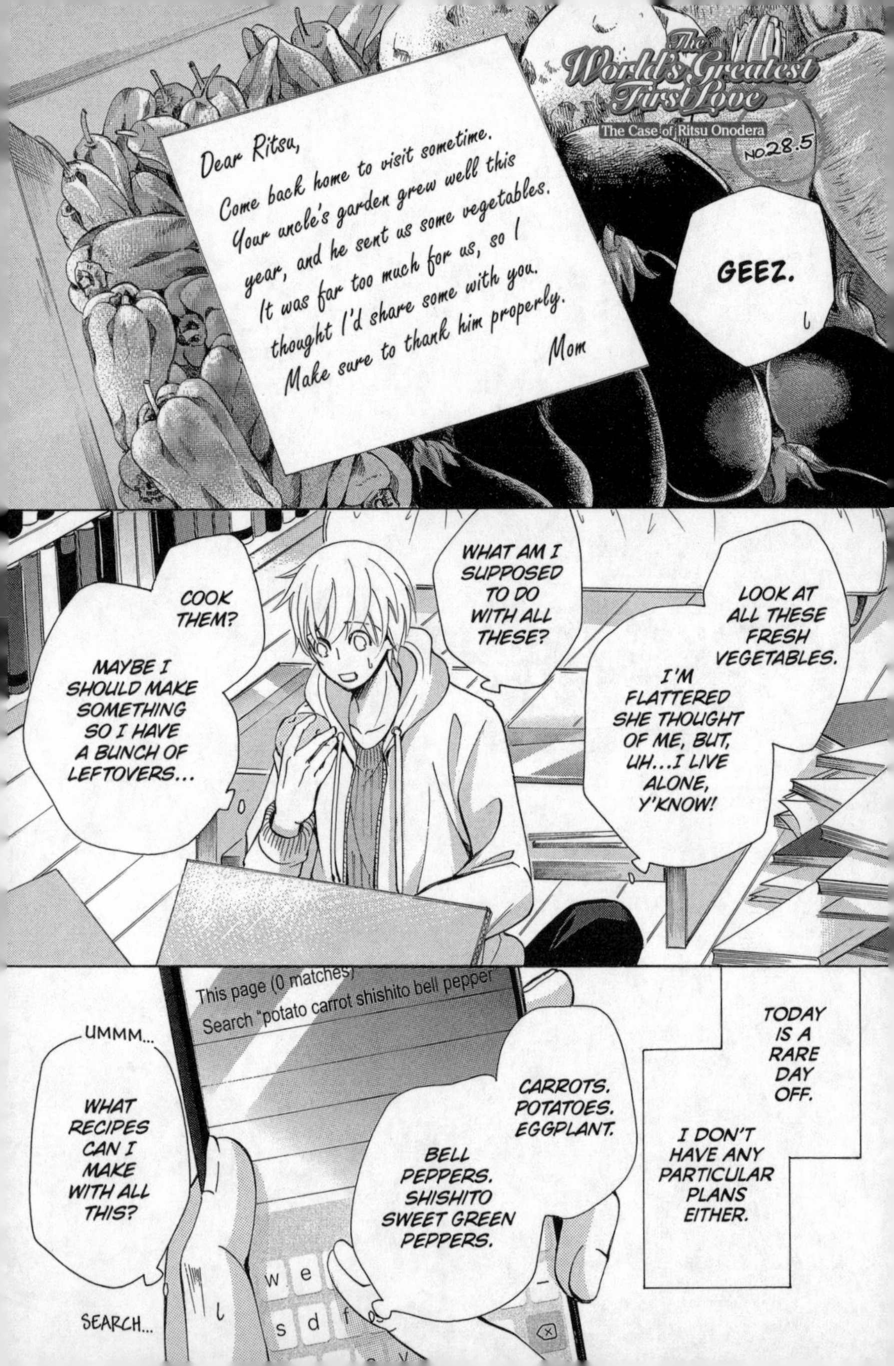
The World's Greatest First Love
The Case of Ritsu Onodera
No.28.5
GEEZ.
Dear Ritsu,
Come back home to visit sometime.
Your uncle's garden grew well this year, and he sent us some vegetables. It was far too much for us, so I thought I'd share some with you. Make sure to thank him properly.
Mom
LOOK AT ALL THESE FRESH VEGETABLES.
I'M FLATTERED SHE THOUGHT OF ME, BUT, UH...I LIVE ALONE, Y'KNOW!
WHAT AM I SUPPOSED TO DO WITH ALL THESE?
COOK THEM?
MAYBE I SHOULD MAKE SOMETHING SO I HAVE A BUNCH OF LEFTOVERS...
TODAY IS A RARE DAY OFF.
I DON'T HAVE ANY PARTICULAR PLANS EITHER.
CARROTS. POTATOES. EGGPLANT.
BELL PEPPERS. SHISHITO SWEET GREEN PEPPERS.
This page (0 matches)
Search "potato carrot shishito bell pepper
UMMM...
WHAT RECIPES CAN I MAKE WITH ALL THIS?
SEARCH...

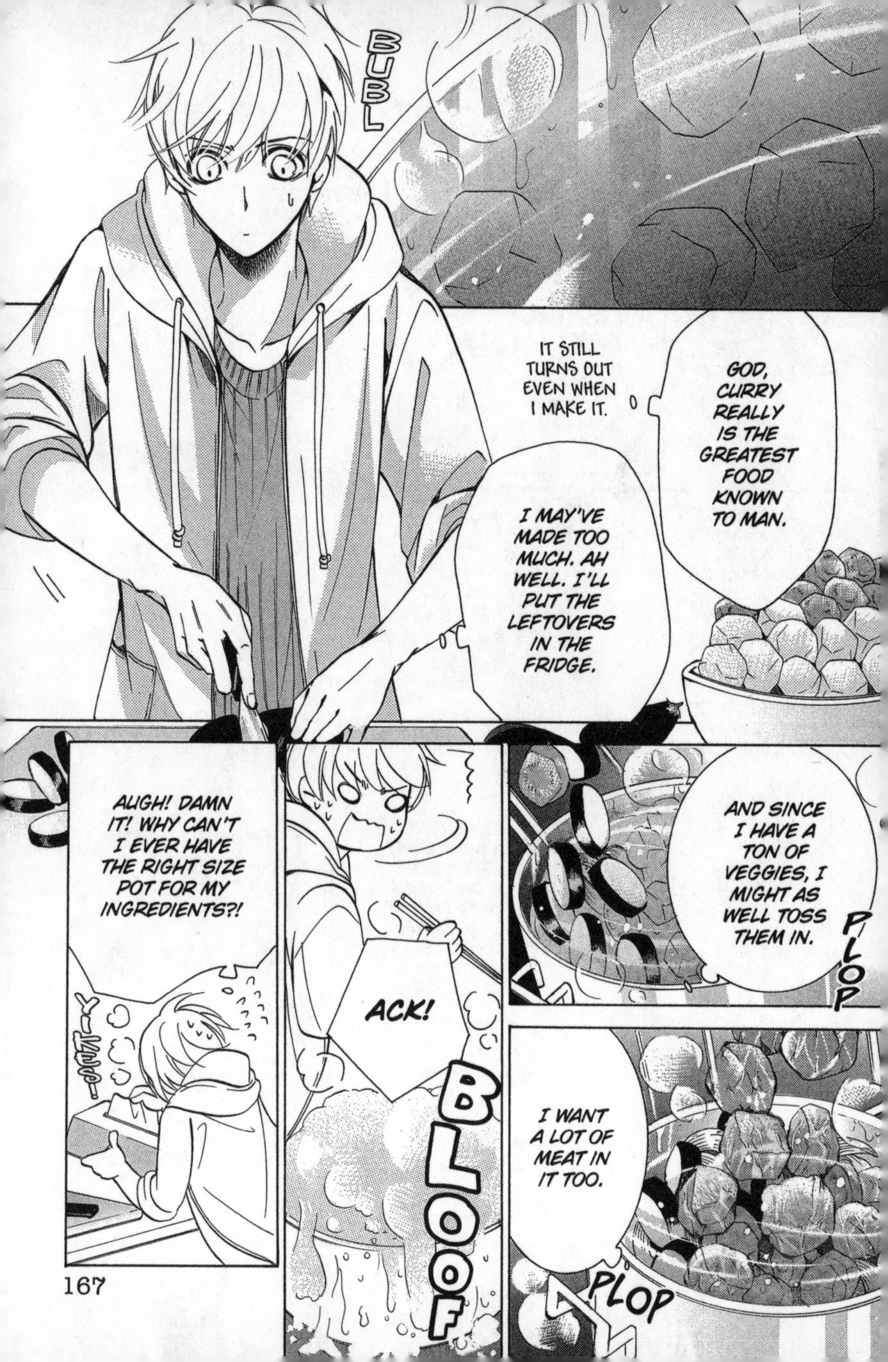
BUBL
GOD, CURRY REALLY IS THE GREATEST FOOD KNOWN TO MAN.
IT STILL TURNS OUT EVEN WHEN I MAKE IT.
I MAY'VE MADE TOO MUCH. AH WELL. I'LL PUT THE LEFTOVERS IN THE FRIDGE.
AND SINCE I HAVE A TON OF VEGGIES, I MIGHT AS WELL TOSS THEM IN.
PLOP
I WANT A LOT OF MEAT IN IT TOO.
PLOP
ACK!
BLOOF
AUGH! DAMN IT! WHY CAN'T I EVER HAVE THE RIGHT SIZE POT FOR MY INGREDIENTS?!

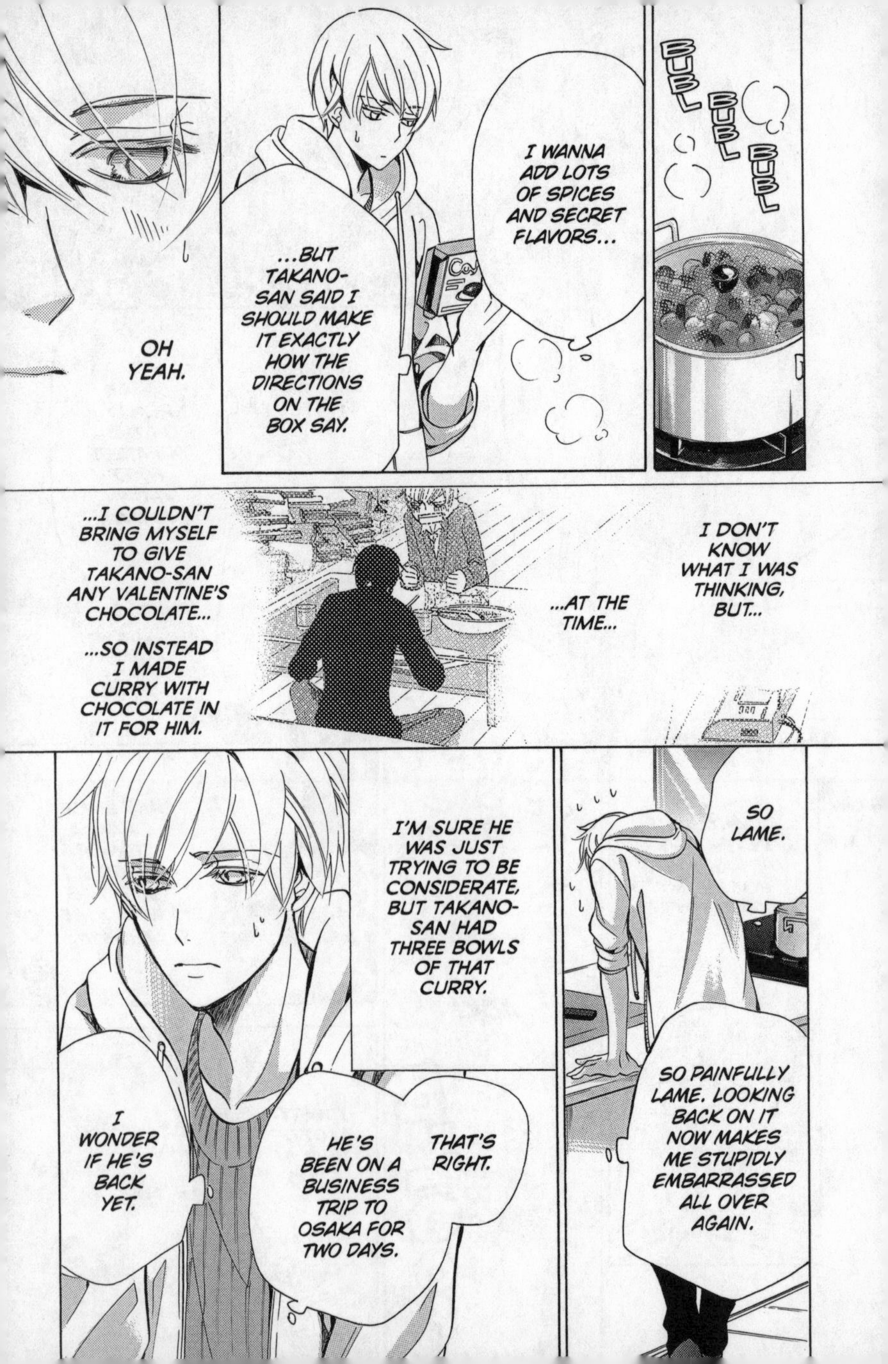
BUBL BUBL BUBL
I WANNA ADD LOTS OF SPICES AND SECRET FLAVORS...
...BUT TAKANO-SAN SAID I SHOULD MAKE IT EXACTLY HOW THE DIRECTIONS ON THE BOX SAY.
OH YEAH.
I DON'T KNOW WHAT I WAS THINKING, BUT...
...AT THE TIME...
...I COULDN'T BRING MYSELF TO GIVE TAKANO-SAN ANY VALENTINE'S CHOCOLATE...
...SO INSTEAD I MADE CURRY WITH CHOCOLATE IN IT FOR HIM.
SO LAME.
SO PAINFULLY LAME. LOOKING BACK ON IT NOW MAKES ME STUPIDLY EMBARRASSED ALL OVER AGAIN.
I'M SURE HE WAS JUST TRYING TO BE CONSIDERATE, BUT TAKANO-SAN HAD THREE BOWLS OF THAT CURRY.
THAT'S RIGHT.
HE'S BEEN ON A BUSINESS TRIP TO OSAKA FOR TWO DAYS.
I WONDER IF HE'S BACK YET.

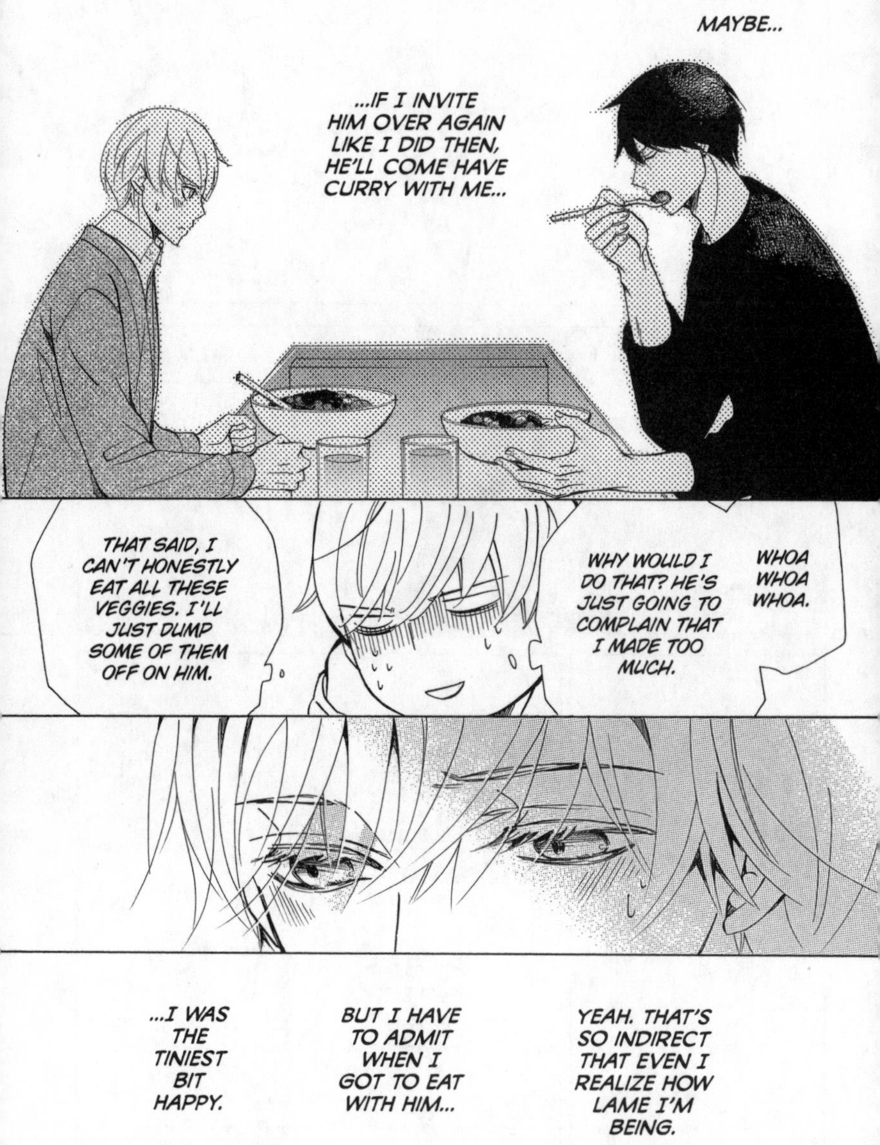
MAYBE...
...IF I INVITE HIM OVER AGAIN LIKE I DID THEN, HE'LL COME HAVE CURRY WITH ME...
WHOA WHOA WHOA.
WHY WOULD I DO THAT? HE'S JUST GOING TO COMPLAIN THAT I MADE TOO MUCH.
THAT SAID, I CAN'T HONESTLY EAT ALL THESE VEGGIES. I'LL JUST DUMP SOME OF THEM OFF ON HIM.
YEAH. THAT'S SO INDIRECT THAT EVEN I REALIZE HOW LAME I'M BEING.
BUT I HAVE TO ADMIT WHEN I GOT TO EAT WITH HIM...
...I WAS THE TINIEST BIT HAPPY.

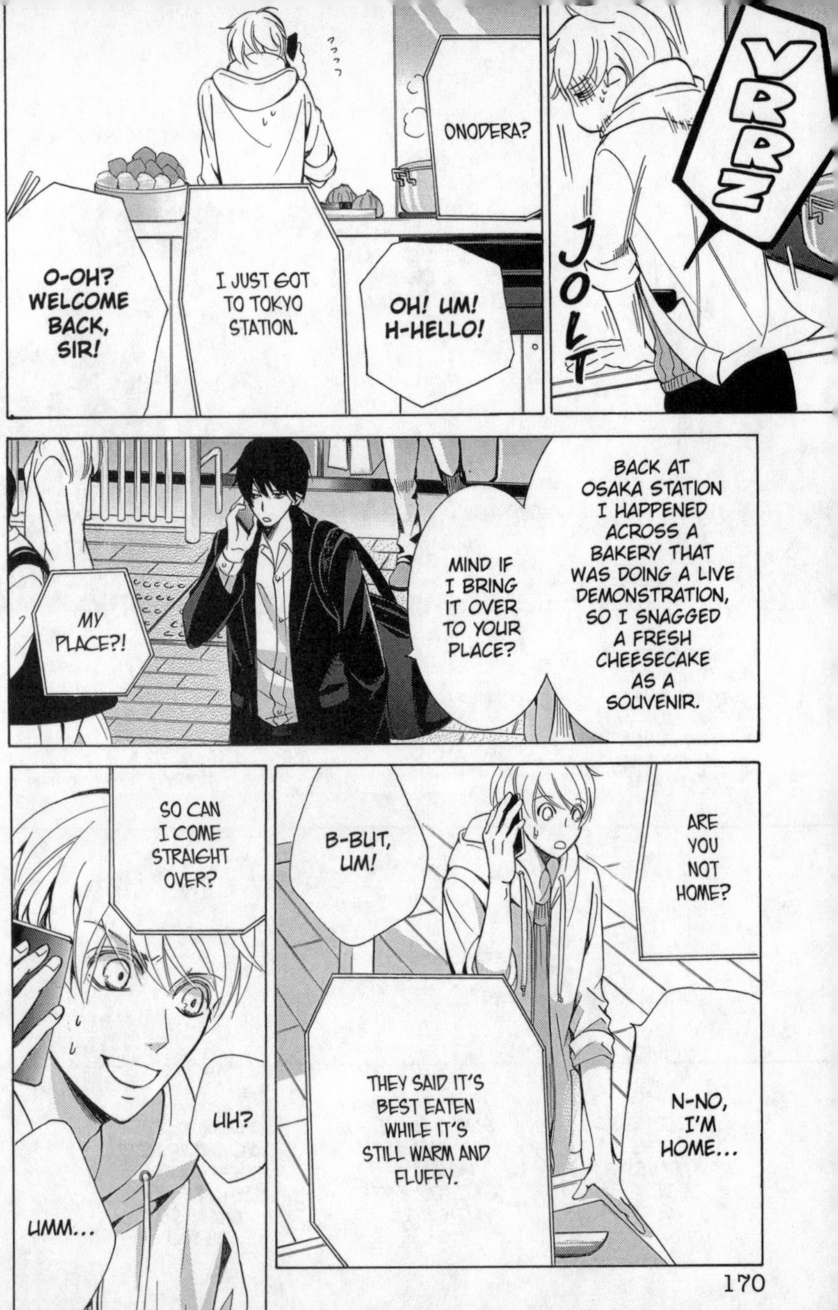
VRRZ
JOLT
ONODERA?
OH! UM! H-HELLO!
I JUST GOT TO TOKYO STATION.
O-OH? WELCOME BACK, SIR!
BACK AT OSAKA STATION I HAPPENED ACROSS A BAKERY THAT WAS DOING A LIVE DEMONSTRATION, SO I SNAGGED A FRESH CHEESECAKE AS A SOUVENIR.
MIND IF I BRING IT OVER TO YOUR PLACE?
MY PLACE?!
ARE YOU NOT HOME?
B-BUT, UM!
N-NO, I'M HOME...
THEY SAID IT'S BEST EATEN WHILE IT'S STILL WARM AND FLUFFY.
SO CAN I COME STRAIGHT OVER?
UH?
UMM...

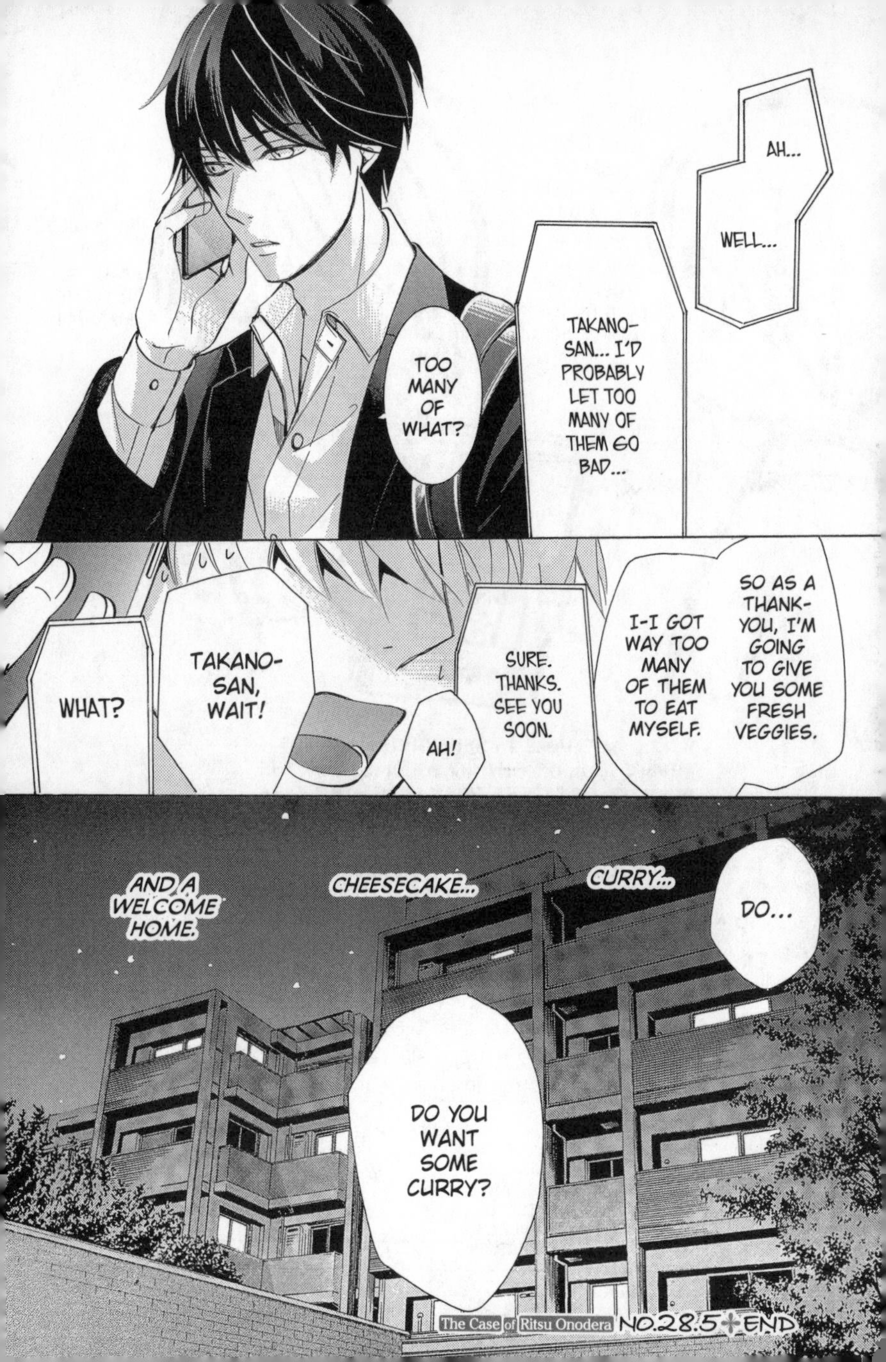
AH...
WELL...
TAKANO-SAN... I'D PROBABLY LET TOO MANY OF THEM GO BAD...
TOO MANY OF WHAT?
SO AS A THANK-YOU, I'M GOING TO GIVE YOU SOME FRESH VEGGIES.
I-I GOT WAY TOO MANY OF THEM TO EAT MYSELF.
SURE. THANKS. SEE YOU SOON.
AH!
TAKANO-SAN, WAIT!
WHAT?
DO...
CURRY...
CHEESECAKE...
AND A WELCOME HOME.
DO YOU WANT SOME CURRY?
The Case of Ritsu Onodera NO.28.5 END

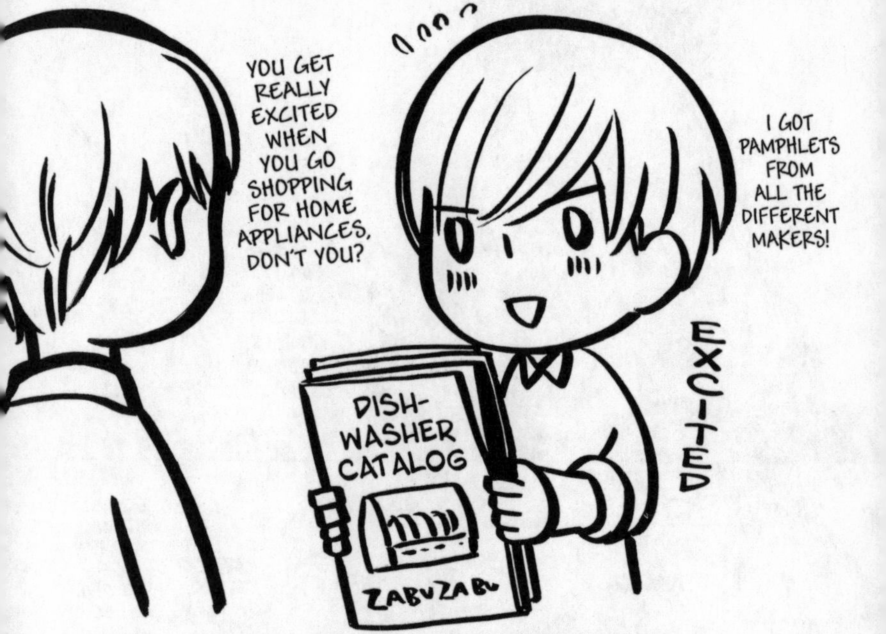
I GOT PAMPHLETS FROM ALL THE DIFFERENT MAKERS!
EXCITED
YOU GET REALLY EXCITED WHEN YOU GO SHOPPING FOR HOME APPLIANCES, DON'T YOU?
DISH-WASHER CATALOG
ZABUZABU

HELLO. MY NAME IS SHUNGIKU NAKAMURA. THANK YOU FOR BUYING VOLUME 14 OF THE WORLD'S GREATEST FIRST LOVE ~THE CASE OF RITSU ONODERA~! THANKS TO EVERYONE'S GENEROUS SUPPORT, WE'VE MADE IT ALL THE WAY TO VOLUME 14 ALREADY. THINGS HAVE BEEN A LITTLE UNEASY FOR A WHILE, BUT I HOPE YOU WILL CONTINUE READING. THANK YOU VERY MUCH.

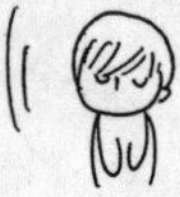

SHUNGIKU NAKAMURA

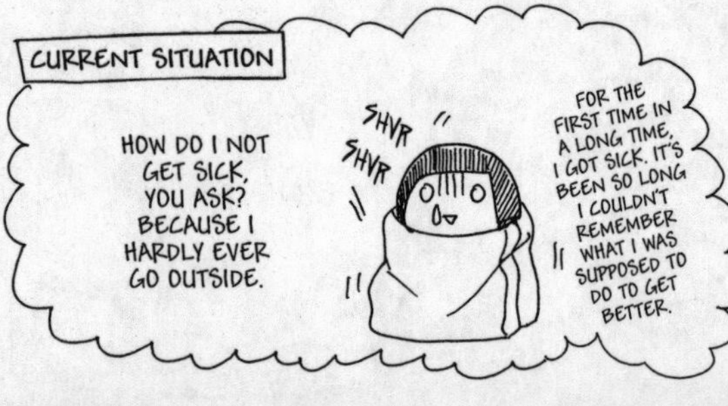
CURRENT SITUATION
FOR THE FIRST TIME IN A LONG TIME, I GOT SICK. IT'S BEEN SO LONG I COULDN'T REMEMBER WHAT I WAS SUPPOSED TO DO TO GET BETTER.
SHVR
SHVR
HOW DO I NOT GET SICK, YOU ASK? BECAUSE I HARDLY EVER GO OUTSIDE.

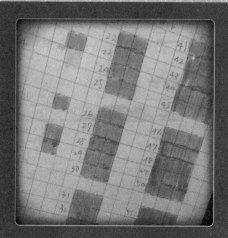

I draw progress charts like this
each time, but as deadlines loom
closer, I feel like I shouldn't be
wasting time coloring them in.
I've never finished a single chart.

About the Author

Shungiku Nakamura
DOB December 13
Sagittarius
Blood Type O

The World's Greatest First Love: The Case of Ritsu Onodera

Volume 14
SuBLime Manga Edition

Story and Art by **Shungiku Nakamura**

Translation—**Adrienne Beck**
Touch-Up Art and Lettering—**Eric Erbes**
Cover and Graphic Design—**Shawn Carrico**
Editor—**Jennifer LeBlanc**

SEKAIICHI HATSUKOI ~ONODERA RITSU NO BAAI~ Volume 14
© Shungiku Nakamura 2019
First published in Japan in 2019 by KADOKAWA CORPORATION, Tokyo.
English translation rights arranged with KADOKAWA CORPORATION, Tokyo.

ASUKA
COMICS
CL D X

Printed in the U.S.A.

Published by SuBLime Manga
P.O. Box 77010
San Francisco, CA 94107

10 9 8 7 6 5 4 3 2 1
First printing, April 2021

 PARENTAL ADVISORY
THE WORLD'S GREATEST FIRST LOVE is rated M for Mature and is
recommended for mature readers. This volume contains graphic
MATURE imagery and mature themes.

www.SuBLimeManga.com

The customer is always right.

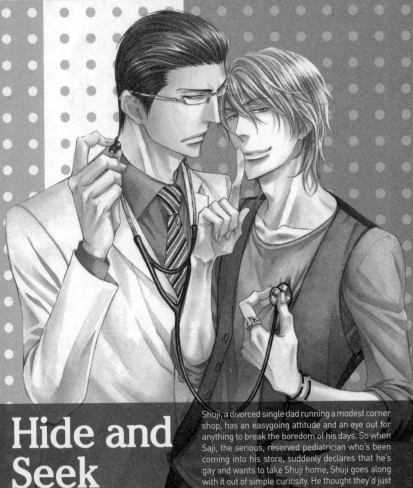

Hide and Seek

Story & Art by Yaya **SAKURAGI**

Shuji, a divorced single dad running a modest corner shop, has an easygoing attitude and an eye out for anything to break the boredom of his days. So when Saji, the serious, reserved pediatrician who's been coming into his store, suddenly declares that he's gay and wants to take Shuji home, Shuji goes along with it out of simple curiosity. He thought they'd just mess around, have some fun, and that would be that. But he gets a lot more than he bargained for in this story of opposites in love!